SUPERFOODS

FOR WOMEN

Also by Dolores Riccio

Superfoods

SUPERFOODS
FOR WOMEN

---

300 Recipes That Fulfill
Your Special Nutritional Needs

DOLORES RICCIO

A Time Warner Company

Superfoods for Women is not intended to offer medical advice.
As with any change in your diet, check your plans with your physician.

Warner Books, Inc., 1271 Avenue of the Americas, New York, NY 10020

W A Time Warner Company

Printed in the United States of America

ISBN 0-446-51795-X

Book design by Giorgetta Bell McRee

This book is dedicated to
my daughter Lucy-Marie with love . . .
and to all daughters and their mothers
in the hope that they will
take good care of themselves—
just as they take good care of others.

CONTENTS

ACKNOWLEDGMENTS

My warmest thanks to the wonderful people who have helped to make this book possible.

I'm grateful to my editors at Warner: Liv Blumer for the warmth of her interest in this project, her skillful direction in completing it, and her discriminating touches throughout; and Caryn Karmatz for her boundless enthusiasm, her discerning insights, and her careful editing.

I'd like to express appreciation, also, to my indefatigable agent Blanche Schlessinger for her comforting encouragement, her wisdom, and the continued pleasure of our friendly association.

As always, I'm thankful to my husband, Rick, whose love, pride, and patience have sustained me during the long process of completing this book.

INTRODUCTION: SUPERFOODS FOR WOMEN AND THE PEOPLE THEY LOVE

Vitality, intelligence, beauty! Healthy babies, graceful aging, and a joyful life at any age! Super nutrition really does help a woman achieve these goals, and this is a cookbook dedicated to showing how every woman can enhance her life in many ways through healthy eating.

Although *Superfoods for Women* is designed to promote overall good health, you'll find many references throughout the book to food "prescriptions" for specific deficiencies and conditions. You'll also find food strategies for meeting the nutritional challenges of every stage of a woman's life.

TAKING CARE OF OURSELVES AS WELL AS OTHERS

Traditionally, women have been responsible for most of a family's informal home health care, from nursing a cold to deciding when a trip to the doctor is in order. They've also been responsible for managing family meals and making sure that everyone is adequately nourished. Although these family roles have become more flexible, we're still giving loving thought to the health and well-being of our home circle. In this book, I want to suggest that women combine that concern about others with attention to themselves.

Every food we put into our bodies contains nutrients and chemicals that act on it in ways that will be important to us, if not today or tomorrow, then some year soon. As women, each of us has a unique potential to fulfill. We are needed by our families, friends, coworkers, and community, so we simply cannot afford to ignore our own nutritional needs or to diet our way into incipient malnutrition and low spirits.

WOMEN'S NUTRITIONAL NEEDS DO DIFFER FROM MEN'S

Although all humans share the same basic requirements for foods that will promote growth, strength, energy, and healing, there are some significant female differences and requirements that should be kept in mind as we decide what we're going to eat three times each day. Women are more liable to suffer from diabetes, depression, osteoporosis, and anemia, for instance. All the woes attendant to premenstrual syndrome and menopausal problems are ours alone. Managing nutrition for two during pregnancy and nursing is also a woman's challenge.

Then there are some interesting paradoxes in the female-male health picture. Women live longer than men; they have a lower mortality rate from every cause except diabetes. But women have a higher illness rate and use more health care.

Some female sex advantages have narrowed, however, with changing life conditions. Subject to the same workplace stresses as men, and smoking more than in previous decades, women are suffering from more cardiovascular and respiratory ailments. Heart disease is now the leading cause of female mortality, more than all the cancers. Defensive eating patterns, such as you'll find in this cookbook, can help to keep you from becoming part of this alarming statistic.

WOMEN'S HEALTH—A SPECIALTY WHOSE TIME HAS COME

In recent years a new emphasis has been placed on the neglected specialty of women's health—and it's about time! No longer the passive recipients of any system—whether it be government, medical, social, or corporate—we women are taking charge of our lives and our bodies.

In the past, research on women's health has focused chiefly on the reproductive system rather than on the entire package of femaleness. Often we have been excluded from research trials for fear that our reproductive and menstrual cycles would skew the results. The Seven Countries Study, a landmark in linking diet and heart disease, was conducted entirely with male subjects.

Aware that we are the chief consumers of the health-care system, women today are insisting that the special female concerns, needs, problems, and symptoms be given more careful attention, including being the subject of separate studies. We want more from medical research than the assumption that male test results will apply equally to female biological systems.

In response, a $625 million, fifteen-year project, called the Women's Health Initiative, involving 160,000 women ages 50 to 79, is being undertaken by the National Institutes of Health to address some of the inequities that exist in research involving women. Large-scale clinical trials will focus on diseases that disable and kill women: heart disease, cancer, and osteoporosis.

SUPERFOODS DEFEND AGAINST CANCER AND OTHER DISEASES

A diet change toward more super fruits, vegetables, grains, and beans does in itself constitute a major defense against cancer. Recently, it's been estimated that 35 percent of all cancers in the United States are probably caused by diet and are therefore preventable. When 200 studies on the vegetables-and-fruits connection to reducing the risk of cancer were analyzed, significant protection was found in 128 of 156. In cancers of the cervix, ovary, and endometrium, 11 studies out of 15 showed a connection.

But animal foods (especially fish!) have their place in a healthy diet, too. In a praiseworthy attempt to avoid fat, women sometimes lose sight of the fact that lean meats in reasonable portions are important sources of many nutrients, among them iron and folate (a B vitamin also known as folic acid and folacin)—and that dairy foods really deliver the calcium that will keep our bones strong.

For women who choose a vegetarian diet, care must be taken to include plant sources of calcium, folate, and iron in their meals, and to combine grains and legumes in dishes because these two foods eaten together form a complete protein equal to meat protein. Still lacking in a strict vegan diet (no animal products at all), however, will be vitamin B_{12}, which should be added as a vitamin supplement to avoid nerve damage.

GOOD NUTRITION ENHANCES EVERY STAGE OF A WOMAN'S LIFE

Some nutritional needs change throughout a woman's life, and some remain constant. Women of childbearing years need more iron than men, and women of every age have a special requirement for calcium. The surgeon general's recent report recommends that women's intake of both minerals be increased. Yet even among women concerned about fitness, more attention may be given to exercise than nutrition. One study found that over 80 percent of women recreational runners were not obtaining their Recommended Daily Allowances (RDAs) of iron, calcium, and zinc.

Although it's self-evident that pregnant and nursing women have specialized nutritional requirements, recent research has been zeroing in on what and why. Studies have found that even a deficiency in a single nutrient—zinc, iron, vitamin B_6, or selenium are among those that have been studied—can compromise an unborn child's immune system. A diet rich in folate, consumed *before* as well as after a woman becomes pregnant, helps prevent cases of spina bifida and other neural tube defects. And recent research shows that the omega fatty acids found in seafood are essential nutrients to the development of a child's brain, both as a fetus and as a nursing infant.

Young girls on marginal diets may achieve their proper growth at the expense of beginning their reproductive years with a deficiency in both iron and vitamin A. Nutritionists speculate that this may cause profuse bleeding at menses and, in girls who become pregnant, a disproportion between the size of the child's head and the young woman's pelvis.

Nutrition also has an important role in protecting women from the effects of menopause and aging. Calcium and some companion minerals help to stave off osteoporosis and high blood pressure associated with a woman's older years, and other vitamins and minerals promote immunity from infection and disease. Vitamin C, which among other good effects is responsible for forming and maintaining collagen, plays a role in keeping the skin looking young. Antioxidants, like vitamin C, in general are active in sponging up free radicals—molecules that cause much of the damage we associate with aging.

LIVE LONGER—AND MORE ABUNDANTLY!

If our goal is not only to live longer but also to live more abundantly, still able to enjoy intellectual pursuits and to participate in joyous activities, there is every reason to believe that good nutrition, meaning *good food*, will make the most of whatever our genetic inheritance has decreed. Yet a study of older Americans showed that 40 percent of women over 65 had intakes of vitamin E, calcium, and zinc that were two-thirds below the RDA. Some scientists have gone out on a limb (see References) to make the suggestion that healthy older Americans should take a basic multivitamin and mineral supplement. It's hard to believe, with all the evidence, that this is still considered a controversial recommendation. Until very recently, it's been fashionable to be as skeptical of nutritional discoveries as if they were reports of out-of-the-body experiences.

Fortunately, this picture is changing. Although our chief health institutions rarely, except for pregnancy, espouse vitamin supplements, they *are* more than ever before recommending nutritious foods as a means of preventing diseases.

A DESIGNER DIET FOR OPTIMUM NUTRITION

In 1989, the National Academy of Sciences urged broad changes in American eating habits: Reduce total fat consumption to 30 percent or less of total calories per day. Reduce cholesterol to less than 30 milligrams a day (slightly more than the amount in one egg). Eat five or more servings a day of vegetables or fruits, especially green and yellow vegetables and citrus fruit. Eat six or more servings a day of starches and complex carbohydrates. Limit protein intake to 6 ounces (180 grams) a day. Limit salt intake (including what's already in prepared foods) to 6 grams (one teaspoon) a day. Be moderate about alcoholic beverages.

What constitutes a serving? One cup of greens or ½ cup of other vegetables; 1 medium whole fruit, such as apple or banana;

½ cup diced fruit; or ¼ cup dried fruit. And in starches or grains, it's ½ cup pasta, 1 slice bread, ½ bagel or muffin. The USDA's *Dietary Guidelines for Americans* describes moderate drinking as no more than one drink a day for women, two for men. (The difference is not explained.) One drink is 5 ounces of wine, 12 ounces of beer, or 1½ ounces of 80-proof liquor.

In a study of over a thousand women ages 19 through 50, it was found that the most healthful diets were those of middle-income women who ate more than 70 percent of their meals at home, whereas those who had higher incomes and ate out in restaurants more often consumed the most fat . . . *even more* than teenaged girls in the "fast-food eating pattern." Eating the greater proportion of one's meals at home is definitely the best way to control one's nutrition.

YOU DON'T HAVE TO CHOOSE BETWEEN WEIGHT LOSS AND GOOD HEALTH

A survey of thirty-nine states and the District of Columbia revealed that 40 percent of the female population was currently striving to lose weight, as compared to 25 percent of the male population—although, on average, both sexes wanted to lose about 30 pounds. Women need fewer calories than men; we lose weight less easily, owing to slower metabolism. This can be so frustrating that a woman resorts to extreme measures like fasting or simplistic cure-alls like replacing real food with diet shakes.

Constant dieting is one of the reasons why women are more liable to be malnourished than men. Healthful weight loss should involve replacing processed foods full of fat, sugar, and salt with fresh vegetables and fruits, plus legumes and grains, thus keeping vitamin and mineral intake high.

REAL FOOD—NO SUBSTITUTES—FOR THE HEALTH OF BODY AND MIND

Nature intended us to nourish ourselves with actual food, not just vitamin supplements or juices extracted from fruits and vegetables. Food, after all, contains both the nutrients that have been discovered and those that have not; some of a food's benefits may as yet be unknown, and the synergism of its combined elements is not yet fully understood.

One hot new area of nutritional research involves phytochemicals (chemicals that exist naturally in plant foods). All fruits and vegetables contain phytochemicals as well as vitamins. The capsaicin in hot peppers and the sulforaphane in broccoli, both phytochemicals, may have no nutritive value but they are active in preventing cancer. Many of the superfoods on which this cookbook is based are as rich in phytochemicals as they are in nutrients.

Although supplements definitely have a place in specific circumstances—such as pregnancy, certain illnesses, and advancing years—it's the real foods we eat day in and day out that matter most, not only to the health of our bodies but also to our mental states.

Recent research into the connection between nutrients and neurotransmitters has given us some intriguing new possibilities for replacing fatigue, depression, and burnout with alertness, cheerfulness, and focus simply through the combinations of foods we eat and when we eat them.

HOW TO PUT THIS SUPERFOOD COOKBOOK TO WORK FOR YOU

While addressing the nutritional needs of both body and mind, this is first and foremost a cookbook. There are over 300 recipes for healthy dishes arranged in over 80 menus. The menus stress different packages of nutrients, from iron-rich meals to big-fiber dinners to comforting suppers for the really-stressed-out. The choice of ingredients is taken from my earlier book *Superfoods*, published in 1993—they are the foods that offer not just one but multiple nutritional advantages. Most menus can be prepared in an hour or less and serve four to six people, with occasional leftovers in dessert, which is no hardship. Many recipes take less than 30 minutes from start to finish. The ingredients are widely available. Saturated fat has been avoided whenever possible, and in general, the dishes are low-fat or reduced-fat compared to standard recipes. When skim milk or an egg substitute can be used, it's so noted. The results taste so good you'll probably forget these dishes are "health food."

And so you should (once you've carefully chosen those nutritious foods), because the pleasure of dining well is a chief consolation in this stressful world—a consolation that can't be obtained from calorie-controlled frozen dinners, diet drinks, and/or vitamin pills. Stress is, after all, the hidden factor in so many health problems, and I feel strongly that the world always looks better after a good meal.

The menus can be followed just as they are, and they can also be used as patterns for menus of your own devising. Substitutions are always possible, based on the various lists of vitamin and mineral food sources the following chapters provide—as, for example, one orange vegetable can replace another, or different dark leafy greens can substitute for each other, while still maintaining a high level of, say, antioxidants in a specific meal.

I've included many recipes for healthy desserts to complete the menus, but if you're watching your weight or your time in the kitchen, fresh fruit is always a great alternative. I have to admit that I haven't offered any minimalist meals here—selections and portions are generous; that, too, can be adjusted to your particular needs or goals.

Planning is still the most important ingredient in healthy meals, so go ahead and "mix and match" these recipes (and others) in well-balanced meals that really fulfill your body needs for energy, beauty, and good health.

Chapter headings, subheadings, and a comprehensive Index will help you follow up your interest in any particular deficiency or medical condition. The Bibliography and References in the back of this book can be consulted for further reading on the important connection between what you choose to eat and optimum good health. Many studies of the food-health connection are population studies that correlate eating habits with less risk of various diseases. While they don't always show a clear cause and effect, such studies rely on some powerful circumstantial evidence that's worth our while to consider. In some cases, these epidemiological studies have been followed up by *in vitro* (test tube) evidence and animal studies adding additional proof. Thus an excellent "case" for the disease-preventive powers of garlic, broccoli, or yogurt, for example, is built up over time through the efforts of many researchers.

Even when the jury is still out, if a food such as yogurt is enjoyable and shows in convincing preliminary studies the promise of preventing some malady such as yeast infections, we ought to be including yogurt in our diets and not wait for that elusive cause and effect to be demonstrated five or ten years from now. Yogurt is a good illustration because, even if it doesn't protect women against yeast infections, it's still chock-full of the calcium that women need so much, as well as important nutrients like vitamin B_{12}, riboflavin, magnesium, and zinc. We have nothing to lose by enjoying these superfoods, and much to gain.

As an ever-growing body of research testifies to how vital food choices are in delaying aging, retaining good looks and vitality, and preventing diseases, this realization should not be taken to mean that good food can replace medical advice and care. When you move toward a healthier diet, one that more fully meets your needs as a woman, it's a wise idea to consult your doctor in the changes you make and to listen to her advice on how such changes may affect any preexisting conditions you have. No information in this book is meant to be a substitute for appropriate medical attention.

Finally, this is a *YES* book about the life-enhancing foods you should eat—*not* those you ought to give up. The recipes stress fun, fast, fresh, and fabulous food. They are not only good for you but also mostly easy to prepare (even after work!) and great for sharing with friends and family. After all, "food is love"— and nutritious food is intelligent love.

THE SUPERFOODS PANTRY

When you resolve to say yes to the superfoods of high nutrition for body and mind, it's time to take a good, long look at what you're storing in the pantry, on the kitchen shelves, and in your refrigerator. These are the foods that will come to hand when you're inspired to cook or just have a sudden attack of the munchies. If what you have stashed away for these emergencies are apples instead of toaster tarts, whole wheat pita bread instead of potato chips, and nonfat yogurt instead of a spray can of whipped cream, it will make keeping your good resolutions infinitely easier.

The list of superfood basics is a long one, and you may not have space in your kitchen for everything—or some items may not be to your taste. Just let the list serve as a guide, fill your pantry with your favorites, and naturally don't expect to have every item in stock all the time. But great supermeals are always possible when you have most of these basics on hand.

Although organic foods have not been proved to be nutritionally superior, they *are* free of some pesticides and hormones that have been implicated in cancer and other diseases. This factor alone makes it worthwhile hunting them down and paying a little more. I think the fruits, in particular, taste better (but don't look as glossy and perfect) and I urge you to try the taste test yourself. To be sure you're getting the genuine article, buy produce labeled "Certified Organic"—if possible from a good "whole foods" market that will also serve as a source of some harder-to-find organic whole grains, beans, and other superfoods. The second choice is locally grown produce in its most abundant season; these fruits and vegetables are less likely to be waxed or treated with chemicals for the purpose of shipping afar.

Organic or not, fruits and vegetables should be cleaned by washing them in warm, then cold water. You can add a drop of dishwashing liquid to the wash water if you rinse very thoroughly afterward. Use a scrub brush for root vegetables. Peel all waxed fruits and vegetables to rid them of pesticides sealed in with the wax. Discard the outside leaves of lettuce and cabbage. Before using in recipes, rinse leafy greens in several changes of water, and if the leaves are curly, hold them open under running water to wash away sand and grit.

STASH THESE IN YOUR PANTRY AND KITCHEN

Handy, Healthy Canned Goods

Chicken and beef broth, reduced-sodium

Tomatoes and tomato paste

Tomato sauce (if you don't make your own)

Beets (for quick pickled beets!)

Roasted peppers (dress up a salad)

Fruits, no sugar added

Fish: choose your favorites from tuna, sardines, salmon, crab, anchovies

Real Cereals

Oatmeal
Cornmeal (refrigerate for
  long storage)
Whole wheat flakes or
  shredded biscuits

Wheat germ, toasted
  (refrigerate after
  opening)

Versatile Pasta

Macaroni, several shapes
  and sizes

Spaghetti, linguine, or
  fettuccine

Crunchies

Nuts, shelled—freeze for
  longer storage
Seeds for snacking—
  pumpkin, squash,
  sunflower

Popcorn, unflavored
Crackers, whole-grain, low-
  salt and low-fat

In the Cookie Jar

Read that ingredient list! Don't buy any that list sugar first.

Oatmeal cookies
Ginger snaps

Fig bars
Molasses cookies

Spices of Life

Try them all!

Herbs: dried leaves,
  everything from basil to
  tarragon
Spices: arrowroot to
  turmeric
Extracts: anise to vanilla, no
  artificial flavors!

Seeds for cooking: caraway
  to sesame
Whole: dried chilies, vanilla
  beans, cinnamon sticks

Baking Ingredients

Freeze or refrigerate whole-grain flours for long storage.

Flours: whole wheat,
  regular and pastry;
  unbleached white; rye
  and/or barley
Canola oil
Fruits, dried
Milk, nonfat dry in the box;
  skimmed evaporated in
  cans

Molasses
Honey
Maple syrup
Cocoa, Dutch-processed

In the Fruit Bowl

Okay at room temperature for a few days.

Apples
Bananas

Pears
Tomatoes

Great Grains

Couscous, whole-grain
(refrigerate or freeze)
Barley
Bulgur and cracked wheat
(refrigerate or freeze)

Rice: brown, white, wild
(refrigerate brown and
wild rice)

Hearty Legumes

Dried beans, peas, and
lentils

Canned beans: chickpeas,
cannellini, red kidney,
pinto, black, and adzuki

Root Vegetables

In a dark, cool, airy storage place.

Onions, shallots, garlic

Potatoes, sweet and white
Winter squashes, in season

Salad Fixings

Olive oil
Walnut and grapeseed oils
(refrigerate after
opening)

Variety of vinegars: wine,
rice, malt, balsamic,
sherry, raspberry, cider,
white

Refrigerator Staples

Yogurt: plain nonfat and
   flavored
Tofu
Eggs and/or prepared egg
   substitute
Milk, skim
Cheeses, low-fat
Carrots

Fruits: citrus, grapes,
   berries, and other
   perishables in season
Greens
Peppers
Cabbage
Frozen vegetables without
   sauce

TRASH THESE LOSERS

Very sugared cereal
Precooked (tasteless) rice
Most canned vegetables
   (except tomatoes, beets, and
   beans)
Highly salted canned and
   dried soups
Canned fruits in heavy syrup
Dried garlic or onion or
   garlic or onion salt (use
   fresh for better nutrition
   and taste)
Poor-quality pasta that
   cooks up mushy

Sauced or breaded frozen
   vegetables
Heavily salted and/or
   sugared prepared foods
   of every description,
   including salty mixes
   intended to "help" cook
   chicken or hamburger
High-fat cookies and cakes
   with more sugar than flour
   (check the labels)
Fruit pastries with more
   pastry than fruit

A GUIDE TO SUPERFOODS FOR SUPERMEALS

Concentrate on the positive: Fill your menus with these superfoods and you won't have much room left for the foods you know you should give up or play down. Each of the following choices offers multiple nutritional benefits as well as many possibilities for fresh, delicious dishes.* Enjoy!

APPLES

Ever since Eve, this crunchy fruit has been tempting snackers. Whether tart or sweet varieties are your choice, you'll benefit from the apple's soluble fiber to help lower LDL cholesterol and from its high boron content for building strong bones. Apples also help to regulate blood sugar, and in test tube experiments, apple juice showed itself hostile to viruses.

About 80 calories in a medium apple.

*Calorie source: U.S. Department of Agriculture. *Nutritive Value of Foods.* Washington, D.C.: U.S. Government Printing Office, 1981.

APRICOTS AND PEACHES

Take a clue from that rich orange color—these delectable summer treats are bursting with beta-carotene, a form of vitamin A that defends against many kinds of cancer, including lung cancer. Dried apricots are rich in iron for energy and in potassium for a healthy heart. All this and sweetness, too!

17 calories in a fresh apricot, 35 in a peach. 1/4 cup dried apricots contains 77 calories.

ARTICHOKES

This spiny thistle, a Mediterranean favorite, has been a luxury vegetable since Ancient Rome. Delightfully messy to eat whole, artichokes are a simply super source of folate to promote healthy births, plus fiber for gastrointestinal health, magnesium for building bones, and potassium for the heart.

Enjoy a whole artichoke for only 55 calories.

ASPARAGUS

This stylish harbinger of spring is a great source of antioxidant vitamins A, C, and E, as well as the B vitamin folate for healthy births and the heart-helping mineral potassium. Asparagus is low in calories and contains practically no fat, so revel in these elegant spears while the season lasts!

8 spears, 30 calories. Wow!

AVOCADOS

Sometimes called "butter pears" because they're undeniably high in fat, and therefore calories. Nevertheless, avocados are a surprisingly heart-healthy fruit. Their fat is monounsaturated, meaning it helps to lower LDL cholesterol, and avocados are extremely rich in potassium to maintain fluid and electrolyte balance. They are also a good source of folate, vital to women in their childbearing years.

A whole avocado weighing ½ pound is 305 calories. Not so bad when you compare to 320 calories for a chili dog with virtually no health benefits.

BANANAS AND PLANTAINS

Stomach-soother supreme! When you're too nervous to eat anything else, a banana will quiet those tummy flutters. At the same time, you'll be consuming vitamin B_6 for an immune-system booster plus potassium and soluble fiber for your heart. All this and a neat package, too! Plantains, the "cooking banana," offer magnesium to help keep bones strong. And these creamy carbohydrate fruits are strictly low-fat.

1 large banana, 105 calories; ½ plantain, 110 calories.

BARLEY

Check into this Cinderella grain—it's been around since biblical times but only recently recognized for its great fiber content; clinical tests show that it lowers LDL cholesterol as well as or better than oats. Barley is also rich in magnesium to keep bones strong and in several B vitamins to help the nervous system to function at its best. A staple grain in Middle Eastern cooking but rarely used in American kitchens, it needs only a little imagination to become a great grain salad or delectable pilaf.

About 270 calories in 1 cup of cooked barley.

BEANS AND PEAS

If you're not "into" bran, here's the best way to spoon in the most fiber for the health of your heart and digestive system. In addition, beans offer low-calorie protein for energy, B vitamins for your nerves, calcium for your bones, and beautiful complex carbohydrates for calmness and endurance. Because beans are digested slowly, they're an excellent food for diabetics. The best of food bargains!

Depending on variety, beans range around 225 calories a cup.

BEETS

Outstanding in their folate content, a B vitamin that's vital to healthy births, beets also contain a respectable amount of fiber. The greens are a potent source of beta-carotene to defend against cancer and of B_2 (riboflavin), the exerciser's vitamin. Despite their high sugar content, beets are an excellent diet food.

Only 55 calories in a cup of sliced beets.

BERRIES

Sweet treats with short seasons (but available frozen all year), berries are plump with good things like vitamin C for defense against infections and cancer and for quick healing of wounds, plus a surprising amount of fiber for the digestive tract. One of nature's great snack foods!

Strawberries, 45 calories a cup; raspberries, 60 calories a cup; blueberries, 85 calories a cup; blackberries, 86 calories a cup; cranberry sauce, 105 calories for 1/4 cup.

BREAD, WHOLE-GRAIN

It's still the staff of life, a chief source of complex carbohydrates for sustained energy. Make it a whole-grain bread to take advantage of all that vitamin B goodness for the nervous and reproductive systems, plus vitamin E for the antioxidant defense against cancer and both soluble and insoluble fiber. Bread helps you to meet the new recommendation for six to eleven servings of grain foods a day.

A slice of mixed grain bread is 65 calories.

BROCCOLI

This five-star vegetable is tops in nutritional benefits! It's a cruciferous vegetable and high in beta-carotene, making it an important part of an anticancer diet. It's also chock-full of vitamin C to boost immunity, calcium to ward off osteoporosis, and potassium for proper functioning of the heart muscle.

45 calories in a cup of chopped broccoli.

CABBAGE AND BRUSSELS SPROUTS

Big and little kings of the cruciferous patch, they're an important part of the vegetable defense against cancer. Cabbage is especially high in vitamin C, which helps to build new tissue and to form and maintain collagen, so important to youthful skin. Sprouts are rich in calcium for the bones and in folate to protect against birth defects. Both vegetables are a good source of fiber.

1 cup of shredded raw cabbage is 20 calories; 1 cup cooked sprouts, 65 calories.

CARROTS

The ubiquitous carrot practically sets the standard for beta-carotene, the plant form of vitamin A. Antioxidants like beta-carotene sponge up free radicals, those unstable molecules that cause many of the ills of advancing years. Among their many benefits, carrots are also noted for helping to prevent cataracts. Never be without them in your refrigerator!

A whole medium carrot is only 30 calories.

CAULIFLOWER

This "flower of the cabbage family" is one of those cruciferous vegetables rich in the cancer-fighting chemical sulforaphane. Cauliflower is also a good source of fiber and potassium to protect against heart disease, as well as vitamin C to stave off infections and folate to promote healthy births.

Just 30 calories in a cup of cooked cauliflower.

CHEESE, LOW-FAT

Although women sometimes avoid cheese for fear of its fat content, dairy products are still the most reliable source of calcium and vitamin D to build those strong bones that will carry us through menopause without fractures. Instead of giving up cheese, seek out the low-fat, skim milk varieties that are becoming more and more available.

1 ounce of part-skim mozzarella is 80 calories; ½ cup of low-fat cottage cheese, about 100 calories; 1 tablespoon of grated Parmesan, 25 calories.

CITRUS FRUITS

The beautiful winter fruits! Synonymous with antioxidant vitamin C, the citrus family defends against infections, cancer, and the outward signs of aging. Less well known, oranges are rich in two B vitamins—folate, especially needed by women of childbearing age, and thiamin, a vitalizer vitamin that enhances energy by helping in the metabolism of carbohydrates. In addition, grapefruit contains a compound that lowers LDL cholesterol.

A whole orange is a mere 60 calories; a half grapefruit, 40 calories.

Corn and Cornmeal

Sweet golden corn, one of our native vegetables, offers a complement of B vitamins to strengthen the nervous system, and both soluble and insoluble fiber to defend against diseases of the heart and digestive system. As a complex carbohydrate food, corn promotes the physical stamina needed by athletes—and by women who are "having it all."

135 calories in a cup of corn kernels; 120 calories in a cup of cooked cornmeal, such as polenta.

Eggplant

A Mediterranean favorite and also a great staple of vegetarian cooking, eggplant contains compounds called protease inhibitors that are thought to inhibit cancer formation. High in both potassium and fiber, this glossy vegetable (called *aubergine* in French) also defends against heart disease. Low in calories, too, if you don't drench it in oil and/or sauces.

Only 25 calories in a cup of eggplant.

Fish and Shellfish

For a healthy heart, think *fish*! Those amazing omega-3 fatty acids in fish lower destructive LDL cholesterol and raise helpful HDL cholesterol. The so-called oily fish like salmon, mackerel, and anchovies have the most, but all fish have their share of these beneficial fatty acids. And it *is* true about "brain food"—pregnant and nursing women are now being urged to eat fish; those same fatty acids are essential nutrients for the development of a child's brain, both as a fetus and as an infant.

A 3-ounce serving of fish or shellfish will range between 65 (shucked clams) to 140 (salmon) calories, depending on kind. (Compare to a cooked ground beef patty of the same weight at 230 calories.)

Fruits, Dried—Raisins, Figs, Dates, Prunes

As a substitute for nutritionally empty sweets, these dense treats are virtual powerhouses. Prunes and raisins are rich sources of iron. Figs contain a compound called benzaldehyde that has shown promise against cancer, and they are rich in thiamin, a B vitamin that plays a vital role in the normal functioning of the nervous system. All the dried fruits, especially dates, are great sources of fiber for the heart and the digestive tract.

5 prunes or dates, 3 figs, or ¼ cup raisins are all about 115 calories. (Compare to a 1-ounce peanut candy bar at 145 calories.)

Garlic, Onions, Leeks, Shallots, and Scallions

All the bulbs in this family are anticancer vegetables and, in general, rev up the immune system against many infections and diseases. Garlic lowers cholesterol and blood pressure. Both garlic and onion inhibit the blood clotting that can lead to strokes. Onion contains compounds that raise the blood level of HDL, the helpful cholesterol.

With all that big flavor, there's just 55 calories in a cup of chopped onion, 9 calories in 2 cloves of garlic.

Grapes

Another natural snack food, grapes contain boron to assist calcium in keeping bones strong, potassium to protect the heart, and the antioxidant vitamin C to lessen some of the affects of aging. In test tubes, grape juice has demonstrated an ability to polish off intestinal viruses.

35 to 40 calories, depending on variety, in 10 grapes. (Compare to 100 calories in an ounce of gumdrops.)

Greens, Dark Leafy

Vegetables with many virtues, dark leafy greens are rich in the antioxidant beta-carotene (masked by green chlorophyll) to ward off degenerative diseases—and also are generally good sources of vegetable calcium, vital for good bone structure. With so many varieties to choose from and so many quick ways to prepare them—salads to stir-fries—it's easy to take advantage of greens' nutritional bonanza.

Average is around 40 calories for a cup of cooked greens, depending on kind.

Kiwifruit

Need a burst of vitamin C? The kiwi's got it! Besides being a good source of fiber, the kiwi contains 74 milligrams of vitamin C in a single fruit, exceeding the RDA for women, which is 60. Whether vitamin C will prevent the common cold is hotly debated, but it has been shown (in doses much larger than the RDA) to relieve the symptoms.

A whole kiwi (5 to a pound) contains 45 calories.

Mangos and Papayas

Revel in these tempting tropical treats that are rich sources of antioxidant vitamins A and C. Unripe papayas contain the enzyme papain, used in meat tenderizers and some digestive aids. Mangos also provide vitamin B_1 and B_6, for energy and immune power.

65 calories in half a mango or a cup of papaya cubes.

MELONS

Not surprisingly, the richly colored cantaloupe (which was known in ancient Egypt as the muskmelon since Cleopatra was a girl) is highest among melons in vitamin A, and also in potassium to protect against degenerative diseases. But watermelon belongs in your food arsenal, too. That big favorite picnic fruit isn't just full of cool juiciness; it's rich in B vitamins as well. All melons are a dieter's dream dessert—lots of sweet flavor but few calories.

¼ of a whole cantaloupe (2⅓-pound size) or 1 cup diced watermelon are each about 50 calories.

MILK, SKIM

Still the standard for calcium and vitamin D, milk is a "must" for pregnant women—and also can be an important part of an osteoporosis prevention program for all women. (Exercise is another key ingredient.) A diet rich in calcium also helps to keep blood pressure under control. Skim milk has slightly more calcium than whole milk—and a lot fewer calories.

Enjoy nonfat or skim milk for 85 calories a cup; whole milk weighs in at 150 calories.

MOLASSES

Molasses earns its place among superfoods by being the one sweetener with real nutrition to offer women—not only is it loaded with iron but 2 tablespoons of blackstrap molasses also contain almost as much calcium as a cup of milk. An old-time treat for children used to be a spoonful of molasses stirred into milk—pumping up the calcium, still a good idea!

85 calories in 2 tablespoons of molasses. (90 calories in 2 tablespoons of sugar, but not much else.)

MUSHROOMS

Mushrooms do much more than add a gourmet touch to dishes. They're rich in B vitamins to keep the whole nervous system in order and are a source of vegetable protein, too. Asian research has produced evidence that the shiitake is an energizer of the entire immune system. The latest advice on mushrooms of all varieties is that they should be cooked; raw mushrooms contain hydrazines, which when consumed in large amounts are associated with tumors in mice.

Only 20 calories in ½ cup of cooked mushrooms.

NUTS AND SEEDS

Nature has filled these little packets of new life with its densest nutrition. Some special relationships are selenium in Brazil nuts; iron in pine nuts; vitamin E in almonds, hazelnuts, and pecans; zinc in peanuts and pecans; and B vitamins plus fiber in the full panoply of nuts. Seeds are just as rich: iron and folate in pumpkin and squash seeds; vitamin E and selenium in sunflower seeds; zinc, copper, magnesium—the works! But, alas, nature made nuts and seeds rich in calories, too.

An ounce of dry-roasted mixed nuts contains 170 calories. Seeds weigh in about the same. If you like to snack on big handfuls of trail mix, it's best to be walking those trails.

OATS

Forget that frosted flake stuff—there's some great soluble fiber for heart health in this old-fashioned cereal; oat bran can lower LDL cholesterol as well as some drugs prescribed for the same purpose. Oatmeal is also a good source of insoluble fiber for the digestive tract, and supplies iron, manganese, and protein as well. You can't beat a bowl of steaming oatmeal for a quick start on a cold morning!

About 100 calories in a serving of cooked oatmeal, ⅔ cup. (Compare to 250 calories in the same amount of a leading ''natural'' granola cereal.)

OLIVE OIL

"Liquid gold"—and the fat of choice throughout the Mediterranean region, monounsaturated olive oil lowers the "bad" LDL cholesterol and raises the "good" HDL cholesterol. Among other healthful oils are walnut and grapeseed, rich in essential fatty acids that feed the brain.

125 calories in a tablespoon of most oils.

PASTA

A marvelous complex carbohydrate food and stress-soother, pasta clears up the "blues" while adding body-building protein and B vitamins for the nervous system to your diet. It's the perfect choice for that T.G.I.F. supper!

190 calories in a cup of al dente spaghetti; 155 calories if cooked to the tender stage. (Compare with 240 calories in a 3-ounce serving of steak.)

PEARS

These delicate beauties, when consumed with their skins, supply soluble fiber to help lower LDL cholesterol, potassium vital to heart health, and the antioxidant vitamin C. Peeled or not, they're also a source of boron, part of the mineral package that helps to prevent osteoporosis.

Sweet, juicy pears are about 100 calories each, at 2½ pears per pound. (Compare with 200 calories in a 5-ounce serving of pudding.)

PEPPERS

Hot or sweet, these zesty accent vegetables are brimming with vitamin C (more even than oranges) as well as flavor. Sweet red peppers are rich in cancer-fighting carotenoids. Capsaicin, the chemical that puts the "heat" in hot peppers, actually signals the brain to produce anesthetic endorphins, causing something like a "runner's high." Hot peppers are also good medicine for the respiratory tract. To reduce that fiery sensation a bit, discard the seeds and use only the flesh of jalapeños and their spicy relatives.

Big flavor bargain: A hot raw chili or a sweet pepper (5 to a pound) contains a mere 20 calories.

PINEAPPLE

This traditional symbol of welcome is a rich source of manganese, an important mineral for the bones. A single serving will meet 25 percent of a woman's RDA of vitamin C. Like papaya, the pineapple contains enzymes that aid digestion.

1 cup of fresh raw pineapple is 75 calories; 1 cup of juice-packed chunks is 150.

POTATOES, SWEET AND WHITE

A quintessential carbohydrate food to banish stress, potatoes are rich in several B vitamins for the whole nervous system as well. Add to this vitamin C for healing, soluble fiber and potassium for the heart, and, in sweet pototoes, loads of beta-carotene to fight cancer.

A large baked potato weighing ½ pound contains 220 calories and gives you the comfortable feeling of having eaten real food. Dress it lightly with plain nonfat yogurt and chopped fresh chives.

RICE—BROWN, WHITE, AND WILD

All varieties are carbohydrate foods for sustained energy and are good sources of the B vitamins thiamin and niacin (brown rice has these nutrients naturally; white rice is enriched with them after they've been milled out). Brown rice contains the antioxidant vitamin E and rice bran, a cholesterol fighter. Wild rice, which isn't a true rice at all but a species of wild grass, is rich in folate, vital to women in their childbearing years.

Cooked rice is about 220 calories a cup.

SQUASH AND PUMPKIN

Plump with cancer-fighting beta-carotene (more than a day's supply in a single serving) and with fiber and potassium for the heart, those sweet winter squashes and pumpkins offer maximum nutrition from soup to dessert.

50 calories in a cup of mashed pumpkin; 80 in a cup of baked winter squash cubes.

TOFU AND SOYBEANS

Staple foods of Asian countries, soybeans and their products, such as tofu, rank as the most complete source of nonmeat protein. Research has associated these two foods with a reduced risk of various kinds of cancer and, in menopausal women, with fewer hot flashes. Soybeans and tofu are high in both iron and calcium, two minerals particularly associated with women's health needs.

1 cup of cooked soybeans contains 235 calories; ½ cup tofu, 95 calories.

TOMATOES

So important to Mediterranean cuisines, it's hard to believe the tomato is native to the Americas! Beautiful tomatoes are rich in potassium for the heart, vitamin C for general body repair, and vitamin A, a cancer fighter.

Good food news: A raw medium tomato is only about 25 calories; a cup of tomato sauce averages 75 calories.

TURKEY

All the poultry products, when skinned, are good sources of lower-fat protein and B vitamins, but turkey is especially rich in the iron and zinc these products share. Zinc is important to the immune and reproductive systems; iron is an energy mineral so often needed in women's diets. Ground turkey should be a great low-fat substitute for ground beef, but check the label to be sure of actual percentages.

1 cup of chopped turkey, mixed light and dark meat, is 240 calories.

WHOLE WHEAT

Super nourishment for body and mind, wheat is rich in B vitamins for the whole nervous system and in vitamin E and selenium—a dynamic duo of the cancer-fighting antioxidant team. It's also a rich source of choline, which may assist memory.

A slice of whole wheat bread contains 70 calories; 100 calories in a cup of wheat flakes.

YOGURT, NONFAT

Besides being a simply great source of calcium to strengthen bones and vitamin B_{12} for proper nerve function, yogurt may help to prevent yeast infections and lessen the risk of endometrial cancer. Nonfat yogurt can substitute healthfully for high-fat dairy foods like sour cream and cream cheese.

8 ounces of plain nonfat yogurt contain 145 calories. (Compare to 495 calories in the same amount of sour cream.)

— 1 —
IRON-RICH FOODS FOR SUPER ENERGY

A Strong Influence on Physical Endurance and Mental Alertness

Have you ever wished for more physical energy and endurance? Quicker comprehension and alertness? Stronger defense against infectious diseases? Livelier hair and stronger nails? Then it's time to consider whether you're eating enough iron-rich foods, because an iron deficiency can adversely affect all of the above. *Yes, all!*

IRON REALLY DOES GIVE YOU YOUTHFUL ENERGY FOR BODY AND MIND

Iron helps to carry oxygen around your body—as hemoglobin in the blood and myoglobin in the heart and skeletal muscles— a process that generates the energy with which life is sustained. Besides this major role, iron helps to oxidize fatty acids and to produce collagen and elastin, needed to maintain connective tissues (so important to good skin tone!) and to support the immune system. And iron promotes the synthesis and release of the neurotransmitter dopamine, the alertness chemical. Dopamine helps you to feel more mentally energetic. Mind and body, iron is part of what keeps you dancing instead of drooping through your day.

It's not that the trace mineral iron is a magic wand you can wave to banish those miserable winter colds or to have the kind of shining hair that models swing about in shampoo commercials. But insufficient stores of iron in a woman's body can quietly and insidiously contribute to a generally lackluster existence in many ways. And when iron stores are depleted to the point of anemia, a woman suffers from listlessness, fatigue, poor work performance, shortness of breath, and impaired muscle function; her hair becomes dull, her nails brittle, her skin pale. (Of course, these symptoms can occur for other reasons and should always be evaluated by a doctor.) But symptoms of iron deficiency such as fatigue, muscle weakness, and decreased alertness also can occur *without* anemia.

WOMEN GET LESS AND NEED MORE IRON THAN MEN DO

Iron deficiency is the most widespread deficiency in the world, chiefly among women. That's because women use and lose more iron than men. During childbearing years, monthly menstruation continually takes its iron toll from women in the form of lost blood. As a result, women normally have stored a quarter to a half of the iron that men have available, although in fact, women of childbearing years require twice as much iron as men. When a pregnancy occurs, even more iron is needed to supply the needs of the unborn child.

While only about 5 percent of American women develop iron-deficiency anemia, a much higher percentage of women are not getting all the iron they need for optimum energy and good health—especially if they're on a vegetarian or low-calorie diet or on a program of strenuous exercise. (Needless to say, if a woman donates blood, that lost iron will have to be replaced, also.) A current U.S. Department of Agriculture survey found that women 19 to 50 years old had intakes below 80 percent of their Recommended Dietary Allowance (RDA), whereas men of the same age met their RDA. These are some of the reasons why the surgeon general's current report urges women to eat more iron-rich foods.

In a sort of "iron irony," a recent report has linked iron overload in Finnish men to increased risk of heart attack. Although American men have an iron intake that is about half that of their Finnish counterparts, they are being warned not to ingest too much in the form of supplements and vitamin-enriched cereals at the same time as American women are being advised to consume more iron. Just one more way in which women's nutrition can be quite different from men's.

THE MORE YOU EXERCISE, THE MORE IRON YOU USE AND LOSE

Iron is stored in the liver, bone marrow, and spleen, and these stores are drawn upon when a woman's diet contributes less than is needed for her daily activities. Exercise, even a moderate aerobic program, while certainly necessary for overall fitness, further decreases iron values. But women whose systems have stored sufficient iron will exhibit more endurance in physical tests. Interestingly, eating iron-rich foods has been shown to be more effective than taking supplements to restore a desirable iron status for physical activity.

IRON IS ESPECIALLY VITAL DURING PREGNANCY

Supplements are definitely indicated, however, when a woman becomes pregnant, and usually 30 to 60 milligrams a day will be prescribed by her obstetrician. Nature favors the unborn, so iron is drained from the pregnant woman's system for the necessary doubling of her blood supply, for the enlargement of the uterus, and for development of the fetus. A pregnant woman's daily requirement for iron soars by an added 20 to 30 milligrams.

Research studies have shown that iron-deficiency anemia in mothers significantly affects their unborn children. The odds of having a low-weight baby are tripled, of having a preterm delivery doubled. Another study revealed that iron supplements taken by mothers while pregnant made it less likely for their children to have brain tumors during their early years.

YOUR IRON REQUIREMENTS CHANGE
AFTER MENOPAUSE

Once a woman passes menopause, some of the nutritional differences between men and women begin to equalize. In the case of iron, when menstruation and childbearing no longer deplete what the body absorbs and stores, the need for extra iron lessens.

Among the elderly, however, good nutrition is sometimes neglected (anything from depression to dental problems can be the cause) and results in an iron deficiency that in turn decreases appetite—a vicious cycle.

IT'S HARDER TO GET ENOUGH IRON FROM VEGETABLE FOODS

Since the most readily absorbed iron (called *heme iron*) comes from animal foods, the problem of keeping up with the need for iron is even greater for vegetarian women who rely on vegetable (*nonheme iron*) sources. But women who aren't pregnant should be able to obtain enough iron for good health by the right selection of foods—without ingesting a lot of unwanted saturated fat from red meat.

Including a 4-ounce serving of fish or poultry in a meal is beneficial, however, because it greatly improves the absorption of the accompanying vegetable iron.

GETTING THE MOST IRON FROM YOUR DIET TAKES SAVVY

To get the most out of your diet, you ought to know what enhances or inhibits iron absorption. When you read the iron content of various foods, that doesn't mean the body will absorb every milligram. In fact, only 10 to 15 percent of the heme iron available in organic foods (meat) is absorbed, and 3 to 5 percent of nonheme (vegetable) iron. The good news is, the more your body needs iron, the more it will compensate by absorbing a larger amount from any given meal.

The RDA for women ages 25 to 50 is 18 milligrams of iron, 10 milligrams for those over 50. But you have to keep in mind that, although a cup of beans may contain 4 to 5 milligrams of iron (depending on what kind of beans), only a percentage of the iron is going to be absorbed. It really takes a number of iron-rich foods each day—and the right combinations of foods—to fulfill the recommended allowance.

Vitamin C is one of the boosters, so if you're having foods rich in vitamin C at every meal (which is a good idea in itself), you're also increasing iron absorption.

Cooking in cast-iron pots adds minute traces of iron to food—but minute is all you need of a trace mineral, so cast-iron cooking is a recommended way of getting more iron into your meals. For beautifully browned foods in very little fat, you can't beat a well-seasoned cast-iron skillet anyway. It's also the perfect pan for quick breads and cakes, such as cornbread and pineapple upside-down cake.

But tea, coffee, egg yolks, and soy products hinder iron absorption. That's not to say they must all be avoided all the time. In fact, soy products are an important source of protein in a vegetarian diet. Fortunately, tofu, which is especially rich in iron, somehow doesn't share the inhibiting effect of other soy products. Then, of course, a cup of tea or coffee can be a real comfort many of us wouldn't want to give up. But extra iron will be needed to offset the iron-inhibiting foods and beverages.

Some vegetables, such as spinach, are high in iron but also high in oxalic acid, which inhibits the iron's absorption. Including other iron-rich foods, such as meat or fish, in the same meal with dark leafy vegetables like spinach will utilize the greens to best advantage by pumping up absorption.

Diminished gastric acid, which sometimes comes with aging, plus some antacids and some prescription drugs also adversely affect iron absorption.

The foods, the menus, the recipes, even the quick-fixes that help you to enrich your daily fare with plenty of iron follow in this chapter.

Superfood Sources of Iron

Beans and peas
Dried fruits: apricots,
   prunes, raisins
Greens, dark leafy: beet
   greens, collards, mustard
   greens, spinach, turnip
   greens
Molasses
Nuts
Potatoes with their skins

Pumpkin
Sardines
Seeds: pumpkin and squash
Shellfish: clams, mussels,
   oysters, scallops, shrimp
Sardines
Tofu
Tuna in oil
Turkey, dark meat

Note: While they're not included in my list of superfoods, pork, beef, and chicken are good sources of iron—and any kind of liver is an excellent source but high in cholesterol. If cholesterol is not a problem, an occasional snack of chopped chicken liver boosts iron intake in a big way.

A FAST IRON BOOST FOR A BUSY DAY

A scoop of chopped chicken liver
A sardine sandwich
A glass of prune juice
A shrimp cocktail
A cup of clam chowder or bean soup
A handful of trail mix with pumpkin and squash seeds.
   (Even better, make your own, adding pine nuts and
   raisins.)

Supermeals to Pep Up Your Iron Stores

Recipes indicated by a ♦ follow the menus.

AN INDOOR-OUTDOOR DINNER
FOR FOUR

Peppery Grilled Pork Chops
with Oranges and Orange-Ginger Sauce♦
Steamed New Potatoes in Jackets
Spinach Salad with Pecans♦
Molasses-Mocha Frozen Sandwiches♦

*P*ork chops, potatoes with skins, spinach, and pecans—plus molasses in the cookie "sandwiches"—all contain iron. Vitamin C in the oranges boosts absorption.

Peppery Grilled Pork Chops
with Oranges and Orange-Ginger Sauce

SUPERFOODS: shallots, oranges, onion

4 large loin pork chops, ¾ inch
    thick (about 1¾ pounds
    total)
2 shallots, minced

½ teaspoon each *black pepper*
    and ground ginger
¼ teaspoon ground allspice
Salt

For the sauce

1½ cups orange juice
3 tablespoons brown sugar
3 shallots, minced

1 bay leaf
3 slices fresh ginger
¼ teaspoon ground allspice

For the garnish

4 seedless oranges
1 medium red onion, peeled,
    sliced, and separated into
    rings

Remove as much fat as possible from the chops. Mix the 2 minced shallots, pepper, ginger, and allspice. Rub the mixture into the chops, salt to taste, and let them stand at room temperature for 15 to 20 minutes while heating the grill and making the sauce.

Combine the sauce ingredients in a saucepan, bring to a boil, and continue boiling over medium heat for 10 minutes or until reduced by half and syrupy. Strain the sauce into a sauceboat.

Peel the rind and pith from the oranges, and slice them into rounds.

Grill or broil the chops for 5 minutes per side, or until cooked through but not dry.

Divide the chops, orange slices, and red onion rings among 4 heated plates. Top with sauce.

MAKES 4 SERVINGS

Spinach Salad with Pecans

SUPERFOODS: spinach, onion, pecans

Zinc-rich pecans take the place of the traditional fat-drenched bacon.

10 ounces fresh spinach
⅓ to ½ cup Poppy Seed Dressing
  (see page 531)
⅓ cup crumbled blue cheese (may
  be omitted if you are on the
  fat alert)

½ cup lightly toasted pecans

Wash the spinach in several changes of water, beginning with warm and ending with cold. Spin-dry, discard stems, and tear the leaves into bite-size pieces. You should have about 4 cups. Pour ⅓ cup of the dressing into a large salad bowl. Put the spinach on top, but don't toss the salad yet.

Add the cheese and sprinkle the pecans on top.

The untossed salad can be made several hours in advance and stored in the refrigerator.

Just before serving, toss the salad well, adding more dressing if desired.

MAKES 4 SERVINGS

Molasses-Mocha Frozen Sandwiches

Here's a guiltless treat for your sweet tooth that's actually good for you and low in fat (compared to, say, an ice cream bar).

Spread each of 8 Joe Froggers (recipe follows, or store-bought soft molasses cookies can be substituted) with about ¼ cup mocha nonfat frozen yogurt. Make "sandwiches" by topping each with a second cookie, and store them in a plastic container in the freezer. If you're not going to use them within a day or two, wrap each sandwich separately in plastic wrap.

MAKES 8

JOE FROGGERS

SUPERFOODS: whole wheat flour, molasses

1 cup whole wheat flour

1 cup unbleached all-purpose flour

½ teaspoon each ground ginger, baking soda, and salt

½ cup (1 stick) butter or margarine

½ cup sugar

1 egg or ¼ cup prepared egg substitute

½ cup dark molasses

1 tablespoon dark rum (optional)

Preheat the oven to 375 degrees F.

Sift the flours, ginger, baking soda, and salt into a bowl.

In the work bowl of an electric mixer or by hand, cream the margarine until fluffy; gradually add the sugar, beating until light. Add the egg, molasses, and rum. Stir in the dry ingredients.

Drop the cookie batter by tablespoons onto a greased baking sheet. Allow plenty of space between. Bake in batches on the middle shelf for about 9 minutes. The cookies will rise, then flatten, and are done when they are slightly crisp on the edges (but not too brown).

This crisp cookie is best stored in a cookie jar rather than an air-tight plastic or tin container.

MAKES ABOUT 3 DOZEN

READY-WHEN-YOU-ARE DINNER FOR FOUR

Sole with Raisin-Nut Stuffing♦
Brown and Wild Rice (see page 525)
Yellow Tomato, White Bean, and Frisée Salad♦
Crustless Pumpkin Pie with Amaretti Crumbs♦

Most of this menu can be prepared ahead, except for popping the fish in a hot oven for 20 minutes. The iron in the fish enhances the iron in the raisin-nut stuffing. And there's more iron in the salad beans and the pumpkin pie. Yellow tomatoes add that desirable fillip of vitamin C.

Sole with Raisin-Nut Stuffing

SUPERFOODS: walnuts, raisins, garlic, parsley, sole, scallions

For the stuffing

½ cup finely chopped walnuts
¼ cup each raisins and plain
dry bread crumbs
1 garlic clove, pressed through a
garlic press

1 tablespoon minced fresh
parsley
½ teaspoon dried tarragon

8 fillets of sole* (about ½ pounds
total)
4 scallions, chopped

2 tablespoons olive oil
Paprika
Lemon wedges

Mix the stuffing ingredients. *The stuffing can be made a day ahead. Keep refrigerated, or freeze for longer storage.*

Preheat the oven to 400 degrees F.

Rinse and pat dry the sole fillets.

Put the scallions and 1 tablespoon of the oil into a baking pan large enough to hold the fish, and heat in the oven until sizzling. Remove the pan and brush the fillets with some of the oil.

Moisten the stuffing with just enough water to hold it together. Divide the stuffing among the fillets. Roll the fillets up the long way, and place them, seam side down, in the prepared pan. (If necessary, the rolls can be secured with toothpicks.) Drizzle the remaining 1 tablespoon of oil over the tops, and sprinkle them with paprika.

Bake on the top shelf for 20 minutes or until the fish flakes apart easily. Remove toothpicks. Serve with lemon wedges.

MAKES 4 SERVINGS

*Choose fillets wide enough for rolling and stuffing.

Yellow Tomato, White Bean, and Frisée Salad

SUPERFOODS: white beans, yellow tomato

*1 small head frisée (pale tender
    chicory, about ½ pound)*
*1 cup canned white beans
    (cannellini), drained and rinsed*
*1 large ripe yellow tomato
    (½ pound), diced*

*⅓ cup Honey-Mustard Dressing
    (see page 531)*
*2 tablespoons snipped fresh
    chives*

Wash and spin or shake dry the frisée. Trim off the stems, and break the frisée into bite-size pieces.

In a salad bowl, combine the beans, diced tomato, and dressing; stir. Put the frisée on top, and scatter the chives over that.

The salad can be made several hours in advance, and stored in the refrigerator. To keep the frisée crisp, don't toss the salad until just before serving.

MAKES ABOUT 4 SERVINGS

Crustless Pumpkin Pie with Amaretti Crumbs

SUPERFOODS: pumpkin, skim milk

Thin, twisted slices of seedless orange make a pretty garnish for this no-guilt, iron-and-carotene-rich "pie."

*About 20 amaretti cookies**	*1 teaspoon ground ginger*
1 teaspoon butter, melted	*½ teaspoon ground cardamom*
One 15-ounce can solid-pack	*¼ teaspoon salt*
* pumpkin for pie*	*2 tablespoons molasses*
1 cup sugar	*2 eggs, beaten*
1 tablespoon cornstarch	*1 cup milk (can be skim)*

Preheat the oven to 325 degrees F.

Crush the cookies into crumbs. This can be done most easily in a food processor. You should have about ⅔ cup.

Brush the melted butter over the sides and bottom of a 9-inch glass pie plate. Sprinkle ⅓ cup crumbs over the butter.

Blend the pumpkin with the sugar, cornstarch, spices, and salt. Beat in the molasses and eggs, then the milk. Gently pour the custard over the crumbs. Sprinkle the remaining ⅓ cup crumbs over the top.

Bake for 45 minutes, or until the custard is set to within 1 inch of the center. Cool on a wire rack, then chill in the refrigerator for several hours.

The pie can be made up to 1 day ahead—no crust to get soggy! Keep refrigerated.

To serve, cut into wedges. Carefully remove with a pie server to dessert plates.

MAKES 6 TO 8 SLICES

*Imported Italian almond cookies, very crisp.

SUNDAY SPECIAL FOR SIX

Short-Cut Cassoulet with Tofu♦
Red Cabbage and Green Apple Slaw♦
Indian Pudding♦

*R*elax *and read the newspaper while the oven does its work! An entree with a triple-boost of iron in meat, beans, and tofu. Molasses and enriched cornmeal in the pudding add even more. Vitamin C in the colorful cabbage slaw peps up absorption.*

Short-Cut Cassoulet with Tofu

SUPERFOODS: kidney beans, tofu

A quicker, lighter version of a French oven-baked stew that traditionally cooks for hours. If you wish, you can even omit the customary pork and increase the amount of tofu.

2 pork cutlets, trimmed of fat (about ¾ pound total)

1 whole boneless, skinless chicken breast

3 tablespoons olive oil

¼ cup minced shallots

1 garlic clove, minced

2 tablespoons flour

2 cups (a 13-ounce can) chicken or beef broth

Snipped fresh parsley sprigs and bay leaf

¼ teaspoon each dried thyme leaves and dried basil

Salt and pepper

One 20-ounce can kidney beans, drained and rinsed

½ pound firm tofu, diced

2 cups fresh bread crumbs (2 slices Italian bread)*

Cut the meat and chicken into 1-inch chunks. In a Dutch oven, brown the pork and chicken in batches in the hot oil. At the last minute, add the shallots and garlic; fry until they just begin to sizzle, about 2 minutes. Remove and reserve the meat, shallots, and garlic. Lower the heat, add the flour and keep stirring, letting the flour brown but not burn, 8 to 10 minutes.

In another pan, bring the broth to a boil and add it all at once to the flour, whisking to keep smooth until the sauce bubbles and thickens. Stir in the herbs and spices. Taste the sauce, adding salt and pepper as needed. Add the kidney beans and tofu; top with the meat, pushing it down into the sauce. Sprinkle half the bread crumbs over all.

The recipe can be prepared to this point several hours ahead. Keep refrigerated.

Preheat the oven to 350 degrees F.

Bake uncovered for 1 hour (20 minutes longer if refrigerated first), or until the meat is tender. Halfway through the cooking time, push the crusty crumbs into the sauce and sprinkle the remaining crumbs on top.

MAKES 6 SERVINGS

---

*Make the fresh bread crumbs by tossing chunks of bread down the feed tube of a food processor while the motor is running. Or substitute 1½ cups herb stuffing mix.

Red Cabbage and Green Apple Slaw

SUPERFOODS: red cabbage, apples, yogurt

Red cabbage will keep two weeks or more, wrapped in paper towels and a plastic bag in the bottom of the refrigerator, so if you happen to buy more than you need for this slaw, use it to enliven pale greens such as iceberg, not only with color and bite but also with vitamin C and cruciferous clout.

1 small head red cabbage (1 pound)	⅓ cup plain nonfat yogurt
2 Granny Smith apples, quartered and cored	3 tablespoons mayonnaise
¼ cup rice vinegar	1 teaspoon sugar
	¼ teaspoon each celery salt and white pepper

Shred the cabbage and apples in a food processor, using the coarse shredder. Immediately remove the mixture to a large bowl and toss with the vinegar to prevent the apples from turning brown. (Alternative method: Measure the vinegar into a large bowl. Use a sharp knife to slice the cabbage and apples very thin, adding them to the vinegar and tossing as you work.)

Blend the remaining ingredients to make a dressing. Toss the slaw with the dressing. Marinate an hour or so, refrigerated; toss the slaw before serving. Taste to correct seasoning; you may want more celery salt, pepper, vinegar, or yogurt.

May be made several hours ahead. Store, covered, in the refrigerator. Although this slaw tastes best the day it's made, it's still quite enjoyable the day after.

MAKES ABOUT 1½ QUARTS

Indian Pudding

SUPERFOODS: skim milk, stone-ground cornmeal,
molasses, raisins

*A dessert with a sense of history! The Iroquois boiled cornmeal
pudding in a pot, with maple syrup for sweetening, using a specially
carved stick to stir it. In colonial kitchens, "Indian meal pudding"
was boiled over a slow fire and beaten with a "pudding stick."
Later, long cooking in a slow oven—which method happily required
little watching and stirring—replaced the blackened pudding pot.*

3½ cups milk (can be skim)
½ cup stone-ground cornmeal
1 tablespoon butter
¼ cup granulated sugar
½ teaspoon each ground
    cinnamon, ground ginger,
    and salt
¼ teaspoon each ground allspice,
    ground cloves, and grated
    nutmeg

⅓ cup packed brown sugar
⅓ cup dark molasses
½ cup raisins
Vanilla nonfat frozen yogurt as
    topping (optional)

Preheat the oven to 300 degrees F.

In a saucepan, heat 3 cups of the milk until hot but not boiling.
Gradually add the cornmeal, whisking constantly. Continue to
cook and whisk until the mixture thickens and bubbles, about
3 minutes. Blend in the butter.

Mix the granulated sugar with the spices and salt. Add both
sugars and the molasses to the cornmeal. Spoon the batter into
a buttered 2-quart glass or ceramic baking dish set into a larger
baking pan. Place this on the middle shelf of the oven.

Carefully add hot water to the outside pan. Bake 2 hours.

Stir, blending well. Mix in the raisins. Carefully pour the remaining ½ cup milk over the top of the pudding. Bake 2 hours longer. Cool to room temperature before serving with scoops of frozen yogurt.

The pudding can be made 1 day ahead and stored in the refrigerator. Reheat in a 300-degree oven or in the microwave.

MAKES **6** TO **8** SERVINGS

AFTER-WORK EASY FOR FOUR

Spanish-Style Scallops with White Beans♦
Lebanese Spinach Salad♦
Cantaloupe-Ginger Sorbet♦
or
Fresh Cantaloupe Wedges

*S*callops and white beans double up on iron, in this twenty-minute entree, plus steamed spinach salad in a cold creamy (but nonfat) yogurt dressing. Cantaloupe sorbet for dessert gives that vitamin C boost—be sure to freeze the sorbet ingredients before going to work.

Spanish-Style Scallops with White Beans

SUPERFOODS: scallops, tomato sauce, beans, parsley

1½ pounds sea scallops
¾ cup seasoned bread crumbs
2 tablespoons olive oil
½ cup dry white wine or bottled clam juice
1 cup tomato sauce, homemade (see pages 516–518) or from a jar

½ teaspoon dried thyme leaves
¼ teaspoon Spicy Pepper Mix (see page 539)
One 20-ounce can white beans (cannellini), drained and rinsed
2 tablespoons chopped fresh flat-leaf parsley

Rinse the scallops. Cut any extra-large scallops in half. Put the crumbs in a plastic bag, add the scallops, and shake to coat.

In a large skillet, heat the oil until quite hot, and fry the scallops until they are golden on both sides and cooked through, 4 to 5 minutes. Cut one to see that it's opaque through the center. Remove the scallops.

Combine the wine and tomato sauce in the skillet; add the seasonings. Bring the mixture to a boil, scraping the bottom of the pan. Reduce the heat and simmer 5 minutes.

Add the beans and cook 5 minutes longer. Return the scallops and heat through.

Sprinkle with parsley before serving.

MAKES 4 SERVINGS

Lebanese Spinach Salad

SUPERFOODS: spinach, leeks, olive oil, yogurt, garlic

1½ pounds fresh spinach   *Salt and pepper*
4 small leeks*   *1 cup Yogurt-Mint Dressing*
3 tablespoons olive oil   *(see page 532)*

Wash the spinach in several changes of water, and snip off the tough stems. Steam the spinach in just the water that clings to the leaves until they are wilted, about 3 minutes. Drain well.

Trim the green part from the leeks. Cut them in half lengthwise, and wash between the layers. Drain and chop the leeks.

Put the olive oil into a large skillet, and "sweat" the leeks in it over low heat for 10 to 15 minutes, until they are softened. Don't brown the leeks.

Add the spinach, salt and pepper to taste, and toss well. Remove the spinach and leeks to a salad dish.

Serve the salad at room temperature with the chilled dressing on the side.

MAKES 4 TO 6 SERVINGS

---

*A bunch of scallions can be substituted, in which case omit washing between layers.

Cantaloupe-Ginger Sorbet

SUPERFOODS: cantaloupe

How easy can a dessert be? Once you've frozen the fruit, this super sorbet can be whipped up at a moment's notice. Simply delectable!

4 cups diced cantaloupe (about 2 small cantaloupes)	*½ cup sugar* *1 teaspoon ground ginger*

Combine all the ingredients in a plastic bag. Freeze for about 4 hours.

The fruit can be frozen several days, or even a couple of weeks, in advance. Have it ready for when you absolutely must have a dish of smooth, creamy frozen dessert!

Puree the fruit mixture in a food processor until very smooth. Serve at once.

MAKES 3 CUPS; 4 SERVINGS

A SATURDAY NIGHT SUPPER FOR SIX

Chili Meatloaf♦
Steamed Mustard Greens
Cornbread with Tomatoes, Peppers, and Onions♦
Anise Oranges♦

The meatloaf has a heart of red kidney beans for extra iron. Mustard greens are among the highest in iron of the dark leafy greens. Bake the cornbread in a cast-iron skillet for even more iron. Tomatoes, peppers, and oranges deliver plenty of vitamin C to make the most of every milligram.

Chili Meatloaf

SUPERFOODS: wheat germ, garlic, ground turkey, kidney beans

½ cup chili sauce

1 egg or ¼ cup prepared egg substitute

½ cup herb stuffing mix or fresh bread crumbs

¼ cup wheat germ

2 teaspoons chili powder

1 teaspoon dried cilantro

½ teaspoon each dried oregano and salt

¼ teaspoon Spicy Pepper Mix (see page 539) or black pepper

1 garlic clove, pressed through a garlic press or finely minced

1¼ pounds ground turkey

1 cup canned kidney beans, drained and rinsed

Mix ¼ cup of the chili sauce with the egg, stuffing mix, wheat germ, seasonings, and garlic until well blended. Mix in the meat.

Put about two-thirds of the meat mixture into a loaf pan and pat it up the sides about 1 inch to form a box shape. Spoon the beans into the middle and press them down lightly. Smooth the remaining meat mixture on top, then the remaining ¼ cup chili sauce over all.

The meatloaf can be prepared several hours ahead. Keep refrigerated.

Preheat the oven to 350 degrees F.

Bake 40 to 45 minutes on the middle shelf, until the meat is cooked through. Let stand 10 minutes before slicing.

MAKES 6 TO 8 SERVINGS

Cornbread with Tomatoes, Peppers, and Onions

SUPERFOODS: cornmeal, skim milk, tomatoes, onions, peppers

Bake the cornbread first, then lower the oven temperature for the meatloaf. When the meatloaf comes out, turn off the heat and put the cornbread back in the oven to rewarm while the meatloaf stands.

1 cup stone-ground yellow cornmeal

1 cup unbleached all-purpose flour

1 tablespoon baking powder

1 teaspoon salt

1 cup milk (can be skim)

1 egg or ¼ cup prepared egg substitute

¼ cup vegetable oil

1 cup diced fresh plum tomatoes

¾ cup diced green pepper

½ cup diced onion

1 tablespoon minced fresh or canned jalapeño pepper*

1 tablespoon butter

2 tablespoons grated Parmesan cheese

Preheat the oven to 400 degrees F.

Sift the cornmeal, flour, baking powder, and salt into a large bowl. In another bowl, beat the milk, egg, and oil. Mix the vegetables in a third bowl, taking care to distribute the jalapeño evenly throughout.

Melt the butter in a 10-inch cast-iron skillet over low heat until it sizzles. (Alternatively, use a 2-inch-deep metal baking pan.)

Pour the liquid mixture into the dry ingredients; stir just enough to blend. Fold in the vegetables.

*Use rubber gloves when mincing hot peppers.

Spoon the batter into the hot pan, and sprinkle it with the grated cheese. Bake in the top third of the oven for 35 minutes, or until lightly browned on top and dry inside when tested with a cake tester. Serve warm.

The bread tastes best when made fresh, but leftovers can be warmed in the oven or microwave. Leftover bread should be removed from the pan, wrapped, and refrigerated. It can also be frozen for longer storage.

MAKES 6 WEDGES

Anise Oranges

SUPERFOODS: oranges

6 medium seedless oranges
¼ cup anisette liqueur*
1½ teaspoons finely chopped
   fresh mint

Fresh mint sprigs for garnish
   (optional)

With a sharp knife, peel the oranges right down to the flesh, removing not only the peel but also the white membrane. Slice into rounds; halve or quarter the slices. (The halves look prettier, but the quarters are easier to eat.) Put the oranges in an attractive bowl, and stir in the remaining ingredients. Marinate in the refrigerator for an hour or so before serving.

The compote can be made several hours ahead but tastes best when served the same day.

Garnish with mint sprigs, if desired.

MAKES 6 SERVINGS

*½ teaspoon anise flavoring can be substituted.

A SOUP PARTY FOR SIX

Turkey Pepper-Pot Soup♦
Sliced Tomatoes with Fresh Basil and Olive Oil
Spanakopita Loaf (Spinach, Feta, and Garlic Bread)♦
or
Whole Wheat French Bread
Apricot Rice Pudding♦

Iron-rich turkey gets even richer with the aid of vitamin C in both the peppers and the sliced tomatoes. Homemade bread with a melting spinach filling adds its share, but if you're not into baking, store-bought whole wheat French bread works fine with this menu. Desserts can contribute to good nutrition as well as satisfy that sweet tooth; the apricot is a powerhouse—high in iron, plus tops in beta-carotene.

Turkey Pepper-Pot Soup

SUPERFOODS: green peppers, jalapeño peppers, onion, carrot, turkey, potatoes

A meal in one pot, this version of pepper-pot soup has a pleasantly "creamy" flavor without a bit of cream.

2 tablespoons olive oil

2 green bell peppers, seeded and
  chopped

1 red bell pepper, seeded and
  chopped

1 or 2 jalapeño peppers, seeded
  and minced* (optional)

1 medium onion, chopped

2 celery stalks, chopped

1 carrot, scraped and diced

2 turkey thighs (about 1¾
  pounds total), skinned

5 cups water

¾ teaspoon salt

1 pound potatoes, peeled and
  diced

½ cup cold water

¼ cup all-purpose flour

Pepper and additional salt

Heat the oil in a 4-quart pot, and "sweat" the peppers, onion, celery, and carrot over low heat, stirring occasionally, for 10 minutes. Do not brown the vegetables.

Rinse the turkey in salted water, then plain cold water.

Add the turkey, the 5 cups water, and the salt to the pot. Bring to a boil, lower heat, and simmer 1 hour, until the turkey is tender. Remove the turkey and let it cool slightly.

Meanwhile, add the potatoes to the pot, and cook until they are tender, 5 to 8 minutes. Cut up all or some of the turkey to return to the soup. (It's a lot of turkey! You could put some aside for a salad the next day, or freeze it with a bit of broth for another occasion.)

To thicken the soup, pour ½ cup cold water into a jar, add the flour, cover, and shake well. Strain into the simmering soup, stirring constantly. Simmer 5 minutes to cook the flour.

Taste to correct seasoning; add salt and pepper to your taste.

The soup can be prepared a day ahead, stored in the refrigerator, and reheated. If anything, the flavor improves.

MAKES ABOUT 2 QUARTS

*Use rubber gloves when seeding and cutting hot peppers.

Spanakopita Loaf

(Spinach, Feta, and Garlic Bread)

SUPERFOODS: spinach, garlic

If you like to make bread, you'll enjoy turning out this easy but fancy loaf. The directions look lengthy, owing to the alternatives given, but essentially this dough is no different from a quick pizza dough given an upscale twist.

1 envelope active dry yeast
1 teaspoon sugar
1 cup very warm water
3¼ cups unbleached all-purpose
   flour (whole wheat flour can be
   substituted for part or all of
   the flour)
¾ teaspoon salt
3 tablespoons olive oil
1 10-ounce package frozen leaf
   spinach, thawed; or 1 pound
   fresh spinach, steamed until
   wilted

2 garlic cloves, pressed through a
   garlic press
4 ounces feta cheese, crumbled
12 Kalamata olives, pitted and
   halved
2 tablespoons prepared egg
   substitute*

*Beaten egg mixed with 1 tablespoon water can also be used. I generally choose the substitute for glazing because 1 whole egg is too much.

Stir the yeast and sugar into the warm water. Let it stand 5 to 10 minutes; the yeast should bubble up to show that it's active.

Processor method: Combine the flour and salt in the work bowl of a food processor fitted with the steel blade. Measure 2 tablespoons olive oil. Coat a medium bowl with a little of the olive oil; pour the rest into the flour. Process to blend.

With the motor running, pour the yeast mixture down the feed tube. Process 10 to 15 seconds, until the mixture forms a ball that cleans the sides of the bowl. (If the flour does not adhere in a ball, add a little water, 1 teaspoon at a time.) Continue to process, counting 30 seconds, or until the dough is elastic and springy.

Alternative methods: The ingredients can be combined in an electric mixer fitted with a dough hook. Knead 5 minutes. Or the ingredients can be combined by hand. Knead 10 minutes.

Place the dough in the oiled bowl, turning it around to grease all sides, and cover with plastic wrap. Let it rise in a warm place until doubled in bulk, about 1 hour and 15 minutes. Punch the dough down and roll out to an oblong about 10 × 14 inches.

Put the thawed spinach in a fine-meshed strainer and press out as much moisture as possible. In a small skillet, heat the remaining 1 tablespoon oil and sauté the garlic until it sizzles.

Spread the oil, garlic, and spinach to within 1 inch of the edge of the dough. Sprinkle on the feta and olives.

Roll up the dough like a jelly roll, folding in the ends. Pinch the ends and the edges closed. Place the loaf on an oiled baking sheet sprinkled with cornmeal, curving it slightly into a crescent. With a serrated knife, cut slashes ½ inch deep and 1 inch apart on the top of the loaf. Let the loaf rise until doubled.

Preheat the oven to 375 degrees F.

Brush the loaf with prepared egg substitute. Bake the loaf in the middle of the oven for 30 minutes or until both the bottom and top crusts are golden.

Cool slightly and serve warm.

Wrap and refrigerate leftover bread; use within a day or two. It may be warmed in a 300 degree F. oven.

MAKES 1 LOAF

Apricot Rice Pudding

SUPERFOODS: rice, prunes, skim milk, almonds

1¼ cups cooked plain rice

½ cup chopped dried apricots (or snip them with a kitchen scissors—it's easier!)

3 eggs or ¾ cup prepared egg substitute

½ cup sugar

Scant teaspoon each *almond flavoring* and vanilla extract*

2 cups milk (whole milk recommended), scalded

⅓ cup slivered almonds

Preheat the oven to 325 degrees F. Arrange a buttered 1½-quart casserole in a larger pan.

Stir the rice and apricots together in the casserole.

Beat together the eggs, sugar, and flavorings until the sugar is dissolved and the mixture well blended. Gradually add the hot milk. Pour over the rice, stir, and sprinkle with the almonds.

Put the casserole and surrounding pan in the oven on the middle shelf, and carefully pour hot water in the larger pan.

Bake the pudding for 40 to 50 minutes, until set, stirring once after 20 minutes cooking time. Serve slightly warm or chill in the refrigerator.

MAKES 6 SERVINGS

*Don't settle for imitation almond flavoring; buy the real thing. It's harder to find but worth the effort.

SIMPLY ENTERTAINING FOR FOUR

Smoked Salmon Spread♦
or
Cannellini Puree♦
with Assorted Whole-Grain Dippers
Herb-Crusted Chicken on a Bed of Steamed Spinach♦
Couscous with Golden Raisins♦
Roasted, Scalloped Tomatoes♦
Tropical Mango-Kiwi Trifle♦
or
Sliced Fresh Kiwis and Oatmeal Cookies

Cannellini, salmon, chicken, spinach, and raisins bring the iron to this menu, which tomatoes, mango, and especially kiwi—bursting with vitamin C—make more available. The recipes in this expandable menu are easily doubled.

Smoked Salmon Spread

SUPERFOODS: yogurt, salmon

1 cup Yogurt Cheese (see page 534)
¼ pound smoked salmon pieces
1 tablespoon vodka (optional)

1 teaspoon prepared horseradish
¼ teaspoon freshly ground pepper
Cocktail rye bread or bagel chips

Combine all ingredients except pepper and bread in a food processor, and process until smoothly blended. Stir in the pepper. Chill to develop the flavor.

The spread can be made 1 to 2 days ahead and kept refrigerated.

Let stand at room temperature 20 to 30 minutes before serving with cocktail rye or bagel chips.

MAKES ABOUT 1½ CUPS

Cannellini Puree

SUPERFOODS: garlic, cannellini, lemon juice

2 tablespoons olive oil
1 garlic clove, minced
One 20-ounce can cannellini
   (Italian white beans)

¼ teaspoon each *ground cumin*
   and ground coriander
⅛ teaspoon or more *white pepper*
Juice of ½ lemon

In a small skillet, heat the olive oil slightly, add the garlic, and as soon as it sizzles, remove the pan from the heat. Let the mixture stand at room temperature at least a half-hour.

Drain and rinse the beans. Puree them in a food processor. Now you have a choice: For a mild garlic flavor, add only the flavored oil from the skillet. For a strong flavor, add both oil and garlic. Blend with the beans.

Blend in the seasonings and lemon juice. Taste to correct seasoning, adding more pepper or lemon juice to your taste.

The puree can be made 1 to 2 days ahead. Keep refrigerated.

Serve with crackers, cocktail rye bread, or as part of an antipasto.

MAKES 1½ CUPS

Herb-Crusted Chicken on a Bed of Steamed Spinach

SUPERFOODS: yogurt, whole wheat bread, wheat germ, spinach

The boneless, skinless chicken parts available at today's meat counters are especially convenient for a busy person. This quickly fixed entree for boneless thighs can easily be doubled.

½ cup plain nonfat yogurt
½ teaspoon each dried tarragon
   and dried rosemary
¼ teaspoon white pepper
1 cup fresh crumbs from whole
   wheat bread*
¼ cup wheat germ

2 tablespoons grated Parmesan
   cheese
8 boneless, skinless chicken
   thighs (1½ pounds total)
Paprika
1 pound fresh spinach

Preheat the oven to 375 degrees F.

In a soup dish, blend the yogurt with the herbs and pepper. On a sheet of waxed paper, mix the crumbs, wheat germ, and cheese.

Use tongs to coat the chicken lightly with the yogurt, then the crumbs. Place the pieces on a well-oiled baking sheet. Sprinkle them with paprika.

Bake the chicken in the top third of the oven for 35 to 40 minutes, turning the pieces once after about 20 minutes. Loosen the crust well before turning, and sprinkle the second side with paprika also. Drain off any liquid that has accumulated in the pan.

---

*These are simply made by tossing quarter-slices of bread down the feed tube of a food processor while the motor is running. In fact, it's so easy, why not make some extra and freeze them for another time?

Meanwhile, wash the spinach in several changes of water, beginning with warm and ending with cold. Remove any tough-looking stems. Put the spinach in a large pot, and cook it with just the water that clings to the leaves until they're wilted, about 3 minutes. Drain the spinach well and keep it warm.

Divide the spinach among 4 plates, and top it with the cooked chicken.

MAKES 4 SERVINGS

Couscous with Golden Raisins

SUPERFOODS: onion, green pepper, brown couscous, golden raisins

Light and delicate as is all couscous, the whole-grain variety, some-times called brown couscous, is richer in B vitamins.

1 tablespoon olive oil
¼ cup each *chopped onion and chopped green bell pepper*
2 cups (a 13-ounce can) chicken broth

¼ teaspoon each *dried thyme leaves and ground cinnamon*
1 cup whole-grain couscous*
¼ cup golden raisins

In the top of a large double boiler, heat the oil over direct heat and sauté the vegetables until they are softened, about 5 minutes. Add the broth, thyme, and cinnamon; bring the mixture to a boil. Gradually add the couscous, whisking. Reduce the heat, and stir over low heat until quite thick. Stir in the raisins.

Bring 2 inches of water to a boil in the bottom of the double

*Not quick-cooking. Available in whole-foods markets.

boiler. Cook the couscous over boiling water for 25 to 30 minutes, stirring occasionally. Fluff the couscous before serving.

The couscous can be made ahead and rewarmed in the double boiler or in a glass casserole in the microwave. Fluff it again.

MAKES ABOUT 2½ CUPS

Roasted, Scalloped Tomatoes

SUPERFOODS: tomatoes, onion

Meatier than their juicy round counterparts, plum tomatoes hold their shape well when roasted.

2 tablespoons olive oil
8 large plum tomatoes
¼ teaspoon dried basil
Salt and pepper

1 cup herb stuffing mix (not the
  stovetop variety)
½ cup chopped onion

Preheat the oven to 375 degrees F.

Spread 1 tablespoon of the oil in a quiche pan or 10-inch glass pie plate. Cut the tomatoes in half lengthwise; remove the seeds with a paring knife tip. Lay the tomatoes, cut sides up, in the pan in one layer as much as possible. Season the tomatoes with basil, and salt and pepper to your taste. Salt can be omitted entirely, if you wish, since the stuffing mix is well salted.

Sprinkle the stuffing mix and chopped onion on top and between the tomatoes. Drizzle the remaining tablespoon of oil over all.

Bake about 45 minutes on the middle shelf, until the tomatoes are tender but still hold their shape. If the stuffing gets too brown, lay a sheet of foil loosely over the top.

MAKES 4 SERVINGS

Tropical Mango-Kiwi Trifle

SUPERFOODS: skim milk, mango, kiwi

Once you get accustomed to using an egg substitute in cooking, you'll find it's a bit more convenient to measure and mix than regular eggs.

For the custard

2 cups milk (can be skim)   1 whole egg, beaten
¼ cup cornstarch   ½ cup honey, slightly warmed
½ cup prepared egg substitute or   2 tablespoons rum or 1 teaspoon
   3 egg yolks   vanilla extract

12 plain ladyfingers, halved   ½ cup coconut for garnish
1 ripe mango   (optional)
2 ripe kiwifruit

Pour the milk into a saucepan, and stir in the cornstarch until it's dissolved. Whisk in the egg substitute, whole egg, and honey. Cook over medium heat, stirring constantly, until the custard boils and thickens. Keep stirring 1 minute longer. Remove from the heat, and stir in the rum or vanilla. Let cool slightly.

Choose a glass bowl that holds 6 cups. Line the bottom and sides of the bowl with ladyfinger halves. Use a vertical arrangement for the sides. You should have about 6 halves left over.

Prepare the fruit. Peel and dice the mango. Peel and slice the kiwi.

Gently spoon about ⅔ cup of the custard into the cake-lined bowl. Lay the kiwi slices over that. Add another ⅔ cup of custard, and a layer of ladyfinger halves. Lay the diced mango over the ladyfingers. Smooth the remaining custard over the top.

If desired, lightly toast coconut in an ungreased skillet, stirring constantly, until it begins to turn golden. Sprinkle it over the custard.

The trifle should be made several hours in advance, and stored in the refrigerator. Although it tastes best when served the same day as it's made, leftovers are still delicious.

MAKES 6 TO 8 SERVINGS

A MAKE-AHEAD SUPPER
FOR FOUR

Lentil Soup with a Carrot Swirl◆
Hot Rolls
Shrimp and Broccoli Salad◆
Prune Hermits◆

Soup, salad, and dessert all packed with iron-rich foods, lentils, shrimp, prunes, and molasses. Broccoli, plus a garnish of tomato wedges, gives that helpful dash of vitamin C.

Lentil Soup with a Carrot Swirl

SUPERFOODS: carrots, lentils, parsley

Stewed lentils in the freezer are like money in the bank, there are so many uses for this versatile little legume with the big nutritive value.

4 large carrots
1 teaspoon butter
A few pinches of ground
  cinnamon and white pepper
2 cups (a 13-ounce can) chicken
  broth, or more as needed

3 cups Stewed Lentils (see page
  521), undrained
Fresh flat-leaf parsley for
  garnish

Scrape and slice the carrots. Put them in a saucepan with water to cover and add the butter; boil until tender, 10 to 12 minutes. Drain the carrots; reserve the cooking water.

Puree the carrots in a food processor; add cinnamon, pepper, and enough of the cooking water to make a puree that's thick but pourable. If more liquid is necessary, use chicken broth.

Rinse the work bowl, and puree the lentils, adding chicken broth as necessary to achieve a soup consistency.

The purees can be made a day ahead and stored, covered, in the refrigerator.

Heat the purees separately (a microwave is the easiest method) and whisk each to a smooth texture.

Coarsely snip the fresh parsley for a garnish.

Divide the lentil soup among 4 bowls. Swirl about ¼ cup carrot puree in the center of each, keeping the 2 colors separate. Sprinkle with parsley and serve.

MAKES 4 SERVINGS

Shrimp and Broccoli Salad

SUPERFOODS: broccoli, shrimp, onion, tomatoes

8 large leaves of romaine lettuce
8 spears cooked broccoli
1 pound cooked, cleaned shrimp
1 cup ''Light'' Russian Dressing
(see page 532)

4 very thin slices red onion
2 ripe medium tomatoes, cut into
wedges

Wash and shake dry the lettuce. Tear it into bite-size pieces, and make a bed of it on a round platter or large plate. Arrange the broccoli over the lettuce like spokes of a wheel, florets outward.

Mix the shrimp with the dressing, and heap them in the center. Separate the onion into rings, and arrange them over the shrimp. Tuck the tomato wedges around the broccoli. Chill until ready to serve.

The salad can be made several hours ahead and stored in the refrigerator.

MAKES 4 SERVINGS

Prune Hermits

SUPERFOODS: whole wheat flour, molasses, prunes, walnuts

Spice-flavored baked goods lend themselves especially well to the substitution of whole wheat flour for white flour and monounsaturated canola oil for butter. Extra hermits can be wrapped in foil and frozen for later use.

1½ cups whole wheat flour
1 teaspoon ground cinnamon
½ teaspoon each ground cloves, grated nutmeg, baking powder, and salt
½ cup canola oil
⅔ cup packed brown sugar
2 eggs or ½ cup prepared egg substitute

¼ cup molasses
½ cup chopped pitted prunes
½ cup chopped walnuts

Preheat the oven to 350 degrees F. Butter and flour a 13 × 9-inch baking pan.

Sift the dry ingredients into a large bowl. In another bowl or in a food processor, blend the oil, brown sugar, eggs, and molasses. Pour the liquid ingredients into the dry, and stir to blend. Stir in the prunes and walnuts.

Spoon the batter into the prepared pan and smooth it with a spatula into a uniform layer. Don't worry about little hollows; they will all fill in as the hermits bake.

Bake for 20 minutes on the middle shelf, or until the surface is lightly browned and a cake tester inserted in the center comes out dry. Cool in the pan on a wire rack before cutting into squares.

MAKES 18 TO 24 BARS

———— 2 ————
Fabulous Fish

For a Protein Punch that Guards Against Heart Disease—and Much More!

Fish is such a great food nutritionally that the more we substitute seafood for red meat, the healthier our diets are likely to be. We'll still be getting all the body-building protein we need, but without the fear of raising our LDL (low-density lipoprotein) cholesterol. That's the important figure we're hearing so much about these days, and for good reason. LDLs carry cholesterol from the liver to the bloodstream where it may build up and clog arteries, whereas HDLs (high-density lipoproteins) are thought to sweep excess cholesterol out of the blood and return it to the liver where it's excreted as bile through the intestinal tract.

FISH FIGHTS THE NUMBER ONE KILLER OF WOMEN

We women need to take protective nutrition for a healthy heart very seriously these days. Once thought of as a "man's disease," coronary heart disease is now the number one killer of women, rated above all the breast, ovarian, and cervical cancers combined. While it's still true that heart attacks begin to show up in the male population a decade or so before they do among females, and that men tend to have a higher cholesterol count at an earlier age, the hormonal changes that come with menopause dramatically equalize these potential dangers. Once our bodies begin to register the lack of estrogen, the LDL cholesterol count often rises. Statistically, by age 55 to 60, the average cholesterol count of women surpasses that of men.

First and foremost of the protective nutrition offered by fish is its defense against coronary heart disease. Scientists became excited about the "fish effect" when population studies revealed that Greenland Inuits, Japanese fishermen, and Native Americans of the Pacific Northwest—peoples who dined on fish night after night—rarely developed coronary heart disease, probably because their LDL cholesterol usually was low. On the other hand, their neighbors, the Danes, who ate much less fish, tended to have a higher LDL cholesterol. Further research highlighted the omega-3 fatty acids as the beneficial substances; fish is rich in omega-3 fatty acids; the fatter or "oilier" the fish, the more it contains.

Along with the perceived connection between omega-3 fatty acids and a lower LDL count, these compounds are known to have four other heart-defending effects: They lower the rate at which the liver manufactures triglycerides (fat); they reduce the clotting tendency of blood; they repair arteries damaged by lack of oxygen owing to fatty deposits; and they lower blood pressure. The bottom line is that omega-3 fatty acids deliver some very serious defense against heart attacks and strokes.

But nutritionists and doctors, wary as they often are of any self-prescribed remedy or nutritional fad, warn against our rushing out to dose ourselves with fish oil tablets. What's uniformly suggested, however—by the American Heart Association and other important sources of nutritional information—is that we make fish a regular part of our weekly meals. Some studies have shown that people who dine on fish just two or three times a week have fewer heart attacks than those who do not.

FISH BOOSTS THE EFFECTS OF OTHER CHOLESTEROL-LOWERING FOODS

Adding fish to the diet has other benefits as well. In animal studies, fish oil increased the cholesterol-lowering properties of oat bran (which are greater than those of wheat bran). It's often the case that two or more superfoods—as in this case, fish and oats—accomplish even more when they're teamed up together. Any so-called health diet that emphasizes one type of food and eliminates many others may be missing out on some of these desirable synergistic effects.

EATING FOR TWO? DON'T FORGET THE FISH

As you may imagine, there are substantial increases in protein turnover during pregnancy. "Eating for two," however, doesn't mean eating twice as much; it means that a woman's food choices are going to be twice as important. Her need for protein will rise from 46 to 56 grams daily. (In fact, all her nutrition requirements will rise to varying degrees, with the exception of her requirement for vitamin A.) Fish is an excellent source of "light" protein.

And one other important factor—your mother was right! Fish is "brain food"! Pregnant and nursing women are especially encouraged to eat seafood regularly, because recent research shows that certain of the omega-3 fatty acids are essential nutrients to the development of a child's brain, both as a fetus and as an infant.

A FISH DISH A DAY MAY KEEP ARTHRITIS AWAY

Because the omega-3 fatty acids—found most abundantly in oily fish such as trout, salmon, and mackerel—have been shown to bring about a lessening of painful rheumatoid arthritis symptoms, some scientists believe a diet in which fish replaces red meat would discourage inflammatory reactions in general. In some cases, arthritis may even be caused by red meat (or other "trigger" foods, such as milk, corn, or wheat). The same fish diet that's been demonstrated to reduce the risk of cardiovascular disease may help to stave off osteoarthritis, the painful swelling and crippling of joints that sometimes occurs as we age.

FISH IS A DEFENSE AGAINST OTHER DISEASES

Among older women, it may be that fish also helps to defend against diabetes. Results of a study among women and men in the 64 to 79 years age bracket showed that those who habitually ate a small amount of fish were less likely to develop impaired glucose intolerance and diabetes mellitus.

In another study, the incidence or recurrence of colorectal polyps was lessened, especially for women, if their diets featured fish and chicken rather than red meat.

"OILY" FISH WILL NOT MAKE YOU FAT!

Fish offers an excellent source of protein that, on the average, is lower in calories than the same size serving of meat. For example, 3 ounces of flounder equals 80 calories with 1 gram of fat; 3 ounces of lean broiled hamburger yields 230 calories with 16 grams of fat. Even an oily fish like salmon contains only 140 calories and 5 grams of fat for a 3-ounce portion.

TIPS ON MAKING MORE FISH DISHES

With all these great health benefits going for fish, it's a wonder that we're not all eating more of it! Maybe we depend on the main dishes we've always cooked, the same dishes as our mothers cooked before us, and find it hard to substitute, say, a baked salmon for a roast beef on Sunday. Or perhaps we find it so difficult to locate some really good fresh fish even once a week, we tend to give it up on the other days. Or we're so busy that we're eating (and feeding our families) a lot of that good old American fast fried food—such as double cheeseburgers, French fries, and milk shakes—for about a week's worth of dietary fat at one sitting. (So if you've sat down to that meal more than once a week, you're heading for *big* trouble.)

Rather than alternating between the same fifteen or so entrees we've always cooked, substituting fish in our routine menus can be challenging as well as creative. Getting out of a rut is always exhilarating and keeps us feeling young! Swordfish is delicious on the grill as a break from steak, fresh salmon cakes are an upscale change from hamburgers, and shrimp can be the main course instead of just the "cocktail" before the slab of meat. As a side benefit, the day's calorie count will probably have lightened up considerably along the way.

THE FISH MARKET CHALLENGE

Then there's the problem of buying fresh fish several times a week. If you've been buying fish at the supermarket, you may have been disappointed in it from time to time—perhaps it wasn't kept on ice, or it was kept too long—and those experiences will make you reluctant to make this desirable switch. Or you've tried commercially frozen fish and found it to be about as tasty as salt-flavored wet cotton, unless breaded, in which case the breading may outweigh the fish.

So your first challenge is to find a real fish market with a good, rapid turnover, and make it a habit to stop in there at least once a week (I suggest Thursdays). Buy "fresh," meaning never frozen, fish; good markets always label their products so that you can distinguish. Indulge in more than one kind of fish, enough for two or three meals during that week. Utilize short-term freezing, which does not seem to affect the flavor adversely, for any fish you won't be cooking immediately. (But do not try to freeze live shellfish!) Just rinse the fish under cold running water, pat it quite dry with paper towels, and wrap in plastic wrap followed by foil before freezing. Always thaw at refrigerator temperature, never on the kitchen drainboard.

SPEAKING OF FAST FOOD . . .

Now about that fast food. How fast must it be? Any fillet of fish will bake in 12 to 20 minutes, depending on thickness. Here's the whole recipe: Oil the pan and add a few chopped scallions. Turn a fish fillet—at least 1 inch thick—over in the oil to coat both sides, and top with seasoned bread crumbs. Bake at 400 degrees F. until it flakes apart easily when pressed with the back of a fork. Serve with some kind of garnish, such as lemon or lime wedges, nonfat yogurt with fresh chives, or spicy salsa. How's that for quick and easy?

The smaller shellfish, such as clams and shrimp, will be ready after 5 to 7 minutes of steaming. (According to the latest advice, for safe eating, clams, oysters, and mussels should be cooked 3 to 5 minutes *after* they've opened.) Lobster takes 15 to 20 minutes. Or, for my idea of the ultimate in fast and easy food, buy already cooked, cleaned shrimp from a well-trusted source and do a quick pasta dish or a salad.

In winter, hot fish soups can be whipped up in a few minutes with the aid of the usual invaluable staples: bottled clam juice, imported canned plum tomatoes, olive oil, garlic, and herbs of choice. Chunks of red snapper will be cooked through after simmering about 10 minutes in this savory combination. Making a fish stock from scratch from fish trimmings would be nice in a perfect world where there's nothing else you have to do and a kindly fishmonger has saved you those mythical trimmings.

SOME OTHER HEART SAVERS

Heart-healthy diets ought always to include some other items beside fish—foods that are rich in potassium, magnesium, calcium, and soluble fiber.

Potassium is an essential element in balancing body cells and fluids. Scientists, although uncertain just how it works, have found enough evidence to believe that potassium-rich, low-sodium diets may reduce the risk of stroke among people with high blood pressure. (Processed foods, however, often veer off in the opposite direction: high in sodium and low in potassium. Think "fresh foods" when you think potassium!)

Dietary studies have shown that high blood pressure patients frequently have calcium-poor diets, and that adding calcium-rich foods appears to help regulate the problem. The Italian Nine Communities Study, using women subjects ages 20 to 59, also found an association between a calcium-rich diet and lower blood pressure.

Magnesium helps to regulate vascular tone and is thought to interact with calcium to relieve blood vessel constriction. A deficiency in magnesium may be implicated in cardiac dysrhythmias (disruption of normal heart rhythm).

Anyone undergoing diuretic therapy is going to lose more than water; some magnesium and potassium also will be drained away, making a diet rich in these two minerals especially important.

And finally, fiber is important to heart health, also. A number of studies have shown that soluble fiber significantly lowers cholesterol. It's thought that fibers act in two ways: first, by inhibiting cholesterol synthesis; and second, by binding to cholesterol and carrying it out of the body.

The menus, the recipes, even the quick-fixes that will help you to enrich your daily fare with plenty of fish—in combination with these other heart-healthy elements—follow in this chapter.

Superfish for Omega-3 Fatty Acids

Anchovies	Sardines
Bluefish	Shark
Herring	Swordfish
Mackerel	Tuna
Salmon	Trout

But don't feel restricted to these choices; even lean fish contain enough omega-3 fatty acids to benefit the heart significantly. The important thing is to include fish in your weekly menus, especially as a replacement for red meat.

Superfood Sources of Potassium

Asparagus	Greens: beet, chard, spinach
Bananas	Melons
Beans, dried and green	Milk and yogurt
Cauliflower	Mushrooms
Citrus fruits	Nuts: almonds, peanuts
Corn	Peas
Dried fruits: apricots, figs, prunes, raisins	Potatoes: sweet and white
	Tomatoes
Fish: cod, carp	Vegetables, yellow, such as squash and carrots
Fruits, yellow, such as apricots and peaches	

Superfood Sources of Magnesium

Apricots	Greens, dark, leafy
Artichokes	Milk, skim, and nonfat yogurt
Bananas	
Barley	Nuts and seeds
Beans	Whole grains and wheat bran
Fish	

Sources of calcium and fiber are found in the chapters in which they are featured.

FAST AND EASY FISH FIXES

A cup of clam or fish chowder
Smoked salmon with a whole-grain bagel
Tuna from a can, dressed with rice vinegar
Salmon from a can, with yogurt and dill
A sardine sandwich on rye bread
Anchovies with roasted peppers and part-skim mozzarella

HEART-HEALTHY FISH SUPERMEALS

Recipes indicated by a ♦ follow the menus.

A RELAXED SUMMER DINNER FOR FOUR

Seared Salmon Fillets with Dilled Yogurt Sauce♦
Peas with Shallots and Sautéed Mushrooms♦
Steamed Baby Red Potatoes with Chopped Fresh Chives
Carrot-Date Torte♦
or
Sliced Seedless Watermelon

A traditional Fourth of July menu offers great heart food: salmon plus calcium-rich yogurt and peas. The mushrooms, potatoes, carrots, and dates (or melon) contribute lots of potassium.

Seared Salmon Fillets with Dilled Yogurt Sauce

SUPERFOODS: salmon, onion, yogurt

This quick way of cooking fish seals in the flavorful juices. The method can be adapted to any firm fish.

4 salmon fillets, about 4 ounces
   each
Celery salt and black pepper
2 tablespoons olive oil, or more
   as needed
¼ cup chopped onion

1 cup dry white wine
½ cup plain nonfat yogurt
2 teaspoons cornstarch
2 tablespoons chopped fresh dill
Dill sprigs for garnish

Rinse and pat dry the fillets. Season them with celery salt and pepper.

Heat the oil in a 12-inch skillet until it shimmers. Quickly sauté the fillets, 2 at a time, for about 3 minutes a side, until just cooked through. Keep them warm.

Sauté the onion in the same pan, adding a bit more oil if needed, until it is golden brown, 5 minutes. Add the wine, and stir up browned particles, letting the wine boil up until reduced by half.

In a cup, sprinkle the yogurt with the cornstarch, and whisk it in until well blended. Strain the pan liquid into a small saucepan. Stir in the yogurt mixture. Bring the sauce to a boil, whisking constantly until it thickens. Reduce heat, and simmer 2 to 3 minutes, stirring often. Stir in the dill.

Divide the sauce among the fillets, garnish with dill sprigs, and serve at once.

MAKES 4 SERVINGS

Peas with Shallots and Sautéed Mushrooms

SUPERFOODS: shallots, mushrooms, peas

2 tablespoons olive oil
About 4 ounces fresh
  mushrooms, sliced
¼ cup minced shallots
A few pinches of dried tarragon
Salt and pepper

1½ cups shelled fresh peas
  (1½ pounds peas in shell),
  or one 10-ounce package
  frozen peas

Heat the oil in a large skillet, and stir-fry the mushrooms and shallots until the mushrooms are golden brown, 3 to 5 minutes. Add the tarragon and salt and pepper to taste.

Meanwhile, cook the peas. Drop fresh peas in boiling, salted water; when the water comes to a boil again, cook for 2 to 4 minutes, until barely tender. Drain immediately. (Or microwave 1½ cups fresh peas with 2 tablespoons water for 4 to 5 minutes on high. Or cook frozen peas according to package directions.)

Stir the peas into the mushroom mixture. Serve.

MAKES 4 SERVINGS

Carrot-Date Torte

SUPERFOODS: dates, walnuts, wheat germ, carrots

For the filling

1 cup chopped pitted dates
½ cup coarsely chopped walnuts
½ cup water

1 tablespoon dark corn syrup
1 tablespoon cornstarch dissolved
  in ⅓ cup water

For the torte

1 cup unbleached all-purpose
  flour
½ cup sugar
1 tablespoon toasted wheat germ
1 teaspoon baking powder
½ teaspoon each *ground
cardamom and ground
cinnamon*

¼ teaspoon salt
⅓ cup butter or margarine
½ cup well-mashed cooked
  carrots (2 to 3 whole carrots—
  they really pack down)

Make the filling: Combine the dates, walnuts, ½ cup water, and syrup in a saucepan. Bring to a boil, lower heat, and simmer 5 minutes, stirring often. Blend the cornstarch mixture into the dates. Stir constantly until bubbling and thickened; continue cooking 1 minute longer. Cool completely.

The filling can be made 1 to 2 days in advance and kept refrigerated.

Preheat the oven to 375 degrees F. Bring the filling to room temperature.

Mix the dry ingredients. Cut in the butter until the mixture is mealy in texture. Stir in the carrots to make a stiff batter. Spoon the batter into a tart pan with a removeable rim or buttered 9-inch pie plate. Smooth the batter over the bottom and sides of the pan. Lightly drop spoonfuls of the filling over the batter, and gently spread it as a top layer to within an inch of the edges of the pan. Don't mix the layers.

Bake the torte in the middle of the oven for 25 to 30 minutes; the cake layer should be lightly browned. Cool on a wire rack. When the torte shrinks a bit from the sides of the pan, remove the rim. (If using a pie plate, serve from the pan.) Cut into wedges to serve.

MAKES **6** TO **8** SERVINGS

T.G.I.F. SUPPER FOR FOUR

Baked Haddock with Tomatoes and Peppers♦
Baked Potatoes with Blue Cheese–Yogurt Dressing (see page 534)
Steamed Caraway Slaw♦
Poached Papaya, Pear, and Apricot Compote♦

or

Apricot Halves (canned without sugar)

*P*reparation is minimal—so enjoy a relaxing beverage while the oven does its work! Apricots and yogurt for magnesium, plus tomatoes and potatoes for potassium, rounding out this heart-healthy haddock dinner.

Baked Haddock with Tomatoes and Peppers

SUPERFOODS: tomatoes, peppers, garlic, haddock,
wheat germ

*Marinate the vegetables while giving the baked potatoes a head start
of 30 to 40 minutes in the oven.*

4 ripe medium tomatoes, cut into
   wedges

2 Italian frying peppers, seeded
   and chunked

½ cup pitted Kalamata olives*

2 garlic cloves, chopped

2 tablespoons olive oil

Salt

1½ pounds haddock, preferably
   1 piece

½ cup plain dry bread crumbs

2 tablespoons each wheat germ
   and grated Parmesan cheese

1 teaspoon dried oregano

¼ teaspoon freshly ground black
   pepper

Combine the tomatoes, peppers, olives, garlic, and olive oil in a
deep bowl, and sprinkle with salt to your taste. Let stand at room
temperature about 30 minutes; stir once or twice.

Preheat the oven to 400 degrees F.

Rinse the fish and pat it dry. Place it in a large oiled gratin
dish (or other baking dish from which you can serve) and surround with the tomatoes, peppers, and olives. Pour the marinade
juices over all.

Combine the remaining ingredients and sprinkle the crumbs
over the fish and vegetables.

Bake on the top shelf of the oven for 15 to 20 minutes, or
until the fish flakes apart easily when pressed with the back of
a fork.

MAKES 4 SERVINGS

*Whack the olives with the flat side of a chef's knife for easy pitting. But watch
out that they don't scatter!

Steamed Caraway Slaw

SUPERFOODS: cabbage, scallions

Lightly steamed cabbage has a sweet, fresh flavor. In medicinal folklore, caraway seeds, a mild stimulant, were chewed to prevent sleepiness during long church services.

½ large head green cabbage
* (1½ pounds), shredded*
½ cup thinly sliced scallions
¼ cup rice vinegar

2 tablespoons grapeseed oil
1 teaspoon caraway seeds
Salt and freshly ground pepper

Using a steamer basket, steam the cabbage over vigorously boiling water for 3 to 4 minutes, until barely wilted. Remove from the heat and drain. Put all the ingredients in a salad bowl and toss while the cabbage is still warm. Taste to correct seasoning; you may want more vinegar or pepper.

Serve the slaw at room temperature.

MAKES 4 TO 6 SERVINGS

Poached Papaya, Pear, and Apricot Compote

SUPERFOODS: papaya, pears, apricots

1 ripe papaya
2 large ripe pears
1 cup water

½ cup sugar
1 cinnamon stick
8 dried apricots

Peel and seed the fresh fruit. Cut the papaya and pears lengthwise into slices about the size of fat French fries.

Combine the water, sugar, and cinnamon stick in a saucepan. Bring to a boil, uncovered. Stir until the sugar is dissolved. Add the fresh fruit and all the remaining ingredients. Simmer 20 to 30 minutes, until tender, stirring occasionally.

The compote can be made 1 to 2 days ahead. Keep refrigerated.

Serve at room temperature or chilled, perhaps with a plate of ginger snaps on the side.

MAKES 4 SERVINGS

A SUNDAY DINNER FOR FOUR

Spinach-Filled Pasta Shells♦
Gamberi alla Mario (Shrimp with Peppers)♦
Salad of Chicory and Sweetened Red Onion Rings (see page 524)
with Vinaigrette
Banana-Hazelnut Cake♦
or
Sliced Bananas with Brown Sugar

Plenty of potassium in the tomatoes, spinach, and bananas, plus a calcium bonus in the pasta dish. Milk and feta cheese add magnesium. Bananas are also a good source of soluble fiber, another heart plus.

Spinach-Filled Pasta Shells

SUPERFOODS: garlic, spinach, pasta, tomato sauce,
wheat germ

Richly flavorful, even with skim milk—and richly nutritious.

1 tablespoon olive oil

1 garlic clove, pressed in a garlic
   press

One 10-ounce package frozen leaf
   spinach, thawed

1 cup milk (can be skim)

3 tablespoons flour

¼ teaspoon white pepper

½ cup loosely packed, crumbled
   feta cheese

About 20 jumbo pasta shells

2 cups Brown Mushroom-
   Tomato Sauce (see page 518)
   or from a jar

2 tablespoons grated Parmesan
   cheese

1 tablespoon toasted wheat germ

Heat the olive oil and garlic in a medium skillet until sizzling.
Add the spinach, and cook over low heat 3 to 5 minutes.

Chop the spinach coarsely, and add ½ cup of the milk to the
pan. Heat but don't boil the mixture. Combine the remaining ½
cup of the milk with the flour and pepper in a jar. Cover and
shake until there are no lumps. Pour all at once into the spinach,
and cook over medium heat, stirring until the mixture bubbles
and thickens. Reduce heat and simmer 3 to 5 minutes to cook
the flour.

Stir in the feta cheese, and let the mixture cool and thicken.
It will be quite thick.

The filling can be made up to 1 day ahead. Keep refrigerated.

Cook the shells in salted water according to package directions.
(I usually throw in a few extra, in case of breakage.) Rinse them
in cool water, and lay them on waxed paper in a single layer.

Spoon ½ cup sauce into a nonreactive baking dish, about 8 × 12 inches. Fill the shells with rounded tablespoons of the spinach mixture, and place them in the dish. Top with an even layer of the remaining sauce. Sprinkle with Parmesan cheese and wheat germ. Cover the dish with tented foil in which you've cut several slits.

The shells can be prepared several hours or 1 day ahead. Keep refrigerated. If chilled, allow 10 minutes extra cooking time.

Preheat the oven to 350 degrees F.

Bake the shells on the middle shelf for 40 minutes, or until bubbling throughout. Remove the foil during the last 10 minutes of cooking, and bake until golden.

MAKES **20** JUMBO SHELLS

Gamberi alla Mario

(Shrimp with Peppers)

SUPERFOODS: shrimp, olive oil, peppers, onion

3 tablespoons olive oil

2 Italian frying peppers, seeded and diced

1 celery stalk, diced

½ cup chopped scallions

1 to 1¼ pounds shelled, cleaned shrimp* (see also Note)

¾ cup dry vermouth or dry white wine**

Black and cayenne pepper

---

*Use rubber gloves when handling raw shrimp, to prevent an allergic reaction.
**Alcohol evaporates during cooking, leaving only the lovely flavor. The better the quality of the vermouth or wine, the better the taste of the finished dish.

In a large skillet, heat the oil and sauté the peppers, celery, and scallions until they are softened, about 5 minutes. Add the shrimp and wine, and simmer 8 to 10 minutes, stirring often, until the shrimp are pink and tender. Sprinkle with pepper to your taste.

Note: You can substitute already cooked, cleaned shrimp, in which case, reduce the wine to ½ cup and the cooking time to 3 to 4 minutes.

If you double this recipe, use 2 skillets or cook the dish in 2 batches.

MAKES 4 SERVINGS

Banana-Hazelnut Cake

SUPERFOODS: bananas, hazelnuts

2¼ cups sifted unbleached
   all-purpose flour
1 teaspoon each ground
   cardamom and baking soda
¼ teaspoon each baking powder
   and salt
4 small to medium bananas
   (1⅓ pounds total)

1 cup granulated sugar
2 eggs or ½ cup prepared egg
   substitute
½ cup vegetable oil
⅓ cup plain nonfat yogurt
A heaping ½ cup shelled whole
   hazelnuts*
Confectioners' sugar

Preheat the oven to 350 degrees F. Butter and flour a 10-inch tube pan with a removeable rim.

Sift together the flour, cardamom, baking soda, baking powder, and salt into a large bowl.

---

*In need of some decadence? Substitute or add some chocolate chips.

Puree 3 of the bananas. Whisk in the granulated sugar, eggs, oil, and yogurt. (This step is easily done in a food processor.) Pour the banana mixture into the dry ingredients, and blend well.

Slice the remaining banana. Fold the banana slices and the nuts into the batter.

Pour the batter into the prepared pan, and smooth the top. Bake on the middle shelf for 45 minutes or until the cake shrinks a bit from the sides of the pan and a tester inserted in the thickest part comes out dry.

Cool on a wire rack for 5 minutes. Loosen the sides and center; remove the pan rim. When completely cool, remove the cake from the bottom of the pan. Dust the cake—through a sifter—with lots of confectioners' sugar.

The cake can be made 1 day ahead. Keep in a cool place, covered.

MAKES 12 SERVINGS

AUTUMN ON CAPE COD MENU
FOR FOUR

Curried Cod with Brown and Wild Rice♦
Baked Acorn Squash
with Spinach and Raisins♦
Sliced Cucumbers Dressed with Rice Vinegar and Mint
Apple Bread Pudding♦

Along with being a source of magnesium and potassium, nonfat yogurt is tops in dairy products rich in calcium, minus the cholesterol. Squash, spinach, and raisins may be found in the potassium line-up. And cod, besides its omega-3 fatty acid benefit, is also a potassium star.

Curried Cod with Brown and Wild Rice

SUPERFOODS: scallions, cod, yogurt, red pepper, brown rice

Any time you want to make brown rice special, just toss in some wild rice. Happily, they cook in the same amount of time.

1 tablespoon olive oil	*½ teaspoon curry powder*
4 scallions with green tops, chopped	*⅛ teaspoon cayenne pepper*
1¼ to 1½ pounds cod fillets	*½ cup plain nonfat yogurt*
1½ teaspoons cornstarch	*¼ cup finely chopped red bell pepper*
1 tablespoon chopped fresh cilantro or ½ teaspoon dried	*Hot cooked Brown and Wild Rice (see page 525)*

Preheat the oven to 400 degrees F.

In a pan that will fit the fish in one layer, combine the oil and scallions. Heat it in the oven until the scallions are sizzling but not brown. Remove the pan.

Turn the fish over in the scallion oil to coat both sides.

Blend the cornstarch, cilantro, spices, and yogurt. Stir in the red pepper. Spread this mixture over the fish.

Bake the fish on the top shelf for 15 to 20 minutes, or until it flakes apart easily when pressed with the back of a fork. Serve the fish with the rice.

MAKES 4 SERVINGS

Baked Acorn Squash with Spinach and Raisins

SUPERFOODS: acorn squash, spinach, raisins, yogurt

For a nuttier flavor, bake squash with the cut sides up. Otherwise, the vegetable steams instead of baking—and baking is one of the best ways to add flavor without fat.

A 2-pound acorn squash, seeded
    and quartered*
Grated nutmeg
1 cup cooked (or frozen, thawed)
    spinach, chopped**
3 tablespoons seasoned dry bread
    crumbs

2 tablespoons raisins, plumped
    in hot water
About 2 tablespoons plain nonfat
    yogurt

Preheat the oven to 400 degrees F.

Put the squash in a baking dish with about 1 inch of water, cut sides up. Sprinkle with nutmeg, and bake for 50 minutes to 1 hour, until tender. The water will boil out, but that's okay.

The squash can be baked 1 day ahead. Keep refrigerated.

Preheat the oven to 400 degrees F.

Mix the spinach, bread crumbs, and raisins. Add enough yogurt to make a stuffing that will hold its shape when molded.

Divide the stuffing among the quarters, mounding it up if necessary and pressing it to hold firmly. Sprinkle with more nutmeg, and cover loosely with foil.

*You can substitute two 1-pounders for one 2-pound squash, in which case, cut them into halves instead of quarters.
**Squeeze excess moisture out of the spinach.

Bake for 20 minutes (30 minutes if the squash is cold). Remove the foil and bake for an additional 10 minutes. Push down any raisins that have surfaced, to prevent their overbrowning.

MAKES 4 SERVINGS

Apple Bread Pudding

SUPERFOODS: apples, whole wheat bread

Leftover bread pudding, warmed or cold, makes a pleasing quick breakfast food. And much better for you than a toaster tart.

3 cooking apples, peeled, cored,
   and sliced into rounds
2 tablespoons butter or
   margarine, melted
Cinnamon Sugar (see page 540)
3 eggs or ¾ cup prepared egg
   substitute

½ cup sugar
¼ teaspoon each ground
   cinnamon and grated
   nutmeg
2 cups milk
2 cups diced whole wheat bread
   (2 to 3 slices)

Preheat the oven to 350 degrees F.

Brush the apple slices with melted butter, lay them on a baking sheet, and sprinkle with cinnamon sugar. Bake for 15 minutes or until tender.

Meanwhile, beat the eggs until light; beat in the sugar and seasonings. Mix in the milk.

Put the bread into a 2½-quart glass baking dish (preferably flat rather than round) set into a larger baking dish. Pour the egg-milk mixture over, pressing the bread down. Let stand for 15 minutes.

When ready to bake, layer the apples in overlapping rows over the bread mixture. Put the pans on the middle shelf of the oven, pour hot water into the outer pan, and bake 40 to 45 minutes (up to 1 hour for the egg substitute), until set at the center.

Serve warm or at room temperature. Refrigerate leftover pudding for another time. If you wish, rewarm by placing pudding in a warm oven for about 10 minutes, but not long enough to cook it further.

MAKES 8 SERVINGS

LUNCH ON THE VERANDA FOR FOUR

Gratin of Crab
with Whole Wheat Toast Points♦
Sugar Snap Peas
Melon Salad♦
Butternut-Lemon Sponge Cake♦

Crabmeat is high in selenium as well as the omega-3 fatty acids—and whole wheat toast is a serving of magnesium. Watermelon, so sweet and light, is secretly heavy on the potassium, as is butternut squash.

Gratin of Crab with Whole Wheat Toast Points

SUPERFOODS: crabmeat, scallions, skim milk, wheat germ,
whole wheat bread

*Since good fresh crabmeat is not always available or affordable, a
top-quality frozen crabmeat can be substituted. But beware of lesser
products that are both fibrous and tasteless.*

*This spicy crabmeat can also be served with plain rice, white or
brown, or as a topping for large "blossomed" baked potatoes.*

1 pint best-quality fresh or frozen
crabmeat, thawed and
drained
1 tablespoon olive oil
4 scallions, chopped
½ cup dry vermouth, dry white
wine, or clam broth
1 tablespoon tomato paste
1 tablespoon cornstarch
½ cup milk (can be skim)

¼ teaspoon each dried tarragon,
dry mustard, and white
pepper
Cayenne pepper
¼ cup grated Gruyère or Asiago
cheese
Paprika
4 slices toasted whole wheat
bread, cut into triangles

If necessary, remove any cartilage in the crabmeat and cut any
large lumps into smaller pieces.

Heat the oil in a medium skillet, and sauté the scallions until
they are soft but not brown, about 3 minutes. Stir in the crabmeat;
add the wine or broth and tomato paste. Simmer over very low
heat for 3 minutes.

Stir the cornstarch into the milk until it is dissolved. Stir in
the seasonings and cayenne to taste. Pour the mixture all at once
into the crabmeat, stirring constantly until the sauce bubbles and
thickens. Simmer 3 minutes, stirring often.

Spoon the crab mixture into a buttered 8-inch oval gratin dish. *The recipe can be prepared several hours ahead to this point and refrigerated, covered.*

Preheat the oven to 375 degrees F.

Top the gratin with the cheese and paprika. Bake it in the upper third of the oven for 15 to 20 minutes (25 to 30 if the dish is taken from the refrigerator), until the top is brown and the crab bubbles around the edges.

Stand the toast points around the edges of the gratin.

MAKES 4 LUNCHEON SERVINGS; 2 DINNER PORTIONS

Melon Salad

SUPERFOODS: watermelon, cantaloupe, raspberries

2 cups diced seedless watermelon, in bite-size chunks
2 cups diced cantaloupe, in bite-size chunks
2 tablespoons minced fresh mint
Salt
¼ cup raspberry vinegar
4 large leaves red leaf lettuce, torn into bite-size pieces
Fresh raspberries and mint sprigs for garnish

Combine the melons, mint, a sprinkling of salt, and the vinegar in a bowl, and stir to blend. Chill well.

Line 4 cold salad plates with lettuce. Divide the melon among the plates, and garnish with fresh raspberries and mint sprigs.

MAKES 4 SERVINGS

Butternut-Lemon Sponge Cake

SUPERFOODS: butternut squash

This feather-light cake with a hint of nutmeg is a pleasant companion to hot or iced tea.

In choosing a pan, keep in mind that this cake cools upside down, and the surface of the cake must not touch the counter. Angel food pans are designed for this purpose, with legs. Otherwise, you must improvise by resting the edges of the cake pan on two other pans.

1 cup sifted unbleached all-purpose flour	¼ teaspoon cream of tartar
1¼ teaspoons baking powder	1 cup sugar
¼ teaspoon grated nutmeg	2 tablespoons lemon juice
¼ teaspoon salt	½ cup mashed, cooked butternut squash
4 eggs, separated	1 teaspoon grated lemon rind

Preheat the oven to 325 degrees F. Use an ungreased angel food cake pan or 10-inch tube pan with a removeable rim. Sift together the flour, baking powder, nutmeg, and salt. Put the mixture back in the sifter, standing in a small bowl, ready to sift again.

In an electric mixer bowl or a deep medium bowl, beat the egg whites until frothy. Add the cream of tartar, and continue beating until soft peaks form. Gradually add ¼ cup of the sugar, and beat until stiff but not dry.

In a large bowl, whisk the egg yolks and lemon juice together until thick and pale. Gradually beat in the remaining ¾ cup sugar, then the squash and lemon rind.

Gently stir one-fourth of the egg whites into the yolk mixture. Spoon the remaining egg whites onto the yolks. Sift the dry ingredients on top. Fold the egg whites and flour into the egg yolks until combined.

Spoon the batter into the prepared pan, and bake on the middle rack for about 45 minutes, until the cake shrinks a bit from the sides of the pan and the top springs back when lightly pressed with a finger. Turn the cake pan upside down to cool. Remove from the pan when cold.

The cake can be made 1 day ahead. Keep in a cool place, covered.

MAKES 8 TO 10 SLICES

A MAKE-AHEAD CHOWDER SUPPER FOR FOUR

Fresh Tuna Chowder♦
Lentil Salad♦
Whole Wheat Pita Bread
Apricot Mousse with Concord Grape Sauce♦

As an oily fish, tuna is especially high in those important omega-3 fatty acids. Skim milk in the chowder adds calcium, potatoes add potassium—plus apricots for more. Whole wheat pita bread and lentils have magnesium—and lentils are a good source of soluble fiber, too.

Fresh Tuna Chowder

SUPERFOODS: onion, potatoes, tuna, skim milk

2 tablespoons olive oil

1 medium onion, chopped

1½ pounds potatoes, peeled and
   sliced

1 pound fresh tuna steak

1 cup water

½ teaspoon salt

Sprigs of fresh thyme and
   tarragon*

3 cups milk (can be skim)

3 tablespoons flour

¼ teaspoon white pepper

1 tablespoon butter

⅛ teaspoon cayenne pepper, or to
   taste

Chopped fresh parsley for
   garnish

Heat the oil in a 4-quart pot, and sauté the onion until it's yellow and softened, about 3 minutes. Add the potatoes, tuna, water, salt, and herbs. Bring to a boil, lower heat, cover, and simmer over very low heat until the potatoes are tender and the fish flakes apart when pressed with the back of a fork, 10 to 15 minutes.

Remove the potatoes and tuna. Cut the tuna into chunks.

Add 2 cups of the milk to the pan juices, and heat but don't boil the milk.

In a jar, combine the remaining cup of cold milk with the flour and white pepper. Cover and shake until there are no lumps. Strain the flour mixture into the hot milk, and stir constantly over medium heat until the mixture bubbles and thickens. Simmer 3 to 5 minutes to cook the flour.

Stir in the butter and cayenne to your taste. Return the potatoes and tuna to the chowder. Discard herb sprigs.

The chowder can be made several hours to 1 day ahead. Use very fresh fish and refrigerate promptly. Reheat carefully to avoid sticking.

Serve the chowder in bowls, garnished with chopped parsley.

MAKES 1½ QUARTS

*Squeeze excess moisture out of the spinach.

Lentil Salad

SUPERFOODS: lentils, scallions, red pepper

3 cups Stewed Lentils, drained   1 red bell pepper, diced
   (see page 521)   1 tablespoon minced fresh basil
2 celery stalks, diced   ½ cup or more Caper Vinaigrette
4 scallions with green tops, thinly   (see page 530)
   sliced   Belgian endive leaves

Combine all the ingredients except the endive in a bowl and toss gently. Marinate for at least 1 hour.
   Can be made 1 day ahead. Keep refrigerated.
   Before serving, taste to see if you need to add more vinaigrette. Line each salad dish with endive leaves, and spoon the lentils on top.

MAKES 4 SERVINGS

Apricot Mousse with Concord Grape Sauce

SUPERFOODS: apricots, yogurt

One 1-pound can pitted apricot   1 tablespoon lemon juice
   halves*   ½ teaspoon grated lemon rind
2 tablespoons (2 packages)   1 cup plain nonfat yogurt
   unflavored gelatin   ½ cup Concord grape jelly
5 tablespoons sugar   ¼ cup orange juice

*It's important to use the no-sugar-added variety. Otherwise, the dessert will be too sweet.

Strain the apricots, reserving the juice. Put the juice in a small saucepan, and sprinkle the gelatin on top. When the gelatin has softened, add the sugar, and gently heat the mixture, stirring, until the gelatin and sugar have dissolved.

Puree the apricots in a food processor. Blend in the gelatin mixture, lemon juice, and lemon rind, then the yogurt.

Remove to a bowl, and chill in the refrigerator until very thick but not firm, about 1 hour. Whip the mousse with a whisk, electric or hand, until light and smooth in texture. Return it to the refrigerator until ready to serve.

The mousse can be made up to 1 day ahead. Keep refrigerated.

About 1 hour before serving, heat the jelly until it's liquid, and stir in the orange juice. Let stand at room temperature, covered, until cool, stirring occasionally. When cool, it will be syrupy.

The sauce can be made several hours ahead and held at room temperature—or 1 day ahead, refrigerated.

Spoon the mousse into stemmed dessert dishes, and pour some sauce on each serving.

MAKES 4 SERVINGS

AFTER-WORK EASY DINNER FOR FOUR

Broiled Swordfish with Lime and Mint♦
Steamed Broccoli
Tomato 'n' Potato Salad♦
Warm Banana "Splits" with Blueberries♦

*B*roccoli must truly be the queen of vegetables. For the heart, it offers calcium, potassium, and soluble fiber (plus something nutritious for every other part). There's more potassium in the tomatoes and potatoes, plus the bananas for dessert. The yogurt dressing is rich in both magnesium and potassium.

To save time, cook the potatoes a day ahead and refrigerate them until needed.

Broiled Swordfish with Lime and Mint

SUPERFOODS: swordfish

Juice of 2 limes*
3 tablespoons olive oil
About 15 fresh mint leaves,
  minced
2 slices fresh ginger, minced

4 serving-size pieces swordfish
  (1½ to 2 pounds total)
Freshly ground black pepper
2 limes, quartered, and mint
  sprigs for garnish

*Cover the juice limes with warm water for 15 minutes before squeezing them to obtain the most juice possible.

On a platter, combine the lime juice, oil, mint, and ginger. Turn the swordfish over in this mixture several times. Marinate the swordfish for 30 minutes, turning once.

Preheat the broiler or prepare a grill.

Sprinkle the swordfish liberally with black pepper. Broil or grill 6 minutes per side, or until the fish flakes apart when pressed with the back of a fork.

Serve the swordfish with lime quarters, garnished with mint sprigs.

MAKES 4 SERVINGS

Tomato 'n' Potato Salad

SUPERFOODS: tomatoes, potatoes, onions, yogurt

If the potatoes are organically grown, leave well-scrubbed skins on for extra nutrition. But be sure to remove any sprouts from the eyes of the potatoes; potato sprouts and any portions of skin and flesh that have turned green contain a naturally occurring toxin called solanine.

6 large ripe plum tomatoes, sliced

2 pounds sliced, cooked potatoes, with or without skin

½ cup chopped red or sweet white onion

½ cup plain nonfat yogurt

2 tablespoons mayonnaise

¼ cup crumbled Gorgonzola cheese

¼ teaspoon white pepper

Paprika

Combine the tomatoes with the potatoes and onion in a salad dish.

Blend the yogurt, mayonnaise, cheese, and white pepper. Toss the salad with the dressing.

Let the salad stand at room temperature for 15 to 20 minutes. Toss again before serving. Garnish with a sprinkle of paprika.

MAKES ABOUT 1 QUART

Warm Banana "Splits" with Blueberries

SUPERFOODS: bananas, blueberries

1 tablespoon butter	*Ground cinnamon*
2 medium bananas	*4 scoops mocha-flavored nonfat*
1 cup fresh or frozen blueberries	*frozen yogurt*
¼ brown sugar	

Preheat the oven to 350 degrees F. While it's heating, melt the butter in a gratin dish.

Peel and slice the bananas in half lengthwise, then in half crosswise. Put them in the gratin dish, and turn to coat all sides with the melted butter.

Scatter the blueberries on top. Sprinkle with the brown sugar and a liberal dusting of cinnamon.

Bake for 25 to 30 minutes, turning once to coat the blueberries with the melted brown sugar.

Cool a bit. Divide the warm fruit among 4 dessert dishes, top with frozen yogurt, and serve immediately.

MAKES 4 SERVINGS

A CANDLELIGHT DINNER FOR FOUR

Sole with Lobster Newburg Filling♦
Brown Basmati Rice (see page 524)
Green Beans with Almonds
Sliced Tomatoes with Olive Oil and Fresh Basil
Blueberry Whole Wheat Cake♦
or
Fresh Blueberries
with Nonfat Frozen Peach Yogurt

If you make the cake and get the fish ready early in the day, the rest is so easy that you will be able to relax and enjoy the day. There's potassium in the green beans, almonds, and tomatoes, olive oil to lower cholesterol, and whole grains in the rice and dessert for magnesium. Two kinds of fish, of course, are the stars of this heart-healthy menu.

———————

Sole with Lobster Newburg Filling

Superfoods: lobster, wheat germ, sole

For the filling

1¼ cups finely diced, cooked
   lobster meat
¾ cup herb stuffing mix
   (not stovetop)
2 tablespoons toasted wheat germ
3 tablespoons dry sherry

2 tablespoons butter, melted
¼ teaspoon dried tarragon
Freshly ground black pepper
Dash of cayenne pepper

For the fish rolls

1 tablespoon olive oil
2 large or 4 small
   scallions

8 medium fillets of sole (1¼ to
   1½ pounds total)*
Paprika

Blend the filling ingredients. If the mixture appears dry, add a teaspoon or so more sherry.

Oil a pan that will just fit the fish rolls, preferably one from which you can serve. Scatter the scallions on the bottom of the pan.

Put a heaping tablespoon of the filling onto each fillet, roll it up the long way, and place it open side down in the pan. If necessary, secure the rolls with the wooden picks. Push any leftover filling in between the rolls.

The recipe can be prepared to this point a few hours in advance. Keep covered and chilled in the coldest part of the refrigerator.

Preheat the oven to 400 degrees F.

---

*Ask the clerk for medium but uniform fillets to make roll-ups. No torn or ragged fillets.

Sprinkle the dish with paprika, and bake on the top shelf for about 15 minutes, until the fish flakes apart when pressed with the back of a fork. If you have used wooden picks, remove them before serving.

MAKES **8** FISH ROLLS; **4** SERVINGS

Blueberry Whole Wheat Cake

SUPERFOODS: blueberries, whole wheat

It's a big cake! But you can always freeze part of it for another occasion.

1 pint blueberries (small ones are best)
1¾ cups sifted whole wheat pastry flour
1¾ cups sifted unbleached all-purpose flour
4 teaspoons baking powder
½ teaspoon each ground cardamom, ground cinnamon, and salt

2 eggs or ½ cup prepared egg substitute
1½ cups milk (can be skim)
½ cup butter, softened
1½ cups sugar
Cinnamon Sugar (see page 540)

Preheat the oven to 350 degrees F. Butter and flour a 9 × 13 × 2-inch baking pan.

Pick over and wash the blueberries; shake off the moisture and mix them with 2 tablespoons of the all-purpose flour.

Sift the remaining flours with the baking powder and seasonings into a medium bowl.

In another bowl, beat the eggs with the milk.

In the work bowl of an electric mixer (or by hand), cream the butter until fluffy, and gradually add the sugar, beating until light and well mixed. Add the dry and liquid ingredients alternately, beginning and ending with the dry.

Remove the bowl from the mixer and fold in the blueberries. Spoon the batter into the prepared pan, sprinkle with cinnamon sugar, and bake on the middle shelf for about 45 minutes. The cake is done when it's risen, golden brown, and shrinks a little from the sides of the pan. A cake tester inserted in the center should come out dry.

Cool the cake in the pan on a wire rack before cutting.

MAKES 12 TO 18 PIECES

DINNER FOR SIX IN THE KITCHEN

Cioppino with Fennel♦
Whole Wheat French Bread
Tossed Green Salad with Olive Oil Vinaigrette
Apple Shortcakes with Ginger Biscuits
and Yogurt Custard Sauce♦
or
Warm Applesauce with Ginger Sugar (see page 539)

Plenty of fish in the soup—with tomatoes, of course, for potassium and olive oil to lower cholesterol. There's magnesium in the whole wheat bread, so necessary with a good soup. Apples are a source of heart-helping soluble fiber.

Cioppino with Fennel

Superfoods: clams, leek, olive oil, garlic, tomatoes,
red snapper

*Fennel adds a different flavor to this spicy soup, traditionally a
combination of fish and shellfish—whatever was the catch of the
day. And you can still vary it to suit the ''catch'' at the fish market.
It's a cinch to double the recipe, too—just use a larger pot.*

2 pounds steamers (small
  soft-shell clams)
3½ cups water
1 leek
3 tablespoons olive oil
½ fennel bulb, coarsely chopped
2 garlic cloves, minced
3 large ripe tomatoes (1½
  pounds), peeled and diced
4 slivers orange rind (with no
  white pith)

3 sprigs fresh parsley
1 teaspoon fresh thyme leaves,
  or ¼ teaspoon dried
½ cup dry vermouth or dry white
  wine*
1½ pounds red snapper
½ teaspoon or more hot pepper
  sauce
Salt and freshly ground pepper

Prepare the clams. Wash them well, discarding broken ones. Put
them into a pot with the water, bring it to a boil, and simmer
until the shells have opened, about 2 minutes. Simmer 3 minutes
longer. Scoop out the clams with a slotted spoon, reserving the
broth.

As soon as they can be handled, remove the clams from the
shells, discarding any that haven't opened with the rest. Slip off
and discard the rough neck skins, rinsing the clams in the clam
broth as you work; refrigerate the clams until needed.

---

*The alcohol will have evaporated by the time the soup is done.

Strain the broth: use an clean old dish towel, well rinsed, or a paper coffee filter set into a close-meshed strainer over a bowl. Cheesecloth isn't fine enough for this job.

The clams and broth can be prepared several hours ahead and stored separately in the refrigerator.

Make the soup. Slice the leek lengthwise, and rinse it between the layers. Chop the white part; discard the green. Heat the oil in a 4-quart pot, and sauté the leek, fennel, and garlic until softened. Add the tomatoes, orange rind, parsley, thyme, and vermouth; simmer 10 minutes.

Cut the fish into 1-inch chunks. Add the fish, the strained clam juice, and the hot pepper sauce. Cook 5 to 10 minutes longer, until the fish is opaque.

Taste to correct seasoning. Add freshly ground pepper, salt, and more hot pepper sauce to your taste. Stir in the clams and simmer 1 minute more before serving.

While this soup is best served the same day as it's made, so that the fish and clams will be very tender, leftovers are so good as the flavors continue to marry that one might be tempted to prepare too much soup on purpose.

MAKES 2 QUARTS

Apple Shortcakes
with Ginger Biscuits and Yogurt Custard Sauce

SUPERFOODS: apples, apricots, skim milk, yogurt

For the filling

4 large cooking apples, such as
   Granny Smith, peeled and
   sliced
½ cup snipped dried apricots

½ cup water
½ cup packed brown sugar
¼ teaspoon ground cinnamon

For the shortcakes

1½ cups unbleached all-purpose
   flour*
¼ cup granulated sugar
2 teaspoons baking powder
1½ teaspoons ground ginger

¼ teaspoon salt
¼ cup (½ stick) cold butter or
   margarine
½ cup milk (can be skim)

Ginger Sugar (see page 539)

Double recipe of Yogurt Custard
   Sauce (see page 535)

Make the apple filling: Combine the apples, apricots, water, brown sugar, and cinnamon in a medium saucepan. Bring to a boil, stirring; reduce the heat and simmer until the fruit is tender but not mushy, 10 to 15 minutes. Stir occasionally while cooking.

The filling can be made 1 day ahead. Keep refrigerated. Bring to room temperature before serving.

Make the shortcakes: Preheat the oven to 450 degrees F.

Sift the flour, granulated sugar, baking powder, ginger, and salt into a large bowl. Cut in the butter. Stir in the milk. Knead the dough right in the bowl, just enough to form it into a ball.

*Can be as much as half whole wheat flour.

With a table knife, cut the dough into 6 even pieces. Knead each to form a smooth biscuit, and put the balls of dough into a buttered 9- or 10-inch pie plate. Sprinkle with ginger sugar. Bake on the top shelf of the oven for 15 minutes or until risen and golden.

The biscuits can be prepared several hours ahead and rewarmed, but they taste best when eaten the same day they're made.

To serve, split the warm biscuits, spoon the apple mixture onto the bottom half, put the top on, and spoon the custard sauce over all.

MAKES 6 SERVINGS

3

THE CRUCIFEROUS KINGDOM

Super Cancer Fighters in Your Corner

Strong flavors and equally potent effects characterize the cruciferous kingdom. From the Latin *Cruciferae*, the name for this family of vegetables (also called *Brassicaceae*) means "cross"; its flower forms a Greek cross with four petals. Hardy and prolific, cruciferous vegetables have been the mainstay of peasant diets from Asia to the Mediterranean throughout the ages, conferring on farm folk those same healthy qualities.

BROCCOLI AND ITS COUSINS— DEFENDERS AGAINST CANCER

Modern science, with suitable fanfare, has discovered that brash broccoli and humble cabbage are rich in nitrogen compounds called *indoles*. Research suggests that indoles may be effective fighters against cancer, especially of the stomach and large intestine.

Researchers at the Johns Hopkins University School of Medicine have isolated another anticancer chemical in broccoli and other cruciferous vegetables, which they call *sulforaphane*. This chemical stimulates the cells to generate "guardian" enzymes that bond to toxins and prevent them from reaching the cell's vital genetic material.

In the Iowa Women's Health Study, high intakes of all vegetables and fruits, all vegetables, or all leafy green vegetables were each associated with approximately halving the risk of lung cancer.

Scientists are working to isolate some of the cruciferous protective compounds for use in future chemoprevention. One experiment, focusing on lung cancer, is assessing the precursor of a known anticarcinogenic found in watercress.

Population studies in a mining community in the Yunnan province of China credited three classes of foods for a protective effect against lung cancer: the cruciferous vegetables, the beta-carotene foods, and the allium family (garlic, onion, etc.).

ALL THIS . . . PLUS ANTOXIDANTS AND FIBER, TOO!

Many cruciferous vegetables also contain antioxidants, such as beta-carotene and vitamin C, that sponge up free radicals (unstable molecules that are implicated in the diseases and disorders of aging) while the guardian enzymes are attacking toxins. You can find more information about cleaning up free radicals in Chapter 4.

The cruciferous family is rich in fiber, as well—a nonnutrient that's important as a cancer fighter and a defender against many other disorders of the digestive system. All this adds up to a pretty powerful package of prevention.

INTRODUCING MORE RESISTANCE FIGHTERS INTO YOUR DIET

Meanwhile, the National Cancer Institute recommends that we include plenty of cruciferous vegetables in a varied diet. If you've been hooked on the cruciferous family right along, you've been enjoying some of nature's best resistance fighters. If you're just getting into broccoli and its many relatives, you may want to introduce them into your diet slowly (but persistently) to avoid intestinal gas. A bay leaf or two in the pot helps to negate the well-known cruciferous cooking odors.

Quick fixes and menu suggestions for cruciferous supermeals follow.

Cruciferous Superfoods

Broccoli and broccoli rabe
Brussels sprouts
Cabbage, including green, red, napa, savoy, bok choy
Cauliflower
Collards

Kale
Kohlrabi
Mustard greens
Radishes and horseradish
Turnips, rutabagas, and turnip greens
Watercress

CRUCIFEROUS QUICKIES . . .

A plate of crudités: broccoli, cauliflower, radishes, and/or baby turnip slices
A cup of kale soup
A salad of cooked cauliflower and chunks of tomato
A sauerkraut topping on a sandwich, or cole slaw on the side
Pasta with quickly sautéed broccoli, garlic, and olive oil
Plenty of grated horseradish on anything
A watercress tea sandwich on brown bread

SUPERMEALS FROM THE CRUCIFEROUS KINGDOM

Recipes indicated by a ♦ follow the menus.

A HEARTY HARVEST DINNER
FOR FOUR

Chicken and Broccoli Pie with Bruschetta♦
Mashed Potatoes and Rutabaga♦
Lemon Sponge Puddings♦
or
Watermelon Wedges

*B*roccoli and rutabaga are both cruciferous vegetables. Other cancer fighters in this menu are tomatoes, potatoes, and lemon, for
helpings of vitamin C—topped off by carotenoids in the broccoli
and tomatoes. In red fruits like tomatoes and watermelon, the
carotenoid is called lycopene, and it's as potent a cancer-fighter
as beta-carotene.

Chicken and Broccoli Pie with Bruschetta

SUPERFOODS: olive oil, onion, carrot, broccoli, tomatoes

This is a "from scratch" version, but the dish is also a savory way to use leftovers—cooked chicken or turkey! Easy bruschetta (Roman garlic bread) takes the place of a pastry or biscuit topping.

2 pounds bone in, skinless
   chicken breasts
1 tablespoon olive oil
1 medium onion, chopped
1 large carrot, cut into 4 pieces
1 celery stalk with leaves,
   chopped

Sprigs of fresh parsley and thyme
2 cups (a 13-ounce can) reduced-
   sodium chicken broth
3 tablespoons instant flour*
Salt and pepper
12 lightly cooked broccoli spears

For the bruschetta

4 slices Italian bread
2 tablespoons virgin olive oil
1 garlic clove, crushed

2 large plum tomatoes, seeded
   and finely diced
Pinches of mixed Italian herbs

Wash the chicken in salted water, rinse, and pat dry. Heat the oil in a 4-quart pot, and sauté the onion and chicken until the onion is golden, turning the breasts once.

Add the carrot, celery, herb sprigs, and broth. Cover and simmer about 25 minutes, until the chicken is cooked through. Drain and reserve the chicken and vegetables. Discard herb sprigs.

Measure the broth and return it to the pot. If you have more than 1½ cups, boil rapidly to reduce to that amount. Add the flour mixed with a little cold water, stirring constantly until the mixture boils. Reduce the heat, and simmer 3 to 5 minutes. Taste the sauce, adding salt and pepper as needed.

*Nice to have on hand for no-fuss sauces!

Assemble the casserole. Lay the broccoli spears on the bottom of a 2-inch-deep casserole. Remove the chicken from the bone in large pieces, and lay them over the broccoli. Scatter the carrot pieces in between. Pour the sauce over all.

The recipe can be made up to this point several hours ahead. Keep refrigerated.

Preheat the oven to 350 degrees F.

Make the bruschetta: Brush the bread with oil, and rub with crushed garlic. Divide the tomatoes among the slices, and sprinkle with herbs. Lay the bruschetta on top of the chicken but don't immerse them in the sauce.

Bake in the middle of the oven for 30 minutes, or until the casserole bubbles and the bruschetta are golden at the edges. If the casserole was taken from the refrigerator, cook 15 minutes before adding the bruschetta—45 minutes total time.

MAKES **4** SERVINGS

Mashed Potatoes and Rutabaga

SUPERFOODS: potatoes, rutabaga

I prefer to add salt to the potato cooking water (as with pasta) rather than to add it afterwards. Most of the salt is then drained off with the water, leaving a lightly salted vegetable.

2 cups peeled cubed potatoes	2 tablespoons butter or
2 cups diced rutabaga	margarine
2 teaspoons salt	Skim milk as needed
1 tablespoon white vinegar	1 tablespoon minced fresh chives
White pepper	

Put the potato and rutabaga cubes in separate saucepans. Cover each vegetable with water. Add 1 teaspoon salt to each pot, and pour the vinegar into the potatoes. Bring both pans to a boil (or start the rutabaga earlier because it takes longer) and cook uncovered until the vegetables are tender, 30 to 35 minutes for the rutabaga, 10 to 15 minutes for the potatoes.

Drain them both very well. Add 1 tablespoon butter and white pepper to taste to each. Mash them to the desired consistency. Add skim milk as needed to make the potatoes quite creamy so that they will swirl easily. Stir in the chives.

Spoon the potatoes into a serving dish. Spoon the rutabaga into the center, and swirl the 2 together in a marble pattern.

MAKES 4 SERVINGS

Lemon Sponge Puddings

SUPERFOODS: lemon juice, skim milk

2 eggs, separated	*¼ cup fresh lemon juice*
Pinch of cream of tartar	*¼ cup all-purpose flour*
2 tablespoons butter, softened	*⅛ teaspoon salt*
½ cup sugar	*1 cup milk (can be skim)*
2 teaspoons grated lemon rind	

Arrange 4 glass or ceramic baking cups of 1¼-cup capacity in a large baking dish. Preheat the oven to 350 degrees F.

In a deep medium bowl, beat the egg whites until frothy. Add the cream of tartar, and continue beating until stiff peaks form.

In another bowl, cream the butter with the sugar. Blend in the yolks, lemon rind and juice, flour, and salt. Blend in the milk. Fold in the beaten whites.

Divide the pudding among the prepared cups. Half-fill the baking pan with hot water, and bake the puddings on the middle shelf for about 30 minutes, until they are golden brown and slightly puffed.

Remove the cups from the baking pan to cool. Serve at room temperature.

Lemon-Kiwi Sponge Puddings: For a twice-tart taste (very refreshing!), garnish the puddings with sliced kiwifruit.

MAKES 4 SERVINGS

DINNER FOR FOUR WITH AN ITALIAN FLAIR

Fusilli with Cauliflower, Anchovies, and Pine Nuts♦
Salmon with Roasted Broccoli Rabe♦
Whole-Grain Garlic Bread
Banana-Fig Torte♦
or
Fresh Figs with Sliced Red Bananas

Cauliflower and broccoli rabe are numbered among the cruciferous vegetables. Tomatoes and garlic in the pasta and figs in the dessert are other cancer fighters. The latter contain a substance called benzaldehyde, which some animal studies have shown to inhibit the growth of tumors.

Fusilli with Cauliflower, Anchovies, and Pine Nuts

SUPERFOODS: olive oil, garlic, anchovies, tomatoes, cauliflower, nuts, pasta

A bay leaf added to the pot seems to dimish the pungent aroma of cooking cauliflower. It also adds a pleasant flavor to the vegetable.

¼ cup olive oil
1 garlic clove, finely minced
4 flat anchovy fillets
1 dried hot red pepper
1½ cups peeled, chopped fresh tomatoes or canned crushed Italian tomatoes
½ cup pitted black olives
½ teaspoon dried oregano

¼ teaspoon freshly grated black pepper
2 to 3 cups loosely packed, cooked cauliflower florets
½ pound fusilli
⅓ cup pine nuts, lightly toasted
2 tablespoons chopped fresh flat-leaf parsley

Heat the olive oil in a large skillet, and sauté the garlic, anchovies, and red pepper over very low heat, stirring occasionally, until the anchovies have dissolved into the oil. (If the heat is too high, the anchovies will crisp instead of softening, in which case you will have to chop them into small pieces and proceed.)

Add the tomatoes, olives, oregano, and black pepper. Simmer, uncovered, stirring occasionally, for 10 minutes. Add the cauliflower and heat through.

The recipe can be prepared to this point 1 to 2 hours ahead and held at room temperature.

Cook the fusilli according to package directions.

Stir the pine nuts and parsley into the sauce. Toss with the hot cooked fusilli.

MAKES 4 SERVINGS

Salmon with Roasted Broccoli Rabe

SUPERFOODS: salmon, broccoli rabe, garlic

½ pound broccoli rabe
½ cup water
2 tablespoons olive oil
1 garlic clove, minced

2 salmon steaks (about 1½
pounds total)
Freshly ground black pepper

Wash the rabe well and chop it coarsely, discarding any thick, tough ribs. In a large pot, steam the rabe in the water until it's limp. Remove the pot from the heat immediately, and drain the rabe.

Preheat the oven to 400 degrees F.

In a glass or ceramic baking dish, combine the oil and garlic. Drain the rabe, and toss it with this oil as if it were a salad. Lay the salmon steaks over the rabe.

Bake on the top shelf of the oven for 20 minutes or until the salmon flakes apart easily at the center. Divide each of the steaks into 2 portions. Season with black pepper to your taste, and serve immediately.

MAKES 4 SERVINGS

Banana-Fig Torte

SUPERFOODS: figs, banana, almonds

For the filling

1 cup snipped Calimyrna dried
 figs (use a kitchen scissors)
½ cup water

2 tablespoons honey
1 tablespoon cornstarch,
 dissolved in ⅓ cup water

For the torte

1 ripe medium banana
¼ teaspoon almond extract
⅞ cup unbleached all-purpose
 flour (1 cup minus 2
 tablespoons)
½ cup sugar

¼ cup ground blanched almonds
1 tablespoon toasted wheat germ
1 teaspoon baking powder
¼ teaspoon salt
⅓ cup butter

Make the filling: Combine the figs, water, and honey in a sauce-pan. Bring to a boil, lower the heat, and simmer 5 minutes, stirring often. Blend the cornstarch mixture into the figs. Stir constantly until bubbling and thickened, and continue cooking 1 minute longer.

The filling can be made 1 to 2 days ahead. Keep refrigerated.

Preheat the oven to 400 degrees F. Bring the filling to room temperature.

Make the torte: Mash the banana to a puree, and measure it. You should have ½ cup. If not, add enough plain yogurt or milk to make up the difference. Stir in the almond extract.

Mix the dry ingredients. Cut in the butter until the mixture is mealy in texture. (This can be done in a food processor.) Stir in the mashed banana to make a stiff batter.

Spoon the batter into a tart pan with a removeable rim (a buttered 9-inch pie plate can be substituted). Smooth the batter over the bottom and sides of the pan. Lightly drop spoonfuls of the filling over the batter, and gently spread it as a top layer to within 1 inch of the edges of the pan. Don't mix the layers.

Bake the torte in the top third of the oven for 25 to 30 minutes, until golden brown. Cool on a wire rack. When the torte shrinks a bit from the sides of the pan, remove the rim. (If using a pie plate, simply serve from the pan.) Cut into wedges to serve.

MAKES **6** TO **8** SERVINGS

A MOSTLY MAKE-AHEAD MENU FOR FOUR

Marinated Vegetable Appetizer♦
Kale-Stuffed Chicken Breasts with Walnut Sauce♦
Whole Wheat French Bread
Easy Golden-Baked Peaches♦

Cruciferous vegetables can wear many guises. In this make-ahead menu, broccoli (or cauliflower) in the appetizer and kale in the stuffing are two more ways to serve them. Carrots in the appetizer and peaches in the dessert are bright with beta-carotene.

Marinated Vegetable Appetizer

SUPERFOODS: carrots, broccoli

These delightful fresh pickles (a nice change from the ubiquitous raw veggies) can accommodate many substitutions, such as cauliflower and tender green beans—in fact, whatever is available—simply by adjusting the blanching time to suit the vegetable.

3 carrots, scraped and
  sliced diagonally ½ inch
  thick
Florets from 1 bunch broccoli
1 small zucchini, sliced into
  ½-inch rounds

¼ teaspoon each dried basil,
  dried dill, celery seed, freshly
  grated black pepper, hot red
  pepper flakes, and salt (or adjust
  amounts to your taste)
1 cup rice vinegar*

Bring a large pot of water to a boil. Have a large bowl of ice water ready.

Parboil the vegetables separately: 2 minutes for the carrots, 1 minute for the broccoli, and a scant 15 seconds for the zucchini. Remove each with a slotted spoon, and immediately plunge the vegetable into the ice water.

When chilled, drain the vegetables well and sprinkle them with the seasonings. Put them in a quart jar. Pour the vinegar over all.

Marinate in the refrigerator for 3 to 4 hours to develop flavor; shake several times. Drain before serving. (The leftover seasoned vinegar makes a flavorful addition to a vinaigrette.)

These fresh pickles can be made several hours or 1 day ahead—but they will lose color the second day.

MAKES 1 QUART

---

*A mild flavor, so you can use a lot of it.

Kale-Stuffed Chicken Breasts
with Walnut Sauce

SUPERFOODS: kale, onion, walnuts

*1 pound kale, well-washed,
  stemmed, and chopped
1 cup chicken broth
2 tablespoons tomato paste
1 garlic clove, crushed*

*2 whole boneless and skinless
  chicken breasts
Seasoned bread crumbs
Paprika*

For the walnut sauce

*1 tablespoon walnut oil (olive oil
  can be substituted)
¼ cup finely chopped onion
1 cup chicken broth
½ cup dry white wine (or
  increase the broth ½ cup)*

*Pinch of dried thyme
1 tablespoon cornstarch,
  dissolved in ¼ cup cold water
½ cup walnut halves or pieces*

In a large pot, simmer the kale with the broth, tomato paste, and garlic until tender, about 15 minutes. Remove and discard the garlic. Drain the kale well.

Cut the chicken breasts in half. Flatten the halves with a mallet into cutlets, roughly 8 inches in diameter. Arrange a layer of kale (approximately ¼ cup) over each cutlet to within ½ inch of the edge. Pull opposite edges of the cutlet together so that they overlap to make a roll. Pin each roll together with a metal skewer, or tie it with kitchen twine. Put the rolls, cut side down, in an oiled baking dish. Sprinkle with bread crumbs and paprika.

The recipe can be prepared up to this point several hours ahead. Keep refrigerated. Allow about 5 minutes more cooking time if the chicken has been chilled.

Preheat the oven to 350 degrees F.

Bake the chicken for 20 to 25 minutes, until just cooked through.

Make the sauce: Heat the oil in a small saucepan, and sauté the onion until softened, 3 minutes. Add the broth, wine, and thyme. Bring to a boil and cook for 5 minutes, reducing the volume by one-third. Add the cornstarch mixture, and stir constantly until thickened. Add the walnuts, and simmer about 3 minutes, stirring occasionally.

Remove the skewers or ties. Spoon the sauce over the chicken rolls.

MAKES 4 SERVINGS

Easy Golden-Baked Peaches

SUPERFOODS: peaches

Try serving these warm with a spoonful of nonfat frozen yogurt melting on top!

1 tablespoon butter	*About ¼ cup dark corn syrup*
4 ripe peaches, peeled, halved,	*Cinnamon Sugar (see page 540)*
and pitted	

Preheat the oven to 350 degrees F.

Put the butter in a baking dish that will fit the 8 peach halves in 1 layer, and melt the butter in the heating oven. Lay the peaches, cut sides up, in the buttered pan. Brush the halves with the syrup, and sprinkle them with cinnamon sugar.

Bake the peaches for 20 to 25 minutes, until tender. Serve warm or at room temperature.

The peaches can be made up to 1 day ahead. Keep refrigerated. Allow them to come to room temperature before serving.

MAKES 4 SERVINGS

SUPPER FOR FOUR ON THE PORCH

Capered Tuna Cakes♦
Brussels Sprouts and Potato Salad♦
Sweet 'n' Sour Pepper Relish♦
Sliced Honeydew and Kiwi
with Lime Juice and Crushed Mint

Crucerifous Brussels sprouts give a new twist to an old favorite, teaming two cancer-fighting vegetables. Peppers, honeydew, and kiwi add a big boost of vitamin C. Tuna is rich in selenium, another great antioxidant—and niacin, as well.

Capered Tuna Cakes

SUPERFOODS: potato, tuna, onion, green pepper, olive oil

If you double this recipe, no need to double the oil. Just add a little more to the pan if it seems dry.

1 cup mashed potato

2 tablespoons mayonnaise

1 tablespoon Dijon mustard

1 cup cooked tuna, or a 7-ounce can, drained

¼ cup each *finely chopped onion and green bell pepper*

1 tablespoon drained capers

About 1 cup plain or seasoned dry bread crumbs

¼ cup olive oil

Blend the potato, mayonnaise, and mustard. Stir in the tuna, onion, green pepper, and capers. Using 2 tablespoons, form the mixture into 8 cakes (¼ cup each).

Pour the bread crumbs onto a sheet of waxed paper. Place each cake in turn on the crumbs, and turn to coat all sides. Flatten the cakes, put them on a plate, and chill them.

The recipe can be made several hours ahead to this point. Keep refrigerated.

Heat the oil in a large skillet, and fry the cakes slowly until they are golden on both sides, about 6 minutes.

MAKES 4 SERVINGS

Brussels Sprouts and Potato Salad

SUPERFOODS: potatoes, Brussels sprouts, onion, olive oil,
parsley

*1 to 1¼ pounds baby red potatoes
(larger ones can be
substituted; just cut them into
sprout-size chunks)
Salt
1 tablespoon white vinegar
One 10-ounce package frozen
Brussels sprouts, or 1 pint
fresh small sprouts*

*¼ cup chopped red onion
6 tablespoons olive oil
3 tablespoons red wine vinegar
2 tablespoons minced fresh
flat-leaf parsley
Freshly grated lemon pepper or
black pepper*

Scrub the potatoes well, cutting out any defects. Halve the potatoes and put them into a steamer. Salt them to taste. Add the white vinegar to the water in the bottom of the steamer, and steam for 10 to 15 minutes, until quite tender. Remove them from the heat.

Cook the frozen sprouts according to package directions. If using fresh sprouts, trim off outer leaves, cut an *X* in the stem end of each, and steam the sprouts until tender, about 10 minutes.

In a salad bowl, mix the sprouts and onion with 1 tablespoon of the oil to keep the sprouts from turning color when the vinegar is added. Add the potatoes and stir in the wine vinegar, which will penetrate the potatoes for a nice vinaigrette flavor. Last, add the remaining 5 tablespoons olive oil, parsley, and pepper, and toss the salad well.

Serve warm, chilled, or at room temperature. Taste to correct seasoning; you may want more salt, vinegar, or oil.

The salad can be made several hours or 1 day ahead. Keep refrigerated.

Note: There are a number of possible additions to this salad, all delicious, but dependent on what else you're having: anchovies, walnuts, and/or sun-dried tomatoes packed in oil.

MAKES ABOUT 2 QUARTS

Sweet 'n' Sour Pepper Relish

SUPERFOODS: garlic, red peppers, raisins

2 tablespoons olive oil	*¼ cup raisins*
1 to 2 garlic cloves, finely minced	*2 tablespoons balsamic vinegar*
3 red bell pappers (about 1¼ pounds), cut into thin strips	*Freshly ground black pepper, 8 to 10 grinds*

Heat the oil and garlic in a 10-inch skillet. When the garlic barely begins to sizzle, add the peppers. "Sweat" the peppers over low heat until they are tender, 10 to 15 minutes. Stir often to prevent browning.

Add the raisins and vinegar; cook over low heat 3 minutes longer. Remove from the heat, grind the black pepper over the relish, and stir. Cover and let stand at room temperature for about 1 hour to develop the flavor. Taste to correct seasoning; you may want more vinegar, black pepper, or a sprinkle of salt.

The relish may be made a day ahead, refrigerated, and brought to room temperature before serving.

MAKES ABOUT 2 CUPS

SOUP 'N' PIZZA FOR SIX

Aunt Sheila's Soup♦
Broccoli Pizza with Red Pepper and Feta♦
Salad with Watercress and Crisp Red Radishes
Clementines and Assorted Nuts

A nice Sunday night supper, particularly if you've (providentially) made the soup earlier. This menu is simply studded with cruciferous vegetables. Besides those pureed in the soup, there's broccoli on the pizza plus watercress and radishes in the salad.

Aunt Sheila's Soup

SUPERFOODS: Everything that goes into this soup is super!

This recipe came from Ellen Steinbaum's family repertoire. Isn't that just the way you get some really good recipes? Handed along from one family member to another. Make this soup on a day when you're feeling creative and/or you want to clean out the refrigerator from a too-optimistic purchase of vegetables. Nothing is measured—that's the creative part!

Any assortment of

Green beans	*Turnips*
Carrots	*Rutabagas*
Tomatoes	*Potatoes*
Onions	*Several sprigs (a handful) of*
Mushrooms	*fresh parsley and dill*
Zucchini	*Salt and pepper*
Parsnips	

Peel, cut, and otherwise prepare the vegetables. You can use any assortment and amount, but the parsley and dill are a constant.

Put the vegetables in a large pot with broth or water to cover. Cook until tender, then puree in a food processor or blender. If you use a food processor, puree the vegetables separately; then add them to the liquid. If a blender, puree *with* the liquid.

The soup can be made a day or so ahead. Keep refrigerated, or freeze for longer storage.

Serve hot, sprinkled with grated Parmesan cheese, or cold. I like to add a dollop of plain nonfat yogurt to the chilled version.

SERVING NUMBER VARIES WITH THE INGREDIENTS, BUT IT'S ALWAYS A LOT!

Broccoli Pizza with Red Pepper and Feta

SUPERFOODS: olive oil, garlic, red pepper, broccoli

Allowing the shaped pizza to rise again yields a thicker, breadlike crust to hold the vegetables.

Pizza dough, homemade (recipe follows) or store-bought	*10 broccoli stalks, cooked*
3 tablespoons olive oil	*½ cup pitted Kalamata olives*
1 large garlic clove, finely minced	*4 ounces feta cheese, thinly sliced or crumbled*
1 red bell pepper, seeded and diced	*½ teaspoon dried oregano*

Punch down and roll out the dough to fit a 15-inch round pizza pan—or oblong to fit a jelly roll pan—that has been coated with oil and sprinkled with cornmeal. Or fit the dough onto a cornmeal-dusted pizza paddle for baking on a heated stone according to manufacturer's directions.

Flute the edge and let the pizza rise in a warm place for 30 to 45 minutes, until double-thick. Meanwhile, prepare the topping.

In a medium skillet, heat the oil and sauté the garlic and red pepper until the red pepper just begins to soften, about 3 minutes. Use a brush to "paint" the dough with oil remaining in the pan. Sprinkle the dough with the red pepper and garlic. Arrange the broccoli in a wheel-spoke pattern. Scatter the olives on top, then the cheese and oregano.

Preheat the oven to 400 degrees F.

Bake the pizza for 20 to 25 minutes on the bottom shelf of the oven, or until the bottom crust is nicely browned; lift with a spatula to check it.

MAKES 12 SLICES

PIZZA DOUGH

1 envelope active dry yeast
1 teaspoon sugar
1 cup very warm water
3¼ cups unbleached all-purpose
  flour (whole wheat flour can be
  substituted for part or all of
  the flour)

¾ teaspoon salt
2 tablespoons olive oil

Stir the yeast and sugar into the warm water. Let it stand 5 to 10 minutes; the yeast should bubble up to show that it's active.

Processor method: Combine the flour and salt in the work bowl of a food processor fitted with the steel blade. Coat a medium bowl with a little of the olive oil; pour the rest into the flour. Process to blend. With the motor running, pour the yeast mixture down the feed tube. Process 10 to 15 seconds, until the mixture forms a ball that cleans the sides of the bowl. (If the flour does not adhere in a ball, add a little water with the motor running, 1 teaspoon at a time.) Continue to process, counting 30 seconds, or just until the dough is elastic and springy. Do not overprocess.

Alternative methods: The ingredients can be combined in an electric mixer fitted with a dough hook. Knead 5 minutes. Or the ingredients can be combined by hand. Knead 10 minutes.

Place the dough in the oiled bowl, turning it around to grease all sides, and cover with plastic wrap. Let it rise in a warm place until doubled in bulk, about 1 hour and 15 minutes. Punch the dough down and proceed with the pizza recipe.

MAKES 1 LARGE OR 2 SMALL PIZZAS

A FIRESIDE DINNER FOR SIX

Broccoli Rabe (Rapini) and Macaroni Casserole♦
Perch with Braised Fennel♦
Whole-Grain Italian Bread
Fresh Pears with Gorgonzola Cheese

*P*asta and cruciferous vegetables seem to be a natural combination, as in this macaroni and rabe casserole. The menu is rich in calcium, as well, with the rabe, milk, and cheese each contributing its share.

Broccoli Rabe (Rapini) and Macaroni Casserole

SUPERFOODS: broccoli rabe, garlic, skim milk, macaroni

Of all the hard *cheeses, Parmesan has the most calcium, yet is lowest in cholesterol. The amount of grated cheese in this recipe equals about 1 ounce but gives a great deal of flavor.*

1- to 1¼-pound bunch broccoli
    rabe
2 tablespoons olive oil
1 garlic clove, minced
1 cup chicken broth or water
1 cup milk (can be skim)

3 tablespoons flour
¼ teaspoon each salt* and
    pepper
¼ cup grated Parmesan cheese
⅓ pound elbow macaroni

For the topping

2 tablespoons seasoned bread
    crumbs

1 tablespoon each grated
    Parmesan cheese and wheat
    germ

Wash the rabe well; cut it coarsely. Heat the oil in a 4-quart pot, and sauté the garlic until it sizzles. Add the rabe and broth or water. Simmer 10 minutes, or until tender. Remove the rabe with a slotted spoon.

Combine the milk, flour, salt, and pepper in a jar. Shake well and strain into the simmering broth, stirring constantly. Continue cooking for 5 minutes to cook the flour. Stir in the cheese and the rabe.

Meanwhile, cook the macaroni according to package directions. Combine the rabe, sauce, and macaroni in a buttered 2½-quart casserole.

Blend the topping ingredients, and sprinkle them on the casserole.

The casserole can be made several hours ahead. Keep refrigerated.

Preheat the oven to 375 degrees F.

Bake 30 minutes (45, if refrigerated) until bubbly throughout.

MAKES 2 QUARTS

---

*You can omit the salt, if you wish, since the cheese is salty.

Perch with Braised Fennel

SUPERFOODS: olive oil, tomato sauce, perch

Fennel with its distinctive licorice flavor is wonderful braised (hot or cold) as well as raw in salads. Unlike celery, fennel turns brown when cut, so it must be protected from exposure to air by immediate dousing in whatever sauce or dressing the recipe calls for.

2 tablespoons olive oil	6 serving-size perch or sole fillets
1 large fennel bulb, cored and	(about 2 pounds total)
cut into sixths	Flour for dredging
1½ cups tomato sauce,	Salt and pepper
homemade (see pages	Olive oil for frying
516–518) or store-bought	

Preheat the oven to 325 degrees F.

Heat 2 tablespoons oil in a Dutch oven on the range top, and sauté the fennel until the pieces are lightly browned. Add the tomato sauce, and bring to a simmer.

Cover and bake on the middle shelf of the oven for 1 hour or until tender.

May be made a day ahead. Keep refrigerated. Reheat on the range top.

Dredge the fillets in flour; shake off excess. Salt and pepper them to taste. Fry in a large skillet, preferably cast-iron, in a thin coating of olive oil, until golden on both sides, about 6 minutes. Transfer fillets to a platter. Surround with the fennel and serve.

MAKES 6 SERVINGS

A SIMPLY SUPER SUNDAY DINNER FOR EIGHT

Poached Chicken with Red Pepper Sauce♦
"Creamed" Broccoli and Potatoes♦
Whole Wheat Baking Powder Biscuits♦
Fruit Sorbet with Ginger Snaps

Turnips cooked with the chicken and broccoli are the cruciferous vegetables. Potatoes are a source of vitamin C, plus compounds called protease inhibitors, thought to help prevent tumor formation. There's beta-carotene, too, in carrots and broccoli, to round out the defense against cancer.

Poached Chicken with Red Pepper Sauce

SUPERFOODS: leeks, carrots, turnips,
green and red peppers, garlic

One 3½- to 4-pound chicken
2 sprigs each *fresh rosemary and
  fresh thyme or sage*
4 medium white turnips
4 carrots
2 leeks, white part only, or 1
  medium onion

2 celery stalks
2 cups chicken broth
  (a 13-ounce can)
2 cups water
1 cup dry white wine*
½ teaspoon salt

For the red pepper sauce

2 tablespoons olive oil
1 cup finely chopped celery,
  onion, and green pepper
2 garlic cloves, minced
1 cup chicken broth**
½ cup dry white wine or broth

1 large roasted red pepper***
1 tablespoon tomato paste
¼ teaspoon each cayenne
  pepper, black pepper, and
  salt

Discard any fat from the chicken cavity, wash the bird in salted water, rinse, and drain. Put 1 sprig of each of the herbs in the cavity.

*The alcohol will evaporate during the poaching, leaving only the flavor, but broth can be substituted.
**After the chicken is cooked, this can be taken from the poaching liquid.
***From a jar, measure ¾ cup, or use homemade (see page 523).

Peel the turnips; leave them whole. Scrape the carrots; cut them in half. Wash, peel, and slice the remaining vegetables. Put half the vegetables in the bottom of a large pot, add the chicken, the rest of the vegetables and herbs, and the broth, water, wine, and salt. Bring to a boil, reduce the heat, and poach at a low simmer, with cover slightly ajar, for 45 minutes, or until juices from the thigh run clear, not pink. (When in doubt, cut the joint.)

The chicken can be made 1 day ahead. Separate the chicken, vegetables, and broth. Cool the chicken and vegetables for 20 minutes or so before refrigerating. Cool the broth to room temperature before chilling, lest the refrigerator get too warm from all this hot food.

Make the sauce: In a medium skillet, heat the oil and sauté the chopped vegetables and garlic until they are yellowed but not brown, about 5 minutes. Add the broth and wine, and boil rapidly until reduced to 1 cup (including the vegetables). Puree the mixture with the roasted pepper, adding all the remaining ingredients. Return the sauce to the skillet, and continue to cook over low heat, stirring often, until it's as thick as salsa. Once reduced to this point, the sauce is quite spicy, but taste it to see if you want more pepper.

The sauce can be made up to 3 days ahead. Keep refrigerated.

Serve the chicken (heated in a little broth, if made ahead) with the turnips and carrots; pass the sauce on the side. Save the poaching liquid for a terrific soup.

MAKES 8 SERVINGS

"Creamed" Broccoli and Potatoes

SUPERFOODS: broccoli, potatoes, skim milk, scallions

"Creamed" without any fat at all. Leftovers from this recipe can be pureed with chicken broth to make a tasty soup the next day.

1 bunch fresh or 2 10-ounce packages frozen broccoli
16 small new potatoes
3 cups skim milk
¼ cup all-purpose flour

2 teaspoons ground cumin
¼ to ½ teaspoon white pepper
Salt
8 scallions, chopped

Wash, trim, and slice the broccoli stems. Leave the florets whole. Steam the fresh broccoli until tender, 3 to 5 minutes. Or cook frozen broccoli according to package directions; drain.

Scrub the potatoes well, trim them of defects, but leave them unpeeled. Boil them separately until tender, about 10 minutes. Drain.

Heat 2 cups milk in a saucepan until scalded but not boiling.

Meanwhile, combine the remaining cup of cold milk with the flour and seasonings in a jar. Cover and shake well to blend. Strain into the hot milk, and cook over medium heat, stirring constantly, until thick and bubbling. Simmer over low heat 3 to 5 minutes, stirring often, to cook the flour.

Gently stir in the broccoli, potatoes, and scallions.

MAKES **8** SERVINGS

Whole Wheat Baking Powder Biscuits

SUPERFOODS: whole wheat flour, skim milk

The oils in whole wheat can develop a rancid taste in summer or after long storage. Keep the flour fresh-tasting by refrigerating or freezing it until needed.

2 cups whole wheat flour	*¼ cup (½ stick) butter or*
4 teaspoons baking powder	*margarine*
1 tablespoon sugar	*About ⅞ cup skim milk (1 cup*
¼ to ½ teaspoon salt	*less 2 tablespoons)*

Preheat the oven to 425 degrees F.

Sift the flour, baking powder, sugar, and salt into a bowl. Cut in the butter with a pastry blender until the mixture looks like coarse meal. (These two steps can be accomplished in a food processor.)

Add enough milk to make a soft dough. Knead in the bowl to form a ball. Turn out onto a floured surface, and pat into a ½-inch thickness. Cut biscuits with a 2-inch cutter or with a floured drinking glass of the same size, rerolling scraps. Lay the biscuits in a buttered baking pan, and bake on the top shelf for 12 to 14 minutes or until lightly browned. Serve warm.

The biscuits can be made ahead and rewarmed in a 300 degree F. oven.

Note: Some optional additions are grated cheese, finely chopped parsley, herbs, and/or minced onion.

MAKES 8 TO 10

DINNER FOR FOUR IN A HALF-HOUR

Baked Salmon Fillets with Garlic and Lemon♦
Mustard Greens with Chickpeas and Cherry Peppers♦
Sliced Cucumbers and Finely Shredded Red Cabbage
with Yogurt-Mint Dressing (see page 532)
Rye Bread
Chilled, Assorted Seedless Grapes

Cruciferous mustard greens and red cabbage join other superfoods in this quick dinner, made speedier if you delegate some of the washing and shredding chores. Other immunity boosters are vitamin E–rich salmon, garlic, and yogurt.

Baked Salmon Fillets with Garlic and Lemon

SUPERFOODS: salmon, wheat germ, garlic

1½ to 2 pounds salmon fillets
Olive oil
½ cup plain bread crumbs
2 tablespoons wheat germ
2 tablespoons grated lemon rind
2 garlic cloves, pressed in a garlic press

½ teaspoon dried tarragon
Salt and freshly ground pepper
1 egg, beaten, or ¼ cup prepared egg substitute
Paprika
Lemon wedges

Preheat the oven to 400 degrees F.

Rinse and pat dry the salmon fillets. Place them in 1 layer in an oiled baking dish, skin sides down.

Combine the crumbs, wheat germ, lemon rind, garlic, tarragon, salt, and pepper, and rub the mixture between your fingers to distribute the garlic evenly throughout.

Use a brush to paint the tops of the fillets with the egg. Press the crumbs evenly on top. Drizzle a little olive oil over the crumbs. Sprinkle with paprika.

Bake for 20 minutes on the top shelf, until the fish flakes apart easily at the center.

Serve with lemon wedges.

MAKES 4 SERVINGS

Mustard Greens with Chickpeas and Cherry Peppers

SUPERFOODS: mustard greens, leeks, olive oil, chickpeas

"Some like it hot!" If you're one of them, just add more cherry peppers.

1 bunch mustard greens
2 large leeks
3 tablespoons olive oil
½ cup chicken broth or water

1 cup drained and rinsed canned
   chickpeas
2 to 4 hot cherry peppers,
   quartered, or halved if small*

*For a milder flavor, seed the peppers.

Wash the mustard greens. Remove tough stems and chop the greens coarsely.

Cut almost all the green tops off the leeks. Wash them very well, including between the rings, and chop them.

Spoon the oil into a large pot, cover, and sweat the leeks in it over low heat for about 10 minutes.

Add the greens and broth or water. Simmer until the vegetable is almost tender, 5 to 8 minutes.

Stir in the chickpeas and cherry peppers. Simmer an additional 5 minutes or more to develop the flavor.

MAKES 4 TO 6 SERVINGS

AFTER-WORK EASY DINNER FOR FOUR

Braised Chicken with Brussels Sprouts and Figs♦
Turnip and Tomato Salad with Mint♦
Buttered Whole Wheat Noodles
Maple-Baked Apple Rings♦

Cruciferous Brussels sprouts and sweet young turnips are not the only defenders in this menu. Vitamin C–rich tomatoes and antitumor figs also qualify.

Braised Chicken with Brussels Sprouts and Figs

SUPERFOODS: olive oil, shallots, Brussels sprouts, figs

A skillet dinner you can have ready in a little more than a half-hour.

4 large boneless, skinless chicken thighs
One 10-ounce package frozen Brussels sprouts, thawed to separate
2 tablespoons olive oil
¼ cup chopped shallots
¼ teaspoon dried thyme leaves
Salt and pepper
4 dried Calimyrna figs
¼ cup balsamic vinegar

Wash the chicken in salted water, rinse, and pat dry. Cut the thighs in half lengthwise. If the Brussels sprouts are still frozen, thaw them fast in a strainer under running cool water.

Heat the oil in a large skillet, and sauté the shallots until they are softened, about 2 minutes. Add the chicken, sprinkling it with thyme, salt, and pepper to taste. Sauté for about 20 minutes, turning once, until the chicken is just cooked through.

Add the Brussels sprouts. Cut the figs in half, removing and discarding the small hard stem. Add the figs. Continue to sauté for about 5 minutes, or until the sprouts are tender.

Spoon the balsamic vinegar over all before serving.

MAKES 4 SERVINGS

Turnip and Tomato Salad with Mint

SUPERFOODS: turnips, tomatoes, onion, parsley, olive oil

Small turnips prepared this way almost taste like crisp radishes.

*½ pound fresh, young, small
    purple-topped turnips
1 pound ripe tomatoes (2 large),
    sliced
4 slices red onion, separated into
    rings
Salt*

*4 fresh parsley sprigs, chopped
About 8 fresh mint leaves,
    minced
3 tablespoons olive oil
1 tablespoon white wine vinegar
    or lemon juice*

Peel and slice the turnips as thin as possible. Put them into a shallow salad dish with the sliced tomatoes and add all the remaining ingredients. Toss the salad gently, and allow it to stand for about 30 minutes at room temperature, turning occasionally.

MAKES 4 SERVINGS

Maple-Baked Apple Rings

SUPERFOODS: apple, walnuts

*4 red baking apples, such as
    Rome or Gala
½ cup pure maple syrup
¼ cup brown sugar*

*½ cup walnut halves
½ teaspoon natural maple
    flavoring (optional)*

Preheat the oven to 350 degrees F.

Peel and core the apples. Slice them into rings. Put them into a casserole with all the remaining ingredients, stir gently but well, and bake for 30 minutes, stirring 2 or 3 times during the cooking time. Serve warm or at room temperature.

MAKES **4** SERVINGS

EASY WAYS WITH VEGETABLES FOR FOUR

Chicken Cutlets
with Red Pepper and Braised Carrots♦
Roasted Cauliflower♦
Sweet 'n' Sour Cabbage♦
Whole Wheat Toast
Blackberry Fool♦

Braising, roasting, and skillet-steaming are three easy ways to cook vegetables, and each gives a flavor sweeter than the more traditional boiling. Techniques that yield a lighter flavor are especially important when increasing the cruciferous vegetables in your menus (cauliflower and cabbage in this case).

Chicken Cutlets with Red Pepper and Braised Carrots

SUPERFOODS: red pepper, carrots

*2 whole boneless, skinless
  chicken breasts*
Flour
8 small or 4 large carrots, peeled
1 cinnamon stick
3 or more tablespoons olive oil

*1 red bell pepper, seeded and cut
  into triangles*
*Salt and Spicy Pepper Mix (see
  page 539)*
*About ½ teaspoon dried
  rosemary*

Cut each chicken breast into 4 pieces lengthwise. On a wooden board, flatten each chicken piece to about ½ inch thick. I use an old-fashioned wooden potato masher, but you can use any heavy mallet or the flat side of a cleaver. Lightly flour the chicken, and refrigerate it until ready to cook.

Cut the carrots into 2-inch pieces diagonally. Put them in a saucepan with the cinnamon stick and 2 inches of water. Boil until tender, about 10 minutes. Drain. (Rinse, dry, and save the cinnamon stick for another use.)

Heat 1 tablespoon of the oil in a large skillet, and sauté the pepper until tender, about 3 minutes. Remove the pepper. Save the oil in the skillet.

The recipe can be prepared several hours ahead to this point.

Add a tablespoon of oil to that which is already in the skillet. Heat it until quite hot and shimmering. Cook the chicken pieces, 2 or 3 at a time, until golden and cooked through, about 3 minutes per side over medium-high heat. Add more oil as needed. Just before turning the chicken to the second side, sprinkle with salt, pepper mix, and a pinch of rosemary leaves. Keep the cutlets warm on a platter.

When all the chicken is cooked, quickly and lightly brown the carrots in the hot oil, shaking and stirring often. Add the pepper pieces to heat them through.

Spoon the braised vegetables onto the platter, and serve.

MAKES 4 SERVINGS

Roasted Cauliflower

SUPERFOODS: cauliflower

Serve hot as a vegetable, or at room temperature as an appetizer with Honey-Mustard Dressing (see page 531).

4 cups cauliflower florets	1 bay leaf, broken into 2 or 3
2 tablespoons olive oil	pieces
1 garlic clove, crushed	Salt and pepper

Preheat the oven to 375 degrees F.

Put the florets in a large glass or stainless steel roasting pan in which they will fit more or less in one layer. Pour 1 tablespoon oil into the pan, and turn the florets around in it. Add the garlic and bay leaf.

Roast in the top third of the oven for 15 to 20 minutes, until the desired tender-crispness is reached. Stir and turn the florets every 5 minutes while cooking, adding the remaining tablespoon of oil if the florets seem dry.

When cooked, season the cauliflower with salt and pepper to your taste.

MAKES 4 SERVINGS

Sweet 'n' Sour Cabbage

SUPERFOODS: onion, tomato sauce, cabbage

1½ tablespoons olive oil	*2 tablespoons brown sugar*
1 medium onion, sliced into	*4 cups finely sliced green cabbage*
* rounds*	*2 to 3 tablespoons water*
½ cup tomato sauce, homemade	* (optional)*
* (see page 516) or store-bought*	*Salt and cayenne pepper*
¼ cup red wine vinegar	

Heat the olive oil in a large skillet, and sauté the onion rounds until they separate into rings and soften, about 5 minutes.

Add the tomato sauce, vinegar, and brown sugar, and simmer 2 to 3 minutes, uncovered. Add the cabbage.

The recipe can be prepared to this point several hours ahead. Cool slightly; refrigerate in the skillet, covered.

Toss the cabbage with the sauce, and add a little water if the mixture seems dry. Cover and steam for 5 minutes or until the cabbage is just tender. Do not overcook.

Add salt and cayenne pepper to taste. Serve immediately.

MAKES 4 SERVINGS

Blackberry Fool

SUPERFOODS: yogurt, blackberries

1 cup plain nonfat yogurt	¼ teaspoon salt
2 tablespoons cornstarch	¼ cup Chambord (black
1 cup whole milk	raspberry liqueur), or 1½
2 eggs, beaten	teaspoons vanilla extract
½ cup sugar	1 cup blackberries, rinsed

In a small bowl, sprinkle the yogurt with the cornstarch, and whisk it in until very well combined.

In a saucepan, whisk together the milk, eggs, sugar, and salt over low heat until the sugar is dissolved. (Do not boil yet.) Whisk in the yogurt mixture, and keep whisking over medium heat until the mixture bubbles and thickens. Cook about 1 minute longer.

Remove the sauce from the heat and stir in the liqueur or vanilla.

Remove 4 blackberries for garnishing. Stir the rest into the yogurt custard. Divide the custard among 4 dessert dishes; top with reserved berries. Chill until set before serving.

MAKES 4 SERVINGS

A STIR-FRY DINNER
FOR FOUR TO SIX

Beef with Broccoli and Tomatoes♦
Bok Choy, Pepper, and Scallion Stir-Fry♦
Hot Brown Rice (see page 524)
Gingered Figs♦

Asian-style fast methods of cooking and distinctive flavors go well with cruciferous vegetables—broccoli and bok choy in this menu. The latter is one of the mildest tasting of the cruciferous family. Antioxidant vitamin C in the tomatoes and broccoli plus allium in the scallions underscore the immunity theme. Asian tea is a harmonious accompaniment that also boosts immunity.

Beef with Broccoli and Tomatoes

SUPERFOODS: broccoli, garlic, cherry tomatoes

Have all the ingredients prepared in advance for these two super-speedy stir-fries.

1¼ pounds steak tips
2 tablespoons cornstarch
3 cups fresh broccoli florets
⅓ cup each oyster sauce and
    chicken broth
3 tablespoons sake or dry
    vermouth (or increase broth)

2 tablespoons soy sauce
½ tablespoon brown sugar
2 tablespoons vegetable oil
2 garlic cloves, minced
8 to 10 cherry tomatoes, halved

Trim and thinly slice the meat across the grain. Toss it with the cornstarch.

Blanch the broccoli in boiling water 2 minutes. Immediately rinse it in cold water.

Mix together the oyster sauce, broth, sake or vermouth, soy sauce, and brown sugar until the sugar is dissolved. Set this mixture aside.

Coat a nonstick skillet or wok with 1 tablespoon vegetable oil, and brown the beef. Remove it with a slotted spoon. Add the remaining tablespoon of oil, and stir-fry the broccoli with the garlic until tender-crisp. Remove the vegetables from the pan.

Add the sauce mixture to the pan, bring it to a boil, and simmer, stirring constantly, for 2 minutes. Return the meat and vegetables, and just heat them through. Stir in the tomatoes.

MAKES 4 TO 6 SERVINGS

Bok Choy, Pepper, and Scallion Stir-Fry

SUPERFOODS: scallions, red peppers, jalapeño peppers,
bok choy, tofu

1 bunch scallions	*1 cup diced firm tofu*
2 red bell peppers	*¼ cup each water and soy sauce*
4 fresh jalapeño peppers	*2 teaspoons cornstarch*
8 large stalks bok choy	*¼ cup dry white wine**
1½ tablespoons vegetable oil	

Prepare the vegetables. Cut the scallions into 1-inch lengths, using the white and pale green parts. Seed the red peppers and cut them into triangles. Using rubber gloves, seed the jalapeño peppers and cut them into quarters lengthwise. Coarsely chop the bok choy leaves, slice the stems; you should have 6 cups, loosely packed.

Heat 1 tablespoon oil in a large skillet or wok. Stir-fry the scallions, red peppers, and jalapeños for about 3 minutes, until almost tender-crisp. Add the bok choy, and continue cooking until the leaves have wilted but the stems are still crisp, about 2 minutes. Remove the vegetables to a serving dish.

Add the remaining ½ tablespoon of oil to the pan, and quickly brown the tofu over high heat. Add this to the vegetables.

In a cup, mix the water, soy sauce, and cornstarch until there are no lumps. Deglaze the pan with the wine, and add the cornstarch mixture. Cook, stirring constantly, until the glaze is thick and bubbling.

Return everything to the pan, toss with the glaze, and reheat briefly.

MAKES 4 TO 6 SERVINGS

---

*Chicken broth or water can be substituted for the wine.

Gingered Figs

SUPERFOODS: figs, ginger, molasses

One 8-ounce package golden
* dried figs**
3 cups water

½ cup sugar
6 slices fresh ginger
2 tablespoons molasses

Combine all the ingredients in a saucepan. Bring to a boil, reduce heat to simmer the fruit over low heat, with cover ajar, for 40 minutes.

Cool the figs and ginger in their syrup before chilling them in the refrigerator.

The figs can be made up to 5 days ahead. Keep refrigerated.

MAKES 20 TO 24 POACHED FIGS

*Not black figs. Golden figs by the name of Calimyrna are especially nice, but any light-colored fig will do.

A ROBUST BRUNCH OR LUNCH
FOR SIX

Broccoli Frittata♦
Mushrooms with Radicchio♦
Whole Wheat Scones♦
Assorted Fresh Plums

For those who like "real food" in the morning, start the day with a helping of cruciferous broccoli! Include some mushrooms— boosters of the immune system—along with plums, a source of antioxidant vitamin A, and you'll be well defended.

Broccoli Frittata

SUPERFOODS: broccoli, onion, red pepper

6 stalks cooked broccoli
3 eggs
¾ cup prepared egg substitute*,
  or 3 additional eggs
½ tablespoon minced fresh
  flatleaf parsley
Pinch of dried oregano

Salt and pepper
1½ tablespoons olive oil
¼ cup chopped onion
½ red bell pepper, diced
2 tablespoons grated Parmesan
  cheese

Cut the broccoli lengthwise so that the stalks are the thickness of pencils.

Beat the eggs, egg substitute, and seasonings together.

Heat 1 tablespoon of the oil in a 10-inch skillet, preferably nonstick. Sauté the onion and red pepper until they are tender, about 5 minutes.

Lay the broccoli in the pan like the spokes of a wheel, florets outward. Press them down with a spatula. Pour the egg mixture over all. Sprinkle with 1 tablespoon of the cheese.

Cook over very low heat until the egg has set, about 5 minutes, lifting the edges from time to time to let the uncooked portion seep underneath.

To invert, loosen the entire frittata with a spatula. Place a large plate over it, and turn the pan and plate together.

Put the pan back on the heat, add the remaining ½ tablespoon of oil, and slide the frittata back into the pan to brown on the second side, which will take only 1 or 2 minutes. Sprinkle the top with the remaining tablespoon of cheese.

Cut into wedges and serve immediately.

Note: The idea is to introduce a prepared egg substitute without sacrificing real egg flavor. But 3 more eggs can be used instead of the egg substitute, or another ¾ cup of the substitute can be used in place of the whole eggs. The total egg mixture should equal 6 eggs.

MAKES **6** WEDGES

Mushrooms with Radicchio

Superfoods: mushrooms, onion, radicchio

*12 ounces assorted fresh
  mushrooms**
2 tablespoons olive oil
*1 medium onion, finely
  chopped*

¼ teaspoon each *dried tarragon
  and dried basil*
*2 cups loosely packed, shredded
  radicchio***
Salt and pepper

Wash the mushrooms well, and shake them dry in a salad spinner or towel. Remove tough portions of stems, and slice the mushrooms.

Heat the oil in a large skillet, and fry the mushrooms, stirring often, until their moisture evaporates and they begin to brown. Add the onion and stir-fry for 2 to 3 minutes.

Add all the remaining ingredients, and stir-fry just until the radicchio wilts, about 5 minutes. Remove from the heat. Serve warm or at room temperature.

MAKES ABOUT 1½ CUPS

*Include 1 or 2 fresh shiitake mushrooms, one of the most potent of mushrooms in stimulating the body's natural defenses.
**Finely shredded red cabbage can be substituted.

Whole Wheat Scones

SUPERFOODS: whole wheat flour

1½ cups whole wheat flour	*¼ teaspoon salt*
1½ cups plus 2 tablespoons	*½ cup (1 stick) unsalted butter*
unbleached all-purpose flour	*or margarine*
⅓ cup sugar	*1 cup plain nonfat yogurt*
2 teaspoons baking soda	*About 3 tablespoons milk*
2 teaspoons cream of tartar	*Cinnamon Sugar (see page 540)*

Preheat the oven to 425 degrees F.

Processor method: Put all the dry ingredients in the work bowl, and process to blend well. Add the butter, in 8 pieces. Cut in the butter with on/off turns of the motor until the mixture resembles coarse meal. Spoon the mixture into a large bowl.

Alternative method: Sift the dry ingredients into a large bowl. Cut in the butter with a pastry cutter.

Stir in the yogurt. Cautiously add just enough milk to make a soft but manageable dough.

Use about 2 tablespoons of flour to handle the dough. Divide the dough in half, and pat the halves into rounds. With a bread knife, cut each round into 6 wedges. Sprinkle with cinnamon sugar.

Using a broad spatula, place the wedges on a greased jelly roll pan or baking sheet. Bake in the top third of the oven for 12 to 14 minutes, until dry inside when tested with a cake tester. Serve warm, or cool the scones on wire racks.

Although the scones taste best when eaten the same day as baked, they can be made as much as a day ahead and kept in plastic bags, refrigerated. Heat them in a warm oven. Extra scones can be frozen.

Cranberry-Wheat Scones: After the dough is mixed, gently work in ⅔ cup dried sweetened cranberries (found in the produce section of many supermarkets).

MAKES 12 SCONES

_____ 4 _____
ANTIOXIDANTS TO THE RESCUE

Revving up Our Defense Against Diseases While Slowing down the Aging Process

W hy we age and eventually die is a question that has occupied scientific inquiry throughout the ages. Theories about aging and remedies for this seemingly inevitable process have been proposed since before the pyramids were built (which, as we know, were designed to protect the immortality of pharaohs). We must be doing something right, since our life expectancy has risen from an average 45 years in 1900 to an average 75 years today. Those of us who live to be oldest may celebrate 110 years, but that seems to be our limit. So far. Fortunately, science is never satisfied with the status quo.

FREE RADICALS CITED AS THE CULPRITS IN AGING

A current theory receiving a great deal of attention is that many of the disabling or unlovely aspects of aging are caused by unstable oxygen molecules—called _free radicals_—cruising around our bodies. Highly reactive, a free radical carries an unpaired electron and seeks out another molecule with which to combine. And there's no avoiding them! These roving marauders are an inescapable by-product of the cellular process that uses the oxygen we breathe for energy—and about as welcome as rust on your car, another by-product of contact with oxygen. Free radicals are spewed out constantly by every cell in the body as a natural part of the living process.

But we wouldn't want to rid ourselves of them entirely, because free radicals are essential for many of our vital metabolic processes. Even the immune system depends on free radicals to help kill invaders. But like free-roving mercenaries, when not productively employed, they're liable to cause mayhem wherever they lodge. If they happen to bed down in DNA, for instance, they can cause damaging chain reactions—the kind that lead to cancer.

The body has mechanisms for controlling free radicals, but as we get older or are exposed to too much stress or too many external irritants (such as polluted air, cigarette smoke, radiation, and X-rays), more free radicals are able to escape the body's safeguards. Free radicals on the rampage have been blamed for everything from the unattractive sags and bags of advancing years to the degenerative diseases that crop up along the way: osteoporosis, cancer, heart disease, Parkinson's disease, and cataracts.

ANTIOXIDANTS DEFEND AGAINST THE RAVAGES OF TIME

Fortunately, current research suggests that we have some powerful nutritional defenses—called *antioxidants*, meaning "against oxidation"—to help protect us from the unwanted actions of free radicals. Sponging up or neutralizing free radicals, breaking up their chain reaction and rendering them harmless, antioxidants are associated with lowering DNA damage, preventing malignant transformation and other cell ravages, and lowering the incidence of degenerative diseases.

KEEPING MOBILE WITH ADVANCING YEARS

Mobility is an important factor to the quality of life, but, with age, rampant free radicals cause a reduction of muscle mass and the ability to exercise without undue muscle strain. Antioxidant vitamins C and E and selenium have been shown to reduce oxidative harm sufficiently to delay the onset of this "old age" slowdown.

FROM BROWN SPOTS TO SENILITY . . .

Another unwanted free-radical effect is the production of lipofuscin, a brown pigment that's been related to senility as well as to those dark patches on the hands and face sometimes known as "liver spots." Research shows that antioxidants may offer some protection from these effects of aging.

SHIELDING WOMEN AGAINST CANCER, TUMORS, AND ULCERS

A diet rich in antioxidants will feature generous amounts of fruits, vegetables, and whole grains. Endometrial cancer has been shown to be inversely associated with a diet high in fruits, yellow and green vegetables, whole-grain bread, pasta, and low-fat dairy products—that is, those who eat plenty of these good foods are less at risk.

In a Hungarian study, natural antioxidants, vitamins A, C, and E, demonstrated a protective effect in the treatment of gastroduodenal ulcer. Another study, conducted in China, found that those who took a powerful antioxidant combination were less at risk for stomach cancer.

Vitamins C and E and foods rich in those vitamins consumed by mothers while pregnant appear to protect young children from brain tumors during their early years.

GETTING ENOUGH OF THIS NUTRIENT GROUP THROUGH DIET IS VITAL

Organizations like the National Cancer Institute and the U.S. Department of Agriculture (USDA) have been advocating the whole-food route to antioxidant defense. Although it would seem a basic good-health move to eat fruit and vegetables every day, a recent population study revealed that 45 percent of the people interviewed had consumed no fruit or fruit juice on that day and 22 percent no vegetables. As for the recommended five to nine servings of fruits and vegetables a day, only 9 percent of Americans are actually following that guideline.

It takes three carefully balanced meals a day to fulfill even the basic recommendations. Sometimes it may seem easier just to pop a few vitamin pills, but supplements cannot substitute for a well-rounded diet. They are just what the name implies—a way to *supplement* when more is needed than can be derived from food. We women ought to pay close attention to our antioxidant intake (plus calcium, folate, and iron, as well). *Good food first . . .* and then, whether a diet needs additional fortification with supplements is an individual decision, which should be arrived at with the help of medical advice.

THE ANTIOXIDANT FAMILY

Because of the press interest this family of nutrients has generated, the term *antioxidants* is now basking in the public's attention. Manufacturers of multivitamin tablets are emblazoning "antioxidants" and/or "beta-carotene" on their packaging; some are coloring their pills an attractive shade of pale orange to emphasize the carotenoids subliminally. But if you turn the box over and read the fine print for content, you'll find a list of some old friends who've been around for a while but who are finally getting the research respect they deserve.

Some of those familiar names follow. If they've always been a big part of your diet, you probably look young for your age, have a good resistance to illness, and can look forward to living several years longer than those who are subsisting on processed and fast foods. But if you're just getting into the swing of the antioxidant defense, you'll find, later in this chapter, supermeal menus to inspire you further. Because enjoying a diet that offers abundant antioxidants—to protect you from disease and to keep you looking younger longer—is not only easily possible but is the delicious wave of the future.

VITAMIN C, FOR THE INNER AND OUTER YOU

Strengthening the blood vessels, forming and maintaining collagen to bind cells together, healing wounds, and helping to resist infection are some of the primary functions for which vitamin C is best known.

THE COLLAGEN CONNECTION

The term *collagen* should ring a bell for women; it's often part of the blurbs for anti-aging skin creams. Collagen is a protein fiber that keeps skin strong and flexible; when collagen fibers begin to break down, as they do after the age of 25, the skin holds less water, becomes dry, and allows gravity to have its way. Nutrient creams layered on the skin will not prevent this from happening; treating the whole body to good nutrition is the best defense against the aging of various parts, including the skin. So, besides all the great things it does for you on the inside, vitamin C is vital to an attractive skin and healthy gums. In fact, the very signs of a vitamin C deficiency are dry, rough skin, bleeding gums, and easy bruising.

THE IDEAL COMPANION NUTRIENT

As a helpful companion, vitamin C (a.k.a. ascorbic acid) boosts and enhances the power of other vitamins and minerals. It aids in the absorption of iron, and when included in the same meal, it even reverses the effects of inhibiting substances such as tea. Calcium, too, is absorbed better from foods when vitamin C accompanies the meal. Vitamin C is also interrelated with the performance of the B vitamins. A deficiency in vitamin C has been suspected to cause some anemias by impairing the metabolism of folate (a B vitamin vital to women of childbearing age). Vitamin C even assists vitamin E, another antioxidant, to work better at sparring with free radicals.

GETTING EXPOSED TO SOME RAYS? DRINK ORANGE JUICE FIRST . . .

In animal studies, vitamin C exerted a protective effect on albino rats subjected to irradiation, and it lessened the effect of ultraviolet rays on pig skin. In another study, mice given orange juice or vitamin C injections before exposure to X-rays suffered only half as much damage. We might be encouraged by this study to enjoy a large glass of orange juice before having dental X-rays or mammography or even sunbathing. An 8-ounce serving of orange juice contains more than 150 percent of the U.S. RDA for vitamin C. Since this water-soluble vitamin can't be made by the body or stored for any length of time, starting any day with citrus fruit or juice is a smart move.

VITAMIN C HELPS WOMEN AVOID HEART DISEASE

Scientists may not have figured out how vitamin C works to protect the heart, but they have noted that people who have a high intake of vitamin C also have a reduced risk of death from cardiovascular disease. Some researchers suggest that increasing vitamin C consumption has a good effect on total cholesterol. In a study by the National Center for Health Statistics, women in the highest vitamin C intake group (300 milligrams daily— the present RDA is 60 milligrams) were 25 percent less likely to die of heart disease or stroke.

GETTING ENOUGH VITAMIN C IS EASY

It's not all that difficult or fattening to eat your way to 300 milligrams of vitamin C. If in one day you consume, say, an average serving each of orange juice, broccoli, bell peppers, tomatoes, and cantaloupe, that would put you way over the top. It would also constitute the five daily servings of fruits and vegetables that the USDA has been recommending.

Vitamin C supplements are among the most popular of supplements, often consumed in megadoses. Many people swear that extra vitamin C protects them against the common cold in winter. Notably, Nobel Prize winner Linus Pauling claimed for years that vitamin C in megadoses helps prevent not only the cold but also cancer. Independent research has not confirmed Pauling's claims, but there are glimpses here and there, such as the Iowa Women's Study in which high intakes of vitamin C–rich fruits and vegetables were associated with a lower risk of lung cancer—and in other studies, vitamin C has been shown to inhibit cancer cell metabolism and proliferation. In combination with vitamin E, vitamin C was found to protect against air pollution.

Smoking uses up one's supply of vitamin C at a fearful rate, however—so a combination of quitting smoking and getting plenty of vitamin C, as well as beta-carotene and vitamin E, would be an even better lifestyle protection for the lungs. Sometimes women tend to think of lung cancer as a "man's disease," but in fact, more women die of lung cancer than of breast cancer.

This book, however, is addressing our ability to get most of the vitamins and minerals we need for optimum health through an intelligent, enjoyable diet, rather than through supplements. The good thing about getting nutrients from food rather than megadoses of this or that is that it's exceedingly difficult to overdose. (Some of the side effects of vitamin C megadoses are diarrhea and/or bladder irritation.)

Strawberries, raspberries, and cranberries—besides being rich in vitamin C—also contain a naturally occurring substance called ellagic acid, which doesn't break down when the berries are cooked. Preliminary evidence suggests that ellagic acid may have cancer-prevention properties. It's a pleasure to be able to feel nutritionally correct while enjoying some glorious dessert, such as fresh raspberry pie or poached pears with cranberries.

Perhaps the bottom line here should be that people who maintain a high intake of vitamin C simply live longer than those who do not, according to a study of the dietary habits of 10,000 people in their seventies. Statistically, women gain an extra year, men gain five years. But before you begin to think nature is being unfair to us, remember that women outlive men by seven years anyway.

Superfood Sources of Vitamin C

Asparagus
Berries
Broccoli
Cabbage and Brussels
  sprouts
Cauliflower
Citrus fruits
Kale

Kiwifruit
Mango and papaya
Melons
Peppers, including hot
  peppers
Potatoes, especially sweet
  potatoes
Tomatoes

FOR A QUICK BOOST OF VITAMIN C

A glass of orange, grapefruit, or cranberry juice
A tangerine (or two, if they're small)
A half grapefruit
A wedge of cantaloupe or honeydew
Raw broccoli and/or cauliflower with a low-fat, calcium-
  rich cheese dip
A snack of cherry tomatoes
A dish of strawberries or raspberries
A side of cole slaw with that luncheon sandwich

VITAMIN E AND SELENIUM, A DYNAMIC DUO FOR WOMEN

Like a good marriage, antioxidants vitamin E and selenium have a synergistic relationship. Selenium, an important mineral that's part of the antioxidant package inside the body, brings out the best in vitamin E. Vitamin E has the distinction of being our oldest recognized antioxidant—actually a group of fat-soluble compounds. Because they were discovered to have an important role in animal reproduction, these compounds were named *tocopherols*, from the Greek "to carry and bear offspring" (but this role has not been shown to carry over to humans).

Owing to a plethora of unconfirmed health claims made for vitamin E in the past, scientists tended to stay away from these muddy waters until rather recently. But new research has confirmed some very real benefits that vitamin E confers.

Strengthening the Immune System Against Cancer

Both substances are immune-system stimulants, working well in tandem. In animal studies, antibody production was boosted thirtyfold when a combination of vitamin E and selenium was administered.

Vitamin E has been demonstrated to serve as a chain-breaking antioxidant, meaning it protects against runaway chain reactions of free radicals that are implicated in membrane and cellular aging processes as well as many diseases such as cancer.

Research results are mixed on whether vitamin E foods or supplements lessen the risk of breast cancer. A Chinese study found a combination of vitamins E, A, and selenium inhibited breast cancer cells in lab experiments. A study of postmenopausal women in Boston found the risk of breast cancer was decreased among those who had the highest intake of vitamin E from food, but not from supplements. Vitamin E supplements of 600 milligrams have been used to treat fibrocystic breast disease with a 70 percent success rate. But the extensive Harvard Medical School's Nurses' Health Study found that those taking vitamin E and C supplements were as likely to get breast cancer as those who were not taking the supplements.

Along with beta-carotene, vitamin E may protect against mouth and throat cancer, according to a recent study. Researchers involved in this investigation believe that the combination of vitamin E and beta-carotene has a potential role in chemoprevention of these malignancies.

Although population studies have shown that there is a relationship between low selenium status and deaths from cancer of the breast, digestive tract, liver, and respiratory organs, scientists still feel there is insufficient evidence to support a recommendation for taking selenium supplements as a cancer-preventive method.

VITAMIN E DEFENDS AGAINST HEART DISEASE

Since a number of studies have confirmed that women are less at risk for heart disease if their intake of vitamin E is high, there's every reason to keep up one's intake of this antioxidant while the jury is still out on the breast cancer effect. Preliminary evidence gathered in that same nurses' study has shown that vitamin E supplements are associated with a decreased risk of heart attacks in women. In another study, vitamin E supplements of 500 milligrams elevated the helpful HDL cholesterol by 14 percent.

SUN WORSHIPPERS TAKE NOTE

Of course, we've all learned by now that too much exposure to the sun's rays in search of that perfect tan ages the skin prematurely and puts us in danger of skin cancer. (On the other hand, a moderate amount of sunlight is needed for the body to manufacture vitamin D. So often moderation, considered a bit dull, is the key to best results.) In animal studies, vitamin E has actually reversed the effects of ultraviolet light irradiation on the skin.

The topical application of vitamin E to cuts and skin abrasions to minimize scarring has found some favor with the general public, but research hasn't established these claims as valid.

LACK OF SELENIUM COULD BE IMPLICATED
IN SUDDEN INFANT DEATH SYNDROME

Produce grown locally or animals fed on grains grown where the soil is rich in selenium are the major sources of this trace mineral in the diet. New Zealand, recognizing a health problem inherent in its severely selenium-deficient soil, has done considerable research on the effects of selenium deficiency. One extensive survey has implicated the selenium-poor milk of New Zealand cows in sudden infant death syndrome (SID).

VITAMIN E'S EFFECT ON MENOPAUSAL AND PMS SYMPTOMS

Nancy Woods, in her *Complete Book of Women's Health*, comments that little attention is given to the problems of menopausal women, "especially what might have prevented symptoms." For one of the most distressing symptoms—hot flashes—Dr. Woods lists self-help approaches women can try, including vitamin E and ginseng, an Asian herb. She cites a study suggesting that estrogen replacement therapy, the most commonly prescribed remedy, seems to postpone rather than avert the problem. The hot flashes reappear when one stops taking the hormone.

There have been some very promising results in the use of vitamin E to relieve symptoms of premenstrual syndrome, but it's still early days in this research and the tests need more confirmation. Meanwhile, a diet rich in vitamin E has so many benefits—might as well keep those vitamin E levels up with good food during "hell week," too.

ABOUT SUPPLEMENTS

If you're dosing yourself with supplements, keep in mind that vitamin E is toxic in megadoses, as is selenium. One more instance of, "if a little is good, it doesn't mean that a lot is better." Consult your doctor for a recommendation on the amount that's right for you. In the wake of recent promising heart studies, some doctors are prescribing 400 international units (IUs) of vitamin E to their patients.

Recent USDA surveys find that women 19 to 50 years of age average less than 90 percent of the RDA for vitamin E (which is only 10 milligrams) while men consume nearer 100 percent. But you can increase your intake of vitamin E and selenium just by eating the right foods—and good food is a pleasure in itself!

Superfood Sources of Vitamin E

Asparagus
Fish: mackerel, salmon
Greens, dark leafy
Nuts: almonds, hazelnuts,
  peanuts
Oils, vegetable

Shellfish: shrimp, scallops,
  clams
Soybeans
Sunflower seeds
Wheat germ and whole-
  grain foods

Superfood Sources of Selenium

Brazil nuts
Fish: swordfish, tuna,
  flounder
Mushrooms
Shellfish: lobster, oysters,
  crabmeat, shrimp

Sunflower seeds
Wheat germ and whole-
  grain foods

QUICK LUNCH FOODS RICH IN VITAMIN E

Peanut butter on whole wheat toast
Salmon salad on a whole-grain bun
A cup of clam chowder
Chilled asparagus tips with an olive-oil vinaigrette
A snack of whole almonds
A couple of hazelnut cookies

FAIRLY FAST FOOD FULL OF SELENIUM

A tuna sandwich on rye
A crabmeat salad (the real thing, not imitation)
Stuffed mushrooms (even better if homemade with wheat
  germ in the stuffing!)
A couple of Brazil nuts (yes, that's plenty for one day—
  these nuts are especially rich!)
A snack of sunflower seeds

VITAMIN A AND THE CAROTENOID BONUS

Vitamin A has been a headline grabber for the past two decades, and for good reason—some of the health and beauty claims made for this nutrient border on the downright miraculous. But as population, animal, and laboratory studies affirming its wonders continue to be published, we find there's more than "an ounce of prevention" in vitamin A worth our attention—especially against cancer.

Vitamin A comes to us from nature in two forms: animal and vegetable. The former (technically, *retinol* or *retinyl esters*) found in organ meats and dairy products, is known as *preformed vitamin A*. It's immediately available for use in the body; it's also a fat-soluble nutrient that is stored in the liver, and too high a dose—such as you might get from supplements, not food—can be quite toxic. The vegetable form, called *provitamin A*, is a precursor substance that your body has to convert to a usable form. Provitamin A includes the carotenoids, found in dark green and orange plant foods, of which beta-carotene is the most widely publicized. Too much beta-carotene is not considered to be poisonous, except to heavy drinkers, but it might turn your skin yellow—a condition that reverses itself when the overdose is discontinued.

Besides beta-carotene, some lesser known carotenoids working against cancer are: alpha-carotene, notable in carrots; beta-cryptoxanthin, big in oranges and tangerines; lycopene, associated with a red color, such as in tomatoes and strawberries; plus lutein and zeaxanthin, found in those dark leafy greens.

VITAMIN A WARDS OFF INFECTION

Vitamin A does a multitude of great things for the body. For one, it wards off infection on a day-to-day basis. Giving vitamin A to lab animals boosted their immunity by increasing antibody activity and speeding up the production of various disease-fighting cells. It's something to keep in mind when the cold and flu season is at hand.

A VITAMIN FOR THE EYES, SKIN, HAIR, NAILS

Definitely the eye vitamin, vitamin A helps to avert night blindness, corneal lesions, and cataracts.

It's a beauty vitamin, too. Carotenoid-rich foods are needed to keep skin, hair, and nails looking their best. Topically, vitamin A derivatives have been used in several forms to cure acne and psoriasis; and (this was the big beauty news!) Retin A, sometimes called the "miracle skin restorer," has lessened fine wrinkles and sun-damaged skin in older women. (These topical treatments must be prescribed by a physician.) Vitamin A is also needed to maintain bones, teeth, gums, and glands.

PREVENTING CANCER AND BIRTH DEFECTS

Lately, the role of beta-carotene, precursor to vitamin A, in forestalling cancer has taken the limelight. Research results on the beta-carotene–cancer link are so promising that the USDA and the National Cancer Institute, among others, are urging the

American public to consume some beta-carotene every day in order to lessen the risk of developing cancer. Beta-carotene has been especially linked with the prevention of lung, mouth, and throat cancers, but it plays a role in protecting against other cancers, also.

The Nurses' Health Study, evaluating the diets of thousands of women over eight years, found a slightly reduced risk of breast cancer in those who consistently ate foods rich in carotenoids. Modest servings of fruits and vegetables containing beta-carotenes—such as one carrot or a third of a cantaloupe or a half-cup of broccoli—seemed to reduce the rate of developing breast cancer by 20 percent. You might think that most women already ate those amounts, but in this survey, one-fifth of the women didn't. Women who ate great quantities of these same foods did not reduce their risk of breast cancer any further.

Studying the food choices of over a thousand elderly Massachusetts residents, researchers discovered a significantly lowered risk mortality from all cancers among those who ate the most green and yellow vegetables.

Tretinoin, a derivative of vitamin A, has been used to treat a form of leukemia with some success, apparently restoring a regulatory mechanism to runaway cancerous cells.

Preliminary studies suggest that women whose diets include beta-carotene and other carotenoids are less at risk of bearing children with birth defects.

THE BEST WAY TO GET ENOUGH VITAMIN A

Although large amounts of preformed vitamin A are found in dairy foods and organ meats, current nutritional research recommends fruit and vegetable sources because they offer a number of other anticancer compounds and beneficial fiber without raising cholesterol.

The new U.S. Department of Agriculture guidelines call for at least two servings of fruit and three of vegetables every day. A medium-size raw fruit, a 6-ounce glass of juice, or ½ cup vegetable each constitute one serving. Easy enough? With good planning, yes, which we'll get to later in this chapter.

Superfood Sources of Carotenoids

Apricots
Broccoli
Cabbage, red
Cantaloupe
Carrots
Cherries
Greens: beet, chicory, cress,
    parsley, spinach, turnip

Mango
Papaya
Peaches and nectarines
Pepper, red bell
Potatoes, sweet
Pumpkin
Squashes, winter
Tomatoes

Superfood Sources of Preformed Vitamin A

Dairy products: skim milk,
    part-skim ricotta cheese,
    nonfat yogurt

A CAROTENOID QUICK-FIX IS A CINCH!

A handful of dried apricots
Fresh cherries
A wedge of cantaloupe
Carrot sticks or raw broccoli (with a low-fat cheese dip for
    extra vitamin A, plus calcium)
A baked sweet potato (about 7 to 9 minutes in a micro-
    wave)
From the salad bar: Ignore that iceberg stuff! Choose spin-
    ach, cress, chicory, tomatoes, carrots, or red cabbage
    slaw.
Munch up that parsley garnish!

ZINC ROUNDS OUT THE ANTIOXIDANT PACKAGE

When a potent antioxidant package including zinc as well as vitamins A, C, E, and selenium was administered in a recent study to over a thousand older people with age-related diseases such as diabetes, arthritis, vascular disease, and hypertension, the combination proved to have promising results in improving the conditions of most patients, encouraging researchers to continue with more controlled clinical trials. Although this is only preliminary evidence, it's an indication that those who want to continue enjoying an active, disease-free life—and that's everyone—ought to enrich their diets with the antioxidant helpers, including zinc.

ZINC FORTIFIES THE IMMUNE SYSTEM

Established as a protector of the immune system, zinc is an important disease fighter. Effects of aging that result from immune impairment can be partly repaired by zinc. Studies show that even children whose immune systems have been challenged by protein-calorie malnutrition can be helped simply by being given zinc supplements.

Known to accelerate wound healing, zinc supplements are often given to patients after surgery.

WANT TO GET PREGNANT? FEED ZINC TO YOUR PARTNER!

A woman who is trying to get pregnant would do well to feed zinc-rich foods to her partner. Some cases of infertility in men have been traced to a zinc deficiency. A new USDA study has found a man's semen volume decreased by as much as 30 percent when he's restricted to a zinc-deficient diet.

ZINC NEEDED FOR GOOD DELIVERIES AND HEALTHY BABIES

Studies have tied low zinc levels in women to abnormal deliveries, nervous-system malfunctions, and low-birth-weight babies. On the other hand, taking self-prescribed zinc supplements poses serious dangers for a woman of childbearing years. Stillbirths and birth defects have been traced to taking megadoses of zinc in the third trimester of pregnancy. Unless supplements are prescribed by a physician, a safer route is to fulfill your RDA for zinc with zinc-rich foods.

USDA surveys find that men 19 to 50 years old average about 95 percent of their RDA for zinc. Many women, however, are getting less than 70 percent of their RDA.

ZINC DEFICIENCY MAY FIGURE IN DEPRESSION

There may be some link between depression and zinc levels, as indicated by a recent study comparing these levels in depressed and control patients. Values were significantly higher in patients who recovered than in those who remained depressed.

BON APPÉTIT . . . WITH ZINC

Zinc may be the gourmet's mineral. It's present in many enzymes that are essential to digestion and metabolism. The alteration of taste and smell can be an early sign of zinc deficiency, and zinc is essential to the growth and differentiation of taste buds, an important note for those of us who enjoy the subtleties of cooking . . . and eating.

Superfood Sources of Zinc

Diary products: skim milk,
  part-skim ricotta cheese,
  nonfat yogurt
Nuts: pecans, pine nuts,
  Brazil nuts, peanuts
Seeds: pumpkin, squash,
  sunflower

Shellfish, especially oysters
Turkey, dark meat
Wheat germ and whole-
  grain foods

Note: While cocoa isn't exactly a "health food," it's reassuring to know it does offer the chocolate lover a good supply of zinc. Cocoa is a better choice than chocolate, by the way, because it contains much less fat.

A NO-FUSS HELPING OF ZINC

Sliced turkey (dark meat) on whole wheat bread
A plate of oysters on the half-shell
A scoop of ricotta cheese drizzled with honey and sprinkled
  with toasted pine nuts
A cup of cocoa made with skim milk
A handful of trail mix with nuts and seeds
A cup of fruit-flavored yogurt

SUPERMEALS TO KEEP YOUR ANTIOXIDANT LEVEL HIGH

Recipes indicated by a ◆ follow the menus.

VEGETARIAN PLEASURES FOR FOUR

Pasta Autunno◆
Spinach-Stuffed Mushrooms◆
Whole-Grain Focaccia (Italian Flat Bread)
Marbled Pumpkin Bars◆

*T*omatoes, green peppers, carrots, and broccoli in the pasta sauce yield a double-bonus of vitamin C and beta-carotene. There's more beta-carotene in the spinach, and, of course, in those pumpkin bars, with walnuts adding zinc. Wheat germ in the mushroom stuffing and olive oil in the pasta are good sources of vitamin E, and there's selenium in the mushrooms.

ANTIOXIDANTS AND THEIR HELPERS AT A GLANCE

NUTRIENT vitamin A

RDA for Females
800 retinol
pregnant: same
Benefits
Helps to keep skin, hair, nails, and eyes healthy
Defends against infections
Carotenoids may protect against lung cancer and related cancers
Sources
Orange and red-fleshed fruits and vegetables, dark green vegetables
Warnings
Provitamin A (carotenoids) is not toxic but too much can turn skin yellow
Megadoses of vitamin A supplements (retinol) can be toxic, can cause birth
  defects

NUTRIENT vitamin C

RDA for Females
60 mg
pregnant: +10 mg
Benefits
Builds collagen to bind cells together
Promotes strong blood vessels
Helps to heal wounds
Maintains healthy gums
Enhances other nutrient, especially calcium
Reduces risk of heart disease
Part of an overall cancer-prevention diet
Sources
Berries, broccoli, cabbage, citrus fruits, kale, kiwi, mango, papaya, peppers,
  tomatoes
Warnings
Megadoses can cause diarrhea, urinary tract irritation, and kidney stones

NUTRIENT vitamin E

RDA for Females
8 mg
pregnant: +2 mg

BENEFITS
Needed for healthy red blood cells and muscles
Protects against heart disease
Stimulates immune system
May help prevent mouth and throat cancer
Protects against sun damage
May relieve some menopausal symptoms
SOURCES
Asparagus, fish, dark greens, nuts, soybeans, vegetable oils, wheat germ,
   whole grains
WARNINGS
Megadoses can be toxic

NUTRIENT selenium

RDA FOR FEMALES
55 mcg
pregnant: +10 mcg
BENEFITS
Works with vitamin E to prevent cell damage and stimulate the immune
   system
SOURCES
Brazil nuts, fish, mushrooms, wheat germ, whole grains
WARNINGS
Megadoses can be toxic

NUTRIENT zinc

RDA FOR FEMALES
12 mg
pregnant: +3 mg
BENEFITS
Part of an antioxidant enzyme
Essential to taste, digestion, and metabolism
Needed for health of reproductive system
SOURCES
Dairy products, nuts and seeds, oysters and shellfish, turkey (dark meat),
   wheat germ, whole grains
WARNINGS
Megadoses can cause intestinal disturbances, premature labor, and still-
   births

Pasta Autunno

SUPERFOODS: tomatoes, olive oil, onion, green pepper, garlic, carrots, broccoli, parsley, pasta

1½ *pounds ripe tomatoes*
¼ *cup olive oil*
1 *medium onion, chopped*
1 *green bell pepper, seeded and*
  chunked
2 *garlic cloves, minced*
½ *teaspoon salt*
Several pinches of hot red pepper
  flakes, plus more to pass
1 *large carrot, scraped and sliced*

¼ *pound broccoli florets*
¼ *pound green beans, sliced into*
  2-inch pieces
¾ *pound penne or ziti*
¼ *cup coarsely chopped flat-leaf*
  parsley
1 *cup diced Bel Paese cheese**
2 *tablespoons grated Romano*
  cheese, plus more to pass

Pour boiling water over the tomatoes and let them stand until the skins loosen. Slip off skins; chop the tomatoes.

Heat the oil in a large skillet. Sauté the onion, green pepper, and garlic until they have softened but not browned. Add the tomatoes, salt, red pepper flakes, and carrot. Cook over medium-high heat until the tomatoes are reduced to a sauce consistency, 10 to 15 minutes.

Add the broccoli and green beans. Cover and simmer until the vegetables are just tender, 5 to 8 minutes.

Meanwhile, cook the penne according to package directions. Toss the penne and parsley with the vegetable sauce. Stir in the Bel Paese and Romano cheeses.

Pass additional red pepper flakes and Romano cheese at the table.

MAKES 4 SERVINGS

*Ricotta salata (not the soft variety) or feta can be substituted.

Spinach-Stuffed Mushrooms

SUPERFOODS: spinach, garlic, mushrooms, wheat germ

10 ounces fresh spinach	1 tablespoon toasted wheat germ
2 garlic cloves, crushed	2 tablespoons grated Parmesan
12 "stuffing" mushrooms	cheese
(about 14 ounces)	⅛ teaspoon salt
3 tablespoons plain dry bread	Freshly ground black pepper
crumbs	Olive oil

Wash the spinach in several changes of water and remove any tough stems. Put the garlic in a large pot; add the spinach, and steam it in just the water that clings to the leaves, until wilted, about 5 minutes. Reserve the garlic.

Drain the spinach, and press out as much moisture as possible. You should have about ¾ cup. Mash the garlic into the spinach, distributing it evenly throughout. (Fingers work best.)

The recipe can be prepared to this point several hours or 1 day ahead. Keep refrigerated.

Preheat the oven to 375 degrees F.

Wash the mushrooms and remove the stems. (Save the stems for another use, such as soup or omelet.) Place the caps in an oiled baking dish that will fit them in 1 layer.

Mix the spinach and garlic with the bread crumbs, wheat germ, cheese, salt, and black pepper to your taste. Stuff the mushrooms with the mixture, about 1 heaping tablespoon each, mounding the filling up. Drizzle a little olive oil on each.

Bake on the top shelf of the oven for 25 minutes. Serve warm or at room temperature.

MAKES 4 SERVINGS

Marbled Pumpkin Bars

SUPERFOODS: pumpkin, molasses, walnuts

½ cup light cream cheese, softened

2 tablespoons granulated sugar

2 eggs, beaten, or ½ cup prepared egg substitute

¾ cup solid-pack unflavored canned pumpkin

¾ cup packed brown sugar

2 tablespoons molasses

½ teaspoon each ground ginger and ground cinnamon

¼ teaspoon each ground cloves, ground allspice, and salt

⅓ cup vegetable oil

1 cup unbleached all-purpose flour

1 teaspoon baking powder

½ cup coarsely chopped walnuts

Grease a 9 × 12-inch baking pan. Preheat the oven to 350 degrees F.

In a food processor or by hand, blend the cream cheese, granulated sugar, and 2 tablespoons of the egg. Remove and reserve this mixture. (No need to wash the work bowl.)

In the same bowl, blend in the pumpkin, brown sugar, molasses, spices, and salt. Blend in the remaining egg and the oil.

If using a processor, add the flour and baking powder to the bowl. Process with on/off turns of the motor until just blended. If mixing by hand, stir until smooth.

By hand, fold the walnuts into the batter, and spoon it into the prepared pan.

Spoon the cream cheese over the top. Use a paring knife in a back-and-forth motion through the batter to make a marbleized effect. Don't overmix or you'll lose the distinctly different colors.

Bake on the middle shelf of oven for 35 minutes or until a cake tester inserted in the center comes out clean.

Cool in the pan on a rack. They may fall a little, as brownies do. Cut into 12 squares.

MAKES 12 BARS

AN EASY AND HEARTY DINNER FOR SIX

Grilled Veal Chops with Orange-Tomato Sauce♦
"Shuffled" Chard and Potatoes♦
Carrot Salad with Ginger Vinaigrette♦
Raspberry Crumble♦
or
Fresh Raspberries

Especially easy if you delegate some of the vegetable preparation! Top vitamin C sources in this menu are the tomatoes, oranges, potatoes, and raspberries. Carrots are fairly bursting with beta-carotene, and chard adds even more. Yogurt is a zinc food. Grapeseed oil in the salad and almonds in the dessert are quite high in vitamin E.

Grilled Veal Chops with Orange-Tomato Sauce

SUPERFOODS: tomatoes, yogurt, oranges

1 cup orange juice	*3 sprigs flat-leaf parsley,*
½ cup dry vermouth, dry white	*stemmed*
wine, or chicken broth	*1 scant teaspoon grated orange*
¾ cup peeled, seeded, and	*rind*
chopped fresh tomatoes	*6 large veal loin chops*
1½ tablespoons cornstarch	*3 seedless oranges, peeled and*
¾ cup plain nonfat yogurt	*sliced*
6 basil leaves	*Basil sprigs for garnish*

In a small saucepan, combine the orange juice and wine or broth. Boil until reduced to 1 cup. Add the tomatoes and simmer for 3 minutes; remove from the heat.

Blend the cornstarch into the yogurt. Whisk the yogurt into the hot orange-tomato sauce; stir constantly over medium heat until the mixture is thick and bubbling. Simmer 1 to 2 minutes longer.

Snip the herbs; stir the herbs and grated rind into the sauce and remove it from the heat.

The sauce can be made several hours or 1 day ahead, kept chilled, and reheated when needed. It can also be frozen, thawed, and reheated as a quick sauce for almost any broiled meat.

Grill or broil the chops in a heated broiler until medium-rare, about 5 minutes per side.

To serve, divide the sauce among 6 warm plates and top each with a chop. Garnish with orange slices and basil sprigs.

MAKES 6 SERVINGS

"Shuffled" Chard and Potatoes

SUPERFOODS: potatoes, chard, garlic

This is an Italian-style "home-fries with greens." Other greens, such as broccoli rabe or spinach, can be easily substituted.

2 pounds boiling potatoes, such as red potatoes
1 pound Swiss chard
2 tablespoons olive oil
1 large garlic clove, minced

Salt and freshly ground black pepper
2 or more tablespoons balsamic vinegar

Peel the potatoes and cut them into ¼-inch-thick half-rounds. Boil them in salted water until tender, about 8 minutes. Drain well.

Wash the chard. Remove any large stems and dice them. Put the leaves and chopped stems into a large pot, and steam in just the water that clings to the leaves until the vegetable is tender, about 3 minutes. Add more water if necessary. Drain well, pressing out moisture with the back of a spoon.

Heat the olive oil in a large skillet, add the potatoes, and fry them until they begin to brown. Add the garlic; cook 1 minute. Add the greens, and "shuffle" them together until piping hot and fragrant.

Season with salt and pepper to your taste, and sprinkle with balsamic vinegar.

MAKES 6 SERVINGS

Carrot Salad with Ginger Vinaigrette

SUPERFOODS: carrots, grapeseed oil, garlic, ginger

Grapeseed and walnut oils are great sources of vitamin E—as well as adding their distinctive flavors to salad dressings.

4 medium carrots   1 large cucumber

For the vinaigrette

⅓ cup grapeseed or olive oil   ⅛ teaspoon each white pepper,
¼ cup rice vinegar*   salt, and sugar
1 tablespoon finely grated fresh
   ginger

Scrape and coarsely grate the carrots. (This can be done quickly in a food processor.) Peel and scrape the seeds out of the cucumber; cut it into julienne strips. Combine the vegetables in a shallow salad dish.

Combine the vinaigrette ingredients in a jar and shake well. Dress the salad with the vinaigrette, and let the mixture stand at room temperature while you prepare the rest of the menu.

MAKES 6 SERVINGS

*If you use seasoned rice vinegar, omit salt and sugar.

Raspberry Crumble

SUPERFOODS: raspberries, almonds

This "humble crumble" homestyle dessert has the same flavor combination as a sophisticated Linzer torte—but can be tossed together in just a few minutes! You will need a food processor, however, to prepare the topping.

4 cups unsweetened frozen whole
   raspberries, partly thawed
½ cup sugar

3 tablespoons quick-cooking
   tapioca

For the topping

½ cup blanched whole almonds
¼ cup all-purpose flour
3 tablespoons sugar

2 tablespoons unsalted butter
¼ teaspoon almond extract*

Preheat the oven to 375 degrees F.

Combine the raspberries, sugar, and tapioca in a 12-inch glass pie plate or 10-inch glass cake pan, and stir to blend.

In a food processor, grind the almonds fine, then blend in the flour, sugar, and butter. Last, add the almond flavoring. The topping should have the texture of rough meal.

Sprinkle the topping evenly over the raspberries, and bake for 30 to 35 minutes, until bubbly throughout. If the topping gets brown too fast, cover the crumble with a sheet of foil, not tucked in. Serve warm or at room temperature.

MAKES 6 SERVINGS

*Real, not artificial flavoring. Usually found in kitchen equipment stores or whole-foods markets.

A COMFORTING SOUP SUPPER FOR FOUR

Butternut and Lentil Soup with Chilies♦
Tuna and Mixed Greens Salad♦
Whole Wheat Rolls, homemade♦ or bakery
Melon Balls (frozen, thawed) and Ginger Snaps

Whole wheat gives you plenty of vitamin E, selenium, and zinc (and many other benefits), and tuna is one of the greatest sources of selenium. The chili-spiced soup is rich in flavor—and in beta-carotene, thanks to the butternut squash! Dark leafy greens add more, plus vitamin E. Refreshing, low-calorie melon is nonetheless plump with vitamin C and beta-carotene.

Butternut and Lentil Soup with Chilies

SUPERFOODS: onion, garlic, lentils, tomato sauce, butternut squash, chilies

You'll probably have a bonus of leftover soup, which can be served on another day or frozen for later use. Suggestions for reheating are included in the recipe.

2 tablespoons olive oil
1 large onion, chopped
1 celery stalk with the leaves, chopped
1 garlic clove, minced
6 cups chicken broth*
1 cup lentils, picked over and rinsed

1 cup tomato sauce (an 8-ounce can)
4 cups peeled and diced butternut squash
One 4-ounce can chopped mild chilies, drained
1 teaspoon each dried cilantro and ground cumin

In a large pot, heat the oil and sauté the onion, celery, and garlic until they have softened, about 5 minutes. Add all the remaining ingredients.

Simmer the soup for about 1 hour, until the lentils are quite tender but the squash still retains its shape, stirring occasionally, more often toward the end of the cooking time. Taste to correct seasoning; you may want some salt, depending on the broth you used.

The soup can be made 1 day ahead. Keep refrigerated. Reheat carefully, because thick soups tend to stick. A microwave takes the worry out of this procedure.

MAKES 2½ QUARTS

*In a pinch, you can substitute 6 cups water and 4 bouillon cubes.

Tuna and Mixed Greens Salad

SUPERFOODS: tuna, dark leafy salad greens, onion

I don't use any oil in this salad, because the oil that clings to the drained tuna seems enough.

One 6-ounce can imported
   Italian tuna (tonno) packed
   in oil*
3 tablespoons red wine vinegar
4 cups bite-size dark greens:
   choose at least 2 from
   romaine lettuce, escarole,
   tender spinach, chicory

About ½ cup Sweetened Red
   Onion Rings (see page 524)
Freshly ground black pepper

Drain the tuna. Put it into a salad bowl and flake it slightly. Sprinkle it with the wine vinegar. Put the greens and drained red onion rings on top.

The salad can be made several hours ahead. Don't toss it until ready to serve. Keep refrigerated.

When ready to serve, grind some pepper on top, to your taste, and toss the salad well.

MAKES 4 SERVINGS

*No substitutes.

Whole Wheat Rolls

SUPERFOODS: whole wheat flour

One of the easiest of yeast bread recipes!

1 envelope active dry yeast	*1 scant teaspoon salt*
2 teaspoons sugar	*2 tablespoons olive oil*
1 cup very warm water	*1 egg, beaten, or ½ cup prepared*
1½ cups whole wheat flour	*egg substitute*
1½ cups unbleached all-purpose	
flour	

Add the yeast and sugar to the water, and allow it to stand for 5 minutes. The yeast should bubble up.

Combine the flours, salt, and olive oil in the work bowl of an electric mixer fitted with a dough hook. (Don't substitute a food processor; this dough gets so elastic, it may stop the blades from turning and overheat the motor.) Stir in the yeast mixture. Knead the dough with the dough hook for 5 minutes or until it forms a smooth, elastic ball that springs back when pressed. (Alternatively, combine the ingredients in large bowl. Knead by hand on a floured board for about 10 minutes.)

Put the dough in an oiled bowl, cover with plastic wrap, and let it rise in a warm place until doubled, about 1½ hours.

Oil a 9 × 13-inch baking pan and sprinkle it with cornmeal. Knead the dough briefly, and form it into a rope. Cut the rope into 12 pieces, and form the pieces into plain round rolls. Put them into the pan in 4 rows of 3 rolls each. Let them rise, covered with a towel, until doubled, about 1 hour.

Preheat the oven to 375 degrees F.

Brush the rolls with the egg wash, and bake them for 25 to 30 minutes, until they are brown and sound hollow when tapped.

Garlic Rolls: Add 1 to 2 finely minced garlic cloves to the dough. Blend well.

Cheese Rolls: Add 1 cup loosely packed, coarsely grated Parmesan cheese to the dough. If you substitute the powdery store-grated cheese, use less: ⅔ to ½ cup.

Fennel and Black Pepper Rolls: Add 1 teaspoon *each* coarsely grated black pepper and fennel seeds to the dough.

MAKES 12 ROLLS

A SPICY CHICKEN DINNER FOR FOUR

African Chicken Stew♦
Brown Basmati Rice (see page 524)
Salad of Bitter Greens (Chicory, Dandelion, Radicchio)
with Herb Vinaigrette (see page 530)
Golden Cornmeal-Carrot Cake♦
or
Sliced Fresh Papaya

*P*eanuts, a favorite African flavoring, are a great source of zinc. Besides peanut butter, the other stew ingredients—tomatoes and peppers—contribute their share of vitamin C, while dark leafy greens in the salad yield beta-carotene. And so do carrots in the golden cake (or papaya). Rice bran, found in brown rice, scores high in vitamin E.

African Chicken Stew

SUPERFOODS: green pepper, onions, garlic, tomatoes, peanut butter, brown rice

Although nutritious, peanut butter is high in fat. The rest of this menu is low in fat, but if you're watching those grams closely, you can reduce the amount of peanut butter in half.

8 skinless chicken thighs	*½ teaspoon salt*
3 tablespoons vegetable oil	*¼ teaspoon black pepper*
1 cup chopped green bell pepper	*1 dried hot chili pepper*
½ cup chopped onion	*½ cup creamy peanut butter*
1 teaspoon minced garlic	*Hot red pepper flakes*
One 14-ounce can tomatoes with juice	

In a 12-inch skillet (or in 2 batches), brown the chicken pieces in the oil and remove them. Add the green pepper, onion, and garlic; sauté until softened but not brown, about 5 minutes.

Add the tomatoes, salt, black pepper, and chili. Simmer the sauce uncovered for 10 minutes, stirring occasionally and breaking up the tomatoes.

Add the chicken, cover, and cook over low heat for 20 to 30 minutes, until the chicken is cooked through. Remove chicken and whisk in peanut butter until smooth.

The stew can be made up to a day ahead. Keep refrigerated. Reheat over very low flame, stirring often.

Add hot red pepper flakes to your taste, and simmer 3 minutes.

MAKES 4 SERVINGS

Golden Cornmeal-Carrot Cake

SUPERFOODS: cornmeal, carrots, yogurt

Quite unlike the usual moist, dark version, this carrot cake is light and lemony, with an interesting crunch of barely cooked carrots.

1¼ cups sifted unbleached all-
  purpose flour
½ cup stone-ground yellow
  cornmeal
2 teaspoons baking powder
½ teaspoon grated nutmeg
¼ teaspoon salt
4 eggs
Pinch of cream of tartar

1 cup granulated sugar
½ cup vegetable oil
¼ cup plain nonfat yogurt
¼ cup lemon juice
1 tablespoon loosely packed,
  grated lemon rind (1 lemon)
1½ cups coarsely grated carrots
  (about 2 medium)
Confectioners' sugar

Preheat the oven to 350 degrees F. Butter and flour a 12-inch springform pan.

Sift together the dry ingredients. Separate the eggs.

With an electric mixer, beat the egg whites to a froth, add the cream of tartar, and continue beating until soft peaks form. Remove and reserve the egg whites.

Beat the egg yolks until light, gradually adding the sugar. Beat in the oil, yogurt, lemon juice, and rind.

Remove the egg yolks from the electric mixer, and stir in the dry ingredients. Fold in about one-fourth of the beaten egg whites to lighten the batter, then fold in the rest. Fold in the carrots.

Spoon the batter into the prepared pan, and bake the cake on the middle shelf for 30 to 35 minutes, until a cake tester inserted in the center comes out dry. If the cake begins to get too brown, lay a piece of foil across the top during the last few minutes of cooking.

Cool 5 minutes in the pan on a wire rack before removing the pan's rim. When the cake is cold, sprinkle it liberally with confectioners' sugar through a sifter.

MAKES **12** SERVINGS

A CLASSIC SUMMERTIME MENU FOR FOUR

Fresh Salmon Cakes with Mango♦
Peas and Summer Squash with Mint♦
Steamed New Potatoes with Garlic♦
Sliced Strawberries
with Strawberry Nonfat Frozen Yogurt

Salmon is a simply super fish—rich in vitamin E (plus B vitamins and vitamin D)! It's easy to recognize the beta-carotene in mangos, but did you know that peas are another fine source? Vitamin C for this menu is found in the peas, potatoes, mango, and especially the strawberries!

Fresh Salmon Cakes with Mango

SUPERFOODS: salmon, mango

This recipe calls for poaching salmon, but leftover cooked salmon or canned salmon could be substituted.

2 fresh salmon fillets (6 to 8 ounces each)
Sprigs of fresh dill
2 tablespoons to ½ cup dry white wine or clam broth
2 cups fresh bread crumbs*
2 tablespoons chopped fresh chives

2 teaspoons chopped fresh dill
1 egg, beaten, or ¼ cup prepared egg substitute
Salt and pepper
2 tablespoons cornmeal
About 2 tablespoons olive oil
1 ripe mango, peeled and sliced

Poach the salmon fillets. *Microwave method:* Place them in a glass dish, lay sprigs of dill over them, and add 2 tablespoons of wine. Cover and microwave on medium for about 5 minutes or just until the fish flakes apart easily. *Range-top method:* Poach them on the range top in a covered skillet, increasing the wine to ½ cup, at a low simmer for 8 to 10 minutes. Remove from the heat as soon as the fish flakes apart.

Cool slightly. Discard skin and bones; chop the fish coarsely. You should have about 2 cups.

(If substituting cooked or canned salmon, begin here.)

Mix the salmon, crumbs, chives, dill, egg, salt, and pepper. Form the mixture into 8 balls, ¼ cup each. Lay the balls on a plate, and flatten them into cakes. Sprinkle them with half the cornmeal; turn and sprinkle the rest on the other side. Cover and chill.

The recipe can be prepared to this point several hours in advance. Keep refrigerated.

*Don't substitute dry crumbs.

Coat a large skillet with 1 tablespoon of the oil, and fry the cakes until they are brown on both sides, adding more oil if necessary. Remove the cakes and keep them warm. Lay the mango slices in the pan just long enough to warm them slightly.

Divide the cakes and mango slices among 4 plates.

MAKES 4 SERVINGS

Peas and Summer Squash with Mint

SUPERFOODS: peas

Fresh mint grows so lustily that the smallest garden or windowbox or windowsill could be home to a useful mint plant. In fact, if you buy a bunch of mint in the supermarket and keep a few sprigs of it in a vase of water, you may find it sprouting roots and ready for planting in a few days' time.

1 small summer squash, diced	*⅛ teaspoon white pepper*
¼ cup water	*½ tablespoon finely minced fresh*
1½ tablespoons butter	*mint, or ½ teaspoon dried*
One 10-ounce package tiny	
frozen peas*	

Combine the squash, water, and butter in a saucepan, and bring it to a simmer. Cover and cook 5 minutes or until tender.

Stir in the remaining ingredients, and bring to a boil. Cover and remove from heat; let stand 5 minutes to finish cooking the peas. (If using fresh peas, cook them with the squash and omit standing time.)

MAKES 4 SERVINGS

*By all means, substitute fresh peas (1½ pounds before shelling) if you can find good ones.

Steamed New Potatoes with Garlic

SUPERFOODS: potatoes, garlic

If your family is squeamish about garlic, the flavor of steamed garlic is surprisingly mild.

1¼ pounds small new potatoes*	4 garlic cloves
1 tablespoon white vinegar	Freshly ground black pepper
1 teaspoon salt	

Scrub the potatoes well; cut off any imperfections, but otherwise leave them unpeeled.

Put the potatoes into a steamer over 2 inches of water to which you've added the vinegar and salt. Cut the root end off the unpeeled garlic cloves, and add them to the steamer. Steam until the potatoes are tender, about 15 minutes. Season with freshly ground black pepper.

Serve the steamed garlic as a condiment. Slit the skins and spread the soft flesh on the potatoes.

MAKES 4 SERVINGS

---

*Organic potatoes are preferable, since they will be served in their jackets. New potatoes can be large or small; the important thing is that they have thin skins and a firm waxy texture. If all you can find are the large variety, cut them into the desired size.

A CHOWDER SUPPER ON THE PORCH
FOR FOUR TO SIX

Corn, Tomato, and Oyster Chowder♦
Whole-Grain French Bread
Asparagus Vinaigrette♦
Peach-Almond Skillet Cake♦
or
Fresh Peaches

A combination of zinc, selenium, chromium, copper, and riboflavin makes oysters an especially potent seafood. Tomatoes and green peppers in the chowder yield vitamin C, and peaches are yet another delectable beta-carotene food. Asparagus, whole wheat, flour, and almonds are rich in vitamin E. And as a bonus, there's lots of B vitamins and fiber in the corn.

Corn, Tomato, and Oyster Chowder

Superfoods: onion, green pepper, tomatoes, potatoes, corn, oysters

This chowder couldn't be easier; the preparation is a cinch, and it cooks in about 30 minutes.

2 tablespoons olive oil

1 small onion, chopped

1 green bell pepper, seeded and diced

2 cups peeled and chopped fresh tomatoes*

2 cups water

1 teaspoon ground coriander

½ teaspoon salt

2 large potatoes, peeled and diced

¼ teaspoon black pepper

2 cups fresh corn kernels cut from the cob**

8 ounces shucked oysters and their liquor

2 teaspoons cornstarch

½ cup cold water

6 leaves fresh basil, shredded

Heat the olive oil in a 4-quart pot, and sauté the onion and green pepper until sizzling, about 2 minutes. Add the tomatoes, water, coriander, and salt. Bring to a simmer, and cook with cover ajar for 10 minutes.

Add the potatoes; simmer until tender, about 10 minutes.

Add the black pepper and corn; simmer 5 minutes.

The recipe can be made to this point 1 day ahead. Keep refrigerated.

Add the oysters and their liquor; simmer until the edges of the oysters curl, about 2 minutes.

Stir the cornstarch into the cold water until there are no lumps. Pour the mixture into the soup, and cook, stirring constantly, until the soup bubbles and thickens. Simmer 3 minutes more.

Stir in the basil. Taste to correct seasoning. You may want more salt.

Corn and Tomato Chowder: Simply omit the oysters for a vegetarian soup with a really rich flavor.

MAKES ABOUT 2 QUARTS

---

*Canned tomatoes can be substituted.

**Much depends on the flavor of fresh corn to give this soup its "creamy" sweetness. Cut the kernels from leftover cooked ears or raw ears.

Asparagus Vinaigrette

SUPERFOODS: asparagus, red pepper, onion, olive oil

Besides being a harbinger of spring, asparagus is a powerhouse of vitamins C, E, folate, chromium, and potassium.

1½ *pounds asparagus*
1 *roasted red bell pepper, from a jar or homemade (see page 523)*
1 *tablespoon drained capers*
½ *cup Sweetened Red Onion Rings (see page 524)*

¼ *cup olive oil*
2 *tablespoons white wine vinegar*
1 *teaspoon Dijon mustard*
Freshly ground black pepper

Wash the asparagus, and cut off the tough stem ends. Lay the asparagus in a large skillet with ½ inch water in the bottom. Bring the water to a boil, and steam the asparagus, covered, until tender-crisp, 3 to 5 minutes. Drain and rinse the asparagus in cold water. Cool.

Arrange the asparagus on a platter. Dice the red pepper. Sprinkle the red pepper and capers on the asparagus. Lay the drained red onions over all.

Put the oil, vinegar, mustard, and pepper in a jar, and shake well until blended. Pour the dressing evenly over the asparagus. Chill until ready to serve.

The salad can be made several hours ahead. Keep refrigerated.

MAKES 4 TO 6 SERVINGS

Peach-Almond Skillet Cake

SUPERFOODS: peaches, almonds

The skillet needed for "skillet cakes" is a well-seasoned, 10-inch cast-iron frying pan. If you don't have such a pan, you can substitute a heavy cake pan of the same size and depth.

My favorite cast-iron skillet is over 40 years old; I'd say such a pan is a worthwhile investment.

2 tablespoons butter or margarine	*1½ teaspoons baking powder*
½ cup firmly packed brown sugar	*¼ teaspoon salt*
¼ cup silvered almonds	*3 eggs or ¾ cup prepared egg substitute*
1½ cups sliced peaches, fresh peeled or canned, drained	*½ cup granulated sugar*
1 cup unbleached all-purpose flour	*1½ tablespoons juice from peaches or orange juice*
	¼ teaspoon natural almond flavoring

Preheat the oven to 350 degrees F.

Melt the butter in a 10-inch cast-iron skillet. Remove it from the heat, add the brown sugar, and smooth it into an even layer. Scatter the almonds over the melted brown sugar, and arrange the peach slices in a pinwheel design on top of the almonds.

Sift the flour with the baking powder and salt.

Beat the eggs until thick and fluffy. Gradually add the granulated sugar, beating until light and spongy. Blend in the flour, peach juice, and almond flavoring. Pour the batter over the peach slices.

Bake the cake in the middle of the oven for 35 minutes, or until a cake tester inserted in the cake comes out dry.

Let the cake stand in the pan on a rack for 10 minutes. Loosen the edges, place a round serving plate face down on top of the pan, and carefully invert the pan and plate together.

Serve warm or at room temperature the same day as made.

MAKES **6** TO **8** SLICES

A HEARTWARMING CURRIED STEW DINNER FOR FOUR

Pork and Squash Curry on Noodles♦
Broccoli with Sautéed Garlic Crumbs♦
Mango-Honey Tart♦
or Fresh Sliced Mangos

This menu is absolutely loaded with beta-carotene—in the butternut squash, the mangos, and the broccoli—and the last two add vitamin C. Peanuts in the stew, plus yogurt and milk in the dessert, are high in zinc.

Pork and Squash Curry on Noodles

SUPERFOODS: butternut squash, red pepper, onion, garlic, noodles, peanuts

Put the boneless chops in the freezer for a few minutes for easy slicing.

1 medium butternut squash

2 cups (a 13-ounce can, reduced-sodium) beef broth

1 tablespoon vegetable oil, or more

1 to 1¼ pounds boneless pork chops, trimmed of fat and thinly sliced

1 large red bell pepper, seeded and sliced

1 large onion, sliced

1 garlic clove, minced

1 tablespoon cornstarch

2 teaspoons curry powder

½ teaspoon dry mustard

⅛ teaspoon cayenne pepper

½ pound fresh Chinese noodles* (found in the produce section of many supermarkets)

¼ cup unsalted peanuts, lightly toasted

Cut slices of squash from the unseeded end, approximately 4 inches in diameter and ¾ inch thick. (Save the rest for another use.)

Combine the slices with 1½ cups of the beef broth in a saucepan, bring to a simmer, and cook, covered, until the squash is tender but not mushy, about 10 minutes. Peel the squash using a fork and sharp paring knife to handle the hot vegetable. Cut the slices into quarters. Reserve the broth.

In a 12-inch skillet, heat the oil and stir-fry the pork until it is lightly browned and cooked through, 3 to 5 minutes. Remove and reserve the pork.

Add more oil if needed. Stir-fry the red pepper, onion, and garlic for 2 minutes. Add the reserved beef broth.

*Spaghetti can be substituted.

Mix the remaining ½ cup cold broth with the cornstarch and seasonings until there are no lumps. Pour the sauce into the vegetables, and cook, stirring constantly, until the sauce bubbles and thickens, then cook on low 3 minutes longer. Taste to correct seasoning, adding more curry or cayenne if desired.

Stir in the reserved pork and squash. Remove from the heat. Just before serving, bring the mixture to a simmer, but don't cook it any longer.

Meanwhile, cook the noodles according to package directions. Put them in a large pasta serving dish, and stir in some of the curry sauce. Top with the pork mixture and sprinkle with the peanuts.

MAKES 4 SERVINGS

Broccoli with Sautéed Garlic Crumbs

SUPERFOODS: broccoli, shallots, whole wheat bread

4 cups broccoli florets	1 cup fresh whole wheat bread
2 tablespoons olive oil	crumbs (2 slices)
2 garlic cloves, minced	¼ cup grated Parmesan cheese

Parboil the florets in boiling water for 3 minutes or until just tender. Immediately plunge them into ice water to stop the cooking action. Drain well.

Heat the oil in a 12-inch skillet, and sauté the garlic until softened. Add the crumbs, and stir-fry until golden-brown.

Add the broccoli and cheese, and stir-fry until the broccoli is heated through.

Leftovers are great as a salad—on a bed of romaine with Honey-Mustard Dressing (see page 531).

MAKES 4 SERVINGS

Mango-Honey Tart

Superfoods: yogurt, skim milk, mango

Mango flesh clings to the stone in a devilish way. A flexible fruit knife (for food preparation, not tableware) with a thin serrated blade is most helpful in this task.

1 cup plain nonfat yogurt

1 cup whole milk

2 eggs

¼ cup honey

2 tablespoons cornstarch

¼ teaspoon ground allspice* or
    more as needed

1 large mango, peeled and sliced

A baked 8- or 9-inch pie shell
    (see page 538)

In a food processor or bowl, combine the yogurt, milk, eggs, honey, cornstarch, and ¼ teaspoon allspice, and blend the mixture well.

Pour the mixture into a deep saucepan (twice as big as you think you'll need) and bring it to a boil over medium heat while stirring constantly. When the filling is thick and bubbling, cook 1 minute longer. Watch out for splatters of hot filling.

Cool the filling to warm. Lay the mango slices in the pie shell to form a wheel. Smooth the filling over them. Sprinkle with a bit more allspice, and chill the tart for several hours, until firm.

The pie shell can be made 1 day in advance. Keep it in a breadbox or on the kitchen counter, covered with waxed paper rather than plastic wrap.

The tart tastes best when served the same day it's made.

MAKES 6 TO 8 SLICES

*Preferably freshly ground.

A TRADITIONAL SUNDAY DINNER
FOR EIGHT

Easy Roast Chicken with Sweet Potatoes◆
Spinach and Brown Rice Tian◆
Romaine, Fennel, and Apple Salad
with Honey-Mustard Dressing (see page 531)
Raspberry Trifle with Chocolate Meringue◆

Homey roast chicken for Sunday dinner, with sweet potatoes and plenty of dark leafy greens for beta-carotene, raspberries for vitamin C, olive oil and brown rice for vitamin E, and (yes!) cocoa in the meringue for zinc!

Suppose you do have leftovers? Welcome them as a bonus for the first of the week! Leftover roast chicken, well wrapped in foil, can also be frozen for later use.

Easy Roast Chicken with Sweet Potatoes

SUPERFOODS: sweet potatoes

One 6- to 7-pound roasting   Paprika
  chicken   Ground thyme
2 garlic cloves, crushed   2 bouillon cubes
Sprig of fresh rosemary*   4 large sweet potatoes
Sprig of fresh thyme*   Salt and pepper
1 lemon, sliced

Remove the giblets and internal fat, if any, from the chicken. Wash the bird in salted water, rinse, and drain.

Preheat the oven to 350 degrees F.

Insert the garlic and fresh herbs into the chicken cavity. Squeeze the lemon slices slightly into the cavity before adding them to the garlic and herbs.

Rub the outside of the chicken all over with generous amounts of paprika and thyme. Tie the legs together. If there was fat in the cavity, skewer that on top of the breast with toothpicks.

Put the chicken on a flat rack in a large roasting pan that will also fit the potatoes. Add 1 inch of water and the bouillon cubes to the pan. Lay a sheet of foil over the top, but don't tuck it in.

Roast the chicken for 1 hour, basting once at the half-hour. Meanwhile, wash and quarter the sweet potatoes. Salt and pepper them to your taste.

Remove the pan from the oven, and add the unpeeled sweet potato quarters, cut sides up. Baste the potatoes and chicken, and return the pan to the oven to cook 1 more hour, basting again at the half-hour. When pricked, the thigh juices should run clear, not pink; the potatoes should be tender. If you're using a meat thermometer, the thigh meat should reach 180 degrees F.

MAKES **8** SERVINGS

*A half-teaspoon of dried herbs can be substituted for either or both.

Spinach and Brown Rice Tian

SUPERFOODS: brown rice, spinach, garlic, wheat germ

About 1½ pounds fresh spinach

2 tablespoons olive oil

2 garlic cloves, minced

Salt and pepper

2½ cups cooked brown rice
   (see page 524)

2 tablespoons seasoned bread
   crumbs

1 tablespoon wheat germ

2 tablespoons grated Parmesan
   cheese

Paprika

¼ cup chicken broth or water

Wash the spinach in several changes of water. Remove any tough stems. Steam it in just the water that clings to the leaves until it has wilted, about 3 minutes. Remove spinach from the heat; drain but *do not press it dry.* Season the spinach with oil, garlic, salt, and pepper.

Layer half the spinach in the bottom of an oiled 12-inch glass pie pan or other round baking dish. Make a layer of all the brown rice, and top it with the remaining spinach. Sprinkle the tian with bread crumbs, wheat germ, cheese, and paprika.

The recipe can be prepared to this point up to 1 day ahead. Keep refrigerated.

Preheat the oven to 350 degrees F.

Drizzle the broth over the tian, and bake on the middle shelf for 30 minutes (5 to 10 minutes longer if cold). Let stand 10 minutes before slicing into wedges.

MAKES 8 SERVINGS

Raspberry Trifle with Chocolate Meringue

Superfoods: raspberries

12 plain ladyfingers
½ cup mascarpone or cream
cheese, softened
¼ cup apricot preserves, melted

2 cups fresh or frozen
unsweetened whole
raspberries
2 tablespoons sugar

For the meringue

⅓ cup sugar
2 tablespoons unsweetened cocoa

¾ cup egg whites
¼ teaspoon cream of tartar

Line the sides and bottom of an 9-inch glass pie pan with split ladyfingers, rounded sides down. Spread the ladyfingers with cheese, and drizzle on the apricot preserves. Add the raspberries in one layer, pressing down slightly, and sprinkle them with 2 tablespoons sugar. Let the dessert stand at room temperature 30 minutes or so, until the raspberries give up their juice.

Or the recipe can be made ahead to this point and refrigerated for several hours.

Preheat the oven to 400 degrees F.

Make the meringue: Sift the sugar and cocoa together through a tea strainer to blend. In a deep bowl, beat the egg whites until frothy, add the cream of tartar, and keep beating until soft peaks form. Gradually add the sugar mixture, beating until the meringue is thick and glossy.

Spread the meringue right to the edges of the trifle dish (which keeps it from shrinking). With a rubber spatula, lift small peaks of meringue here and there for an attractive topography.

Bake 7 to 8 minutes on the middle shelf, until browned. It would brown faster on the top shelf, but this method will cook the egg white through.

Cool to room temperature before serving. Cut with a wet knife into wedges.

MAKES 8 SERVINGS

SIMPLY ELEGANT DINNER FOR FOUR

Carrot and Celery Soup with Anise♦
Lobster and Conchigliette Salad with Peas♦
Whole Wheat French Bread
Diced Papaya with Yogurt Custard Sauce (see page 535)

Carrots, of course, are a standard for beta-carotene. Peas add more—and with papaya are the vitamin C foods in this menu. But lobster? Yes, for its great selenium content! Yogurt for zinc, and whole wheat for practically everything: vitamin E, selenium, and zinc.

Carrot and Celery Soup with Anise

SUPERFOODS: carrots, shallots, skim milk

Because celery and carrots are both naturally high in sodium, and beef broth is salted (although less in the recommended reduced-sodium varieties), no additional salt should be needed in this soup. Other sodium-high vegetables are beets, artichokes, and many dark leafy greens, such as kale and mustard greens.

1 pound carrots, scraped	*1 teaspoon anise seeds*
2 cups (a 13-ounce can, reduced-sodium) beef broth	*1½ tablespoons cornstarch*
1 cup water	*1½ cups milk (can be skim)*
4 large celery stalks	*Freshly ground black pepper*
¼ cup minced shallots	*A few dashes of grated nutmeg*
2 tablespoons olive oil	*Finely minced celery leaves*

Cut the carrots into uniform pieces, and put them into a 3-quart saucepan with the broth and water. Simmer the carrots until very tender, about 20 minutes.

Meanwhile, in a medium skillet, sauté the celery and shallots in the oil over very low heat for about the same amount of time; the vegetables should be golden but not brown. Two minutes before taking them from the heat, stir in the anise seeds.

In a food processor, puree the carrots, broth, and celery mixture. If necessary, do this in 2 batches; don't fill the work bowl more than half full of hot food or it will bubble over when processed.

The recipe can be made ahead to this point. Keep refrigerated.

Put the soup back into the saucepan and bring it to a simmer. Stir the cornstarch into the cold milk until there are no lumps. Whisk the milk into the soup, stirring constantly until it bubbles and thickens. Simmer at least 3 minutes. If the soup seems too thick, it can be thinned with milk or broth.

Add black pepper and nutmeg to taste. Garnish with minced celery leaves.

MAKES ABOUT 1½ QUARTS

Lobster and Conchigliette Salad with Peas

SUPERFOODS: pasta, peas, lobster, olive oil

1 cup conchigliette (smallest shell pasta)

1 cup frozen peas

1½ cups finely diced cooked lobster meat

4 scallions with some of the green tops, chopped

⅓ to ½ cup Honey-Mustard Dressing (see page 531)

Cook the conchigliette according to package directions. Drain and rinse with cold water until the pasta is cool to the touch.

Bring the peas to a boil according to package directions, but immediately remove them from the heat, drain, and rinse them in cold water.

Combine the pasta, peas, lobster, scallions, and ⅓ cup dressing. Toss well, and refrigerate until ready to serve.

The salad can be made several hours ahead.

Taste to correct dressing; add 2 tablespoons more if needed.

MAKES 4 SERVINGS

A MOSTLY MAKE-AHEAD DINNER
FOR SIX

Turkey Stew♦
Whole Wheat and Cranberry Pilaf♦
Tomato, Green Bean, and Watercress Salad♦
Orange Frangipane♦
or
Clementines and Assorted Nuts

The stew and pilaf can be made a day ahead, the salad and dessert several hours ahead. Versatile turkey is noted for its zinc content. Sweet potatoes in the stew and watercress in the salad add beta-carotene. Whole wheat pilaf, salad oil, and almonds (in the frangipane) for vitamin E, tomatoes and oranges for vitamin C. There's no reason why desserts can't add extra nutrition to a meal!

Turkey Stew

SUPERFOODS: onion, turkey, sweet potato, spinach, cracked wheat, cranberries

Don't be put off by the length of this recipe or the number of ingredients. Essentially an easy dish, like most stews, it can be prepared in stages.

1 medium onion, chopped	2 carrots, scraped and sliced
2 celery stalks, chopped	1 large sweet potato, peeled and
1½ tablespoons olive oil	cut into 1-inch chunks
2 skinless turkey thighs	½ cup cold water
(2 pounds total)	3 tablespoons flour
6 cups water	Pepper
¾ teaspoon salt, or more to taste	Optional additions: fried
Bouquet of fresh herbs, such as	mushrooms and/or sautéed
thyme, marjoram, and sage*	red bell pepper

In a large pot, sauté the onion and celery in the oil until the vegetables sizzle. Add the turkey, water, ¾ teaspoon salt, and herbs. Simmer until the turkey is very tender, about 1 hour. Strain, reserving the broth.

The recipe can be prepared to this point up to 1 day ahead. Cool the turkey only slightly (20 minutes) before refrigerating. Cool the broth longer to preserve refrigerator coldness. When you refrigerate warm foods, put them on the bottom shelf, while keeping perishable items like milk on the top shelf.

*Pinches of the dried herbs can be substituted.

You should have at least 4 cups of broth. Set 2 cups aside for the pilaf, and put 2 cups back in the pot. Dice the turkey and add that, along with the carrots and sweet potato. Simmer, covered, until the vegetables are tender, 10 minutes. If desired, mushrooms and/or red peppers can be added at this point

Combine ½ cup cold water and flour in a jar. Cover tightly and shake well. Strain into the simmering stew, stirring constantly until the gravy thickens. Simmer 5 minutes to cook the flour. Taste to correct seasoning, adding salt and pepper as needed.

The entire stew can be made 1 day in advance, refrigerated, then reheated. In which case, cook the turkey on the same day, not a day ahead.

Serve the stew with the pilaf on the side.

MAKES 6 SERVINGS

Whole Wheat and Cranberry Pilaf

2 cups turkey broth   ½ cup dried sweetened
1 cup cracked wheat   cranberries

Microwave method: Combine broth and cracked wheat ingredients in a 1½-quart casserole. Microwave on high for 8 minutes or until boiling. Stir in the cranberries, reduce setting to medium, and cook an additional 10 to 12 minutes, until the cracked wheat is tender enough for your taste.

Double boiler method: Heat the broth to boiling in the top of the double boiler over direct heat. Gradually add the cracked wheat, whisking. When the mixture is thick and bubbling, place it over simmered water and continue cooking for about 30 minutes, until it tastes done. Stir in the cranberries during the last 10 minutes.

The pilaf can be made 1 day ahead. Keep refrigerated. Because of the gelling properties of turkey broth, this cold pilaf can be sliced before reheating, which looks very nice. Place overlapping slices on a glass pie pan and microwave for 3 to 5 minutes, or bake at 300 degrees F. for 20 minutes, until piping hot.

MAKES 6 SERVINGS

Tomato, Green Bean, and Watercress Salad

SUPERFOODS: watercress, olive oil, green beans, tomatoes

If good fresh green beans aren't available, use a 10-ounce package of frozen Italian beans, cooked.

1 bunch watercress	1 large or 2 small ripe tomatoes
½ cup Greek-Style Salad	(½ pound), chopped
Dressing (see page 529)	
2 cups cooked green beans, cut	
into 2-inch pieces	

Wash the watercress. Discard the lower stems and chop the rest.

Pour the dressing into a salad bowl, and stir in the green beans and tomatoes. Put the watercress on top.

The salad can be made several hours ahead. Keep refrigerated.

Toss just before serving.

MAKES 6 SERVINGS

Orange Frangipane

SUPERFOODS: oranges, almonds

All nuts are nutritious, but almonds are especially high in vitamin E, as well as some important B vitamins.

2 to 3 seedless oranges	*¼ teaspoon baking powder*
1 tablespoon butter or margarine	*¼ cup ground almonds (can be*
2 egg whites	*done in a food processor)*
Pinch of cream of tartar	*2 tablespoons orange juice*
⅓ cup sugar	*½ teaspoon natural almond*
¼ cup all-purpose flour	*flavoring*

Peel the oranges, removing all white membrane. Cut them into slices, then dice them. You should have 2 cups. Drain them in a strainer set over a pitcher. Use the accumulated liquid for the juice needed in the recipe.

Preheat the oven to 350 degrees F.

While the oven is heating, put the butter into a 9-inch glass pie pan or quiche dish and melt it in the oven; don't let it brown.

Layer the oranges in the melted butter.

Beat the egg whites until they're frothy. Add the cream of tartar and continue beating until soft peaks form. Gradually beat in the sugar.

Mix the flour and baking powder together. Fold the mixture into the egg whites. Fold in the ground almonds. Gently whisk in the juice and flavoring.

Pour the batter evenly over the oranges, and use a spatula to spread it right to the edge of the dish. Bake the cake in the middle of the oven for 25 to 30 minutes, or until the top is golden and springs back when pressed.

Serve warm or at room temperature. It falls a bit in cooling.
The cake can be prepared several hours ahead but tastes best when eaten the same day it's made.

MAKES 6 SERVINGS

BRUNCH OR LUNCH FOR FOUR
ON A BIG DAY

Sliced Kiwi and Honeydew with Lime Wedges
Salmon and Potato Frittata♦
Carrot-Bran Muffins♦

Rev up for the day with beta-carotene in the honeydew and carrots, vitamin C in the kiwi and potatoes, vitamin E in salmon and bran. For those with normal blood cholesterol, the American Heart Association allows 3 to 4 eggs per week.

Salmon and Potato Frittata

SUPERFOODS: potatoes, salmon

Italians are fond of egg dishes and will add almost any leftovers to a frittata, which is why there are so many varieties of frittata. If you're short on cooked potatoes, you could add some peas with the egg mixture. Frittatas call for flexibility.

2 tablespoons olive oil
2 cups cooked and sliced potatoes
1 cup canned or cooked salmon
4 eggs or 2 eggs plus ½ cup
   prepared egg substitute

2 tablespoons water
¼ teaspoon dried rosemary
Salt and freshly ground black
   pepper

Heat 1½ tablespoons of the oil in a 10-inch skillet, preferably nonstick. Fry the potatoes, turning often, until most of them are browned on one side, about 7 minutes.

Pick over the salmon to remove any bones, but don't mash it; keep the flakes large.

Beat the eggs with the water, rosemary, salt, and pepper to taste. Pour the egg mixture over the potatoes. Scatter the salmon on top, pressing the flakes into the egg with the back of a spoon.

Cook over very low heat until the egg has set, lifting the edges from time to time to let the uncooked portion seep underneath. The top of the frittata will still be moist.

To invert, loosen the entire frittata with a spatula. Place a large plate over it, and turn the pan and plate together.

Put the pan back on the heat, add the remaining ½ tablespoon of oil, and slide the frittata back into the pan to brown on the second side, which will take only a minute or two. Cut into quarters and serve immediately.

MAKES 4 SERVINGS

Carrot-Bran Muffins

SUPERFOODS: bran, orange juice, carrots, raisins

1½ cups unbleached all-purpose
  flour
¼ cup sugar
1 teaspoon each ground
  cinnamon and baking soda
½ teaspoon each ground ginger,
  baking powder, and salt
¼ teaspoon ground allspice

½ cup wheat bran*
⅔ cup orange juice
¼ cup vegetable oil
1 egg or ¼ cup prepared egg
  substitute
1 cup finely grated carrots
⅓ cup raisins

Spray a nonstick 12-cup muffin tin with cooking spray, or grease a regular muffin tin, or use paper liners.

Sift together into a large bowl all the dry ingredients except the bran. Stir in the bran.

In a medium bowl, whisk together the orange juice, oil, and egg. Grate the carrots (very easy in food processor). Measure the carrots and raisins.

The recipe can be made ahead to this point and held for several hours or overnight. Refrigerate the liquid ingredients and carrots until needed.

When ready to cook, preheat the oven to 400 degrees F. Stir the liquid ingredients into the dry until just blended. Fold in the carrots and raisins.

Divide the batter among the muffin cups, and bake on the top shelf for about 20 minutes. The muffins are done when they're risen, brown, and a cake tester inserted in the center of a muffin comes out dry.

As soon as they can be handled, remove the muffins from the pan and cool them on a wire rack. Serve slightly warm or at room temperature.

*Not the cold cereal. Unprocessed wheat bran is sold in jars or boxes in the cereal section of the supermarket, near the toasted wheat germ.

Homemade muffins will keep for 3 to 4 days in a plastic container in the refrigerator—or may be frozen for longer storage.

MAKES 12 MUFFINS

A LAZY SUNDAY BRUNCH
FOR FOUR

Grapefruit Sections
with Honey and Toasted Pine Nuts
Lazy Sunday Ricotta Quiche♦
Apricot-Oatmeal Muffins♦

Another brunch—this one with lots of zinc in pine nuts and ricotta (calcium in the low-fat cheese, too!). Get your beta-carotene in apricots, vitamin C in grapefruit, and vitamin E from whole grains in the muffins.

Lazy Sunday Ricotta Quiche

SUPERFOODS: ricotta, skim milk

Whipped up in a processor or blender, this quiche makes its own crust. What could be easier?

1 cup part-skim ricotta	⅛ teaspoon white pepper
½ cup milk (can be skim)	Salt*
3 eggs	½ cup loosely packed, slivered
½ cup all-purpose flour	prosciutto (or any ham)
½ teaspoon baking powder	¼ cup loosely packed, coarsely
	grated Parmesan cheese

Preheat the oven to 375 degrees F. Generously butter a 9-inch glass pie pan.

In a food processor or blender, blend the ricotta, milk, eggs, flour, baking powder, and seasonings. Pour the mixture into the prepared pan.

Scatter the ham on top, and sprinkle with the Parmesan cheese.

Bake on the middle shelf for about 20 minutes, until set at the center. The quiche will puff up, then fall when removed from the oven. Serve warm or at room temperature.

MAKES 4 TO 6 SERVINGS

*Can be omitted, since the ham and cheese are salty.

Apricot-Oatmeal Muffins

SUPERFOODS: oats, wheat germ, apricots

Packed with nutrition, two of these muffins make a fine breakfast for those who find the crunch of cold cereal too loud in the morning.

1½ cups unbleached all-purpose
   flour
1 tablespoon baking powder
1 teaspoon ground cardamom
½ teaspoon salt
1 cup quick-cooking oats
½ cup packed brown sugar
   (remove lumps)

¼ cup wheat germ
¾ cup milk
2 eggs or ½ cup prepared egg
   substitute
⅓ cup vegetable oil
½ cup snipped dried apricots

Spray a nonstick 12-cup muffin tin with cooking spray, or grease a regular muffin tin, or use paper liners.

Sift together into a large bowl the flour, baking powder, cardamom, and salt. Stir in the oats, brown sugar, and wheat germ.

In a medium bowl, whisk together the milk, eggs, and oil.

The recipe can be made ahead to this point and held for several hours or overnight. Refrigerate the liquid ingredients until needed.

When ready to cook, preheat the oven to 400 degrees F. Stir the liquid ingredients into the dry until just blended. Fold in the apricots.

Divide the batter among the muffin cups, and bake on the top shelf for 15 to 20 minutes. The muffins are done when they're risen, brown, and a cake tester inserted in the center of a muffin comes out dry.

As soon as they can be handled, remove the muffins from the pan and cool them on a wire rack. Serve slightly warm or at room temperature.

In some homes fresh muffins will disappear in a day, but bear in mind that they'll keep for 3 to 4 days in a plastic container in the refrigerator—or freeze them for longer storage.

MAKES 12 MUFFINS

5

AMAZING YOGURT AND TOFU

Credited with Everything from Preventing Yeast Infections to Lessening Hot Flashes

For women especially, there seems to be something inherently healthful in these two superfoods. Studies keep cropping up in current medical literature linking yogurt or tofu with decreased risks of female disorders ranging from yeast infections and hot flashes to breast and endometrial cancers.

Both superfoods are smooth and silky. Tofu is bland and yogurt mildly tangy, but each is fairly featureless, like an empty canvas, awaiting your creative inspiration to turn them into culinary masterpieces. Tofu is the product of pureed soybeans thickened with a coagulant, yogurt the product of milk thickened by fermentation. Yogurt has the added benefit of being obtainable in a nonfat form, just like skim milk. Reduced-fat tofu is on the market and is worth searching for, but regular tofu may contain as much fat as meat; the firmer it is, the more fat. Yet tofu is a traditional part of low-fat Asian diets, used sparingly but flavorfully in Asian dishes.

YOGURT FIGHTS YEAST INFECTIONS

For many women, yeast infections are a pesky, recurring problem that causes discomfort and embarrassment. How reassuring to learn that yogurt, already a favorite food for fast low-calorie lunches, can be a valuable preventive measure! A cup of yogurt a day, containing active *Lactobacillus acidophilus* cultures, has been found to fight the growth of *Candida albicans* and therefore to lessen the incidence of yeast infections—a threefold decrease in one study.

TOFU MAY RELIEVE MENOPAUSAL SYMPTOMS

"Is it hot in here, or is it me?" is the constant menopausal refrain, with decreased estrogen production bringing on sudden waves of intense heat by day and drenching sweats by night. But current diet research has turned up some promising news. More soybeans and soybean curd (tofu) in their diets is believed to be the reason why Japanese women report fewer hot flashes than women in North America. If you've never cooked with tofu, this could be a good reason to give it a try!

PROVEN ADDITIONS TO THE ANTICANCER ARSENAL

Yogurt with active *L. acidophilus* cultures has been shown to prevent certain bacteria in the large intestine from creating carcinogens from our food. In a Los Angeles study of the relationship of diet to colon cancer, while no individual food could be associated with an increased risk, yogurt was found to be significantly protective.

Another report, published in the *American Journal of Epidemiol-*

ogy, stated that women who ate the most yogurt and skim milk (as well as fruits and vegetables) had the lowest endometrial cancer risk.

Researchers at the National Cancer Institute report that there may be a similar advantage from soybean products, such as tofu. Some population studies have suggested that people who eat soybean foods regularly have less risk of colon and rectal cancer.

Other studies have linked soybean consumption to a reduced breast cancer risk. Chemicals found in soybeans, called *isoflavones,* are thought to prevent the hormone estrogen from stimulating breast tumor growth.

YOGURT MAY BOOST THE IMMUNE SYSTEM

Researchers studying the effects of long-term yogurt consumption in rather large amounts found no negative side effects (not even a rise in cholesterol), but a significant and beneficial increase in calcium levels and an "interesting" increase in the production of gamma-interferon when the yogurt contained live cultures. This could mean a boost to your immune system.

In one experiment, volunteers given 6 ounces of yogurt containing these two cultures experienced a reduction in colds, infectious diarrhea, hay fever, and allergies (reported in *Eating Well,* March/April 1993).

Eating yogurt with active cultures may even help to counterbalance odor-causing bacteria in your mouth, according to Dr. Memory Elvin-Lewis, dentist and professor of biomedicine at Washington University in St. Louis (reported in *American Health,* May 1993).

GOT THE ANTIBIOTIC BLUES? TRY YOGURT

Those potent antibiotics we all have to take from time to time are so efficient at killing off intestinal bacteria, they eliminate some of the "friendly" ones as well. This often results in a case of diarrhea adding to one's woes. There is some medical evidence—plus many anecdotal reports—that the live cultures in yogurt will restore the intestinal balance. A few doctors, when prescribing a big dose of antibiotics, even recommend that a patient snack on yogurt to lessen this distressing side effect.

GREAT CALCIUM, EVEN FOR THE LACTOSE INTOLERANT

If you suffer from cramps, bloating, or diarrhea when you drink milk, you're probably lactose intolerant, meaning your body doesn't do a good job of digesting lactose, a milk sugar. Still, a woman should eat some dairy products for much-needed calcium to help keep her bones strong. Because yogurt (and hard cheese, too) is low in lactose, you may find nonfat yogurt an excellent source of dairy calcium without those intestinal upsets.

Usually thickened with nonfat milk solids, yogurt actually provides more calcium than milk does—400 to 450 milligrams a cup, or one-third to one-half of your RDA. Tofu, a completely nondairy source of calcium, yields 108 milligrams per small slice.

TOFU AS A MEAT SUBSTITUTE

Reduced-fat tofu is a great way to get protein and calcium without saturated fat and cholesterol. Even regular tofu is low in saturated fat; only about 14 percent of the fat it contains is saturated; the larger percent is polyunsaturated. It's a complete protein, too, because soybeans, unlike any other plant food, contain all the amino acids of meat. That makes tofu a fine meat substitute for vegetarians—or anyone wanting to improve that LDL cholesterol count by cutting down on meat.

BUYING AND COOKING WITH YOGURT AND TOFU

Tofu, made from soybeans in a manner similar to the way cheese is produced, could be thought of as an Asian cheese. It's sold in the supermarket packaged in blocks marked soft or firm, with a freshness date stamped on the package. Soft tofu is good for a puree or a shake. Firm tofu can be sliced, diced, or slivered, breaded or marinated, stir-fried, grilled, braised, or tossed in a salad. Like eggplant, tofu needs imagination in preparation and a generous hand in flavoring.

Although a vegetable product, tofu offers a big protein punch for about 65 calories per 3 ounces, compared to a lean ground beef patty of the same weight for 230 calories. Unlike the beef, the fat in tofu is mostly unsaturated, another plus.

In buying yogurt, you'll want a brand that contains those beneficial active cultures. Look for *L. acidophilus* and other live cultures, such as *Streptococcus thermophilus*, listed on the label. At the very least, the yogurt you buy should advertise "active cultures" on the container.

Although live yogurt cultures are destroyed by heat, calcium is retained, so cooking with nonfat yogurt is beneficial in two ways: It adds calcium and it reduces calories and fat. Plain nonfat yogurt contains only about 145 calories per cup; fruit yogurt may contain as much as 7 teaspoons of sugar per "cup" container, and some contain aspartame, an artificial sweetener.

That's why it may make sense for you to buy the large container of plain nonfat yogurt and mix in some fruit and honey when you want fruit yogurt. The fruit will be fresher, and you'll control the amount of sweetness. Meanwhile, you'll also have versatile plain yogurt to use in salad dressings, whipped potatoes, and cool condiments like cucumber sauce.

With very little effort, you also can make yogurt "cheese" to use in place of cream cheese. Yogurt is a tasty coating ingredient (with seasoned crumbs) for oven-fried chicken, and it can be used to make "lighter" custard sauces.

Maybe you should buy *two* large containers.

YOGURT AND TOFU QUICKIES

Marinate tofu in vinaigrette and toss in a salad.
Fold whole cranberry sauce into yogurt.
Make an instant veggie dip by stirring onion soup mix into plain nonfat yogurt.
Blend frozen nonfat yogurt in place of ice cream in a "smoothie."
Top a baked potato with nonfat yogurt and chopped chives—you'll never miss the sour cream!
Whisk 2 tablespoons of your favorite sugarless fruit spread into a cup of nonfat yogurt.
Sprinkle granola on fresh fruit and yogurt for breakfast.
"Lighten" mayonnaise by mixing with 3 parts yogurt.

SUPERMEALS STARRING YOGURT AND TOFU

Recipes indicated by a ◆ follow the menus.

FIRESIDE VEGETARIAN FARE
FOR SIX

"Cream" of Spinach Soup with Garlic Croutons◆
Adzuki Bean Salad with Tofu◆
Whole Wheat Pita Bread
Pineapple Brown Rice Pudding◆

*M*any a former ''cream'' dish can be made with nonfat yogurt, which gives a pleasing tang to the flavor. Fiber-rich beans and brown rice complement each other to offer complete protein without meat, an important consideration when planning vegetarian menus. Tofu (actually a second bean ingredient) adds a satisfying richness and more calcium to the salad.

"Cream" of Spinach Soup with Garlic Croutons

SUPERFOODS: onions, garlic, tomato juice, carrots,
spinach, yogurt

2 tablespoons olive oil
1 medium onion, chopped
1 garlic clove, chopped
3 cups tomato juice
3 cups cider or apple juice
2 carrots, scraped and sliced
1 pound well-washed spinach

1 tablespoon minced fresh dill
¼ teaspoon Spicy Pepper Mix (see
   page 539) or black pepper
1 tablespoon cornstarch
1 cup plain nonfat yogurt
Garlic Croutons (recipe follows)

Heat the oil in a large pot, and sauté the onion and garlic until
tender but not brown, about 5 minutes. Add the tomato juice,
cider, and carrots; simmer until the carrots are very tender, 10
to 12 minutes. Add the spinach, dill, and pepper; cook just until
the spinach has wilted.

Puree the soup in batches in a food processor or blender; don't
fill the work bowl more than half full, since hot liquids tend to
foam up.

Return the soup to the pot, but don't return it to a boil yet.
Whisk the cornstarch into the yogurt. Blend the yogurt into the
soup. Slowly bring to a boil, whisking constantly, and simmer
3 minutes.

Float a garlic crouton on each portion.

MAKES 6 SERVINGS

GARLIC CROUTONS

SUPERFOODS: olive oil, garlic

2 tablespoons olive oil
1 garlic clove, pressed in a garlic press

6 slices French bread, cut diagonally

Preheat the oven to 350 degrees F.
Mix the olive oil and garlic. Brush the mixture on both sides of the bread slices. Bake the slices on a baking sheet, turning once, 10 to 15 minutes or until golden and crisp.

Adzuki Bean Salad with Tofu

SUPERFOODS: adzuki beans, tofu, red onion, green pepper

Light, sweet adzuki beans need no oil at all to make an appetizing salad.

One 15-ounce can adzuki beans, drained and rinsed*
½ cup chopped red onion
1 green bell pepper, seeded and chopped
1 celery stalk with leaves, diced

½ cup seasoned rice vinegar**
½ teaspoon dried cilantro
1 cup diced firm tofu

*Available in specialty stores and whole-foods markets.
**The "seasoning" is salt and sugar, so if you use unseasoned rice vinegar, add a pinch of each.

Combine all ingredients except the tofu, and blend well. Gently stir in the tofu. Marinate at room temperature for 30 minutes or in the refrigerator for an hour or more.

The salad can be made 1 day ahead. Keep refrigerated.

MAKES **6** SERVINGS

Pineapple Brown Rice Pudding

SUPERFOODS: skim milk, brown rice, pineapple

Just the thing for using up leftover rice—old-fashioned, range-top rice pudding, a soothing dessert to pamper the child in you.

2 cups milk (can be skim)
1¼ cups cooked brown rice (see
   page 524)
½ cup sugar
1 cinnamon stick*

One 8-ounce can crushed
   pineapple (no added sugar)
2 tablespoons cornstarch
2 eggs, beaten

In the top of a large double boiler, combine the milk, rice, sugar, and cinnamon stick. Cook over simmering water for ½ hour, taking care that the water doesn't boil out. Stir once or twice at the beginning to dissolve the sugar.

Drain the pineapple, reserving the juice. Mix the cornstarch with ½ cup juice until smooth and blended.

Gradually add about ½ cup of the hot milk to the eggs. Remove the cinnamon stick from the double boiler. Blend the eggs into the milk-rice mixture, stirring constantly, until slightly thickened.

*Much more flavor than merely adding ground cinnamon.

Place the top of the double boiler over direct medium heat, add the cornstarch mixture all at once, and cook until thick and bubbling. Remove from the heat and fold in the pineapple.

Cool 20 minutes or so, then refrigerate to chill. If you wish, you can divide the pudding among 6 dessert dishes before chilling.

MAKES 6 SERVINGS

WATCHING-THE-GAME DINNER FOR SIX

Crudités with Garden Fresh Herb Cheese♦
Beef and Bean Stew with Molasses♦
Whole-Grain Italian Bread
Tossed Green Salad with Avocado-Tofu Mayonnaise♦
Apples and Oatmeal Cookies

No fussing around in the kitchen with this make-ahead (as much as a day ahead!) dinner for hearty appetites, so join the party! Nonfat yogurt cheese is a great substitute for the richer stuff, and avocado-tofu ''mayonnaise,'' while not exactly low-cal, is certainly a nutritious choice on good dark-leaf greens.

Garden Fresh Herb Cheese

SUPERFOODS: carrot, red pepper, yogurt, plus raw
cruciferous vegetables

*A delightfully light dip for fresh veggies such as broccoli florets,
cauliflower, radish roses, and slices of tender purple-topped turnip.*

1 small carrot, scraped	1 cup Yogurt Cheese (see page
½ red bell pepper	534)
2 tablespoons minced fresh chives	4 ounces light cream cheese
Sprigs of fresh oregano, basil,	Dashes of salt, white pepper, and
and/or thyme, stems	cayenne pepper
discarded, minced (about 2	
teaspoons)	

Finely grate the carrot and red pepper. Stir in the chives and
herbs. Whip together the yogurt and cream cheese, and blend
in the vegetable-herb mixture.

The preceding steps can be accomplished in a few minutes
with the aid of a food processor.

Add salt and peppers to your taste. Plenty of pepper is recommended. Refrigerate for a hour or two to blend flavors.

*The cheese can be prepared 1 to 2 days ahead and will be even better.
Keep refrigerated. Bring to room temperature before serving.*

MAKES 1½ CUPS

Beef and Bean Stew with Molasses

SUPERFOODS: onion, carrots, molasses, beans

Having less meat and more beans is a shrewd health move! This sweet-and-sour stew is a good example of how to cut down on beef without feeling deprived.

1 pound stewing beef	*2 tablespoons molasses*
¼ cup all-purpose flour	*¼ teaspoon each ground ginger,*
2 tablespoons vegetable oil	*salt, and pepper*
1 large onion, chopped	*One 15-ounce can navy beans,*
2 large carrots, scraped and sliced	*drained and rinsed*
2 celery stalks with leaves, sliced	
1 cup water, or more	
¼ cup ketchup or chili sauce	
3 tablespoons cider vinegar	

Trim the beef well of fat and gristle. Cut into uniform chunks, about 1 inch square. (The store's cut is usually about 2 inches.) Put the beef into a plastic bag with the flour, and shake to coat. Shake off any excess flour.

Heat the oil in a large skillet, and brown the beef chunks on both sides. Add the onion during the last minute or so of browning.

Add all the remaining ingredients except the beans. Bring the stew to a boil, reduce the heat, and simmer very slowly, covered, for 1½ to 2 hours, until the meat is quite tender. Stir occasionally, adding up to ½ cup water if the gravy seems too thick.

Add the drained beans during the last 10 minutes of cooking. *The stew can be made 1 day ahead and reheated.*

MAKES 6 SERVINGS

Avocado-Tofu Mayonnaise

SUPERFOODS: garlic, avocado, tofu

Serve this dressing with crisp mixed dark-leaf greens. Include both bland (romaine or escarole) and bitter flavors (watercress, chicory, or dandelion).

1 small garlic clove
1 large avocado, very ripe, peeled
  and cut into chunks
5 ounces tofu

3 tablespoons lemon juice or
  white wine vinegar
½ teaspoon salt
⅛ teaspoon cayenne pepper

In a food processor, with the motor running, toss the garlic down the feed tube to mince it. Stop the motor and add all the remaining ingredients. Blend the mixture to a creamy puree similar to mayonnaise. Taste the dressing to correct the seasoning and texture, adding more lemon juice, salt, or cayenne to your taste.

MAKES ABOUT 1½ CUPS

COOL 'N' CAREFREE SUMMER MENU
FOR FOUR

Chilled Shrimp and Cucumber Bisque♦
Chopped Vegetable Salad with Tofu♦
Whole Wheat French Bread
A Platter of Fresh Apricots and Plums

*A*nother *mostly make-ahead menu featuring the creamy magic and good nutrition of yogurt and tofu. An abundance of chopped summer vegetables rounds out the meal with an antioxidant plus—and always, whole-grain bread for a panorama of vitamins B, E, and selenium. Like tofu, vitamin E is a defense against menopausal hot flashes.*

Chilled Shrimp and Cucumber Bisque

SUPERFOODS: onion, carrot, shrimp, yogurt, parsley

1 small onion, chopped
1 celery stalk with leaves,
  chopped
1 tablespoon vegetable oil
1 carrot, chopped
2 8-ounce bottles clam juice
½ cup dry vermouth or white
  wine*
1 tablespoon tomato paste
2 cups shelled cooked shrimp
1½ tablespoons cornstarch

1 cucumber
1 cup plain nonfat yogurt
¼ teaspoon white pepper
Pinch or two of mace (optional)
1 tablespoon each minced fresh
  chives and flat-leaf parsley
Tiny (3-leaf) sprigs of parsley for
  garnish

Sauté the onion and celery in the oil until soft but not brown, about 5 minutes. Add the carrot, clam juice, wine, and tomato paste, and simmer for 10 minutes, or until the vegetables are very tender.

Put aside a few shrimp for garnishing. Puree the rest in a food processor. Scoop up the vegetables with a slotted spoon and puree those with the shrimp. Add the cornstarch. Gradually blend in the pan juices through the feed tube. Return the mixture to the pan.

Bring the soup to a boil over medium heat, stirring constantly until thickened. Simmer 2 to 3 minutes, stirring often. Chill the soup.

The recipe can be made to this point up to 1 day ahead. Keep in the coldest part of the refrigerator.

*Alcohol evaporates during the cooking process.

Peel, seed, and dice the cucumber. Whisk the yogurt, pepper, and mace into the soup, and stir in the cucumber, chives, and parsley.

Serve the soup cold, garnished with the reserved shrimp and tiny sprigs of parsley.

MAKES 1 QUART

Chopped Vegetable Salad with Tofu

SUPERFOODS: tofu, tomato, mixed vegetables, chickpeas, olive oil

Based on a Tunisian dish of finely chopped vegetables, leftovers of this salad will be perfectly at home stuffed into pita bread pockets.

1½ cups diced firm tofu

1½ cups diced ripe tomatoes

2 cups or more of any of the following diced vegetables (or any others that are handy and in season): green bell pepper, tender green beans, young zucchini, celery, green or red onions

1 cup canned chickpeas, drained

¼ cup olive oil

2 tablespoons white wine vinegar

1 tablespoon minced fresh, or ½ teaspoon dried, oregano or mint leaves (the mint is more traditionally Tunisian)

½ teaspoon salt, or to taste

Freshly ground black pepper

Hot red pepper flakes (optional)

Combine all the ingredients in a large bowl. Toss the salad and allow it to marinate to develop flavor—either an hour at room temperature or several hours in the refrigerator.

The salad can be made a day ahead and kept covered and chilled.

Toss again before serving, and taste. You may want a little more oil and/or vinegar.

MAKES ABOUT 2 QUARTS

A CANDLELIGHT DINNER
FOR SIX

Veal Paprika♦
Whole Wheat Spaetzle♦
or
Buttered Whole Wheat Egg Bows
Stir-Fried Asparagus with Tofu and Cashews♦
Sweet Potato Custard♦
or
Steamed Sweet Potatoes
Chocolate Yogurt Cheesecake with Glazed Strawberries♦

This elegant menu pushes all the nutrition buttons, from yogurt and tofu to whole wheat, folate-rich asparagus, and bursting-with-beta-carotene sweet potatoes. After all that goodness, how about a slice of chocolate cheesecake? A smooth, very low-fat version!

Veal Paprika

SUPERFOODS: onion, red pepper, yogurt

*2¼ pounds stewing veal,
trimmed of fat and cut into
uniform pieces
¼ cup all-purpose flour
¼ teaspoon salt
⅛ teaspoon Spicy Pepper Mix (see
page 539) or black pepper
3½ teaspoons sweet
Hungarian paprika
2 tablespoons vegetable oil*

*½ cup chopped onion
½ cup finely diced red bell pepper
1 cup chicken broth or water,
plus more as needed
1 tablespoon cornstarch
1 cup plain nonfat yogurt*

Put the veal in a plastic bag with the flour, salt, pepper, and 1 teaspoon of the paprika. Shake to coat, then shake off excess.

Heat the oil in a 12-inch skillet. Brown the veal on all sides. As the last side is browning, add the vegetables and continue frying for 3 to 5 minutes.

Add the broth or water, cover, and simmer over low heat for 1 hour, until the veal is tender. Stir often, adding more liquid as needed to maintain about ¼ cup.

Remove the veal and keep it warm. Whisk the cornstarch and the remaining 2½ teaspoons of paprika into the yogurt. Blend the yogurt into the pan gravy, and stir constantly over low heat until thick and bubbling gently. Return the veal to the pan, and simmer 3 minutes, stirring very often.

The recipe can be made ahead and rewarmed over very low heat, watching carefully and stirring often. Keep refrigerated.

Serve with spaetzle.

MAKES 6 SERVINGS

Whole Wheat Spaetzle

SUPERFOODS: whole wheat flour

Shaped with a teaspoon instead of sliced, these round spaetzle are more like little dumplings or gnocchi than noodles.

1 cup whole wheat flour	*1 cup water*
1 cup unbleached all-purpose flour	*2 tablespoons melted butter, or more as needed*
½ teaspoon salt	*1 tablespoon minced fresh flat-leaf parsley*
1 egg, slightly beaten, or ¼ cup prepared egg substitute	

Sift together the flours and salt. In another bowl, whisk together the egg and water. Gradually add the flour to the liquids, blending until smooth. The batter should be thick.

About a half-hour before the veal is tender, bring a large pot of salted water to a boil. Drop the batter by ½ teaspoons into the water, dipping the spoon into the boiling water after each. Cook only one layer at a time (about one third of the batter). When the dumplings rise the surface, boil an additional 5 to 8 minutes; taste for desired tenderness. Drain well in a slotted spoon.

Keep the dumplings warm in a serving dish, stirred into the melted butter, until all are cooked. When the veal sauce is finished, stir ⅓ cup of it into the spaetzle. Sprinkle with the parsley.

MAKES 6 SERVINGS

Stir-Fried Asparagus with Tofu and Cashews

SUPERFOODS: asparagus, garlic, tofu, cashews

A 10-minute dish that could be an agreeable luncheon entree at another time.

1 bunch thin asparagus (about 1¼ pounds)	1 cup diced firm tofu
2 tablespoons olive oil	½ cup unsalted cashews
1 garlic clove, finely minced	A liberal sprinkling of freshly ground black pepper
1 tablespoon white wine or water	

Break off the tough ends from the asparagus stalks, and slice them on the diagonal into 2-inch pieces.

Heat the oil and garlic in a large skillet or wok. Stir-fry the asparagus over medium-high heat until nearly tender-crisp, 3 to 5 minutes. Add the wine or water, and allow it to evaporate, about 1 minute, to finish cooking the asparagus. It should be slightly crunchy.

Add the tofu and cashews, stir-frying until the cashews brown just slightly, 1 to 2 minutes.

The dish may be made an hour or so ahead and rewarmed in the skillet.

Sprinkle with pepper and serve.

MAKES 6 SERVINGS

Sweet Potato Custard

SUPERFOODS: sweet potato, skim milk

This is delicious with sweet potato, but keep in mind that the recipe also can be made with any mashed orange-colored vegetable you happen to have cooked and on hand.

1 tablespoon butter, melted	*¼ teaspoon each grated nutmeg,*
1½ cups mashed sweet potato	*ground allspice, and salt*
(2 medium potatoes)	*Freshly ground black pepper*
½ cup milk (can be skim)	
2 eggs	

Preheat the oven to 375 degrees F. Coat a 9-inch glass cake or pie pan with the butter. Blend all the remaining ingredients, and spread them in the prepared pan.

Bake 30 to 35 minutes or until set.

The recipe can be made several hours ahead for later baking, or it can be baked ahead and reheated in a microwave (3 to 4 minutes) or in a 300 degree F. oven (15 to 20 minutes).

MAKES 6 SERVINGS

Chocolate Yogurt Cheesecake with Glazed Strawberries

SUPERFOODS: yogurt, strawberries

⅔ cup sugar
¼ cup unsweetened cocoa*
2 tablespoons cornstarch
1 cup nonfat Yogurt Cheese (see page 534)
1 cup ricotta

2 eggs
1 teaspoon vanilla extract
¼ teaspoon almond extract
1 pint fresh strawberries
½ cup red currant jelly, melted

Preheat the oven to 325 degrees F. Butter an 8-inch glass cake pan or pie plate, and sprinkle it with 1 tablespoon of the sugar.

Blend the remaining sugar with the cocoa and cornstarch. Combine the yogurt cheese, ricotta, sugar-cocoa mixture, eggs, and flavorings, and beat until well blended. Spoon the batter into the prepared pan.

Bake the cheesecake on the middle shelf for 35 to 40 minutes or until set at the center. Cool completely.

The cheesecake can be made 1 day ahead; keep it covered and refrigerated.

Cut the strawberries in half and dip them in the melted jelly, using tongs. Arrange them on top of the cheesecake in an attractive pattern. Chill long enough to set the jelly, but serve soon afterwards, since the berries will begin to "weep" after an hour or so.

Note: If strawberries are not in season, this cheesecake is scrumptious topped with half a can of prepared cherry pie filling. (Freeze the rest for another occasion.)

MAKES 6 SLICES

*A good-quality Dutch-processed cocoa is preferable.

EXOTIC BUT EASY DINNER
FOR FOUR

Braised Chicken with Curried Yogurt Sauce and Sweet Potatoes♦
Brown Basmati Rice (see page 524)
Sautéed Spinach and Tofu♦
Last-Minute Baked Bananas with Dates♦

Yogurt is a terrific complement to sweet, spicy curry. Tofu adds even more calcium to the menu. Also look for beta-carotene in the potatoes and the spinach, great B vitamins in the rice, important fiber in the bananas and dates for dessert.

Braised Chicken with Curried Yogurt Sauce and
Sweet Potatoes

SUPERFOODS: sweet potatoes, onion, red pepper, yogurt,
peanuts

A one-pot dinner that requires little attention as it braises—a nice time for the cook to relax. Bake the easy dessert alongside the chicken during the last 20 minutes of its cooking time.

4 small sweet potatoes	1 cup chicken broth
2 tablespoons olive oil	2 tablespoons cornstarch
8 skinless chicken thighs	1 tablespoon curry powder
½ cup chopped onion	1 cup plain nonfat yogurt
½ cup chopped red bell pepper	¼ cup chopped unsalted peanuts (optional)

Preheat the oven to 350 degrees F.

Peel the potatoes and cut them into chunks.

Heat the oil in a Dutch oven on the range top, and brown the chicken pieces on both sides. Add the onion and red pepper when turning to the second side.

Put the potatoes around and under the chicken, pour the broth over all, and bring it to a boil. Cover and bake on the middle shelf for 45 minutes, or until the chicken is cooked through and the potatoes are tender.

The recipe can be made 1 day ahead to this point. Keep refrigerated.

Remove the chicken and potatoes from the Dutch oven, and keep them warm on a platter. (Reheat them first if they've been refrigerated.)

Blend the cornstarch and curry powder into the yogurt. Whisk the mixture into the pan juices (which should be about ½ cup) over medium heat and stir constantly until the sauce is thick and bubbling. Simmer for 3 minutes.

Pour the sauce over the chicken and potatoes, sprinkle with peanuts if using, and serve.

MAKES 4 SERVINGS

Sautéed Spinach and Tofu

SUPERFOODS: shallots, tofu, spinach

2 tablespoons olive oil	1 tablespoon chopped fresh dill
¼ cup chopped shallots	Freshly ground pepper
½ cup diced firm tofu	2 tablespoons broth or water
¼ cup pitted black Moroccan olives	10 ounces fresh spinach, well washed

Heat the olive oil in a large skillet, and sauté the shallots until they just begin to brown. Add the diced tofu, olives, and seasonings. Stir-fry 3 minutes. Remove and reserve the tofu and olives.

Add the broth and spinach to the pan, and steam the vegetable, stirring constantly, until wilted; this only takes a minute or two. Return the tofu and olives, and heat through.

MAKES 4 SERVINGS

Last-Minute Baked Bananas with Dates

SUPERFOODS: bananas, dates

Toss this together in a jiffy anytime you simply must have a dessert. Keeping dried fruits, nuts, spices and the like on hand makes possible these last-minute inspirations.

A spoonful of nonfat frozen yogurt melting on top is a heavenly addition.

4 small bananas	*Pinches of ground cloves, allspice,*
12 pitted dates	*and cinnamon*
¼ cup brown sugar	*1 tablespoon butter*

Peel and slice the bananas into a bowl. Toss with the dates, brown sugar, and spices.

Preheat the oven to 350 degrees F.

While oven is heating, allow the butter to melt in a baking dish (a soufflé dish works well). Spoon the fruit into the dish, and bake for 25 to 30 minutes. Cool slightly before serving.

Leftovers are still delicious the next day.

MAKES **4** SERVINGS

6

THE
MEDITERRANEAN
SECRET

An Easy-Going Cuisine that Protects Against Cancer, Heart Disease, and Infections

*T*i *voglio bene* . . . is the way Italians say "I love you." Yet its literal meaning, "I wish you well," extends beyond personal intimacy to embrace happiness, health, and the whole goodness of life. This phrase seems to me to be inextricably woven into the Italian lifestyle, where "food is love" assumes more importance than "a diamond is forever."

Other countries besides Italy to which nutritionists usually refer when they use the term *Mediterranean diet* are Greece, coastal Spain, and the south of France. (Additionally, North Africa has had its influence on Southern Italian fare, adding nuts and raisins to savory fillings and citrus to meats, and inspiring other delicious concoctions.)

In all these "Mediterranean diet" countries, the same theme abounds around family tables; love is expressed in the pleasurable, relaxed, and unhurried sharing of vegetables, fruits, fish, grains, beans, and wine that Mediterranean coastal regions provide in abundance. Now that scientists are looking at the Mediterranean diet as a model for the world, those who adopt it may enjoy even more health benefits if they could include the warm, easy-going, yet hard-working lifestyle with the pasta, beans, and fish stew.

NUTRITIONISTS "DISCOVER" THE MEDITERRANEAN DIET

Revelations about the Mediterranean diet began in the late 1950s when nutrition expert Dr. Ancel Keys—and a team of scientists from various countries—studied the relationship between diet and heart disease in what came to be called the Seven Countries Study. At the time, it was considered good science and sufficiently accurate to confine the study to male subjects. The comparative countries were Italy, Greece, the United States, Japan, Yugoslavia, Finland, and the Netherlands. All told, 14,000 men were involved, ages 40 through 59. The plan was to determine the actual incidence of coronary heart disease in contrasting populations. Case histories of 10,000 men were followed up at the end of ten years. The overwhelming conclusion was that the Mediterranean populations, although consuming a good percentage of their calories in fat, were enjoying unique protection from heart disease.

IT'S THE *KIND* OF FAT THAT COUNTS

These researchers had discovered a significant aspect of the Mediterranean secret—that it wasn't the *amount* but the *kind* of fat in the diet that predicted the risk of heart disease. For example, there were villages in Crete and southern Italy where calories might consist of 30 percent or more of fat from olive oil, but butter was virtually unheard of—and so was heart disease! Cholesterol figures ranged under 200. On the Costa del Sol in Spain, where eggs and shellfish were served plentifully but meat and milk were scarce, the incidence of heart attacks was still much lower than in the United States.

A GOOD WORD FOR EGGS

Ancel Keys concluded that it was not damaging for people with a blood cholesterol below 220 to eat three to four eggs a week, including in the count those eggs that are hidden in cooked dishes. (These are the same guidelines given by the American Heart Association today.)

It's important to remember that cholesterol and fat are not the same thing. Although eggs are high in cholesterol, the amount and type of fat you eat affects blood cholesterol more than the cholesterol in your food—called *dietary cholesterol.* Limiting your intake of saturated fats lowers blood cholesterol better than limiting dietary cholesterol. Fat is high in the American diet—37 percent of our calories—the largest portion of which comes from meat and whole-milk dairy products.

OLIVE OIL—THE GOLDEN HEART OF MEDITERRANEAN HEALTH

It's not that olive oil merely plays a passive part in not being damaging to the heart; Homer's "liquid gold" actually takes an active role in preventing heart disease. Olive oil (as well as other monounsaturated oils such as canola and some nut oils) lowers the damaging LDL cholesterol and raises the heart-healthy HDL cholesterol.

The more recent Italian Nine Communities Study on Atherosclerosis Risk Factors (this time with female subjects) also concluded that butter consumption increases cholesterol and olive oil decreases it. Although olive oil and most other fats have about 125 calories per tablespoon and 14 grams of fat, monounsaturated fats help to prevent the build-up of artery-clogging LDL cholesterol. The ideal would be to reduce the amount of fat in our typical American diet, and to make olive oil the fat of choice. (Other good choices are canola, walnut, and grapeseed oils.)

Some studies have indicated that olive oil even may lower

blood pressure, control blood sugar levels, and exert a radiopro-tective effect as well.

BESIDES LOVE AND OLIVE OIL, WHAT ELSE IS ON THE MENU?

In addition to a lavish helping of love and monounsaturated olive oil, the Mediterranean diet is characterized by the following: a frugality with meat and dairy products resulting in a low intake of animal fats; plentiful complex carbohyrate foods like pasta, beans, and bread; fresh vegetables and fruits galore; garlic and onions in practically everything. Fish, shellfish, poultry, eggs, cheese, and yogurt are the main sources of complete protein in those countries that border the Mediterranean. Wine is a staple beverage.

GARLIC AND ONIONS, FROM FOLK WISDOM TO MEDICAL FACT

Garlic and onions have enjoyed a reputation for being miracle healers since around 3000 B.C. in Babylonia and Egypt. It's doubt-ful if the pyramids would have been built to last the ages if the early Egyptians hadn't fed their workers garlic, onions, leeks, melons, barley, and fish. The Bible recounts that the Israelites, while wandering in the desert after their escape from Egypt, remembered those foods with nostalgic appreciation.

The fame of these two odoriferous relatives of the lily family moved onward through the ancient worlds of the Romans, Chi-nese, and Indians. The Greeks criticized garlic for being too com-mon, but fed it to their athletes as a stimulant. In China, onion tea was prescribed for fevers and infections. In India, garlic was used in an antiseptic wash. Throughout the generations, garlic has been credited with dispelling everything from worms and headaches to tumors and vampires.

Remedies that stand the test of time earn the right to be taken seriously. And it seems that time and scientific inquiry have not dimmed the luster of garlic, onions, and scallions—along with their upscale relatives, leeks and chives. Not only do these piquant flavor agents pep up one's culinary efforts but they also rev up the immune system against cancer and viral infections and stave off the risk of heart disease.

Garlic and its flavorful cousins contain a substance called *alliin*. Alliin is odorless, but when crushed, it exudes scores of aromatic substances, including a sulfur compound called *allicin* which can bring tears to the eyes. Nothing to cry about, allicin is antibacterial, antiviral, antifungal, and antitumor. (To keep your eye makeup intact, slice onions underwater or refrigerate them briefly before chopping.)

PUNGENT BULBS FOR CARDIOVASCULAR HEALTH

Garlic has been shown to lower LDL cholesterol and raise protective HDL cholesterol levels in humans. Substances in garlic keep the blood from being "sticky" and therefore liable to form clots, and, in addition, step up the clot-dissolving ability of the blood, thus helping in two ways to prevent strokes.

ALLIIN VEGETABLES VS. CANCER

Studies in China and Italy have indicated that those who eat the most alliin vegetables have the least incidence of stomach cancer. According to Dr. Terrance Leighton, chairman of microbiology and immunology at the University of California-Berkeley, onions and garlic contain "incredible levels" of one of the most powerful anticancer agents ever discovered. Called *quercetin*, this substance, which scientists are attempting to isolate, is also present in broccoli, squash, and other fruits and vegetables.

WORRIED ABOUT THAT ODOR?

Despite the many amazing properties of garlic and onion, we women often worry about exhaling that pungent odor toward those near and dear to us. Unfortunately, the beneficial effects of garlic are best obtained from fresh unprocessed garlic, and no breath sweetener can dispel the aroma of fresh garlic and/or onions until they have been digested. One solution is to enjoy these pungent bulbs *en famille* and feed them to everyone around you. (Don't forget the family pet, for garlic, along with Brewer's yeast, helps to discourage fleas.) Essence of garlic clinging to the cook's fingers, although resistant to mere soap, can be eliminated by rubbing briskly with a lemon wedge.

"TAKE TWO CLOVES ..."
WHAT EXACTLY IS THE PRESCRIPTION?

Guidance about just how much garlic is needed to defend against diseases, disorders, and evil spirits is contradictory—anywhere from half a clove to seven cloves a day. Most women are not going to be able to manage the high side of that recommendation, but a dish a day that includes a sautéed minced clove or two or three is perfectly possible if the Mediterranean diet is adopted.

WINE—CONTROVERSIAL HEART HELPER
OF THE MEDITERRANEAN RX

The most controversial part of the Mediterranean lifestyle, especially for women, is the drinking of wine.

First the good news. Much has been said and written about a phenomenon known as the French paradox. Although a high intake of saturated fat goes hand-in-hand with coronary heart disease in most countries, in France the situation is reversed. Their diet may be higher in saturated fat than in other Mediterranean countries (think of pâté de foie gras!), but mortality from heart disease is low in France compared to most countries outside the Mediterranean area. This has led researchers to take a closer look at the effects of wine drinking; and it's been found that the clotting ability of the blood, which is related to coronary heart disease, is reduced by wine. Also, red wine in particular raises the helpful HDL cholesterol; the active ingredient is thought to be a chemical called *resveratrol.*

A study of the effects of alcohol consumption on estrogen levels in postmenopausal women found that those levels were increased with moderate use, suggesting that this might prove to be a protective effect with respect to postmenopausal cardiovascular disease risk. (Before menopause, women enjoy some defense from heart disease because their bodies are producing heart-protecting estrogen.)

Now for the bad news. Women who drink over 1½ drinks a day may be increasing their risk of breast cancer. That's probably because the wine-induced increase in estrogen appears to promote the growth of breast tumors.

One study showed this effect only in premenopausal, not postmenopausal, women. Another study, by Dr. Terrance Leighton, in which laboratory rats were given high doses of alcohol in the form of red wine, did not show the same increase in breast cancer—possibly because red wine contains quercetin (mentioned previously in connection with garlic). It should be noted, however, that the results of any one study cannot be considered conclusive; future research into the alcohol-cancer connection should be carefully followed by women.

There is very strong evidence that consumption of alcohol by pregnant women can cause birth defects in their infants. Scientists are now trying to determine how much alcohol is safe to drink and at what point in the pregnancy the risk is greatest. They want to learn, for instance, if the risk is higher during the first month, or the first trimester . . . or if a single incidence of high alcohol consumption does as much damage as day-by-day imbibing.

In the meantime, the National Institute on Alcohol Abuse has warned that there is a definite risk of full fetal alcohol syndrome if a pregnant woman drinks 3 fluid ounces or more (two to six drinks) of alcohol a day—and other possible abnormalities involved for lesser amounts. Mothers who drink even 1 ounce or less of alcohol a day have been observed to have a higher rate of stillbirths and low-weight babies.

Apart from pregnancy, in deciding whether your Mediterranean fare is going to include a glass of wine, you may want to consider your family's individual medical history and, of course, discuss the matter with your physician.

To sum up these conflicting reports, it appears that heart disease—the greatest threat to women's health—is inhibited by alcohol, but women who drink may be at a 40 percent (or more) greater risk of breast cancer. It's possible that red wine may turn out to be exempt from this worrisome statistic, but the jury is still out.

That heart-protecting chemical resveratrol, by the way, is also found, in reduced amounts, in red grape juice; also in raisins that *haven't* been sun-dried (check the label). Resveratrol is produced by the fruit to ward off disease; regrettably, grapes grown for the table don't produce very much of it.

A DIET THAT'S RICH IN FLAVOR AND SUBSTANCE

The Mediterranean diet's other gloriously healthy, delicious, and satisfying foods—fish, vegetables, fruits, beans, and pasta—are covered in more detail in other chapters in this book. The potent combination produces a fresh, fast, homestyle (not high-style) cuisine that seems to be popular with everyone.

Menus and recipes for Mediterranean supermeals follow. *Buon' Appetito!*

Mediterranean Superfoods

Artichokes
Beans, lentils, peas, and
  green beans
Broccoli
Cabbage
Citrus fruits
Eggplant
Figs
Fish and shellfish
Garlic, onions, leeks,
  scallions, chives
Grapes and wine, raisins
Greens, dark leafy: spinach,
  broccoli rabe, chicory,
  dandelions

Melons
Mozzarella cheese and
  ricotta (part-skim)
Mushrooms
Nuts: almonds, walnuts,
  chestnuts
Okra
Olive oil
Pasta
Peaches
Peppers
Tomatoes

MEDITERRANEAN QUICKIES

From the antipasto salad bar: chickpeas, Roman beans, marinated artichoke hearts, stuffed mushrooms, roasted peppers, tuna, part-skim mozzarella (skip the salty cheese and salami)

A bowl of Italian chicken soup with escarole

White bean salad with chopped onion, olive oil, and vinegar

Broccoli salad with lemon juice, olive oil, and hot pepper

A plate of Spanish garlic soup (sautéed garlic and toasted bread with chicken broth poured over)

A slice of pizza made with part-skim mozzarella

Chunked tomatoes, onions, garlic, basil, and olive oil (as a salad or as an uncooked pasta sauce)

A Greek salad with whole wheat pita bread

Melon with fresh or dried figs

HEALTH-BUILDING MEDITERRANEAN SUPERMEALS

Recipes indicated by a ♦ follow the menus.

FAST AND FRESH PASTA 'N' FISH FOR FOUR

Scallops with Tomato Pesto and Vermicelli♦
Broccoli with Oil and Lemon♦
Whole-Grain Italian Bread
Crustless Almond Pizza Dolce♦
or
Sliced Fresh Peaches with Toasted Almonds

*P*asta and fish may be the quintessential Mediterranean dinner! With heart-healthy benefits derived from fish and complex carbohydrates offered by pasta, it's a satisfying, nutritious combination (with literally hundreds of versions). Our menu adds five-star broccoli, and either ricotta for extra calcium or peaches for beta-carotene. Almonds are rich in vitamin E and several B vitamins.

Scallops with Tomato Pesto and Vermicelli

Superfoods: tomatoes, garlic, olive oil, scallops

For the tomato pesto

4 ripe tomatoes (1½ pounds)

2 cups loosely packed fresh basil
   leaves

1 large garlic clove, halved

¼ cup olive oil

½ teaspoon salt

Freshly ground pepper

1 pound vermicelli, cooked
   according to package
   directions

For the scallops

1½ pounds sea scallops

⅓ cup seasoned dry bread crumbs

3 tablespoons cornmeal

2 tablespoons olive oil, or more

1 pound vermicelli, cooked
   according to package
   directions

Pour boiling water over the tomatoes; let them stand 5 minutes. Drain, peel, seed, and finely dice the tomatoes.

Make the pesto. Mince the basil leaves (this is most easily done in a food processor); they should be reduced to ½ cup. Combine the basil with the tomatoes and the remaining pesto ingredients. Allow the pesto to marinate at room temperature for 30 minutes, stirring occasionally. Remove the garlic before using.

The pesto can be made several hours in advance. Store, covered, in the refrigerator. Bring to room temperature before combining with the vermicelli.

Prepare the scallops. Rinse and drain the scallops well, cutting any extra-large ones in half. Mix the crumbs and cornmeal in a plastic bag. Shake with the scallops to coat them. Shake off excess coating. Refrigerate until ready to cook.

Heat the oil in a large skillet until it's very hot (shimmering). Lower heat to medium, and brown the scallops on both sides, loosening with a spatula frequently, 5 to 7 minutes. Add more oil if needed. Check a large scallop for doneness; it should separate easily when halved with a fork.

Mix the hot vermicelli with the pesto in a serving dish; a platter works best. Put the scallops on top.

MAKES 4 SERVINGS

Broccoli with Oil and Lemon

SUPERFOODS: broccoli, olive oil, lemon juice

Served warm, at room temperature, or chilled, this is one of our favorite broccoli dishes—and its simplicity is typical of the fast, fresh Italian way with vegetables.

1 bunch broccoli (about 1 pound)	About ¼ teaspoon hot red pepper
1½ teaspoons salt	flakes (optional)
3 to 4 tablespoons olive oil	Juice of 1 lemon

Wash the broccoli well, and trim off the tough ends of the stalks, leaving about 3 inches. Peel the remaining stalks. If they are thick, cut them lengthwise into thinner stalks (½ inch wide) with florets attached.

Bring a large pot of water to a rapid boil. Add the salt and broccoli. So much cold vegetable will stop the boiling for a minute or two; count the cooking time from the water's second boil. Cook the broccoli only 2 to 3 minutes or until barely tender-crisp.

Meanwhile, have ready a large bowl of ice water. Scoop out the broccoli and plunge it into the ice water. When it is cool to the touch, drain it well, and put it into a flat serving dish. Dress it with the oil and red pepper, if using; try to scatter the red pepper evenly so that no fiery surprises will lurk among the florets.

Just before serving, pour the lemon juice over all, and turn the broccoli over in the dressing. (Lemon juice added too early discolors the broccoli.)

MAKES 4 SERVINGS

Crustless Almond Pizza Dolce

SUPERFOODS: ricotta, almonds

A rich-tasting dessert you can put together in a few minutes. With a recipe this easy to double, it's a great choice for company; bake in two pie plates or a 9 × 13-inch cake pan.

1 tablespoon fine dry, unflavored
   bread crumbs
1½ pounds whole-milk ricotta
3 eggs
½ cup sugar
½ teaspoon natural almond
   flavoring

2 tablespoons candied citron
2 tablespoons candied orange
   rind
6 candied cherries, chopped
½ cup slivered almonds

Preheat the oven to 325 degrees F. Butter a 9-inch glass pie pan or quiche dish. Scatter bread crumbs over the bottom and sides.

Cream the ricotta in a food processor or by hand. Blend in the eggs, sugar, and flavoring. Stir in the fruit. Spoon the mixture into the prepared pan, smooth the top, and scatter the almonds over all.

Bake for 45 to 50 minutes or until the pie is set 1 inch from the center. Cool completely before cutting.

MAKES 6 TO 8 SLICES

SUMMER DINNER UNDER THE STARS
FOR FOUR OR SIX

Grilled Bruschetta with Walnut Pesto♦
Herb-Marinated Grilled Tuna♦
My Mother's Potato Salad♦
Sautéed Green Peppers and Mushrooms
Fresh Fruit Bowl
Amaretti (Italian Almond Cookies)

The convenient pepper and mushroom sauté, which can be served at any temperature, is typically Italian. Emphasizing fresh produce, especially tomatoes and peppers, Mediterranean menus are generally abundant in vitamin C. And, more often than not, fresh fruit is the dessert of choice. Our menu adds tuna, rich in selenium as well as omega-3 fatty acids, and walnuts, rich in folate.

Grilled Bruschetta with Walnut Pesto

SUPERFOODS: tomato, walnuts, garlic, olive or walnut oil

This makes an easy-going outdoor appetizer when you're getting ready to grill the main course. Second choice to grilling: toast the bread under a broiler instead of in a toaster. Watch it carefully!

4 to 6 slices Italian bread,   1 large ripe tomato, peeled,
* preferably whole wheat   seeded, and finely chopped*
Walnut Pesto (recipe follows)

Grill or toast the bread slices. Spread them with pesto. Top each with a tablespoon of peeled, chopped tomato. Serve immediately.

WALNUT PESTO

Leftover pesto makes a heavenly topping for baked potatoes.

½ cup walnut pieces   ¼ teaspoon freshly ground black
2 garlic cloves, peeled   pepper
2 cups fresh basil leaves, main   About ½ cup virgin olive oil (or
* stems removed   use part walnut oil)*
½ teaspoon salt   ¼ cup freshly grated Parmesan
*   cheese*

Blanch the walnuts in boiling water for 1 minute to remove bitterness. Drain.

Rinse and thoroughly dry the basil leaves.

In a food processor fitted with the steel blade, with the motor running, toss the garlic down the feed tube to mince it.

Stop the motor. Add the basil, walnuts, salt, and pepper. Process until very finely chopped.

With the motor running, slowly pour the oil down the feed tube in a thin stream until the mixture reaches a pastelike consistency, neither too thick to drop off a spoon nor runny.

Transfer the pesto to a bowl, and stir in the cheese.

The pesto can be made 2 to 3 days ahead. Cover with plastic wrap so that it touches the entire surface of the pesto, and store in the refrigerator (it will keep a week, but is best used sooner). Leftover pesto can be frozen for longer storage.

MAKES 4 TO 6 SERVINGS

Herb-Marinated Grilled Tuna

SUPERFOODS: tuna

More vinegar than oil in this marinade gives a refreshing tang to an otherwise oily fish.

4 to 6 serving-size tuna fillets
(about 6 ounces each), ¾ to 1
inch thick
⅓ cup white wine vinegar
2 tablespoons olive oil

1 tablespoon minced shallots
1 tablespoon each chopped fresh
sage and thyme*
¼ teaspoon freshly ground black
pepper

Rinse the fillets and pat them dry. Mix the remaining ingredients. In a deep platter, marinate the fish in this mixture for at least 2 hours in the refrigerator, turning occasionally and gently rubbing the herbs into the fish.

Oil the grill bars. Grill the fish steaks over ash-gray coals or medium-high gas (or broil in an oiled broiling pan in the oven) 4 to 5 minutes per side. The fish should flake apart when pressed with the back of a fork.

MAKES 4 TO 6 SERVINGS

*Or substitute ½ teaspoon *each* dried tarragon, cilantro, and thyme leaves (since only the ground sage is available, not the dried leaves. Unless, of course, you grow and dry your own sage).

My Mother's Potato Salad

SUPERFOODS: potatoes, onion, olive oil, parsley

2 pounds large new potatoes
1 tablespoon white vinegar
1 teaspoon salt
2 tablespoons red wine vinegar
¼ cup chopped red onion
⅓ cup olive oil

1 tablespoon minced fresh flat-
  leaf parsley
½ teaspoon dried oregano,
  or more
Salt and pepper

Wash the potatoes well and put them into a large pot with the white vinegar, 1 teaspoon salt, and water to cover. Bring to a boil, reduce heat, and simmer until tender but not mushy, about 20 minutes for large whole potatoes.

Drain the potatoes. When cool enough to handle, peel and dice them into a large bowl. Sprinkle them with the wine vinegar. Add the onion and olive oil. The potatoes should be shiny throughout from the oil; if needed, add more. Add the parsley, oregano, salt, and pepper, tossing to blend.

The salad improves if chilled for several hours and can be made as much as a day ahead. Keep refrigerated.

Toss and taste to correct seasoning. Serve chilled or at room temperature.

MAKES 2 POUNDS

WINTER SUPPER FOR SIX IN THE KITCHEN

Winter Minestrone♦
Oven-Fried Eggplant Sticks♦
Whole-Grain Italian Bread
Assorted Nuts and Tangerines

A hefty minestrone can be considered a meal in itself. Plenty of cancer-preventive vegetables in this one—onion, garlic, carrots, cabbage, beans, plus a side dish of eggplant. And the same vegetables are a pretty good defense against winter's cold and flu, too! The menu is rounded out with B vitamins and vitamin E in the whole-grain bread, to protect against stress, and healing vitamin C in the tangerines.

Winter Minestrone

SUPERFOODS: onion, garlic, tomatoes, carrots, cabbage, beans, pasta

Minestrone *means "big soup," and this one certainly qualifies! I love the way it fills the kitchen with warm steam and a delicious aroma while cooking, yet it requires little attention. Just the thing to have on the simmer while watching the Super Bowl or Gone With the Wind.*

1 tablespoon olive oil

1 pound stewing beef, trimmed of fat

1 large onion, chopped

1 celery stalk with leaves, chopped

1 large garlic clove, chopped

One 1-pound can Italian tomatoes with basil

2 quarts water

½ teaspoon salt

¼ teaspoon pepper

2 medium carrots, scraped and sliced

2 cups shredded green cabbage

1 cup canned kidney beans, rinsed

1 cup tubettini or 1½ cups penne, cooked according to package directions

2 tablespoons chopped fresh flat-leaf parsley

In a large pot, heat the oil and brown the meat well on all sides. You want plenty of browned bits to give a rich color to the soup. Add the onion, celery, and garlic—plus a bit more oil if necessary—and cook until the vegetables are sizzling, about 2 minutes. Add the tomatoes, water, salt, and pepper. Skim off any gray froth that rises to the surface. Simmer with cover ajar for about 2 hours.

Add the carrots, cabbage, and beans. Simmer until the carrots are tender, about 10 minutes.

The soup can be made to this point 1 to 2 days ahead. Keep refrigerated. Extras can be frozen.

Taste to correct seasoning; you may want more salt. Add the cooked macaroni and parsley; reheat if necessary.

MAKES ABOUT 2½ QUARTS

Oven-Fried Eggplant Sticks

SUPERFOODS: eggplant, wheat germ

A low-fat but flavorful way of cooking eggplant.

1 *medium eggplant*	2 *tablespoons* each *wheat germ*
2 *tablespoons olive oil*	and *grated Parmesan cheese*
⅓ *cup seasoned dry bread crumbs*	

Peel and slice the eggplant crosswise, ½ inch thick. Salt the slices, and let them drain in a colander for 30 minutes to 1 hour. Rinse off the salt, and gently press the moisture out of the slices in a towel.

Preheat the oven to 375 degrees F. Line a baking sheet with foil.

Cut the eggplant slices into sticks similar in size to French fries. Put them into a bowl and toss them with the oil.

Combine the crumbs, wheat germ, and cheese in a plastic bag. Add the eggplant sticks, and shake to coat them with the mixture. Place them in a single layer on the prepared sheet.

The recipe can be prepared in advance to this point. Refrigerate until needed.

Bake the eggplant sticks for 15 to 20 minutes (longer if refrigerated), until golden and tender. If you wish, you can make them crisper and browner by broiling under a heated broiler for 2 to 3 minutes.

MAKES ABOUT 6 SERVINGS

A SPANISH LUNCHEON FOR FOUR

Gazpacho in a Jiffy♦
Spanish Potato Omelet♦
Peas Braised in Lettuce Leaves♦
Crusty Whole-Grain Rolls
Lemon Sherbet with Fresh Mint Sprigs

A Mediterranean favorite and one of nature's small powerhouses of nutrition, peas are a source of calcium, iron, vitamins A, C, and E, plus B vitamins thiamin and folate—and they're rich in fiber, too! Plenty more vitamin C in the refreshing cold soup, along with a shot of infection-fighting garlic in both soup and omelet— and cancer-fighting protease inhibitors in the potatoes.

Gazpacho in a Jiffy

SUPERFOODS: garlic, green pepper, tomatoes

1 garlic clove
½ green bell pepper
1 cucumber
1½ pounds ripe tomatoes
One 5-ounce can tomato juice
1 cup chicken broth
2 tablespoons olive oil
1 tablespoon chopped fresh
   cilantro, or 1 teaspoon dried

¾ teaspoon salt
½ teaspoon to 1 teaspoon hot
   pepper sauce
¼ teaspoon Spicy Pepper Mix (see
   page 539) or black pepper
Chopped scallions and crumbled
   feta cheese or grated
   Monterey Jack for garnish

Prepare the vegetables. Peel the garlic. Cut the green pepper into strips. Seed the cucumber and cut it into fourths. Cut the tomatoes in half lengthwise and scrape out the seeds with a grapefruit spoon; no need to peel them.

With the motor running, drop the garlic down the feed tube of a food processor. Add the green pepper, cucumber, and tomato, and stop the motor the instant they are coarsely chopped.

Add to the work bowl all the remaining ingredients except the scallions and cheese. Process just briefly. The vegetables should be very finely minced but not pureed. Chill the soup to develop its flavor. Serve ice cold, garnished with scallions and cheese. (Aternatively, all this fine chopping and mincing can be done by hand, as it certainly was in earlier generations.)

The soup can be made a day in advance. Store, covered, in the refrigerator.

MAKES 1 QUART

Gazpacho with Corn: Stir in a cup of frozen corn kernels, which will thaw as the soup marinates in the refrigerator. Or if you happen to obtain some very young, very tender fresh corn, you can use raw kernels cut from 1 to 2 ears.

Spanish Potato Omelet

SUPERFOODS: onion, garlic, potato

2 medium to large potatoes	*Salt*
2 tablespoons olive oil	*Freshly ground black pepper*
1 small onion, diced	*6 eggs**
1 garlic clove, minced	*1 tablespoon water*

Peel and slice the potatoes. Cook them in salted boiling water until tender, 5 to 8 minutes. Drain well and pat dry with a towel.

Heat 1½ tablespoons of the oil in a 10-inch skillet, preferably nonstick. Sauté the onion and garlic until translucent but not brown, about 3 minutes. Mix in the potatoes, salt and pepper them to your taste, and flatten them into a neat layer with a spatula. Let them fry for about 5 minutes, stirring and flattening again.

Beat the eggs with the water, and pour them over the potatoes. Cook over very low heat until the egg has set, lifting the edges from time to time to let the uncooked portion seep underneath.

To invert, loosen the entire omelet with a spatula. Place a large plate over it, and turn the pan and plate together.

Put the pan back on the heat, add the remaining ½ tablespoon of oil, and slide the omelet back into the pan to brown on the second side, which will take only 1 or 2 minutes. Cut into wedges and serve immediately.

MAKES 4 SERVINGS

*¾ cup prepared egg substitute can be used in place of half the eggs. Use 3 whole eggs for the other half of the mixture.

Peas Braised in Lettuce Leaves

SUPERFOODS: peas

*1½ cups shelled fresh peas (1½
pounds whole peas in shells),
or one 10-ounce package
frozen peas
1 tablespoon butter*

*4 romaine lettuce leaves
Pinch of dried thyme leaves
½ cup chicken broth*

If using frozen peas, thaw just to separate them in a strainer under cold running water.

Melt the butter in a medium saucepan. Tear the romaine leaves into large pieces and put them in the bottom of the pan. Add the peas and thyme. Pour the broth over all.

Cover and cook over very low heat until the peas are tender, 5 to 8 minutes for frozen peas, 8 to 10 minutes for tender fresh peas, or more for mature peas—braising takes a bit longer than boiling. Taste one to test.

Most of the broth should evaporate, but take care that it doesn't boil out completely during the braising.

MAKES 4 SERVINGS

Peas with Ham: ½ pound chopped ham is often added to braised peas.

A MEATLESS MENU FOR FOUR

Red Lentil Soup with Parsley Pesto◆
Broccoli Rabe Pie◆
Eggplant Salad◆
Crusty Whole-Grain Bread
Almond-Stuffed Figs Dusted with Cocoa Sugar◆

Cruciferous vegetables, like broccoli rabe, are a regular feature of Mediterranean fare, and eggs and/or legumes are often substituted for meat. Heart-helping fiber in the lentils and anticancer compounds in the eggplant and figs round out this ''defensive'' menu.

Red Lentil Soup with Parsley Pesto

SUPERFOODS: onion, garlic, tomatoes, lentils, parsley

2 tablespoons olive oil
1 large onion, chopped
1 celery stalk with leaves, diced
1 to 2 garlic cloves, minced
1 cup chopped tomatoes, fresh or
  canned
6 cups water

1 cup red lentils, picked over and
  washed
1 teaspoon dried cilantro
½ teaspoon salt
¼ teaspoon pepper
4 to 6 teaspoons Parsley Pesto (see
  page 527)*

*Finely minced parsley can be substituted.

Heat the oil in a large pot. Sauté the onion, celery, and garlic until they are softened but not brown. Add the tomatoes, and sauté for 5 minutes.

Add all the remaining ingredients except the pesto. Cook the soup, with cover ajar, stirring occasionally, for 1 hour. Whisk the soup to puree it, or use a food processor (in 2 batches, since hot foods foam up).

Stir a teaspoon of parsley pesto into each serving.

Makes about 5 cups

Broccoli Rabe Pie

Superfoods: whole wheat flour, broccoli rabe, pine nuts, raisins

This is just the kind of dish in which it's actually easier to use an egg substitute—and because the rabe and cheese are strong flavors, the substitution goes unnoticed. Even if you're not watching cholesterol, an egg substitute is a handy item to have around, if only for those times you run out of eggs. The substitute can be frozen for long storage.

1 tablespoon olive oil
1¼ cups fresh whole wheat bread crumbs*
1 cup cooked broccoli rabe, well drained
¼ cup pine nuts
2 tablespoons raisins
4 eggs or 1 cup prepared egg substitute

½ cup plain nonfat yogurt
1 tablespoon cornstarch
Freshly ground black pepper
½ cup coarsely grated Asiago or Gruyère cheese
4 large cherry tomatoes, halved (optional)

*1 whole wheat roll or 2 slices bread, crumbed in the food processor.

Preheat the oven to 350 degrees F. Use the olive oil to grease a 9-inch pie pan or a springform pan.

Lightly toast the bread crumbs in a toaster oven or under the broiler. Spread the sides and bottom of the prepared pan with slightly more than half the crumbs.

Chop the broccoli rabe and mix it with the nuts and raisins. Spread the mixture in the pan without disturbing the crumbs.

Beat together the egg, yogurt, cornstarch, pepper, and cheese. Pour the egg mixture evenly over the greens. Sprinkle the remaining crumbs on top.

Arrange the cherry tomato halves, rounded side up, so that there will be a half in each wedge of the finished pie.

Bake for 30 minutes on the middle shelf of the oven or until set. Cool 10 minutes. Serve cut into wedges, warm or at room temperature. Refrigerate leftovers.

MAKES 8 WEDGES; 4 SERVINGS

Eggplant Salad

SUPERFOODS: eggplant, olive oil, garlic, parsley

2 cups Oven-Sautéed Eggplant
  (see page 522)
⅓ cup red wine vinegar
1 tablespoon finely minced fresh
  flat-leaf parsley

½ teaspoon dried oregano
Hot red pepper flakes
½ cup walnut pieces

Toss all the ingredients to blend well, and let the salad stand at room temperature about 30 minutes before serving. Taste to correct seasoning; you may want more vinegar or pepper.

The salad can be made 1 day ahead. Keep refrigerated, then bring to room temperature.

MAKES 4 SERVINGS

Almond-Stuffed Figs Dusted with Cocoa Sugar

SUPERFOODS: figs, almonds, oranges

Just a hint of chocolate! Intensely sweet (but nutritious) treats like this are great for satisfying that candy-bar craving.

You could, of course, buy the almond paste—but if you have a food processor, do try making it just to see how easy it is! A bag of slivered almonds in the freezer is always ready for adding crunch (plus folate, niacin, and vitamin E) to vegetables and desserts—or for whipping up an almond paste, a favorite ingredient in many a delectable dessert.

*12 soft dried figs, such as
   Calimyrna
About ¼ cup Almond Paste (see
   page 536)*

*Cocoa Sugar (see page 540)
Orange slices for garnish*

Preheat the oven to 350 degrees F.

Trim off the tough little stems from the figs, and cut them down one side. Press the slits open, and stuff each one with about a teaspoon of the almond paste. Gently press them shut and put them into a baking dish. Add ¼ cup water to the dish.

Bake the figs for 15 minutes—they will darken slightly.

Roll them while they are warm in the cocoa sugar. Put them into a serving dish, and sift more cocoa sugar over all. Chill the figs. Before serving, garnish them with orange slices.

MAKES 12

DINNER ON THE PORCH A LA GRECQUE
FOR FOUR

Penne with Tomato-Yogurt Sauce♦
Swordfish Kebabs with Peppers♦
Green Bean Salad à la Grecque♦
Whole Wheat Pita Bread
Fruit and Dates♦

This relaxed collection of recipes is rich in vitamin C in the tomatoes, peppers, and fruit, calcium in the yogurt and cheese, fiber in the green beans and whole wheat, plus, of course, the marvelous heart benefits from swordfish: omega-3 fatty acids, niacin, and selenium.

Penne with Tomato-Yogurt Sauce

SUPERFOODS: tomato, garlic, yogurt, pasta

1½ cups diced ripe tomato
1 tablespoon minced fresh
    oregano, or 1 teaspoon dried
1 garlic clove, pressed in a garlic
    press
¼ teaspoon salt
Freshly ground black pepper

1 cup thickened plain nonfat
    yogurt (see page 534)
½ pound penne or ziti, cooked
    according to package
    directions
½ cup grated Parmesan cheese

Mix the tomato, oregano, garlic, salt, and pepper. Let stand at room temperature for 15 minutes. Stir in the yogurt, and let stand while cooking the pasta.

Toss the pasta with the tomato-yogurt mixture and the grated cheese, and serve at once.

Leftovers should not be rewarmed. Instead, refrigerate the extra portion, then bring it back to room temperature before serving.

MAKES 4 SERVINGS AS A SIDE DISH

Swordfish Kebabs with Peppers

SUPERFOODS: swordfish, peppers

1½ pounds swordfish steak
3 bell peppers of different colors
  (green, red, yellow)
Juice of 1 lemon
¼ cup olive oil

1 teaspoon mixed dried
  marjoram and thyme leaves
Salt and freshly ground black
  pepper

Cut the swordfish into 1-inch cubes. Seed and core the peppers; cut them into chunks.

Thread the swordfish and peppers evenly on four 15-inch skewers. Lay the skewers in a platter or baking dish. Whisk together the lemon juice, oil, and herbs, and brush the mixture on both sides of the kebabs. Salt and pepper the kebabs to your taste. Refrigerate until ready to cook them, turning occasionally and brushing with the marinade.

The kebabs can be made ahead and will be more flavorful from having marinated for 2 hours or more. Keep refrigerated.

Brush the kebabs again with any marinade that has collected in the platter. Grill or broil the kebabs about 5 minutes, until the fish is firm and just cooked through.

To serve, unthread each skewer onto a warm dinner plate.

MAKES 4 SERVINGS

Green Bean Salad à la Grecque

SUPERFOODS: walnuts, green beans, lemon juice, olive oil

½ cup walnut halves
⅓ cup Kalamata olives, pitted
3 cups whole green beans, fresh
* or frozen, cooked*

About ½ cup Greek-Style Salad
* Dressing (see page 529)*
4 ounces feta cheese, crumbled

In a small saucepan, cover the walnuts with water and bring the mixture to a boil. Drain the walnuts. (This will remove any bitter flavor from the walnut skins. For another kind of dish, you might want to toast the walnuts after blanching, but for this marinated salad it's not necessary.)

Pit the olives. To do this the easy way, place a few olives on a bread board and hit them with the side of a wide knife— carefully or they'll fly all over the kitchen! Squeeze out the pits.

Combine the walnuts, olives, and green beans in a salad dish. Add ½ cup dressing, and let the salad stand at room temperature for 30 minutes to 1 hour, stirring occasionally. Taste to correct dressing, adding more dressing if needed.

Top with feta cheese, and serve with whole wheat pita bread.

MAKES 4 TO 6 SERVINGS

Fruit and Dates

This is simply a combination of fresh and dried fruits composed on chilled dessert plates. You might choose to use a few cherries, a halved apricot, and a slice of seedless watermelon, garnished with pitted dates. It's interesting to note that people who will not ordinarily help themselves to a fruit bowl will nevertheless enjoy (and consume!) this kind of attractive presentation. (Also, think about making a platterful for yourself when you're alone. Keep the dish refrigerated, covered with plastic wrap, and ready for the next snack attack!)

FARM-STYLE DINNER A LA FRANÇAIS FOR FOUR

Sauté de Veau Chasseur♦ (Hunter's Veal Stew)
Beet, Potato, and Chicory Salad♦
Whole Wheat French Bread
Apple "Cream" Tart à la Normande♦

These lighter versions of classic French dishes enhance the basic good nutrition of provincial Mediterranean fare. Beets and artichokes are rich in folate, a healthy-birth vitamin; potatoes and mushrooms contain compounds that protect against cancer; apples and whole wheat are sources of soluble and insoluble fiber, respectively; and nonfat yogurt in the pie adds calcium.

Sauté de Veau Chasseur

(Hunter's Veal Stew)

SUPERFOODS: artichoke hearts, olive oil, shallots, mushrooms, tomatoes

A great make-ahead dish for easy entertaining. In Italy, a similar hunter's stew would be called cacciatore.

1½ pounds stewing veal
¼ cup all-purpose flour
3 tablespoons olive oil
6 shallots, minced (½ cup)
8 ounces mushrooms, cleaned
   and sliced
1 cup seeded, chopped tomatoes
   (4 plum tomatoes)
1½ cups chicken broth, or more
   as needed

½ cup dry vermouth or white
   wine
Scant ½ teaspoon dried thyme
   leaves
¼ teaspoon salt
⅛ teaspoon pepper
One 10-ounce package frozen
   artichoke hearts, separated
1 tablespoon minced fresh flat-
   leaf parsley

Trim the veal of any gristle or fat; if necessary, cut it into uniform chunks. Put the veal into a plastic bag with the flour, and shake to coat the meat. Shake off excess flour. Heat 2 tablespoons of the oil in a 12-inch skillet. Brown the veal well in the hot oil.

Add the remaining tablespoon of oil and the shallots and mushrooms to the skillet. Sauté 2 to 3 minutes. Add the tomatoes, and simmer 5 minutes.

Add 1 cup of the broth, the wine, thyme, salt, and pepper. Simmer, covered, stirring occasionally, for 1 hour, until the veal is tender, adding more broth as needed to maintain a cup of gravy, which will be thickened by the flour on the veal.

Taste to correct seasoning. You may want more salt and pepper. *The recipe can be made to this point 1 day ahead and reheated in a skillet or microwave.*

Add the artichokes and simmer, covered, until they are tender, 8 to 10 minutes. Stir in the parsley and serve.

MAKES 4 SERVINGS

Beet, Potato, and Chicory Salad

SUPERFOODS: beets, potatoes, olive oil, chicory

Another make-ahead dish to tuck into the refrigerator!

One 1-pound can baby beets, drained
1¼ pounds baby new potatoes, cooked and peeled*
1 tablespoon Dijon mustard
2 tablespoons white wine vinegar

¼ cup olive oil
1 tablespoon each chopped fresh chives and fresh dill
Several well-washed chicory leaves

Combine the beets and potatoes in a bowl. Whisk together the mustard and vinegar; slowly add the oil while continuing to whisk. Stir in the herbs. Toss the salad with the dressing. Marinate at least 1 hour in the refrigerator.

The salad can be made to this point 1 day ahead. Keep refrigerated.

Line 4 to 6 salad plates with chicory torn into bite-size pieces. Divide the beet-potato mixture among the plates.

MAKES 4 SERVINGS

*Or larger new potatoes, cut to the same size as the beets.

Apple "Cream" Tart à la Normande

SUPERFOODS: apples, yogurt

And not a bit of heavy cream in it!

*Pastry for a 9-inch single-crust
  pie (see page 538)*

For the filling

5 cooking apples (not McIntosh;
  2 to 2¼ pounds)
1 tablespoon white vinegar
1 cup plain nonfat yogurt
1 egg, beaten, or ¼ cup prepared
  egg substitute

⅔ cup sugar
2 tablespoons cornstarch
1 to 2 tablespoons Calvados
  (apple brandy; optional)
½ teaspoon ground cinnamon

For the topping

¼ cup sugar
2 tablespoons all-purpose flour
¼ teaspoon ground cinnamon

1 tablespoon butter or
  margarine, softened

Preheat the oven to 350 degrees F. Roll out the pastry to fit a
9-inch pie pan, and flute the edge. Chill the pastry while preparing the filling.

Peel and thinly slice the apples into a bowl of cold water to
which you've added a tablespoon of vinegar.

Whisk together and blend well the remaining filling ingredients.

In a separate small bowl, mix the topping dry ingredients;
blend in the butter with your fingertips.

Assemble the pie. Drain the apples well and mix them with the yogurt filling. Spoon the filling into the prepared pie shell, and smooth it level and even. Sprinkle the topping over all.

Bake the pie on the middle shelf for 1 to 1¼ hours, until the apples are tender and the filling is set. Cool completely on a wire rack before slicing.

The pie is best served the same day as it's made. Refrigerate leftovers.

MAKES 6 TO 8 SLICES

A SICILIAN COLD SUPPER FOR SIX

Baked Tomatoes with Rice♦
Turkey Fillet with Tuna Sauce♦
Wheat Berry and Tubettini Salad♦
Macedonia di Frutta (Italian Fruit Salad)♦

Turkey is an especially nutritious source of protein, rich in iron, phosphorous, zinc, and a number of B vitamins. Whole wheat, too, offers B vitamins plus vitamin E. Tuna adds those important omega-3 fatty acids and selenium. The dinner is rounded out with carotenoids in the tomatoes, and a burst of vitamins A and C in the dessert.

Baked Tomatoes with Rice

SUPERFOODS: tomatoes, olive oil, garlic, rice

Unbelievably delicious and easy for a dish with so few ingredients, making it typically Italian. Besides serving these fragrant tomatoes at room temperature as light picnic fare, they can be served warm as a side dish at dinner.

6 large ripe tomatoes	¼ teaspoon salt
3 tablespoons olive oil	Several grinds of black pepper
1 garlic clove, pressed in a garlic press or finely minced	6 large fresh basil leaves
9 tablespoons raw arborio rice	

Preheat the oven to 375 degrees F.

Cut the tops off the tomatoes, and reserve them. Scoop out the seeds and juicy pulp into a wire-meshed strainer set over a bowl. Squeeze it with your hands to extract as much juice as possible. Discard the solids.

Mix 1 tablespoon olive oil, the garlic, rice, salt, and pepper into the juice. Blend well to distribute the garlic evenly.

Put a leaf of basil into the bottom of each hollow tomato. Divide the rice mixture among the tomatoes; they'll be about half full of rice and juice. If necessary, add water to reach the halfway mark. Put the tops on as lids, and stand the tomatoes in a baking dish that will hold them upright. Drizzle the remaining tablespoon of olive oil over the tops.

Bake the tomatoes uncovered for 30 minutes. Remove the dish from the oven and, gently lifting the side of each top with a fork, baste the filling with some of the accumulated juices in the dish. Return the dish to the oven and bake 20 to 30 minutes longer, until the rice swells to fill the tomatoes.

The tomatoes can be baked 1 day ahead. Keep refrigerated.

MAKES 6 SERVINGS

Turkey Fillet with Tuna Sauce

SUPERFOODS: turkey, carrots, olive oil, tuna

Turkey tenderloins replace the boned, rolled veal in this classic cold supper dish.

2 turkey tenderloins (about ¾ pound each)*
2 cups (a 13-ounce can) chicken broth
½ cup dry vermouth or white wine
1 small onion, peeled and sliced
2 carrots, scraped and sliced
One 6-ounce can Italian tuna packed in oil, drained

½ cup Lemon-Garlic Mayonnaise (see page 528)
¼ teaspoon hot pepper sauce or to taste
2 teaspoons drained capers
Pitted black olives
Drained anchovies (optional)

Combine the turkey, broth, wine, onion, and carrots in a large saucepan, bring to a boil, and lower heat to barely simmer the turkey fillets for 20 to 25 minutes (allow 10 minutes more if you substitute a single piece of the breast). Cool the turkey slightly; refrigerate to finish cooling in the broth. *The turkey can be made 1 day ahead.*

In a food processor, puree the tuna until it's smooth; add the mayonnaise. The mixture should be pourable but not runny. If it seems too thick, blend in a tablespoon or two of the broth from the turkey. Remove the sauce to a bowl, and stir in the hot pepper sauce and capers. *The sauce can be made 1 day ahead. Keep refrigerated.*

*These are not cutlets, but whole pieces located under the breast; they are shaped something like a large sweet potato. Or use a 1½- to 2-pound piece of boneless, skinless turkey breast.

Slice the cold turkey at an angle, and lay the slices overlapping on a platter. Pour some of the sauce over the slices, and garnish the platter with the cold carrot slices from the broth, black olives, and anchovies, if using. (The leftover broth makes a nice small soup.)

Pass the remaining sauce at the table.

MAKES 6 SERVINGS

Wheat Berry and Tubettini Salad

SUPERFOODS: whole wheat berries, pasta, olive oil, red pepper, scallions

1 cup whole wheat berries*
1 cup tubettini (tiny tubes of pasta)
⅓ cup olive oil
3 tablespoons red wine vinegar
½ teaspoon salt
Several grindings of black pepper
1 cup diced fennel (anise), or 2 celery stalks with leaves, diced

1 red bell pepper, finely diced
4 scallions with green tops, chopped
2 tablespoons chopped fresh herbs: basil, oregano, or marjoram
⅔ cup crumbled ricotta salata**

Cook the wheat berries in a pot of salted water until they are tender, 1 to 1½ hours. Drain and rinse with cold water.

Cook the tubettini according to package directions. Drain and rinse in cold water.

*Available in whole-foods markets.
**This is a solid cheese, very similar to feta.

Combine the wheat berries and tubettini in a salad dish, and stir in the oil, vinegar, salt, and pepper.

Stir in the fennel or celery, red pepper, scallions, and herbs. *The recipe can be made to this point a day ahead. Keep refrigerated.*

Add the cheese. Taste to correct seasoning; you may want more oil, vinegar, salt, or pepper. Allow the salad to stand at room temperature for 30 minutes before serving.

MAKES ABOUT 2 QUARTS

Macedonia di Frutta

(Italian Fruit Salad)

Never the same dish twice, this creative recipe depends entirely on what fruits are in season. In summer, it's melons, peaches, nectarines, mangos, raspberries; in fall, pears, apples, oranges, seedless grapes, pineapple. In winter, cooked dried fruits such as apricots and figs and/or canned fruits such as peaches and pineapple might be added to apples and oranges. The fruit is cut larger than diced, roughly in 1-inch chunks.

Only a few rules apply: A little orange juice or white wine must be added to keep some fruits from turning brown. If you are using berries or sliced banana, add them just before serving.

Italian fruit salad is flavored with a jigger or two of maraschino liqueur (crème de almond), which gives it a rosy color and a delectable almond flavor. Or you can substitute maraschino cherries with some of their juice.

The salad can be made up to 1 day ahead without bananas and/or berries, but I think it tastes best when made the morning of the day it will be served. Keep refrigerated.

It's nearly impossible to make too much Macedonia di Frutta.

SIMPLE DELIGHTS FOR SIX

Salmon à la Turque♦
Roasted Baby Eggplant and Zucchini♦
Tabbouli♦
Sliced Crenshaw Melon

This delightful menu may not seem like "health food," but it's packed with nutrition! As an oily fish, salmon is especially rich in heart-protecting compounds. The calcium in yogurt helps to lower blood pressure. Spinach is rich in vitamin A, with the melon adding more carotenoids. Eggplant, garlic, and whole wheat add cancer defense.

Salmon à la Turque

SUPERFOODS: salmon, spinach, yogurt

The North African influence is felt everywhere in coastal Mediterranean cuisine.

2 tablespoon olive oil
¼ cup chopped shallots
1½ cups cooked and drained
  spinach
¼ cup chopped pitted black olives
2 pounds salmon fillets or steaks
2 teaspoons cornstarch

¼ teaspoon white pepper
Several dashes of grated nutmeg
Pinch of dried thyme leaves
1 cup Thickened Yogurt (see page
  534)
2 tablespoons grated Parmesan
  cheese

Heat the oil in a small skillet, and sauté the shallots until they are softened, about 2 minutes. Spread this mixture over the bottom of a baking dish that will fit the fish and from which you can serve. Layer the spinach and olives over the shallots; then add the fish.

Whisk the cornstarch, pepper, nutmeg, and thyme into the yogurt, and spread the mixture over the fish. Sprinkle everything with the Parmesan cheese.

The dish can be prepared to this point several hours ahead. Keep refrigerated.

Preheat the oven to 400 degrees F.

Bake the fish on the top shelf of the oven until it flakes apart when pressed with the back of fork, about 20 minutes (25 minutes if chilled).

MAKES 6 SERVINGS

Roasted Baby Eggplant and Zucchini

SUPERFOODS: olive oil, eggplant, red pepper, garlic

This easy dish can be served hot, cold, or at room temperature.

3 tablespoons olive oil	¼ teaspoon each dried oregano
5 baby eggplant*	and cilantro
4 small zucchini*	Salt and pepper
2 large red bell peppers	
6 garlic cloves, unpeeled, slightly	
crushed with a chef's knife	
or mallet	

Preheat the oven to 350 degrees F. Pour the oil into the large roasting pan.

Wash the eggplant and zucchini well, and pat dry. Trim off the eggplant stems, cut the vegetables in half lengthwise, and slash the flesh about ½ inch deep, 1 inch apart. Cut the zucchini in half lengthwise. Seed the peppers, and cut them into 8 strips each.

Put the eggplant and zucchini into the pan, and turn to coat all sides with the oil. Add the red peppers and garlic; stir again. Arrange eggplant and zucchini cut sides up. Remove any garlic skins that may have come loose. Sprinkle with herbs and salt and pepper to your taste.

Bake for 1 hour on the middle shelf.

The roasted vegetables can be made 1 day in advance and kept, covered, in the refrigerator.

---

*If baby vegetables are not available, full-size eggplant and zucchini can be substituted. Cut them to the size of baby vegetables. But if you do use full size, it's better to salt the eggplant, drain for 30 minutes, and rinse before cooking.

Roasted Vegetable Sandwiches: Leftover roasted vegetables are a bonus to be savored. Spread 1 clove of carmalized garlic, skin removed, on the inside of a sliced crusty rectangular roll. Add a slice of eggplant, a slice of zucchini, a strip of red pepper, and a slice of mozzarella cheese.

MAKES **6** SERVINGS

Tabbouli

SUPERFOODS: bulgur, olive oil, tomatoes, onions

Bulgur can be bought at a whole-foods market or at a supermarket with a Greek or Middle Eastern foods section; it's wheat that's been processed to cook by soaking in boiling water. Ideally, the mint for tabbouli should be fresh, often sold in bunches at the produce counter. If you must *substitute, use 1 teaspoon dried mint with 2 tablespoons finely minced fresh parsley. The tomatoes may be* au naturel *or peeled and seeded. The latter method yields a less juicy salad.*

1 cup bulgur	*¼ teaspoon salt*
½ teaspoon salt	*Freshly ground black pepper (8*
2 cups boiling water	*to 10 grinds)*
¼ cup olive oil	*2 large ripe tomatoes, cut into*
2 tablespoons lemon juice	*small dice*
3 tablespoons finely chopped	*½ cup chopped sweet onion, such*
fresh mint	*as Vidalia*

Mix the bulgur and salt in a medium bowl. Pour the boiling water over it, stir, and let stand for ½ to 1 hour. Drain the wheat in a fine-meshed strainer, discarding the water. Press out excess water with the back of a spoon, getting out as much as possible. Fluff with a fork.

In a salad bowl, mix the oil, lemon juice, mint, ¼ teaspoon salt, and pepper. Stir in the tomatoes, onion, and drained bulgur. Marinate the salad in the refrigerator for several hours to develop the flavor.

The salad can be made a day in advance, and will be all the better.

Taste to correct the seasoning. You may want more lemon juice, salt, or pepper.

MAKES ABOUT 3 CUPS

THE QUINTESSENTIAL MACARONI SUPPER FOR FOUR

Escarole in Chicken Broth♦
Ziti with Tomato Sauce (see pages 516–518)
Broccoli and Fennel Salad♦
Fresh Grapes and Bel Paese Cheese

While macaroni with tomato sauce has gone out of favor in fashionable places, it has remained a staple of Italian meals and a sure-fire family pleaser. Many times, a simple dish of ricotta is served along with the macaroni, and scoops of the cheese are spooned right on top, rather like an "instant lasagna." If you like this idea, choose part skim ricotta and benefit from the low-fat calcium!

This meal starts with some vitamin A–rich greens in good chicken broth, adds broccoli salad (the Mediterranean way is after the pasta!) for more. As a complex carbohydrate food, macaroni gives calmness to the mind and sustained energy to the body.

Escarole in Chicken Broth

SUPERFOODS: escarole, carrot

1 medium head escarole (1¼ pounds)	1 large carrot, cut into julienne strips
1 quart full-flavored Italian Chicken Broth* (see page 520)	4 slices prosciutto ham, shredded

Escarole leaves are especially curly, so it's best to wash each leaf individually under running warm water. Tear or cut the leaves coarsely.

Bring the broth to a boil, add the escarole, and cook, stirring occasionally, until the escarole is quite tender, 10 minutes. During the last 5 minutes, add the carrot. Just before serving, stir in the ham.

MAKES 4 SERVINGS

*Of course, you can substitute canned, reduced-sodium broth (2 cans), but for an outstanding soup, homemade broth is the best!

Broccoli and Fennel Salad

SUPERFOODS: dark leaves of romaine, broccoli, scallions, olive oil

½ head romaine lettuce
1 small fennel bulb
2 cups cooked broccoli florets*
4 scallions, chopped

⅓ cup olive oil
3 tablespoons red wine vinegar
Salt
Freshly ground pepper

Wash and dry the lettuce in a spin-drier or in a towel. Tear it into bite-size pieces, and put them into a salad bowl.

Trim the fennel bulb, discarding the woody core. Chop the fennel into bite-size pieces. (Save the stalks for another use.)

Add the broccoli, fennel, and scallions to the salad. Toss the salad with the oil, vinegar and salt and pepper to taste. Taste a leaf of lettuce, adding more of any of the dressing ingredients to your taste.

MAKES **4** SERVINGS

AFTER-WORK EASY DINNER FOR FOUR

Broiled Veal Chops with Red Peppers and Sage♦
Greek-Style Okra♦
Arborio Rice (see page 525)
Chicory and Romaine Salad with Carrot Curls
Practically Instant Strawberry Tiramisù♦

*Use fresh broccoli cooked tender-crisp—2 to 3 minutes in rapidly boiling water should do it.

Red bell peppers and strawberries are fairly bursting with vitamin C, and okra is rich in folate for healthy childbearing and magnesium for the heart. Forget the iceberg lettuce and fill the salad bowl instead with the vitamin A–rich dark leafy greens.

Broiled Veal Chops with Red Peppers and Sage

SUPERFOODS: red peppers, garlic

The same whole-foods markets that stock organic vegetables and fruits may also sell meat from animals that have not been shot full of hormones or raised in crates. This "naturally raised" meat costs more, and the veal is not as pale and tender, but I've found its quality to be excellent.

3 tablespoons olive oil	About 20 leaves of fresh sage
4 veal loin chops	(or rosemary sprigs)*
(¾ to 1 inch thick)	2 large red bell peppers
4 garlic cloves, halved	Freshly ground black pepper

Pour the olive oil onto a large platter. Rub the veal chops with the garlic and sage, then add the garlic and sage to the oil.

Quarter the red peppers lengthwise and discard the seeds.

Place the veal chops and the red peppers on the platter, and rub them all over with the oil. Allow them to marinate in the oil for ½ hour at room temperature, turning occasionally.

Heat the broiler, and season the chops with ground black pepper to your taste.

Arrange the chops and red peppers on a large broiler pan. Put

---

*If you don't have a sage plant, look for bunches of fresh herbs sold in many supermarket produce sections.

the red pepper quarters cut sides up with a piece of garlic in each. (If everything doesn't fit, cook the peppers separately, first.)

Broil the chops close to the heat source about 5 minutes per side for veal that will be faintly pink at the center. Turn the peppers when you turn the chops. It's okay if the pepper skins char a bit, but if they seem to be in danger of burning, remove them from the broiler.

Before serving, lightly scrape the charred skin off the peppers with the back of a paring knife. Don't be fussy about it—this dish should look a bit rustic! Include or discard the garlic, according to your taste.

MAKES 4 SERVINGS

Greek-Style Okra

SUPERFOODS: onion, jalapeño pepper, okra, tomatoes

1 tablespoon olive oil	One 10-ounce package frozen
1 medium onion, chopped	whole okra
1 jalapeño pepper, seeded and	Juice of ½ lemon
minced*	Salt and pepper
1 pound ripe tomatoes, diced	12 Kalamata olives, pitted

In a 2-quart saucepan, heat the oil and sauté the onion and jalapeño until softened, about 3 minutes. Add the tomatoes, and continue to cook, uncovered, stirring often, for 10 minutes.

Add the okra, cover, and cook until tender, about 10 minutes more. Stir in the lemon juice, salt and pepper to taste, and olives.

MAKES 4 SERVINGS

*Wear rubber gloves when handling hot peppers.

Practically Instant Strawberry Tiramisù

SUPERFOODS: strawberries

Tiramisù is a pick-me-up (literally, "pull me up"). And this speedy version of the classic Venetian dessert adds the vitamin C boost of strawberries.

1 pint ripe strawberries, hulled
4 tablespoons marsala wine
  (rum or a liqueur can be
  substituted)
12 plain (unfilled) ladyfingers

4 tablespoons mascarpone cheese
4 teaspoons strong brewed
  espresso or coffee
Cocoa Sugar (see page 540)

Reserve 4 pretty strawberries for garnishing. Slice the remaining strawberries.

Pour 1 tablespoon marsala onto each of 4 dessert plates. Place the bottom halves of 3 ladyfingers over the marsala on each plate. Spread each portion with 1 tablespoon mascarpone cheese. Divide the sliced strawberries among the portions.

Top the strawberries with the top halves of the ladyfingers. Drizzle each with 1 teaspoon espresso or coffee. Sprinkle them with Cocoa Sugar. Garnish with reserved strawberries.

The Tiramisù will be just right if it stands at room temperature for an hour or so, while you have dinner. If it's to be kept longer than that, chill in the refrigerator.

MAKES 4 SERVINGS

A SUNDAY DINNER FOR SIX

Artichokes with Anchovy-Wheat Stuffing♦
Loin of Pork with Roasted Root Vegetables♦
Tomato, Broccoli, and Provolone Salad♦
Whole-Grain Italian Bread
Steamed Orange-Fig Cake with Orange Yogurt Sauce♦
or
Anise Oranges (see page 59)

This is a "real" Sunday dinner for times when you feel like throwing yourself into cooking. (But note that both the starter and the dessert can be made a day ahead.) Artichokes are rich in folate, and whole wheat adds more, along with fiber and vitamin E. Lots of cancer-protection in carrots, potatoes, tomatoes, broccoli, and figs!

Artichokes with Anchovy-Wheat Stuffing

SUPERFOODS: artichokes, wheat germ, garlic

A traditional Italian appetizer with a strong anchovy flavor. If you decide to omit the anchovies, substitute chopped, pitted Greek or Italian black olives.

6 large artichokes

3 tablespoons olive oil

3 cups herb stuffing mix (not
   stovetop variety)

½ cup toasted wheat germ

⅓ cup grated Parmesan cheese

2 tablespoons minced fresh
   flat-leaf parsley

½ teaspoon each dried oregano
   and dried basil

¼ teaspoon pepper

One 2-ounce can imported
   Italian anchovies packed in olive
   oil

3 garlic cloves, finely minced

Warm water, about ½ cup

Paprika

Bring a large pot of water to a boil. Add the artichokes and 1 tablespoon of olive oil, and when the water boils again, parboil for 4 minutes. Drain.

Slice off the stems so that the artichokes will stand upright. With a scissors, snip off the spiny tips of the leaves. Open the center of the artichoke and scoop out the fuzzy inner choke with a grapefruit (serrated) spoon, leaving the meaty heart intact.

In a food processor, process the stuffing mix with the wheat germ, cheese, parsley, herbs, and pepper just enough to reduce the mixture to coarse crumbs.

In a small skillet, simmer the anchovies and their oil with the garlic over *very* low heat until the anchovies are dissolved, about 5 minutes. Thoroughly blend the anchovy mixture into the stuffing. Add enough warm water so that the stuffing holds together when pressed.

Preheat the oven to 375 degrees F.

Stuff the centers and leaves of the artichokes, holding them over the bowl. Stand them in a baking dish that will hold them upright. Drizzle the remaining 2 tablespoons of oil over the tops. Sprinkle them with paprika. Add about ½ inch of water to the pan.

Cover the artichokes with a sheet of foil, not tucked in. Bake them in the middle of the oven for about 1 hour, until the hearts are tender when pierced with the point of a paring knife.

May be made 1 day in advance and kept chilled. Reheat, covered, or simply bring to room temperature before serving.

MAKES 6 SERVINGS

Loin of Pork with Roasted Root Vegetables

SUPERFOODS: carrots, onions, potatoes

This is a favorite, never-fail company dinner that doesn't require hanging around the kitchen.

One 3- to 3½-pound boneless loin of pork

2 garlic cloves, slivered

2 teaspoons Italian seasoning (or mix your own dried herbs)

6 carrots, cut in half and parboiled 5 minutes

6 medium to small onions, parboiled 5 minutes

3 or more russet potatoes, cut into quarters lengthwise

1 tablespoon olive oil

Salt and pepper

Preheat the oven to 350 degrees F. Let the loin come to room temperature.

Cut slits in the loin with the point of a paring knife, and insert a sliver of garlic into each. Pat the seasoning onto the roast. Parboil the vegetables.

Arrange the loin on a flat rack in a large roasting pan. In a bowl, toss the vegetables with the oil, then arrange them around the loin. Have the pan large enough to avoid crowding. Salt and pepper the vegetables to your taste.

Roast the loin for 1 hour to 1 hour and 15 minutes, until it reaches an internal temperature of 160 degrees. Turn the vegetables once during the cooking time.

If the vegetables are not perfectly tender, continue cooking them while letting the pork rest 10 minutes or so before slicing.

MAKES 6 SERVINGS

Tomato, Broccoli, and Provolone Salad

SUPERFOODS: onion, broccoli, tomatoes, olive oil

1 medium red onion, sliced and
  separated into rings
2 to 3 cups broccoli florets*
4 to 6 vine-ripened tomatoes,
  sliced

Salt (optional)
1 cup shredded provolone cheese
⅓ cup virgin olive oil

If the onion is strong, soak the rings in ice water for 15 minutes or so.

Blanch the broccoli in boiling, salted water for 2 to 3 minutes or until barely tender-crisp. Drain and cool in ice water. Drain again.

Layer the tomatoes on a platter and salt them to your taste. Arrange the broccoli on top. Scatter the provolone over all. Top with onion rings. Drizzle on olive oil.

Let stand at room temperature for 30 minutes.

MAKES 6 SERVINGS

Steamed Orange-Fig Cake
with Orange Yogurt Sauce

SUPERFOODS: figs, orange juice, yogurt

5 tablespoons butter, softened	2 eggs or ½ cup prepared egg
1 tablespoon sugar	substitute
1 cup sifted all-purpose flour	⅓ cup orange juice
2 teaspoons baking powder	¾ cup snipped dried figs, stems
¼ cup unflavored dry bread	discarded
crumbs	Orange Yogurt Sauce (recipe
½ cup sugar	follows)
1 teaspoon grated orange rind	

Use a tablespoon of butter to grease the inside of an empty coffee can, 1-pound to 13-ounce size. Sprinkle with a tablespoon sugar, close the plastic cover, and shake the can to distribute the coating. Discard the plastic cover.

Arrange a steaming rack or trivet in a covered pan large enough to stand the coffee can upright. Have 2 inches of water at a simmer in the pan.

Sift the flour with the baking powder. In a large bowl, stir the flour into the bread crumbs.

Cream the remaining 4 tablespoons butter with the sugar. Beat the rind, then the eggs, and finally the juice. (This can be done in a food processor.) Add the liquid ingredients to the dry, stirring to blend. Fold in the snipped figs.

Spoon the batter into the prepared can. Make a dome of foil for the top, and secure it on the top of the can with an elastic or string. Place the can in the steamer, close cover, and steam for 2 hours.

Cool the cake on a rack for 5 minutes. Rest the can on its side and open the bottom with a can opener. Use a spatula to push the cake through onto a serving dish.

Serve warm or at room temperature with Orange Yogurt Sauce.

The cake and sauce can be made 1 day ahead. Steam the cake to rewarm it. Reheat the sauce in a pitcher in a microwave or a small saucepan on the range.

MAKES 6 TO 8 SERVINGS

ORANGE YOGURT SAUCE

SUPERFOODS: orange juice, yogurt

1 cup orange juice	*2 tablespoons cornstarch*
½ cup brown sugar	*1 cup plain nonfat yogurt*

In a small saucepan, combine the orange juice and brown sugar; simmer until sugar is dissolved. Whisk the cornstarch into the yogurt. Stir the yogurt mixture into the simmering juice, and whisk until the sauce bubbles and thickens. Continue to cook over low heat, stirring occasionally, for 3 minutes.

MAKES 2 CUPS

7

WHOLE GRAINS AND B VITAMINS FOR THE WHOLE NERVOUS SYSTEM

Protection Against Stress, PMS, Birth Defects, and a Wide Range of Psychiatric Disorders

Having it all" for a woman is a euphemism for combining important personal goals with family considerations, the greatest balancing act in the modern-day circus. Naturally, this is liable to cause inner stress—worry, frustration, anxiety, and anger—especially for those of us who want to have it all *perfectly*. When you add to that basic dilemma the hormonal roulette of PMS, the fears and hopes of pregnancy, the embarrassment and discomfort of menopausal symptoms, or some other female physical event, you have a bevy of good reasons for wanting to keep your nervous system in fighting trim.

The B vitamins are a vital part of the nutritional armor you need when you take on the world . . . or the new job . . . or a child . . . or an in-law . . . or all of the above. Emphasizing whole grains is one good way to be sure that you're getting plenty of B vitamins (with the exception of B_{12}, which is found only in animal products). Suddenly discovering the wonders of a single

B vitamin and taking that trendy number in a high-powered supplement (unless prescribed by a doctor) is like painting a picture of good health from a one-color palette. Why not utilize the entire wide range of B vitamins that whole grains provide? Many nutritionists agree that B vitamins are meant to work in concert. Take advantage of their synergy!

B VITAMINS NOURISH YOUR NERVOUS SYSTEM

A growing number of studies have indicated a definite connection between B vitamin nutrition—often in combinations of two or three—and the health of the nervous system and brain, including muscle coordination, mental health, and learning ability. Preliminary evidence suggests that the B complex may be helpful in the treatment of geriatric depression. Conversely, symptoms of serious B vitamin deficiencies provoke psychiatric symptoms ranging from mild mood changes to full-blown psychosis.

Other superfoods are rich in specific B vitamins, but whole grains—particularly wheat germ—and fortified cereals are an outstanding across-the-board source. Often a number of B-vitamin foods can be combined in recipes and menus for a super defense against "the slings and arrows of outrageous fortune." With a diet rich in B vitamins, here's what you'll have on your side. . . .

Whole-Grain Superfoods

Barley, brown	Oatmeal
Buckwheat	Rice, brown
Bulgur	Rye
Cornmeal, whole-grain	Wheat germ and bran
Couscous, brown	Whole wheat

GET YOUR WHOLE GRAINS EVEN WHEN YOU'RE RUSHED

A bowl of oatmeal or wheat flakes

A bran muffin—with part-skim ricotta (for B_{12}, too!)

A cup of barley soup and a whole wheat roll

Toasted whole wheat French bread rubbed with garlic and
  drizzled with virgin olive oil

Sliced turkey sandwich on whole wheat sandwich bread

Whole wheat crackers (low-fat, low-salt are best)

THIAMIN FOR ALL-AROUND VITALITY

Thiamin (B_1) is a vitalizer vitamin. It enhances energy by helping in the metabolism of carbohydrates and plays a vital role in the normal functioning of the nervous system. The average intake by women has been found to be slightly below the RDA. Simply because alcohol interferes with thiamin, a deficiency is not uncommon in every stratum of our society. Thiamin deficiency can cause a confused mental state, sometimes seen in alcoholics and in the elderly.

There has been some interesting animal research in which the toxic damage of lead poisoning was blocked with thiamin supplements.

Superfood Sources of Thiamin (Vitamin B_1)

Beans and peas
Broccoli
Brussels sprouts
Citrus fruits
Corn
Fish and shellfish
Fruits, dried: dates, figs
Mangos

Melons, especially
  watermelon
Nuts and seeds
Pineapple
Squashes, winter
Wheat germ and whole-
  grain foods

HAVE SOME THIAMIN . . .

A glass of grapefruit or pineapple juice
Chopped dates on whole-grain cereal
A cup of pea soup
Broccoli salad in a whole wheat pita bread pocket
Corn on the cob (5 minutes an ear in a microwave)
A slice of watermelon
A helping of three-bean salad

ATTENTION, FITNESS AFICIONADOS! GET YOUR RIBOFLAVIN

Riboflavin (B_2) is an exerciser's vitamin. Its antioxidant functions are particularly effective in protecting athletes and dedicated exercisers from the stress of free radical damage. Women who exercise vigorously need even more riboflavin than men on similar regimes.

Superfood Sources of Riboflavin (Vitamin B_2)

Beet greens
Broccoli
Dairy products: nonfat
   yogurt, skim milk, low-fat
   cheeses
Fish and shellfish: oyster,
   salmon, sardines
Mushrooms

Nuts: almonds, cashews,
   walnuts
Potatoes, sweet
Pumpkin
Spinach
Turkey and other poultry
Wheat germ and whole-
   grain foods

RIBOFLAVIN THE EASY WAY

Oysters on the half shell
A cup of mushroom soup
Chicken salad sandwich on whole wheat bread
Pasta with spinach, garlic, and olive oil (even better if it's
  whole-grain pasta)
A salad of tender-crisp broccoli and low-fat mozzarella
A slice of pumpkin bread
A cup of yogurt, any favorite flavor (add some chopped
  walnuts!)

NIACIN FOR YOUR HEART AND MIND!

Niacin (B_3) is a heart protector and nerve builder. It's needed for the proper function of a whole range of enzymes and for DNA formation. In high-prescription doses, niacin is known to lower blood cholesterol, reducing the risk of heart disease.

A few researchers claim that niacin has been useful in treating schizophrenia and some other mental disorders, as well as in reducing dependency on drugs and alcohol and aborting migraine headaches, but the wider medical community feels these claims have not been scientifically substantiated.

"Pure" niacin from whole grains and other foods is not the only source of niacin; tryptophan, an amino acid, is converted to niacin in the body. Wheat germ and peanuts contain both niacin and tryptophan; skim milk is a good source of tryptophan. Getting plenty of the other B vitamins enhances the utilization of the niacin in foods.

Thiamin, riboflavin, and niacin are all involved in the conversion of calories into energy, and the RDA for each is raised when a woman gets pregnant. A deficiency in riboflavin has been associated with increased nausea, premature births, and still-births.

Superfood Sources of Niacin (Vitamin B$_3$)

Almonds	Peanuts
Barley	Potatoes
Fish: salmon, swordfish,	Rice, enriched or brown
halibut, trout, tuna,	Turkey and other poultry
sardines	Wheat germ and whole-
Mushrooms	grain foods

NIACIN IN PRACTICALLY NO TIME

A cup of turkey-barley soup
A helping of potato salad (even better if made with yogurt
   and dill instead of high-fat mayonnaise)
Marinated mushrooms
Salmon salad sandwich on whole-grain bread
A handful of peanuts (preferably unsalted, no oil)
A dish of rice pudding

PYRIDOXINE IMPROVES IMMUNITY— AND MAY RELIEVE PMS!

Pyridoxine (B$_6$) is an immune system booster. Animals fed a diet rich in B$_6$ show improved immune response. Various other animal studies have indicated that B$_6$ slows the growth of tumors, including skin cancers. The health of the elderly and diseases of the immune system such as AIDS may profit from this line of research.

Through its effects on various minerals and neurotransmitters, B$_6$ exerts an influence on the nervous system. Although B$_6$ has been reported to relieve symptoms of PMS, this is the result of some rather small studies considered inconclusive. One study reported relief from the irritability, headaches, tender breasts, and water retention that characterize PMS; the other, relief from depression. An interesting avenue of research to keep an eye on—and (why wait?) a good reason to improve B_6 nutrition!

Vitamin B_6 and ginger have both been shown to be effective for nausea and vomiting in early pregnancy. Results of a study on young women indicated improved B_6 nutrition may enhance calcium and magnesium absorption. In addition, abnormalities in sugar metabolism caused by taking an oral contraceptive have been relieved by B_6 therapy.

Unfortunately, B_6 is a problem nutrient. Although most Americans get plenty of niacin, the average intake of B_6 is below the RDA. Women consume even less than men, and senior diets are especially lacking. We ought to take special care to include vitamin B_6 superfoods often in our menus.

Superfoods Source of Pyridoxine (Vitamin B_6)

Bananas
Corn
Fish and shellfish
Mangos
Nuts: peanuts and chestnuts
Potatoes, white and sweet

Prunes
Turkey and poultry
Watermelon
Wheat germ and whole-
   grain foods

EASY-DOES-IT WAYS TO ENJOY PYRIDOXINE

A cup of corn chowder
A crabmeat salad sandwich on a whole wheat roll
Roasted chestnuts
A snack of prunes
Take a banana to work!
Half a mango with a lime wedge
Melon fruit salad

BIOTIN TO PROTECT YOUR HAIR

Biotin could be a hair vitamin! Sorting among unbelievable claims ("prevents graying," for instance—but I wouldn't bet on it!) some interesting facts emerge.

Talk about having a "bad hair day," some children, owing to numerous cowlicks, literally have uncombable hair; it simply sticks out in all directions. This annoying grooming problem has responded well to treatment with biotin.

A biotin deficiency can cause hair loss, which is corrected when biotin nutrition is restored. But baldness *not caused by a deficiency* has shown no response to biotin therapy. Nevertheless, biotin is often an ingredient in hair nutrition products. Besides hair loss, scaly skin is another symptom of biotin deficiency.

As well as being obtained from whole foods such as brown rice and sardines, biotin is manufactured in adequate amounts by intestinal bacteria, so how would you get a biotin deficiency? A continued regime of antibiotics or an extremely low-calorie reducing diet can create a biotin deficiency (of which hair loss could be a symptom). Ingesting raw egg whites practically wipes out the biotin from your system by preventing absorption.

You may not think you're eating any raw egg whites, but here are some possible hidden sources: homemade eggnog with all those raw eggs in it, or one of those instant-chocolate-mousse recipes that uses stiffly beaten raw egg whites, or a Caesar salad made at the table, with a raw egg dramatically tossed into the dressing, or homemade whole-egg mayonnaise, or even a really runny soft-boiled egg.

Raw eggs should be avoided anyway—and not just for the health of your hair. Salmonella has been turning up more often in our egg supply; cooking an egg is good insurance against a nasty digestive disorder.

Superfood Sources of Biotin

Beans   Vegetables, dark green
Rice, brown   Whole grains
Fish: shellfish, sardines

A QUICK BIOTIN BOOST

Sardines on rye toast
A scoop of hummus (chickpea puree) with whole wheat
    pita bread
Canned baked beans with brown bread
A salad of dark, leafy greens and cannellini (white kidney
    beans)

FOLATE DEFENDS AGAINST BIRTH DEFECTS

Folate (folic acid, B_9) is a healthy-birth vitamin. Folate helps the body form red blood cells and aids in the formation of genetic material within every body cell.

There have been some very impressive studies indicating that women who took extra folate *before* they conceived had a reduced risk of neural-tube defect (NTD) or congenital malformations in the infant. Even in women with a previously affected child, supplementation with folate started before conception and continued for the first trimester reduced the risk of NTD by 72 percent.

Women of childbearing years who are not, for any reason, getting sufficient folate in their diets may wish to discuss taking a supplement with their doctors. The evidence of folate's importance to healthy births is based on extensive research, not just a few studies.

Grains, fruit, and vegetables, the best food sources of folate, should be an important part of the diet, not only of women of childbearing years but of *every* woman, because of folate's anti–cervical cancer properties.

FOLATE AND OTHER B VITAMINS GUARD AGAINST CANCER

A deficiency of folate is thought to play a role in causing precancerous lesions in the cervix, a condition that often results in an abnormal Pap test. Folate therapy in prescription doses reduced these lesions in some women—in another study high doses of folate acted favorably on the precancerous lesions in the lungs of smokers. A diet rich in folates seems to reduce the risk of developing adenomas, benign harbingers of colon cancer.

B vitamin–rich whole-grain bread and pasta are two of the foods (along with fruits, vegetables, and low-fat dairy products) that offer women "significant protection, of the order of 40 to 60 percent," from endometrial cancer.

Superfood Sources of Folate
(Folacin, Folic Acid, Vitamin B₉)

Asparagus
Avocados
Barley
Beets
Beans (including green
  beans) and lentils
Broccoli
Brussels sprouts
Cabbage
Corn

Eggplant
Greens, dark leafy
Nuts: almonds, hazelnuts,
  cashews, walnuts,
  peanuts
Oranges
Plantains
Seeds: pumpkin and squash
Whole grains: wheat, rye,
  soy

FOLATE, FAST AND EASY

A cup of borscht (even better with a dollop of yogurt)
An orange or a glass of orange juice
Cashew butter on whole-grain crackers
At the salad bar: spinach, romaine, raw broccoli florets,
    pickled beets, chickpeas, guacamole
Cooked, chilled asparagus spears with vinaigrette dressing
A handful of trail mix with nuts, seeds, and whole grains

SENIORS TAKE NOTE: GET PLENTY OF B_{12}!

Vitamin B_{12} is the senior's friend. It restores vigor, boosts memory, helps in the functioning of the nervous system, and protects against cancer. It also builds genetic material, as well as metabolizing protein and fat in the body.

The decline in cognitive function experienced by the aged has responded well to treatment with vitamins B_{12}, B_6, and folate. Vitamin B_{12} has also proved helpful in relieving some sleep disorders in people of all ages.

Unlike other B vitamins, B_{12} is found only in animal products. Even the milk and eggs used to make various whole-grain baked goods can be a source of B_{12} in a woman's diet. In fact, baked goods contribute as much as 14 percent of the average woman's RDA for B_{12}.

Low levels of B_{12} are also common among people over 60 owing to a condition known as *atrophic gastritis*, which occurs when stomachs are no longer producing sufficient acid to digest properly the meat, fish, and dairy products that are the only food source of this important B vitamin. Neurological symptoms that B_{12}-deficient seniors may suffer from include a whole range of maladies often blamed on plain old age: uncoordinated muscular movements, weakened limbs, and lack of balance; mood changes, disorientation, and various psychiatric disorders.

When these symptoms occur in seniors, it would be advisable to ask a physician to evaluate for vitamin deficiencies along with whatever other tests are indicated.

B_{12} WORKS WITH FOLATE FOR HEALTHY BIRTHS

Tests of women with NTD showed markedly lower levels of vitamin B_{12} in their amniotic fluid. Folate and B_{12} work closely together in the expanding of blood volume required by the growing fetus. Too small an increase can retard the fetus's development. Spontaneous abortion, stillbirth, and low-birth-weight babies can result, as well as the specific defects linked to folate deficiency.

EVALUATE YOUR RISK OF A B_{12} DEFICIENCY

Vegans (strict vegetarians who avoid all animal products) are put at risk of a B_{12} deficiency, which eventually will cause blood and nerve damage. Pernicious anemia and irreversible neurological damage can result from a severe deficiency. There appears to be a relationship between multiple sclerosis and a deficiency of B_{12}, which is currently being researched.

Gastrointestinal disorders like Crohn's disease or taking megadoses of vitamin C can also interfere with one's B_{12} nutrition.

Other B vitamins abound in whole-grain foods, but for vitamin B_{12} a woman needs to include fish and/or meat or dairy foods in her meals. Of course, if she chooses fish and low-fat dairy products, so much the better—and healthier! Vegans can choose a B_{12}-fortified soymilk or cereal, or B_{12} tablets.

Superfood Sources of Vitamin B$_{12}$

Dairy products: skim milk,   Fish and shellfish
low-fat cheese, nonfat
yogurt

Note: While it's not included in my list of superfoods, liver is an excellent source of B$_{12}$ but high in cholesterol. If cholesterol is not a problem, an occasional snack of chopped chicken liver will boost not only B$_{12}$ but also iron intake.

VITAMIN B$_{12}$ FOR A BUSY DAY

A toasted cheese sandwich (even better with tomato on whole wheat bread)
A cup of New England fish chowder
A low-fat cottage cheese dip with fresh veggies
A scoop of nonfat frozen yogurt
A cup of cocoa made with skim milk
A ripe peach with part-skim ricotta and a drizzle of honey

B VITAMINS AT A GLANCE

B VITAMIN thiamine

RDA for Females
1.1 mg
pregnant: +.5 mg
Benefits
Promotes energy
Helps in metabolism
Vital to nerve functioning
Sources
Beans, broccoli, Brussels sprouts, fish, fruits (fresh and dried), nuts, seeds, fortified grains and cereals
Warnings
Megadose of one B vitamin can cause a deficiency in the others

B VITAMIN riboflavin

RDA for Females
1.3 mg
Pregnant: +.3 mg
Benefits
Promotes energy and good vision
Protects exercisers from free radical damage
Sources
Beet greens, broccoli, dairy products, fish, mushrooms, fortified grains and cereals
Warnings
Megadose of one B vitamin can cause a deficiency in the others

B VITAMIN niacin

RDA for Females
15 mg
Pregnant: +2 mg
Benefits
Heart protector, lowers cholesterol
Needed for enzyme and DNA formation
Nerve builder
Sources
Almonds, barley, fish, mushrooms, peanuts, potatoes, rice, poultry, wheat germ, whole grains

WARNINGS
Megadoses can cause heart and organ disorders

B VITAMIN pyridoxine (B6)

RDA FOR FEMALES
1.6 mg
Pregnant: +.6 mg
BENEFITS
Essential to metabolism
Beneficial to nervous system
Boosts immune system
May relieve symptoms of PMS and nausea in pregnancy
SOURCES
Bananas, corn, fish, mangos, nuts, potatoes, prunes, poultry, watermelon, wheat germ, whole grains
WARNINGS
Megadoses can cause nerve disorders

B VITAMIN biotin

RDA FOR FEMALES
NA
BENEFITS
Essential to metabolism
May promote healthy hair
SOURCES
Beans, brown rice, fish, dark green vegetables, whole grains
WARNINGS
Megadose of one B vitamin can cause a deficiency in the others

B VITAMIN folate

RDA FOR FEMALES
180 mcg
Pregnant: +220 mcg
BENEFITS
Helps form red blood cells and genetic material
Prevents some birth defects
May protect against some cancers
SOURCES
Nuts, oranges, plantains, seeds, vegetables, whole grains
WARNINGS
Megadoses can interfere with zinc absorption

B VITAMIN B_{12}

RDA FOR FEMALES
2.0 mcg
Pregnant: +.2 mcg
BENEFITS
Essential to metabolism and formation of red blood cells
Protects nervous system
May relieve sleep disorders
Helps prevent problems of aging
SOURCES
Meats and fish, dairy products
WARNINGS
Megadose of one B vitamin can cause a deficiency in the others

FOLLOW THE FOOD ROUTE TO GOOD B VITAMIN NUTRITION

Although research studies and therapeutic regimes—such as treatment of heart patients with niacin—often use high-dose supplements of only one B vitamin, such programs should always be carried out under the care of a physician.

But keeping up our B complex nutrition through those food choices we make day after day, meal after meal—that's what we should be doing for ourselves, because of all the indications from current research show that not only our bodies but our minds as well will be strengthened by great grains and other B vitamin foods.

The quick fixes, menus, and recipes to help you do this follow.

SUPERMEALS WITH A BONANZA OF B VITAMINS

Recipes indicated by a ◆ follow the menus.

SUPPER FOR FOUR IN THE KITCHEN

Old-Time Corn Chowder◆
with Whole Wheat Crackers
Eggplant "Sandwiches"◆
Rosemary Oranges◆
or
Seedless Orange Segments

*F*eatures folate!—*an important nutrient included in this menu's corn, eggplant, oranges. The skim milk adds vitamin B₁₂; turkey and potatoes heap on vitamin B₆ and niacin. Plus there are assorted B vitamins in the whole-grain crackers.*

Old-Time Corn Chowder

SUPERFOODS: onion, potatoes, corn, skim milk

This one dates back to World War II! One of those ''emergency'' dishes that can be made in a few minutes, equally well with fresh, canned, or canned ''creamed'' corn, and is quite a comfort on a chilly evening.

1 tablespoon butter
1 small onion, chopped
1 pound potatoes, peeled and
   diced
½ cup water
¼ teaspoon salt
2 cups corn, fresh, frozen, or
   canned (1 pound can
   ''creamed,'' undrained, or
   niblets, drained)

2 cups milk (can be skim)
½ cup chopped ham (optional)
White pepper
2 tablespoons instant flour
Minced fresh chives or parsley for
   garnish

In a 2-quart saucepan, heat the butter and sauté the onion until it's softened but not brown, about 3 minutes. Add the potatoes, ½ cup water, and salt, and simmer, covered, until the potatoes are tender, about 10 minutes. With a potato masher, mash the potatoes slightly.

Add the corn, 1¾ cups milk, and ham, if using, and as much pepper as you like. Heat the soup to scalding but don't boil it yet.

Mix the flour with ¼ cup remaining milk, and add this to the soup. Bring to a boil over medium heat, stirring constantly. Reduce the heat and simmer the soup a few minutes to cook the flour. Sprinkle with chives or parsley.

MAKES ABOUT 5 CUPS

Eggplant "Sandwiches"

SUPERFOODS: eggplant, turkey, whole wheat bread, garlic

2 medium eggplants, preferably
  same length

Olive oil

For the filling

1 to 1¼ pounds ground turkey

1 slice whole wheat bread,
  dampened and squeezed dry,
  broken into pieces

1 garlic clove, finely minced

1 egg or ¼ cup prepared egg
  substitute

2 tablespoons grated Parmesan
  cheese

½ teaspoon each dried basil and
  dried oregano

¼ teaspoon each salt and pepper

2 cups tomato sauce, homemade
  (see page 516 or 517) or from a
  jar

Cut each eggplant, unpeeled, into 8 slices. Salt the slices, and let them drain in a colander for 30 minutes or longer. Rinse the slices and gently squeeze them dry.

Preheat the oven to 400 degrees F. Lay the eggplant slices in one layer on an oiled baking sheet. Brush the tops with additional oil. If you happened to have a seasoned olive oil on hand, this would be a good dish in which to use it. Bake the eggplant for 8 to 10 minutes, until just tender.

Mix all the filling ingredients until well blended, taking special care to crumb the bread. Make sandwiches by filling 2 eggplant slices with ¼ cup of the meat mixture. Place the sandwiches in a nonreactive baking dish (glass or stainless steel). Top each sandwich with ¼ cup sauce.

The recipe can be made to this point several hours in advance. Keep refrigerated until ready to cook.

Preheat the oven to 375 degrees F.

Bake for 30 to 40 minutes, until the meat is cooked through but not dry. Test by cutting into the middle of the largest sandwich.

Note: Leftover meat filling can be made into marble-size meatballs and frozen for future soups.

MAKES 8

Rosemary Oranges

SUPERFOODS: oranges

4 large seedless oranges	*3 to 4 1-inch sprigs of fresh*
½ cup water	*rosemary, or ½ teaspoon dried*
⅓ cup honey	*½ teaspoon lemon extract*

With a serrated knife, peel the oranges thickly right down to the flesh, so that all the white membrane is removed. Slice the oranges into half-rounds.

In a medium saucepan, combine the water, honey, and rosemary, and bring the syrup to a boil. Simmer 5 minutes. Add the oranges, bring the mixture to a boil again, and simmer 2 minutes.

Remove the mixture to a bowl, add the lemon extract, and chill until ready to serve.

The compote can be made 1 day ahead.

MAKES 4 SERVINGS

WINTER WARMTH FOR FOUR

Veal Stew with Sweet Potatoes and Dried Fruit♦
Brown Couscous♦
Dill Pickled Beets♦
Oatmeal Cookies

*D*ried fruits are a source of niacin, beets add folate, sweet potatoes are rich in riboflavin. Couscous is the pasta of Morocco, where it's served last, to be sure that no guest goes away from the table hungry. Brown couscous is a whole-grain version that emphasizes the B vitamins. Oatmeal cookies introduce another whole grain in the guise of dessert.

Veal Stew with Sweet Potatoes and Dried Fruit

SUPERFOODS: onion, tomato, sweet potato, dried fruit

1½ to 2 pounds veal stew meat
¼ cup all-purpose flour
2 tablespoons olive oil, or more as needed
½ cup chopped onion
1 large ripe tomato, peeled and diced
1 pound sweet potatoes, peeled, cut into chunks

1 cup chicken broth, or more as needed
8 dried apricots
4 dried peaches, cut in half
Salt and black pepper
Cayenne pepper
A pinch of ground cinnamon
2 sprigs fresh thyme, or ¼ teaspoon dried

Cut the veal into uniform 1-inch pieces, trimming off any gristle. Put the meat into a plastic bag with the flour, and shake to coat. Shake off excess flour.

Heat 1 tablespoon of the oil in a large skillet. Brown the veal over high heat. When you turn it over to brown the second side, add the second tablespoon of oil and the onion. When these have browned, add the tomato, lower the heat, and cook until the tomato softens, 10 minutes.

Add the potatoes, chicken broth, dried fruits, and seasonings. Cover and cook over low heat for about 1 hour, stirring occasionally, and adding more broth as needed, until the veal is quite tender. The flour clinging to the veal will thicken the gravy.

The stew may be made 1 day in ahead. Keep refrigerated. Reheat in a skillet.

MAKES 4 SERVINGS

Brown Couscous

SUPERFOOD: brown couscous

Brown couscous has a light, nutty flavor and a nutritional advantage over the refined variety.

2 cups (a 13-ounce can) chicken   1 cup brown couscous*
   broth

In the top of a double boiler, bring the broth to a boil and add the couscous in a slow stream, stirring. Lower the heat and cook at a simmer until all the liquid is absorbed, about 5 minutes.

*Available in whole-foods markets. If refined couscous is substituted, use a regular saucepan. Refined couscous needs no further cooking after all the liquid is absorbed.

Bring 2 inches of water to a boil in the bottom of the double boiler. Continue cooking the couscous over simmering water for 15 to 20 minutes. Fluff very well before serving.

MAKES 4 SERVINGS

Dill Pickled Beets

SUPERFOODS: beets, onion

Beets are one of the very few vegetables that retain good quality when canned, which is fortunate since they're not available frozen.

¼ cup sugar
½ cup red wine vinegar
1 teaspoon dried dill
¼ teaspoon celery seed

1 pound fresh beets, peeled, boiled, and sliced, or a 16-ounce can small whole beets with juice
1 medium onion, chopped

In a small, deep bowl, stir the sugar into the vinegar until it's dissolved. Stir in the dill and celery seed. Add the beets and ½ cup beet juice. Stir in the onion. Chill for several hours to develop flavor.

The recipe can be prepared up to 3 days ahead and kept refrigerated, covered. The longer it stands, the sweeter the onion will be and the more pickled the beets.

MAKES 4 TO 6 SERVINGS

SUMMER ELEGANCE FOR FOUR

Newport Lobster Salad♦
with Rhode Island Johnnycakes♦
Steamed Asparagus
Fresh Pineapple with Camembert

How ow nice it is to know that luxurious lobster is rich in many nutrients—like vitamin B_{12}, plus zinc and selenium. Even better on a bed of cruciferous watercress! Asparagus and cornmeal are rich in folate, pineapple adds thiamin, and cheese rounds out the menu with more vitamin B_{12}.

Newport Lobster Salad
with Rhode Island Johnnycakes

SUPERFOODS: watercress, lobster

1 bunch watercress
1½ pounds lobster meat, diced
2 tender inner stalks of celery
* with pale leaves, diced*

Green tops of 4 scallions, chopped
Caper Dressing (recipe follows)
Hot Rhode Island Johnnycakes
* (recipe follows)*

Wash the watercress and dry it well in a salad spinner or kitchen towel. Remove the tough stems, and chop the leaves into bite-size pieces. Make beds of watercress on 4 plates.

Combine the lobster, celery, scallions, and ½ cup of the dressing. Taste to see if you want to add the rest.

The salad can be made several hours ahead. Keep refrigerated.

Divide the salad among the plates, and serve it with a platter of johnnycakes.

MAKES 4 SERVINGS

CAPER DRESSING

¼ cup white wine vinegar   *About ¾ cup olive oil*
1½ tablespoons Dijon mustard   *2 tablespoons drained capers*
¼ teaspoon white pepper

Combine the vinegar, mustard, and pepper in a small, deep bowl. Add the oil in a thin stream, whisking constantly, until the dressing is thick and will absorb no more. (A blender makes this task easier.) Stir in the capers.

Can be made a few days ahead. Keep refrigerated. Bring to room temperature before using.

MAKES 1 CUP

RHODE ISLAND JOHNNYCAKES

SUPERFOODS: cornmeal

In my home state, there are as many subtle variables in the recipe for this colonial dish as there are Rhode Island cooks. The consistency of the batter is most important in this otherwise simple recipe; the cornmeal should drop off the spoon to form a cake somewhat thicker than a pancake.

1 tablespoon butter, cut into small pieces	*About 1 cup boiling water*
1 teaspoon each molasses and sugar	*Milk as needed to thin the batter (1 or 2 tablespoons)*
¾ teaspoon salt	*Vegetable oil to coat the frying pan or griddle*
1½ cups cornmeal, white or yellow*	

Use a nonstick or well-seasoned cast-iron frying pan, or an electric griddle.

Put the butter, molasses, sugar, salt, and cornmeal into a deep bowl. Stir in enough boiling water to achieve a mixture the consistency of mashed potatoes. Whisk so that there are no lumps. Let stand about a half-hour.

If using a griddle, heat it to 350 degrees F. Or heat the frying pan. Brush it with oil (even a nonstick surface). Thin the batter with enough milk so that it will drop off a spoon like pancake batter. *Add the milk cautiously;* you want the cakes ⅓ to ½ inch thick, *not runny.*

Drop batter by heaping tablespoons onto pan or griddle. Bake for about 5 minutes per side, until they are golden-brown and cooked through. Keep the cakes warm while cooking the second batch.

MAKES 12 TO 14

---

*Rhode Island stone-ground white cornmeal is highly preferred.

A SKILLET CHICKEN DINNER FOR FOUR

Chicken with Artichoke Hearts and Walnuts♦
Baked Acorn Squash
Basmati Rice Salad with Fennel, Apple, and Ginger♦
or
Basmati Rice Salad with Tomatoes and Gorgonzola♦
Diced Mango with Yogurt Custard Sauce (see page 535)

*S*neak in some richest-in-B-vitamins wheat germ wherever you can, as in this chicken dish. Brown basmati rice adds more B vitamins. Walnuts are a good source of folate, mango offers vitamin B_6 plus thiamin. Acorn squash is another thiamin food. Yogurt adds vitamin B_{12}.

Chicken with Artichoke Hearts and Walnuts

SUPERFOODS: artichokes, wheat germ, walnuts, parsley

Parsley pesto is added when the dish is finished cooking; this retains the most intense flavor of the herb while adding a zinger of raw garlic.

One 10-ounce package frozen
  artichoke hearts
1 to 1¼ pounds boneless, skinless
  chicken breast
¼ cup all-purpose flour
2 tablespoons wheat germ

½ cup walnut pieces
1½ tablespoons olive oil
Salt, black pepper, and cayenne
  pepper
2 tablespoons Parsley Pesto* (see
  page 527)

Thaw the artichoke hearts. In a pinch, this can be done quickly by putting them in a strainer and running warm water over them—or in the microwave on the defrost setting.

Wash the chicken in cold salted water; rinse and drain well. Cut the chicken into chunks about the same size as the artichoke hearts. Combine the flour and wheat germ in a plastic bag. Add the slightly damp chicken, and shake to coat the pieces. Shake off excess coating.

Put the walnuts in a small saucepan with water to cover. Bring the water to a boil, remove the pan from the heat, and drain the walnuts. This will eliminate any bitter flavor in the walnut skins. Dry the walnuts on a paper towel.

Heat the oil in a skillet, and brown the chicken pieces. Do this slowly and thoroughly, leaving room between, about 5 minutes per side.

Add the artichoke hearts and walnuts; stir-fry until the artichoke hearts and chicken are cooked through, 5 to 7 minutes.

Season the dish with salt, black pepper, and cayenne to your taste. Remove from the heat, and stir in the pesto until it is well blended with the other ingredients.

(Because there's less garlic in the pesto than in the substitution of parsley and pressed garlic, if you do make that substitution, you may wish to cook the garlic, adding it to the dish with the walnuts.)

MAKES 4 SERVINGS

*1 tablespoon finely minced fresh flat-leaf parsley plus ½ small garlic clove, pressed in a garlic press, can be substituted.

Basmati Rice Salad with Fennel, Apple, and Ginger

SUPERFOODS: apple, red pepper, brown basmati rice

Spicy and flavorful without the addition of a drop of oil.

5 tablespoons rice vinegar	2 tablespoons snipped fennel
¼ teaspoon each sugar and salt*	leaves
2 tablespoons snipped fresh	1 green apple, peeled and diced
chives	½ red bell pepper, finely diced
1 teaspoon very finely minced	2 cups cooked brown basmati rice
fresh ginger	(about ¾ cup raw) (see page
1 cup diced fennel	524)

In a large salad bowl, mix the vinegar, seasonings, chives, and ginger.

Stir in the fennel, fennel leaves, apple, and red pepper as soon as they are cut, to prevent browning. Allow the mixture to marinate at room temperature for about a half-hour.

Stir in the rice.

The salad be made ahead and held at room temperature for an hour or refrigerated up to 1 day. Bring to room temperature before serving.

Taste to correct seasoning. You may want more vinegar.

MAKES 1 QUART

*If the rice vinegar is described on the label as seasoned, you can omit the sugar and salt.

Basmati Rice Salad with Tomatoes and Gorgonzola

SUPERFOODS: olive oil, tomatoes, brown basmati rice

This colorful version could be a light main dish all on its own.

3 tablespoons olive oil
2 tablespoons lemon juice
2 tablespoons minced fresh
  marjoram, or ½ teaspoon dried
  oregano
½ teaspoon salt*
Several grinds of black pepper
1 large ripe yellow tomato (½
  pound)

1 large ripe red tomato (½
  pound)
10 to 12 Kalamata olives, pitted
  and halved
2 cups cooked Basmati Rice
  (about ¾ cup raw) (see page
  524)
½ cup crumbled Gorgonzola
  cheese

In a large bowl, mix the olive oil, lemon juice, herbs, and seasonings. Stir in all the remaining ingredients except the rice and cheese. Allow the mixture to marinate at room temperature for about a half-hour.

Stir in the rice and cheese.

The salad be made ahead and held at room temperature for an hour or refrigerated for several hours. Bring to room temperature before serving.

Taste to correct seasoning. You may want more oil, lemon juice, or pepper.

MAKES 1 QUART

*If you wish, you can omit the salt, since both the cheese and the olives are salty.

A HEARTY FISH STEW
FOR FOUR

Swordfish Gumbo with Brown Rice♦
Whole Wheat French Bread
Broccoli and Chickpea Salad♦
Sliced Seedless Watermelon

All rice is good for you—it's a complex carbohydrate food with fiber and B vitamins. But brown rice has more of everything that makes rice one of the great grains! Swordfish (with vitamin B_{12}) and brown rice are good sources of niacin; broccoli yields riboflavin, thiamin, and folate; and the chickpeas add more folate. Vitamin B_6 is found in the watermelon. Whole wheat French bread tops off an extremely "rich" menu, not only in B vitamins but also in many nutrients talked about in other chapters.

Swordfish Gumbo with Brown Rice

Superfoods: swordfish, olive oil, green pepper, onion, tomatoes, okra, parsley, brown rice

This quick gumbo is great when you don't have a lot of time (30 minutes cooking time for the gumbo, 45 minutes for brown rice, so start it first). Of course, many substitutes are possible, such as any combination of shelled shellfish for some or all of the swordfish.

1¼ to 1½ pounds swordfish tips*
3 tablespoons olive oil
1 green bell pepper, seeded and diced
1 celery stalk, diced
1 medium onion, diced
2 garlic cloves, minced
¼ cup all-purpose flour
1 cup hot water
2 cups bottled clam juice
2 cups peeled and chopped tomatoes, fresh or canned
One 10-ounce package frozen chopped okra
1 bay leaf
1½ teaspoons Cajun seasoning, or to taste (recipe follows, or use store-bought)
Salt
1 tablespoon minced fresh flat-leaf parsley
Hot cooked brown rice (see page 524)

Trim the swordfish, removing and discarding the skin. Cut the swordfish into uniform chunks. Keep refrigerated.

In a 4-quart pot, heat 1 tablespoon of the oil and sauté the green pepper, celery, onion, and garlic over low heat until softened but not brown, about 5 minutes. Remove and reserve these vegetables.

Heat the remaining 2 tablespoons of oil until smoking hot, reduce the heat, and add the flour, stirring often until it's brown but not burned, 5 to 7 minutes. (It's better to err on the side of golden-brown than to risk a bitter flavor.) Whisk in the hot water, and keep whisking until mixture is thick and bubbling. Blend in the clam juice.

Add the tomatoes, okra, bay leaf, and sautéed vegetables. Simmer for 15 to 20 minutes. Add the Cajun seasoning, ½ teaspoon at a time, tasting as you go, until the desired spiciness is reached. *The gumbo stock can be prepared to this point up to 1 day in advance. Keep refrigerated.*

Add the swordfish chunks and continue to simmer until they are cooked through, 10 minutes. Taste to correct seasoning, adding salt as needed. Remove the bay leaf and stir in the parsley.

---

*Swordfish tips, sold for kebabs, cost less than the steaks. If not available, a swordfish steak can be substituted.

Serve the gumbo in soup bowls with a scoop of hot cooked brown rice in the center.

MAKES 2 QUARTS

CAJUN SEASONING

This Cajun seasoning contains no dried garlic or onion, since those products have such a strong, unpleasantly acrid flavor compared to the real thing. To compensate, add fresh garlic and onion to the dish, as above. Or if using this mixture to season meat or fish steaks, rub the steak with a cut clove of garlic, then the Cajun spice.

3 teaspoons salt
2 teaspoons paprika
2 teaspoons cayenne pepper
1 teaspoon black pepper
1 teaspoon white pepper

1 teaspoon chili powder
1 teaspoon dried oregano
½ teaspoon dried thyme leaves
¼ teaspoon ground cloves

Blend all the ingredients well. Store the seasoning in a shaker with large holes.

MAKES ¼ CUP

Broccoli and Chickpea Salad

SUPERFOODS: chickpeas, onion, olive oil, lemon juice, broccoli

One 15- to 16-ounce can chickpeas, drained and rinsed
½ cup chopped red onion
½ cup Greek-style Salad Dressing (see page 529)

2 cups chopped, lightly cooked broccoli (3 cups raw or frozen)

In a large bowl, mix the chickpeas, onion, and dressing. Chill until serving time. *The recipe can be made to this point 1 day ahead.*

Just before serving, stir in the broccoli (to prevent its discoloration). Taste to see if more dressing is needed.

Note: If desired, the salad can be served in lettuce-leaf cups or on a bed of bite-size chicory pieces.

MAKES 4 TO 6 SERVINGS

AFTER-WORK EASY DINNER
FOR FOUR

Hearty Tomato-Barley Soup♦
Turkey, Broccoli, and Swiss Cheese
in Whole Wheat Pockets♦
Sliced Peaches and Almond Cookies

Homemade soup in less than an hour, thickened with comforting barley, another of those great but sometimes overlooked grains. Barley and whole wheat pita bread supply a range of B vitamins; turkey is high in vitamins B_{12}, B_6, and niacin, with almonds adding more; broccoli is rich in folate. Cheese and yogurt (in the dressing) boost vitamin B_{12}.

Hearty Tomato-Barley Soup

SUPERFOODS: tomatoes, barley, carrots, onion, celery, garlic

3 cups peeled tomatoes (fresh or canned) with their juices
2 cups (a 13-ounce can, reduced-sodium) beef broth
2 cups water
½ cup barley
2 carrots, scraped and sliced
1 medium onion, chopped
1 celery stalk, chopped
1 garlic clove, minced
½ teaspoon each dried basil, dried cilantro, and chili powder
¼ teaspoon each salt and pepper

Combine all ingredients in a 3-quart saucepan, bring to a boil, and simmer over low heat, with cover slightly ajar, for 45 to 55 minutes or until the barley is tender. Stir often during the last 15 minutes.

If the soup seems too thick, thin it with broth or water. Simmer at least 5 minutes after adding liquid.

The soup can be made ahead and reheated. Keep refrigerated.

MAKES ABOUT 1½ QUARTS

Turkey, Broccoli, and Swiss Cheese in Whole Wheat Pockets

SUPERFOODS: whole wheat pita bread, turkey, broccoli, yogurt

4 whole wheat pita ''loaves''
8 slices smoked turkey
4 slices Swiss cheese, cut in half

8 frozen broccoli spears, cooked
''Light'' Russian Dressing (see page 532)

Cut the loaves in half, allowing 2 halves per person. Line each pocket with a folded slices of turkey and Swiss cheese. Tuck in a spear of broccoli. Add dressing to your taste.

MAKES 4 SANDWICHES

AN AFTER-THE-THEATER SUPPER
FOR FOUR

Scampi on Polenta♦
Mixed Mushroom Sauté♦
Peas with Tomatoes♦
Whole Wheat French Bread
Sliced Oranges Flavored with Cointreau

A serving of shrimp provides 50 percent of a woman's RDA for vitamin B_{12}, plus a good amount of niacin and iron. Corn is a source of B_6, mushrooms yield niacin, peas offer thiamin, and oranges are juiced up with that important folate. Add a little whole-grain bread for across-the-board nerve-tonic B vitamins.

Scampi on Polenta

SUPERFOODS: cornmeal, shrimp, garlic, olive oil

Scampi, the Italian word for shrimp, has come to be associated with this quick skillet method of preparing them, which is why you sometimes see the redundant phrase ''Shrimp Scampi'' on menus.

About 2 cups Polenta (see page 519)

3 tablespoons olive oil

1 large or 2 small garlic cloves, finely minced

About 1¼ pounds cooked, shelled, cleaned large shrimp*

¼ cup lemon juice

Several grinds of black pepper

¼ cup chopped fresh flat-leaf parsley

Chill the polenta in an oiled 9- or 10-inch glass pie plate. When firm, cut into 8 pie-shaped wedges. When ready to cook the shrimp, reheat the polenta about 20 minutes in a 350 degree F. oven.

Heat the olive oil in a large skillet. Add the garlic, and cook just until the garlic sizzles; it should not change color. Add the shrimp and cook 2 minutes longer. Remove from the heat, and add the lemon juice and plenty of pepper.

The shrimp can be made several hours ahead. Keep covered and refrigerated.

When ready to serve, reheat the shrimp and add the parsley. Put 2 slices of polenta on each plate, and divide the shrimp among the plates.

MAKES 4 SERVINGS

*You can use anywhere from 1 pound to 1½ pounds shrimp without any other changes in this recipe.

Mixed Mushroom Sauté

SUPERFOODS: shallots, mushrooms

All mushrooms are immune-system boosters, especially shiitakes. Inspect mushrooms carefully before buying; they should be firm and dry, not flabby and moist.

*4 fresh or dried shiitake
    mushrooms*
4 ounces cremini mushrooms
4 ounces white mushrooms
*2 tablespoons olive oil, or more
    as needed*

¼ cup minced shallots
Salt and pepper
*1 tablespoon minced fresh flat-
    leaf parsley*

If using dried shiitakes, soak them in a bowl of warm water for 30 minutes. Drain and pat dry. Fresh or dry, dice them, discarding the stems.

Wash and trim the fresh mushrooms. Wrap them in a kitchen towel to dry. Slice the cremini and white mushrooms thickly, about 3 slices to an average-size mushroom.

Heat the oil in a large skillet, and sauté the shallots until they are sizzling. Add all the mushrooms, and fry them over medium-high heat, during which time they will exude their liquid. Stir often.

When the liquid evaporates and the mushrooms begin to brown, add a little more oil, if needed. Stir constantly until nicely browned. Remove mushrooms from the heat, and salt and pepper them to your taste. Sprinkle with parsley before serving.

The mushrooms can be made several hours ahead and held at room temperature. Lay a sheet of waxed paper over them, not tucked in. Rewarm the mushrooms, if desired.

MAKES 4 SERVINGS

Peas with Tomatoes

SUPERFOODS: onion, tomatoes, peas

A hint of sweetness gives the illusion of just-picked to frozen peas. If there are any leftover peas with tomatoes, combine them with eggs to make an Italian frittata.

1 tablespoon butter	One 10-ounce package frozen
1 tablespoon olive oil	peas
2 tablespoons finely chopped	½ teaspoon sugar
onion	¼ teaspoon dried tarragon
1½ cups seeded chopped fresh	Salt and pepper
tomatoes	

In a large saucepan, heat the butter and olive oil and sauté the onion until it's sizzling. Add the tomatoes, and continue sautéing for 10 minutes, stirring often.

Add the remaining ingredients. Break up the peas with a fork to separate them, stir, and bring the mixture to a simmer. Cover and cook on low heat for 3 minutes. Taste to see if the peas are tender. If not, cook another minute. Immediately remove the peas from the heat.

The peas can be made ahead. Undercook them a little and keep refrigerated. Rewarm when ready to serve.

MAKES 4 SERVINGS

A FORTIFYING BRUNCH
FOR SIX

Pineapple Juice
Banana-Papaya Muffins♦
Scrambled or Poached Eggs
Kasha with Peppers♦
Warm Applesauce with Cinnamon♦

Whole wheat in the muffins and buckwheat groats (kasha) double up the great grains in this menu. Vitamin B_6 in the bananas, niacin in the mushrooms, and thiamin in the pineapple juice round out the menu.

Banana-Papaya Muffins

SUPERFOODS: whole wheat flour, papaya, bananas,
applesauce

*Use some of a quart jar of applesauce for this fat-free recipe and the
rest for the Warm Applesauce with Cinnamon (recipe follows).*

1 cup whole wheat flour	*¼ teaspoon ground allspice*
1 cup unbleached all-purpose flour	*½ cup packed brown sugar**
1½ teaspoons baking powder	*1½ ripe bananas*
½ teaspoon each ground cinnamon, baking soda, and salt	*½ cup prepared egg substitute*
	About ¾ cup applesauce (from a jar is fine)
	⅔ cup snipped dried papaya**

Spray a nonstick muffin tin with cooking spray or line with paper
liners. Preheat the oven to 375 degrees F.

Sift together all the dry ingredients except the brown sugar
into a large bowl. Stir in the brown sugar until well blended.

Puree the bananas and put them into a 2-cup measuring
pitcher. Add the egg substitute and enough applesauce to measure 1¾ cups.

When ready to bake, stir the banana-applesauce mixture into
the dry ingredients, and fold in the papaya. Do not overbeat.

Divide the batter among the muffin cups, and bake on the top
shelf for 20 minutes or until dry inside when tested with a cake
tester. Cool the muffins for 5 minutes on a wire rack before
removing from the pan.

*The muffins can be made up to 1 day in advance and reheated. They
can also be frozen for longer storage.*

MAKES 12 MUFFINS

*Mash out any lumps.
**Dried apricots can be substituted.

Kasha with Peppers

SUPERFOODS: kasha, red peppers, onions

1 egg, beaten, or ¼ cup prepared
  egg substitute
1 cup kasha*
2 cups (a 13-ounce can) chicken
  broth
1 red bell pepper, seeded and
  diced

1 small onion, chopped
2 tablespoons olive or vegetable
  oil
1 tablespoon minced fresh flat-
  leaf parsley

Mix the egg with the kasha, making sure that all the grains are coated. Heat a heavy 10-inch frying pan that has a tight-fitting cover. Dry and separate the kasha kernels by stir-frying them in the pan and breaking them up with a fork for 3 to 4 minutes. The kernels should be hot and toasted.

Meanwhile, bring the broth to a boil in a saucepan. Add it all at once to the kasha (watch out for splattering). Cover, lower the heat, and steam gently for 10 to 15 minutes, until all the liquid has been absorbed.

While the kasha is cooking, separately sauté the red pepper and onion in the oil, using a medium skillet, until they are soft and tender. Stir them into the finished kasha, and sprinkle the parsley on top.

MAKES ABOUT 3 CUPS

*Roasted buckwheat kernels, available in whole-foods markets and most super-markets.

Warm Applesauce with Cinnamon

SUPERFOODS: applesauce

3 cups store-bought applesauce   *½ teaspoon ground cinnamon*
2 tablespoons brown sugar

Mix the applesauce, brown sugar, and cinnamon. Warm in a saucepan on the range or in a microwave-safe serving dish in the microwave. Stir again when the brown sugar melts.

MAKES 6 SERVINGS

A BRUNCH OR EARLY LUNCH FOR FOUR

Ricotta Omelets♦
Puffed Plantains♦
Maple Oatmeal Bread or Maple-Walnut Swirl Bread♦
or
Oatmeal Bread (store-bought) Toast
A Compote of Rosy Grapefruit Segments and Halved Dried Figs

Ricotta is rich in vitamin B_{12}, oatmeal is full of whole-grain B-vitamin goodness, plantains are folate fruits, grapefruit and figs are sources of thiamin.

Ricotta Omelets

SUPERFOODS: shallots, ricotta

*For making omelets, I wouldn't trade my well-seasoned cast-iron
frying pan for any nonstick pan on the market.*

1 tablespoon butter	2 tablespoons water
2 tablespoons olive oil	1 cup part-skim ricotta
¼ cup minced shallots	4 sprigs fresh flat-leaf parsley
10 eggs*	Salt and pepper

All the ingredients are split between 2 omelets. These directions
are for cooking them sequentially, but you could use 2 pans to
cook them both at the same time.

Heat ½ tablespoon of butter and 1 tablespoon of oil in a 10-
inch cast-iron or nonstick frying pan, and sauté half the shallots
on medium-low heat until they are soft but not brown. Meanwhile, beat all the eggs (or egg-and-substitute combination) with
2 tablespoons of water.

Pour half the egg mixture into the sizzling pan. When the
omelet is firm on the bottom, lift it with a spatula to let the
uncooked portion slide underneath. When the omelet is cooked
through but still soft on top, layer ½ cup ricotta over one half,
snip 2 sprigs parsley over it, and salt and pepper the whole to
your taste. Fold the omelet and allow it to cook another 2 minutes
or until the ricotta begins to ooze at the edges.

Remove the omelet to a platter in a warm oven while cooking
the second omelet the same way with the remaining ingredients.
Let the second omelet stand in the warm oven for 2 minutes
before serving both—this finishes heating the ricotta.

MAKES 4 SERVINGS

*1¼ cups prepared egg substitute can be used for 5 of the eggs.

Puffed Plantains

SUPERFOODS: plantains

This is just about the easiest way to cook the "cooking banana."

2 large ripe plantains   Vegetable oil

Preheat the oven to 400 degrees F.
   Rub the plantain skins with vegetable oil. Cut long slits in them lengthwise, plus a few cross slits. Put them in a baking dish, and bake them for 25 to 30 minutes or until the flesh puffs out of the slits. Cut them in half, and serve them in the skins as you would baked potatoes.

MAKES 4 SERVINGS

Maple Oatmeal Bread

SUPERFOODS: oats, whole wheat flour

2 cups boiling water
1 cup old-fashioned or quick-cooking oats (not instant)
2 tablespoons butter or margarine
2 envelopes active dry yeast
½ cup warm water

2 teaspoons salt
½ cup pure maple syrup
¼ teaspoon natural maple flavoring (optional)
3 to 4 cups unbleached all-purpose flour
3 cups whole wheat flour

Pour the boiling water over the oats. Stir in the butter. Let the mixture stand for 30 minutes or longer.

Dissolve the yeast in the warm water, and add it to the oats. Stir in the salt, syrup, and flavoring, if using.

Add 3 cups all-purpose flour and 3 cups whole wheat to form a dough that can be worked. If necessary, add more all-purpose flour.

Knead the dough with an electric dough hook 5 minutes or by hand 10 minutes, until smooth and elastic. (Don't use a food processor; there is too much dough and it's too sticky.)

Put the dough into a buttered bowl, turning it to grease all sides. Cover with plastic wrap, and let rise in a warm place until doubled, an hour or more.

Punch the dough down, and divide it into 2 portions. Roll one half into a 9-inch square. Roll up the square, and place it in a well-buttered 9 × 5-inch loaf pan. Repeat with the remaining dough. With a serrated knife, cut ½-inch slits in the tops of the loaves. Cover the loaves with a tea towel, and let them rise in a warm place until they reach the top of the pans, about 1 hour.

Preheat the oven to 325 degrees F.

Bake the loaves on the middle shelf of the oven for 45 to 50 minutes, until brown on top and shrinking a bit from the sides of the pans. Carefully loosen the loaves with a spatula and turn them out onto wire racks to cool. Do not wrap until completely cold.

Note: Extra bread can be frozen, well-wrapped in foil.

Maple-Walnut Swirl Bread: For sweeter, "coffee cake" breads, blend together ½ cup walnuts, ½ cup brown sugar, and 2 table-spoons butter or margarine in a food processor until the walnuts are finely ground. (Alternatively, chop the walnuts fine, and blend in the brown sugar and softened butter by hand.) If desired, boost the flavor of the filling with 1/2 teaspoon maple flavoring.

When the dough is rolled into 9-inch squares, divide the filling and sprinkle it over the squares to within 1 inch of the edges. Roll up, taking care to pinch the seams shut so that no brown sugar leaks out to burn. Put the loaves in the pans cut side down, and proceed as above.

Sometimes I make one plain loaf (for peanut butter sandwiches) and one "swirl" loaf for breakfast. In that case, the filling ingredients are reduced by half.

MAKES 2 LOAVES

8

CALCIUM AND VITAMIN D

You're Never Too Young to Start Preventing Osteoporosis

If you've been reading and listening to the current health news, you know the two deficiencies that especially endanger women are insufficient iron and calcium. The surgeon general has singled out these two minerals in new recommendations designed for women. In the case of calcium, a possible connection is cited between inadequate dietary intake of this mineral during the first thirty to forty years of life and increased risk of osteoporosis later. You simply cannot afford to neglect calcium if you want to continue to have a straight, strong body capable of participating in all those pleasant activities and satisfying occupations you most enjoy.

Yet according to recent USDA surveys, the average calcium intake by women ages 19 to 34 is 665 milligrams per day, while women ages 35 to 50 consume about 565 milligrams. The National Osteoporosis Foundation recommends 1,000 milligrams a day for premenopausal women, and 1,200 to 1,500 milligrams for pregnant women. For postmenopausal women who are taking estrogen, the recommendation is 1,000 milligrams; for those not taking estrogen, 1,500 milligrams. Women who are on thyroid medication may also have an increased risk of osteoporosis and should check with their physicians about their particular calcium needs.

Just to put these figures in some perspective, a cup of 1 percent milk contains about 300 milligrams calcium—a bit less if it's whole milk. Eight ounces of nonfat yogurt will yield 345 milligrams.

GOOD CALCIUM NUTRITION MAY HELP PMS

Calcium is a useful mineral for women in other ways besides staving off osteoporosis. A study of premenstrual and menstrual women has revealed that symptoms of water retention, various other negative effects, and pain were significantly relieved by treatment with calcium supplements. We don't know yet how simply eating a calcium-rich diet may alleviate those familiar, unwanted symptoms, but the hopeful results of this study certainly add another reason to reach for the nonfat yogurt.

CALCIUM HELPS TO CONTROL BLOOD PRESSURE

Recently, an important link has been found between calcium intake and lower blood pressure. Besides its implications for the general population, this connection affects mothers and children in a significant way. Expectant mothers who take calcium supplements have a reduced risk of high blood pressure during those stressful nine months. Mothers-to-be who eat plenty of calcium-rich foods during their pregnancy give birth to babies who have a lower blood pressure during their first year of life. Three- to 5-year-olds who drink the most milk have the lowest blood pressure.

CALCIUM IS PART OF AN ANTICANCER DIET

An epidemiological study showed that women who regularly eat yogurt, skim milk, and cheese (along with fruits and yellow and green vegetables) seem to have a lower endometrial cancer risk that those who don't. A high calcium intake has also been associated with a decreased risk of colon cancer—and among calcium-rich foods, yogurt was particularly protective.

All very promising indications for women, but the best established reason, by study after study, for including calcium foods in our daily fare is to guard against the osteoporosis threat that looms in our later years.

SERIOUS DEFENSE AGAINST THE CRIPPLER OF WOMEN

Osteoporosis, the most widespread of skeletal disorders, affects about 24 million people in the United States, mostly women. One-third of postmenopausal women have osteoporosis, resulting in 1.3 million fractures each year. A "silent disease" similar to high blood pressure, osteoporosis doesn't betray itself with any helpful warning signs and won't show up on ordinary X-rays. By the time a woman realizes she has those "porous bones," a great deal of damage already will have occurred. The notion that it's time to worry about osteoporosis when the hot flashes begin is very wrong. Although some genetic factors are involved, by and large it's what you do—and what you eat— all through your life that determines how protected you will be after menopause from fragile, brittle bones and "dowager's hump."

Bones are not the stiff, dry sticks they may appear to be. They are living tissue, strong on the outside but spongy inside and constantly changing. Besides keeping you upright, bones are storehouses for the calcium that every cell in the body needs. Calcium regulates muscular contraction and relaxation, including that of the heart muscle. It activates enzymes, as well as aiding in blood clotting and cell adhesion, and being a major component of teeth and bones.

The average woman's body holds between 1½ and 2 pounds of calcium at any given time. This vital mineral moves in and out of her bones as needed, resolving and redepositing. When blood levels are high, the bones absorb the excess. If the blood supply of calcium falls too low, the bones release more to compensate.

During pregnancy, the calcium requirements of the growing fetus are met by drawing calcium from the mother's bones. During the last trimester, the fetus doubles in size and may draw as much as 13 milligrams of calcium an hour from the mother's bones.

Although a woman has accumulated her greatest bone mass by the age of 35, the process of bone formation will continue throughout her life. There are a number of factors that influence bone structure at any age. A calcium-rich diet (with other important minerals, such as magnesium) helps bones stay strong. So does weight-bearing exercise, in which your legs support your body—that is, walking, running, or dancing but, in this case, not swimming.

Bone strength is adversely affected by smoking and by drinking more than two alcoholic drinks daily. A deficiency in vitamin B_6 has been found to lessen calcium retention. And of course, diminished estrogen, whether from an early hysterectomy or later menopause, causes calcium resorption to exceed production, often resulting in dramatic bone mass loss. But like money in the bank, the more bone mass you've built up earlier, the more loss you can tolerate later.

A CASE FOR CALCIUM SUPPLEMENTS

Many physicians are recommending calcium supplements for postmenopausal women who don't opt for estrogen replacement therapy. Early menopausal bone loss is related to a lack of estrogen, which extra calcium cannot prevent, but it does help to prevent the additional, less dramatic bone loss that continues after the first five or six years. In one test, rates of bone loss in postmenopausal women who took no supplements were greater at every skeletal site measured. In another, supplementation with vitamin D and calcium reduced the risk of hip and other fractures in elderly women.

Whether or not you need supplements and how much to take should be discussed with your doctor. Many sources warn against calcium made from bone meal or dolomite, which may contain traces of heavy metals. Of all the kinds of supplements available, calcium citrate is frequently recommended as one that is most easily absorbed and less likely to cause digestive distress or to promote the formation of kidney stones (an occasional problem with excessive calcium) than other supplements. Not as easy to find, though—you may have to turn to a health-food store or a vitamin catalog for calcium citrate.

Supplements that contain less calcium per pill (and thus require you to take more of them) are probably better absorbed; pills that are highly compressed may not dissolve properly—in fact, may pass through the system intact. Since calcium supplements interfere with iron absorption, it's important to take them at meals that don't contain much iron, such as breakfast. After all, you need your iron, too!

SUPPLEMENTS ASIDE, YOU STILL NEED A CALCIUM-RICH DIET

Women who have dense bones because of a lifetime of eating plenty of calcium are better able to withstand the depletion of estrogen. Maintaining a calcium-rich diet throughout life is the ideal, but more often it's a fat-reducing diet that concerns a woman, and she gives up or sharply curtails the very foods that she needs most—milk and milk products. And weight itself is an influence on osteoporosis; after menopause, drastic reducing endangers the bones while a padding of flesh protects them. (So there is a plus side, after all, for the well-rounded figure!)

VITAMIN D ENHANCES CALCIUM ABSORPTION

Vitamin D is the main regulator of calcium absorption—an important point, since only 30 to 40 percent of the calcium in foods may be actually absorbed. Consider this vital factor when you're evaluating your own intake of calcium!

Your skin manufactures vitamin D from sunlight (less of it if you wear a sunscreen), but when winter or fear of skin damage drives you indoors, milk products and dark-fleshed fish will provide the vitamin D you need.

The sunlight "prescription" for vitamin D is five to fifteen minutes twice weekly under the noonday sun. Those who burn easily need less than those who do not. For women who are at risk for skin cancer, one quart of milk equals twenty minutes of sunlight.

CALCIUM DOESN'T DO IT ALONE—OTHER MINERALS ARE ON THE TEAM

Also involved with skeletal strength are the macrominerals phosphorus and magnesium, plus the trace minerals boron and manganese.

Phosphorus is essential to the process of bone mineralization, therefore to its solid structure. Most of the body's phosphorus is teamed up with calcium in the bones and teeth, but phosphorus has other vital functions, too. It's essential to energy production as well as forming cell membranes, genetic material, and many enzymes.

Optimum nutrition requires a balance of calcium and phosphorus in the diet; too much phosphorus in relation to calcium will actually interfere with the latter's absorption. That critical equilibrium is best obtained by eating the superfoods that contain both calcium and phosphorus, such as skim milk, fish, beans, and peas. Foods that contain only phosphorus (also called *phosphates*)—soft drinks particularly—can upset the balance. Women who routinely replace dairy food (and food in general) with diet sodas may be adding to their risk of osteoporosis by consuming too many phosphates.

As is the case with calcium, pregnant women need 50 percent more phosphorous per day.

Magnesium, the second major "bone material," is another team player. Besides aiding in bone growth, magnesium is interlocked with calcium in many bodily processes, including regulation of the heartbeat. Diets low in magnesium have been linked to heart-rhythm abnormalities. Magnesium by itself is involved in every major biologic process.

One trial reported that magnesium (with other minerals and vitamins) was useful in treating premenstrual syndrome. There are insufficient data as yet—but what a promising field for research!

Only a trace is needed of both manganese and boron, but that small amount also affects bone structure.

Manganese is thought to be as essential as calcium to the process of building strong bones. It's also an antioxidant, protecting the body from the dangerous effect of free radicals, those free-roving molecules that age and/or damage bodily systems.

Recent research suggests that boron plays an important role in regulating the body's use of calcium and magnesium. In one study, postmenopausal women who received boron supplements were found to retain more of both calcium and magnesium, suggesting to researchers that boron does help to prevent calcium loss and bone demineralization.

THE "BONE TEAM" IS NICELY PACKAGED BY NATURE IN FOODS

Whether or not you take calcium supplements, you still can benefit by enriching your diet with the real calcium foods, which so often contain many of those other mineral "helpers" in the bargain. Just see how often the same foods appear in the following lists of sources!

Superfood Sources of Calcium

Almonds   Milk and cheese
Beans and peas   Molasses, blackstrap
Broccoli   Sunflower seeds
Figs   Tofu and soymilk
Fish—herring, salmon,   Yogurt, nonfat
   sardines—and shellfish
Greens—collards, kale,
   turnip greens

Superfood Sources of Vitamin D

Milk and cheese   Yogurt, nonfat
Fish, dark-fleshed

Superfood Sources of Phosphorus

Beans and peas   Fish and shellfish
Milk and cheese   Turkey and other poultry
Nuts

Superfood Sources of Magnesium

Apricots   Milk and cheese
Artichokes   Nuts and seeds
Bananas   Whole grains and wheat
Barley   bran
Beans   Yogurt, nonfat
Fish
Greens—dark, leafy

Superfood Sources of Manganese

Beans

Cocoa

Greens—dark, leafy

Nuts

Pineapple

Tea

Whole grains

Superfood Sources of Boron

Fruits—especially apples
  and pears

Vegetables—especially
  broccoli and carrots

SUPERMEALS THAT BONE UP ON CALCIUM AND ITS HELPERS

Recipes indicated by a ♦ follow the menus.

A COSY WINTER DINNER
FOR SIX

Macaroni 'n' Cheese with Salsa♦
Braised Peas and Shallots with Ham♦
Romaine and Arugula Salad
with Honey-Mustard Dressing (see page 531)
Italian Baked Apples♦

There's even more calcium in reduced-fat cheese and skim milk, featured in this spicy macaroni casserole. Lots of vitamin D and phosphorus, too. Less obviously, peas are rich in both calcium and phosphorus. Dark leafy greens are good sources of magnesium and manganese. Apples are tops for boron.

Macaroni 'n' Cheese with Salsa

SUPERFOODS: skim milk, low-fat cheese, pasta, salsa

2 tablespoons butter or
   margarine
2 tablespoons flour
⅛ teaspoon each white pepper
   and cayenne pepper
3 cups skim milk
½ teaspoon salt (optional)
2 cups shredded part-skim
   mozzarella cheese

4 tablespoons grated Parmesan
   cheese
¾ pound elbow macaroni
1 cup medium-spicy tomato salsa
2 tablespoons seasoned or plain
   bread crumbs
Paprika

In a medium saucepan, melt the butter over low heat and stir in the flour, white pepper, and cayenne until smooth. Cook the roux over low heat for 3 minutes, stirring often. Don't let it brown.

Heat the milk separately until it's scalded but don't boil it. Add the hot milk all at once to the roux, raise the heat to medium, and whisk vigorously until the mixture becomes a smooth, bubbly, thickened sauce.

Stir in salt, if using, the mozzarella, and 2 tablespoons of the Parmesan. As soon as the cheese begins to melt, remove from the sauce from the heat, and stir occasionally. The heat of the sauce will continue to melt the cheese.

The sauce can be made up to 1 day ahead. Keep refrigerated. Or it may be frozen for longer storage, which is a great way to use up milk that's reached it's "sell-by" date—and very useful to have on hand. I don't recommend making the casserole ahead of time because the finished dish wouldn't be as "creamy."

Meanwhile, cook the elbows according to package directions. Preheat the oven to 350 degrees F.

Put the cooked elbows into a buttered 2-quart casserole, preferably a flat rather than deep baking dish. Stir in the cheese sauce and salsa. Sprinkle with crumbs, the remaining Parmesan cheese, and paprika. Bake in the middle of the oven for 30 minutes or until the top is lightly brown and the sauce bubbly throughout.

MAKES **6** SERVINGS

Braised Peas and Shallots with Ham

SUPERFOODS: shallots, peas

If you want to make this a meatless meal, you can simply omit the ham. The braised shallots alone give these peas plenty of flavor.

1½ tablespoons olive oil
6 large shallots, peeled and
  halved
½ to 1 cup diced ham

One 16-ounce bag frozen peas
2 tablespoons water
Pepper

In a large skillet, heat the oil and sauté the shallots over very low heat until they are golden and softened, about 5 minutes. Add the ham and continue cooking until the ham is browned. Add the peas and water, and cook uncovered, stirring often, until the peas are tender, about 5 minutes. If necessary, add another spoonful of water. Season with pepper to your taste.

MAKES 6 SERVINGS

Italian Baked Apples

SUPERFOODS: raisins, apples

What makes them Italian? Why, the wine, of course! Italian cuisine includes many fruit-and-wine desserts but few pastries (except for holidays). Keep in mind that alcohol evaporates during the cooking process, in this case leaving a delectable syrup.

6 baking apples (not Delicious or McIntosh)	⅓ cup sugar
About ½ cup raisins	⅔ cup white wine or dry vermouth
6 teaspoons apricot preserves	

Preheat the oven to 350 degrees F.

Wash and core the apples; remove 1 inch of peel from the tops only. Place the apples in a buttered baking dish that will hold them securely upright.

Put some raisins in each apple, add 1 teaspoon preserves, and finish with more raisins. Sprinkle with sugar, and pour the wine over all.

Place the baking dish on the middle shelf with a sheet of foil over the top, not tucked in, and bake them for 40 to 50 minutes, basting once, until quite tender. Cool to just warm. Put the apples into dessert dishes, and spoon the sweet juices from the pan over them.

If you chill the apples before serving, the juices will thicken into a light syrup.

MAKES 6 SERVINGS

INDOOR-OUTDOOR MENU FOR FOUR

Grilled Salmon Steaks
Green Goddess Vegetable and Macaroni Salad♦
Whole-Grain Italian Bread
Almond "Cream" Puddings
with Sliced Fresh Peaches♦

Calcium, vitamin D, and phosphorus in the salmon entree, and also in the salad, with anchovies (especially since those little fillets include soft bones—fish bones are a top nondairy source of calcium), peas, and yogurt. Whole-grain bread is a source of magnesium and manganese. Milk and almonds in the dessert pack in more calcium.

Green Goddess Vegetable and Macaroni Salad

SUPERFOODS: carrot, green pepper, peas, pasta, garlic, yogurt

1 large carrot	*2 cups penne or large elbow*
1 pound zucchini	*macaroni*
1 green bell pepper	*Green Goddess Salad Dressing*
½ cup very small frozen peas	*(recipe follows)*

Prepare the salad dressing.

Prepare the vegetables. Coarsely grate the carrot and zucchini. Cut the pepper into julienne strips. Thaw (but don't cook) the peas. This can be done quickly by putting them into a close-meshed strainer under running warm water. Mix the vegetables with the dressing.

Meanwhile, cook the macaroni according to package directions. Rinse in cold water until cool to the touch; drain very well. Combine the vegetables with the macaroni. Serve at room temperature or chill first.

The salad tastes best when served the same day as it's made; refrigerate leftovers.

MAKES 5 TO 6 CUPS

GREEN GODDESS SALAD DRESSING

Chances are, no one (not even you) will notice the substitution of nonfat yogurt for most or all of the mayonnaise in many favorite salad dressings.

4 anchovy fillets, drained

1 garlic clove, pressed in a garlic
press

Pinch of salt

⅓ cup plain nonfat yogurt

1 tablespoon mayonnaise

2 tablespoons minced fresh flat-
leaf parsley*

White pepper

On a cutting board, sprinkle the anchovy fillets and garlic with the salt, and mash them with the flat of a chef's knife. In a small bowl, mix them with all the remaining ingredients.

The dressing can be made a day ahead. Keep refrigerated.

MAKES A SCANT ½ CUP

Almond "Cream" Puddings with Sliced Fresh Peaches

SUPERFOODS: almonds, yogurt, peaches

½ cup blanched almonds

1 cup whole milk

½ cup sugar

3 tablespoons cornstarch

⅛ teaspoon salt

1 cup plain nonfat yogurt

¾ teaspoon pure almond
flavoring

2 fresh ripe peaches

8 amaretti cookies (Italian crisp
almond cookies; optional)

*This is going to look like a lot of parsley, but the dressing is *supposed* to be green.

Lightly toast and finely grind the almonds; set them aside.

Combine the milk, sugar, cornstarch, and salt in a deep saucepan. Whisk until well blended, then whisk in the yogurt.

Bring to a boil over medium heat while whisking constantly. Reduce the heat to warm, and simmer 2 minutes, whisking.

Remove the pudding from the heat; stir in the almond flavoring and ground almonds. Divide the pudding among 4 dessert dishes. Chill the puddings until set.

Just before serving, peel and slice the peaches, dividing the slices among the desserts. Crush the cookies, if using, to coarse crumbs, and sprinkle them over the peaches.

MAKES 4 SERVINGS

EASY-DOES-IT MENU
FOR FOUR

Baked Chicken in a Chili Crust♦
Scalloped Potatoes and Spinach♦
Grated Carrots with Yogurt-Mint Dressing (see page 532)
Pineapple Slices with Honey and Toasted Pine Nuts

If you marinate the chicken the night before, this could be an easy after-work menu. Like all poultry, chicken is a good source of phosphorus. Yogurt on the chicken and in the salad dressing, plus spinach and milk in the scalloped dish, are all rich in calcium. The spinach, like other dark leafy greens, also contains magnesium and manganese, but the manganese star in this menu is pineapple—especially high!

Baked Chicken in a Chili Crust

SUPERFOODS: yogurt, wheat germ

1 tablespoon chili powder (hot or mild, your choice)

1 teaspoon paprika

½ cup plain nonfat yogurt

2 whole boneless, skinless chicken breasts, each cut into 4 pieces

1 cup plain dry bread crumbs

¼ cup toasted wheat germ

2 tablespoons olive oil

In a large flat dish with a rim, mix the chili powder and paprika with the yogurt. Turn the chicken pieces in the mixture to coat them thickly, cover with waxed paper, and refrigerate for several hours.

Heat the oven to 350 degrees F.

On a sheet of waxed paper, mix the bread crumbs with the wheat germ. Use tongs or 2 forks to dip the chicken in the crumbs, covering all sides.

Brush with oil a large glass or ceramic baking dish that will fit the chicken pieces in one layer. Place the chicken in the dish, and bake on the middle shelf for 15 minutes. Loosen the pieces with a spatula, turn them, and continue cooking for 15 to 20 more minutes, until just cooked through but still moist.

MAKES 4 SERVINGS

Scalloped Potatoes and Spinach

SUPERFOODS: potatoes, spinach, skim milk

4 potatoes
1 cup cooked spinach, chopped
1 tablespoon cornstarch
¼ teaspoon salt
⅛ teaspoon pepper

1 cup milk (can be skim)
1 teaspoon white wine or cider
   vinegar
2 tablespoons chopped fresh dill

Preheat the oven to 350 degrees F.

Peel and cut the potatoes into ¼-inch slices. Put them into a saucepan of salted water to cover, and boil the potatoes until they are tender, 5 to 7 minutes. Drain the potatoes and layer them in a 9 × 9-inch ceramic baking dish or 2-quart casserole.

Put the cooked spinach into a saucepan. Stir the cornstarch, salt, and pepper into the milk, until the cornstarch is dissolved. Pour this mixture into the saucepan with the spinach, and cook over medium-high heat, stirring, until the mixture bubbles and thickens. Stir in the vinegar, then the dill. Pour the creamed spinach over the potatoes. Bake until bubbling throughout, 20 to 25 minutes.

MAKES 4 SERVINGS

CONTINENTAL CALCIUM
FOR SIX

Pastitsio (Greek Meat and Macaroni Casserole)♦
Sugar Snap Peas in Broth♦
Greek Beet Salad♦
Spicy Banana Flan♦

*A*nother comforting creamed dish! There's lots of calcium and vitamin D, plus phosphorus in the ground turkey! Peas, too, are rich in calcium, and there's skim milk in the dessert for more. Beet greens yield magnesium and manganese. Bananas add a share of boron.

———————————

Pastitsio

(Greek Meat and Macaroni Casserole)

SUPERFOODS: turkey, tomato paste, skim milk, pasta

For the meat sauce

2 tablespoons olive oil
1 medium onion, chopped
1¼ pounds ground turkey
½ cup chicken broth
2 tablespoons tomato paste

¼ teaspoon each ground
  cinnamon, ground allspice,
  grated nutmeg, salt, and black
  pepper

For the cream sauce

2 tablespoons butter or
  margarine
3 tablespoons flour
2 cups hot milk (can be skim)
1 cup hot chicken broth
1 tablespoon grated Parmesan
  cheese
¼ teaspoon white pepper

Salt (optional)
2 beaten eggs, or ½ cup prepared
  egg substitute

½ pound penne or ziti
2 tablespoons grated Parmesan
  cheese
Paprika

Make the meat sauce: Heat the oil in a skillet, and fry the onion until it's softened, about 3 minutes. Add the turkey, breaking it up as it fries, and cook until it's no longer pink. Drain off all fat. Add the broth, tomato paste, cinnamon, allspice, nutmeg, salt, and pepper. Simmer gently for 10 to 15 minutes. If the sauce becomes too dry, add more broth.

Make the cream sauce: Melt the butter in a medium saucepan. Stir in the flour, and cook the roux for about 3 minutes over low heat; do not brown it. Add the hot milk and broth, and cook over medium-high heat, whisking constantly, until the sauce bubbles and thickens. Remove from the heat and whisk in the grated cheese, white pepper, and salt to taste, keeping in mind that the cheese is salty. Gradually whisk the hot sauce into the beaten eggs. The sauce will be thin but will thicken when the casserole is baked.

Meanwhile, cook the macaroni according to package directions.

Assemble the casserole. Choose a baking dish with 2½ -quart capacity, preferably a flat rather than round shape. Layer half the macaroni on the bottom, then one-third of the cream sauce, all the meat sauce, another third of the cream sauce, the rest of the macaroni, the remaining third cream sauce. Sprinkle the top with 2 tablespoons grated cheese and paprika.

The casserole can be made to this point several hours or 1 day ahead and kept refrigerated, but it will not be quite as creamy, since the pasta will absorb the sauce. The best plan is to make only the turkey mixture and the cream sauce ahead. Boil the pasta and assemble the casserole when ready to cook.

Preheat oven to 350 degrees F.

Bake the casserole for about 30 minutes on the middle rack (45 minutes if refrigerated) until bubbly throughout and golden brown on top.

MAKES 6 SERVINGS

Sugar Snap Peas in Broth

SUPERFOODS: sugar snap peas

1 pound sugar snap peas, fresh
   or frozen
1 cup chicken broth

1 tablespoon chopped fresh
   chives, or 1 to 2 teaspoons
   chopped fresh mint

If using fresh sugar snaps, wash them and remove the strings. Combine the sugar snaps and broth in a saucepan. Bring to a boil, reduce heat, and simmer, covered, until tender, 2 to 3 minutes. Sprinkle with chives or mint.

MAKES 6 SERVINGS

Greek Beet Salad

SUPERFOODS: beets, beet greens, olive oil

Choose beets with abundant, fresh-looking tops for this dish.

6 to 8 small to medium beets
   with greens attached
   (2 bunches)

½ cup Greek-Style Salad
   Dressing (see page 529)
Grated nutmeg

Cut off the tops, leaving 1 inch or so of stem attached to the beets. Scrub the beets, put them in a saucepan with water to cover, and boil them until tender, 20 to 30 minutes. Drain and cool the beets.

Wash the greens well and chop them coarsely. Remove any large tough stems. In a large saucepan, steam the greens separately from the beets in about ½ cup water until they have wilted and are tender, about 5 minutes.

Drain the greens and arrange them on a platter. Peel and dice the beets; arrange them in the center of the greens. Pour the dressing over all. Sprinkle with a dusting of nutmeg.

The salad can be served at room temperature or made several hours ahead and chilled.

MAKES 6 SERVINGS

Spicy Banana Flan

SUPERFOODS: bananas, skim milk

2 ripe bananas
½ cup sugar
1½ tablespoons cornstarch
½ teaspoon each ground ginger and cinnamon

¼ teaspoon each ground cloves and salt
3 eggs*
2 cups skim milk

*Or 1 egg plus ½ cup prepared egg substitute, in which case, add as much as 15 minutes to cooking time.

Preheat the oven to 325 degrees F. Butter a 12-inch glass pie plate or a 10-inch glass cake pan and sprinkle it with Cinnamon Sugar (see page 540) or granulated sugar.

Puree the bananas in a food processor or mash them very well by hand. Blend in the sugar, cornstarch, and spices. Mix in the eggs and milk. Pour the mixture into the prepared pan.

Bake for 15 minutes on the middle shelf. Reduce the heat to 300 degrees F. and continue cooking until a knife inserted near the center of the flan comes out clean, about 15 minutes more. Chill before serving.

MAKES 6 TO 8 SERVINGS

A MOSTLY MAKE-AHEAD MENU
FOR FOUR

Turkey à la Queen♦
Brown Basmati Rice (see page 524)
Cannellini Salad with Orange Dressing♦
Fig-Almond Cake♦

"Creamed" turkey gets a boost of extra calcium by being paired with Brussels sprouts, which also contain boron. Beans are high in magnesium and manganese. The dessert is chock-full of calcium and vitamin D, with yogurt, figs, and almonds, all excellent sources. Cocoa is high on the list for manganese.

Turkey à la Queen

Superfoods: Brussels sprouts, onion, green and red
peppers, skim milk, turkey

*Occasionally I roast a turkey breast or a wing-and-breast quarter—
which requires no more of the cook than a good instant meat thermometer—not only for a few easy dinners but also for the convenience
of putting away in the freezer pint containers of cooked turkey moistened with broth for dishes like the following.*

One 10-ounce package frozen
  Brussels sprouts
1 tablespoon butter
¼ cup chopped onion
½ green bell pepper, cut into
  strips
1 cup turkey or chicken broth
5 tablespoons instant flour
¼ teaspoon each white pepper
  and salt

2 cups milk (can be skim)
2 cups cold, diced cooked turkey,
  well packed
1 roasted red pepper, cut into
  strips (from a jar or see page
  523)
1 tablespoon balsamic vinegar
1 tablespoon drained capers
⅛ teaspoon dried tarragon

Cook the sprouts according to package directions. Cut them in
half. Keep them warm if using right away.

Melt the butter in a large skillet. Add the onion and green
pepper; stir-fry until the vegetables are nearly tender, about 5
minutes. If the pan gets too dry, add a little vegetable oil.

Add the broth and bring it to a simmer. Blend the flour, salt,
and pepper into the milk, and pour that all at once into the broth.
Stir constantly over medium heat until the mixture bubbles and
thickens. Stir in the turkey and red pepper. Simmer 3 minutes.
Stir in the vinegar, capers, and tarragon, crushing the herb between your fingers.

The recipe can be made 1 day ahead and rewarmed in the top of a double boiler over simmering water or in a microwave-safe dish in the microwave. Cook the sprouts just before serving.

Serve the turkey on the warm sprouts with rice on the side.

MAKES 4 SERVINGS

Cannellini Salad with Orange Dressing

4 cups romaine lettuce, in bite-size pieces

One 20-ounce can cannellini (white beans), drained and rinsed

4 center slices red onion, separated into rings

For the dressing

⅓ cup orange juice

½ teaspoon grated orange rind

⅓ cup All-Purpose Salad Oil Blend (see page 436) or walnut oil

2 teaspoons Dijon mustard

Arrange the lettuce in a salad bowl. Top with the cannellini and onion rings.

Combine the dressing ingredients in a jar. Cover tightly and shake vigorously until emulified.

The recipe can be prepared in advance and stored in the refrigerator.

When ready to serve, shake the dressing again, and pour it over the salad.

MAKES 4 SERVINGS

Fig-Almond Cake

SUPERFOODS: figs, whole wheat flour, almonds, yogurt

1 cup snipped dried figs, well
packed, stems discarded
1¼ cups sifted all-purpose flour
¾ cup sifted whole wheat pastry
flour
3 tablespoons unsweetened cocoa
1½ teaspoons baking powder
½ teaspoon each baking soda,
ground cinnamon, and salt
½ cup finely ground almonds

2 eggs or ½ cup prepared egg
substitute
1 cup plus 2 tablespoons
granulated sugar
½ cup vegetable oil
½ teaspoon pure almond
flavoring
¾ cup plain nonfat yogurt
¼ cup sliced almonds
Confectioners' sugar (optional)

Preheat the oven to 350 degrees F. Oil an angel food cake pan with a removeable rim, and line the bottom with oiled waxed paper cut to fit.

Mix the figs with 1 tablespoon of the all-purpose flour and set them aside.

Sift together the remaining flours, cocoa, baking powder, baking soda, cinnamon, and salt. Stir the ground almonds into the dry ingredients.

Use an electric mixer to whip the eggs well, gradually adding the sugar. Add the oil and flavoring, and continue beating until the mixture is quite light, about 5 minutes.

Reduce speed; add the dry ingredients in 4 batches alternately with the yogurt in 3 batches, beginning and ending with the flour mixture. Do not overbeat at this stage; as soon as one batch is incorporated, go on to the next, scraping the bowl often.

Remove the bowl from the mixer and fold in the figs.

Spoon the batter into the prepared pan. Sprinkle with the almonds. Bake on the middle shelf for 40 to 45 minutes, until the cake springs back when lightly pressed with a finger and a cake tester inserted in the center comes out dry.

Cool in the pan on a rack for 5 minutes. Remove the rim. Finish cooling completely before removing from the rest of the pan and stripping off the waxed paper. If desired, use a sifter to dust the cake with confectioners' sugar.

MAKES 10 SERVINGS

9

COMPLEX CARBOHYDRATES, NATURE'S ATTITUDE ADJUSTERS

Comforting Starchy Foods Relieve Stress and Provide Stamina

How things have changed! Not so long ago, nutritionists and dieticians were advising us to eat more protein and fewer carbohdyrate foods in order to be strong, energetic, lean, and muscular—the very image of the American athlete! Some popular reducing diets carried this principle to uncomfortable extremes, radically excising starchy carbohydrates in favor of meat and fat—a regime that left many dieters feeling hungry and ill-humored.

Today, however, the U.S. government's new Food Guide Pyramid puts complex carbohydrate foods at the hefty base, recommending eight to eleven servings a day. Some of us may even have a difficult time figuring out how to eat that many helpings in the allotted time frame. Still, the effort is mighty enjoyable—because it seems that everyone loves these comforting, bland, filling starchy foods: pasta, potatoes, rice, bread, and cereal in its various guises.

NATURE'S WAY OF STORING ENERGY

Carbohydrates are created by plants through photosynthesis, a process that uses sunlight to convert water and carbon dioxide into glucose (sugar). Whatever glucose is not needed immediately by the plant is converted into starch and conveniently (for the harvester) stored in root, stem, leaf, and/or seed.

Fruits such as pears that grow sweeter after harvesting do so because their starch converts to sugar. On the other hand, when vegetables like corn and peas lose their sweetness after picking, it's because their sugar content has rapidly converted into starch.

While *simple carbohydrates* are sugars, *complex carbohydrates* are molecular chains of many simple sugars. Different combinations of these molecules are responsible for the wide variety in appearance, texture, and taste of the products in nature's complex carbohydrate food basket. In any form, however, these products will consist of starchy granules wrapped in an indigestible cellulose packaging (known as *fiber*, an important nonnutrient). Cooking softens the packaging and releases the starch so that it can be digested.

That starch is humankind's most common source of energy. It's the main theme of every regional and national cuisine. Think of rice in Asia, corn in Central America, potatoes in Ireland, oats in Scotland, yams in Africa, and wheat in this country—those "amber waves of grain."

COMPLEX CARBOHYDRATES FOR SUSTAINED ACTIVITY

While all carbohydrates can be utilized by the body for energy, simple carbohydrates burn up quickly, like kindling, giving a quick bright lift, whereas complex carbohyrates, like well-seasoned logs, burn more slowly, taking longer to break down and giving a more sustained energy for the long haul. This is why a bowl of oatmeal topped with milk (you need protein, too!) can keep you in top form all through the morning, but a sugar-frosted pastry will leave you languishing long before lunch.

The problem with skipping breakfast before going to work is that mid-morning pastry is liable to be more available than real whole food—and hunger will make it harder to resist. If you can't make time to eat, try to take some of those good carbs with you . . . perhaps a banana and a slice of whole-grain bread with cheese or peanut butter.

BALANCING THOSE MARVELOUS CARBS

The recent redemption of unrefined complex carbohydrates has in some quarters bordered on religious fervor, but the most healthful diet, as usual, favors variety and moderation. In fact, we ought to be suspicious whenever a new food guru advises us to limit our regular diet in some drastic way. We need to make carbohydrates the base and bulk of our daily fare without giving up calcium-rich, low-fat dairy products, iron-rich proteins, and sugar-sweet beta-carotene fruits. And we need to know how to manage those carbohydrates so that they can be used to relieve stress or provide stamina for some special physical effort, whether running a marathon or spring-cleaning the garage.

The current recommendation is that more than half of your daily calories should be obtained from carbohydrates, some of which should replace the excess fat in the American diet. Vegetarians, of course, are already getting most of their calories from carbohydrates, but the rest of us might revamp our typical meals to offer smaller portions of meat and more rice or pasta, including some meatless meals along the way. Countries with the lowest rates of heart disease—in the Mediterranean region and Asia—have been eating this way all along.

PASTA IS A GREAT DIET FOOD . . . YES, REALLY!

"Everything you see I owe to spaghetti," Sophia Loren has maintained, so we conclude that enjoying this tasty carbohydrate dish can't be all that bad for the figure.

Since a current survey tells us that 40 percent of the female population is dieting at any given time, it's important to dispel the old myth associating starchy foods with plump bodies. Scientists have come to the conclusion that hardly any carbohydrate turns into bodily fat because it takes so many calories to make this conversion. In fact, carbohydrates are a reliable source of the energy required to burn up bodily fat. It's not sugar and starch that puts on the pounds as much as it's the fat we eat. Increasing fiber and lowering fat intake (plus stepping up exercise) is the basis of the world's easiest no-mathematics, no-food-exchanges, eat-anywhere diet. And starch, unless refined, already comes wrapped in that indigestible cellulose called *fiber*!

STIMULATING PEAK PERFORMANCE

Such a diet modification won't leave you fainting between meals. A low-fat and moderate- to high-carbohydrate diet is currently recommended for athletes and runners. One study determined that soccer players performed better after a carbohydrate-enriched meal. Another study found runners running faster on a treadmill. The Professional Football Athletic Trainer Society reports that more than 70 percent of NFL trainers today are stressing a high-carbohydrate diet for peak performance in competition.

A DRUGLESS TRANQUILIZER RIGHT ON HAND IN THE KITCHEN

Along with fueling the body with energy, carbohydrates influence the brain. It appears that they are natural tranquilizers, inducing calmness and composure.

Some fascinating research done by Judith J. Wurtman, Ph.D., at the Massachusetts Institute of Technology, has revealed how close a connection there is between the foods we eat and changes in our states of mind.

Our brain is known to manufacture chemicals that ferry signals between neurons in the brain, called *neurotransmitters*, from substances such as amino acids in the foods we eat. Three of these chemicals—dopamine, norepinephrine, and serotonin—produce varying states of mind. Serotonin promotes a mood of calmness, relaxation, and cheerfulness, enabling us to focus on the matter at hand without being agitated or distracted by peripheral events. (The effects of dopamine and norepinephrine are explained in the following chapter.)

The amino acid tryptophan activates serotonin. When carbohydrates are eaten *without an accompanying protein*, insulin released from the pancreas prevents some competing amino acids from entering the brain, allowing tryptophan a clear field. This happens quite fast. Within a half-hour or so, a woman may expect to feel a response to increased serotonin.

Of course, it's not necessary to omit the accompanying protein unless that specific mood-lifting effect is urgently sought. About three in the afternoon of a particularly irritating day when you feel like snarling and snapping might be a good time to have that carbohydrate jolt—perhaps a bran muffin with a spoonful of jam. The rest of the time, it's not only okay, it's essential to pour milk on your morning cereal or to toss shrimp with the pasta. In fact, too much unadulterated carbohydrate at lunchtime—such as a large helping of pasta with a light tomato sauce—is liable to find you "sleeping at the switch" later on in the afternoon.

BALM FOR PMS BLUES AND BLAHS

Women in the throes of premenstrual tension and depression or those who are seasonally affected and get the blues as sunlight diminishes each year have been shown to crave more starches, sweets, and chocolate. (And we all know those must-have-chocolate-or-die moods!) Now researchers have made a connection between eating carbohydrate foods—thus increasing serotonin in the brain—and relief from depression. Those PMS cravings are being viewed not as self-indulgence but as an instinctive self-medication to temporarily relieve the misery.

For women who have trouble falling asleep at night—perhaps mentally reliving the day's events or planning those of the following day—1½ ounces of carbohydrate (with *no protein* this time, not even the proverbial glass of warm milk) can function just like a sleeping pill. Nervous distractions simply fade away, allowing natural fatigue to lull you to sleep. If you're in the midst of PMS week, the "dose" might need to be higher, however—about 2½ ounces, according to Dr. Wurtman's research.

In studying PMS, scientists have advanced the theory that the disorder is caused by the interaction of cyclic hormonal changes with other bodily systems, and that serotonin plays an especially important role. One study, which sought to measure various symptoms in women complaining of PMS, concluded that it was potentially relevant that both carbohydrate craving and depression are linked to serotonergic changes in the brain.

A diet high in carbohydrates, moderate in protein, easy on the salt, and rich in seasonal fruits and vegetables is what some researchers are recommending to lessen the effects of PMS and just generally to keep a woman feeling her best.

DIETARY DEFENSE AGAINST CANCER

Because unrefined complex carbohydrate foods are generally cheap and readily available, they're associated with poorer, less sophisticated populations, whereas affluent segments of society have usually chosen to consume more fatty meats, sugars, and refined grains. Some epidemiologists blame this "richer" diet for giving rise to some of the diseases to which we are susceptible: heart disease, cancer, and gastrointestinal disorders.

Complex carbohydrates are even better for you if they are unrefined, whole foods! Endometrial and breast cancer both have been shown to be inversely associated with a diet high in whole-grain bread, pasta, fruit, and vegetables. (There have been mixed results in breast cancer studies; this particular finding was part of the Canadian National Breast Cancer Screening Study, 1982–1987.) A diet high in carbohydrates, plus fibrous fruit and vegetables, has also been shown to protect women—even more than men—from adenomas (precursors of most colorectal cancers). The risk for women was reduced by 60 percent.

A PLEASANT PRESCRIPTION FOR BODY AND MIND

All of this research information is probably only giving you permission to eat what you enjoy anyway—most people just love those starchy comfort foods like mashed potatoes or noodle soup. And pasta, we must remember, is a mainstay of the healthy Mediterranean diet—as rice is of the healthy Asian diet. All we need to do, when reveling in these good foods, is to lighten up their preparation by substituting plain nonfat yogurt for cream or a little olive oil for a lot of butter.

Some light and lovely carbohydrate menus and recipes follow, plus some quick fixes for those inevitable times of stress and strain—or for those rainy-day moods. Nature's attitude adjusters to the rescue!

Superfood Sources of Carbohydrates

Beans, fresh and dried, including lentils
Bread, whole-grain
Cereals: cornmeal, oatmeal, wheat flakes and biscuits
Grains: barley, millet, oats, rye, wheat
Pasta
Rice, brown or white
Vegetables, starchy: corn, peas, potatoes, pumpkin, squash

SUPERFAST CARBOHYDRATE COMFORTERS

A toasted whole wheat English muffin with marmalade (no butter)
A handful of eat-it-from-the-box cereal (without milk)
A cup of noodle-thick soup (no meat)
A slice of cornbread or a corn muffin with jelly
A baked potato with chopped fresh herbs
A cup of hot rice with a topping of Chinese vegetables
Crackers (low-fat) or melba toast with a vegetable pâté
Italian bread toast with chicken broth poured over

Supermeals for Attitude Adjustment

Recipes indicated by a ♦ follow the menus.

A Menu for Four to Unwind With —You Deserve It!

Polenta with Grilled Fresh Tomato Sauce♦
Italian Three-Bean Salad♦
Whole-Grain Italian Bread
Sliced Peaches with Raspberry Sorbet

When a difficult day is finally over, soothe away those stressful thoughts with a very starchy but very low-fat menu. There's a bunch of beta-carotene, as well as comfort, in this combination.

Polenta with Grilled Fresh Tomato Sauce

SUPERFOODS: tomatoes, olive oil, red pepper, onion, garlic

Although actually broiled, this sauce has a nicely grilled flavor and the slight crunch of al dente peppers and onions. Start the polenta before marinating the sauce ingredients.

4 ripe fresh tomatoes (1¼ pounds)	½ teaspoon salt
3 tablespoons olive oil	⅛ to ¼ teaspoon black pepper
½ cup chopped red bell pepper	Hot red pepper flakes (optional)
¼ cup chopped red onion	2 teaspoons snipped fresh basil
1 garlic clove, finely minced	About 3 cups hot Polenta (see page 519)

Peel, seed, and chop the tomatoes. You should have about 1½ cups.

Combine the tomatoes with all the remaining ingredients except the red pepper flakes and basil. Marinate a half-hour at room temperature.

Preheat the broiler.

Spoon the sauce into the pan portion of a small nonstick broiler (about 7 × 11 inches) or similar nonreactive metal pan. Broil under heated broiler on top shelf for 5 minutes. Stir. Repeat twice: 3 stirrings, 15 minutes total cooking time. If a few pieces of onion and pepper, emerging from the moist tomato, become slightly charred, this is all to the good.

Remove from heat and stir in the red pepper flakes, if using, and basil.

The sauce may be made ahead and rewarmed in a small saucepan.

Smooth the polenta onto a platter (or 4 plates). Top with sauce.

MAKES ABOUT 1½ CUPS SAUCE; 4 SERVINGS

Italian Three-Bean Salad

SUPERFOODS: garlic, green beans, cannellini, pinto beans, red pepper, scallions

In designing a low-fat menu, salad dressing is sometimes an over-looked (but important) factor. This sweet-and-sour salad is dressed with much less oil than vinegar.

½ cup red wine vinegar
2 tablespoons sugar
½ teaspoon salt
¼ cup olive oil
1 garlic clove, finely minced
Freshly ground black pepper
One 10-ounce package frozen Italian green beans
One 15- to 16-ounce can cannellini (white kidney beans), drained and rinsed

One 15- to 16-ounce can pinto beans, drained and rinsed
½ red bell pepper, seeded and slivered
A bunch of scallions with green tops, chopped
2 tablespoons chopped flat-leaf parsley
1 tablespoon chopped fresh marjoram, or 1 teaspoon dried oregano

In a small saucepan, heat the vinegar slightly, and stir in the sugar and salt until dissolved. Remove from the heat immediately. Cool; add the oil, garlic, and black pepper.

Cook the green beans according to package directions, but slightly undercooked. Rinse them in cold water.

In a large bowl, mix the dressing with all the other ingredients, taking care that the garlic is blended throughout. Chill to develop the flavor.

The salad can be made 1 day ahead. Keep refrigerated.

MAKES ABOUT 1 QUART

A VEGETARIAN BURGER MENU FOR SIX

Lentil Burgers♦ on Whole Wheat Hamburger Buns
Baked Sugar Pumpkin♦
Watercress Salad with Chopped Red Onions
Poached Pears with Cranberries♦

Here are complex carbohydrate foods to promote a calm, focused mind and sustained energy. The lentil burger mix takes time but can be prepared ahead, as can the pumpkin (either version) and the pears. The amino acids in lentils and brown rice complement each other to produce the complete protein that you might expect from a beef burger, with none of the fat to weigh you down.

Lentil Burgers

SUPERFOODS: lentils, brown rice, onion, whole wheat
bread, wheat germ

Basic burger mix

1 tablespoon olive oil	2 eggs or ½ cup prepared egg
1 medium onion, finely chopped	substitute
1 cup lentils	1 cup fresh crumbs from whole
½ cup brown rice*	wheat bread
4 cups water	¼ cup wheat germ
¾ teaspoon salt	¼ teaspoon pepper

In a large saucepan, heat the oil and sauté about half the onion
until it softens, about 3 minutes. Add the lentils, rice, water,
and salt, and bring to a boil. Cook 45 minutes, covered, stirring
occasionally, especially toward the end of the cooking time.

Drain the mixture in a close-meshed strainer. (Most of the
liquid will have been absorbed.) Mash the lentil mixture and
blend in the remaining basic ingredients, including the remaining
chopped onion. A food processor makes this easier.

Follow either of the 2 variations given below.

The burgers can be made 1 day in advance and stored in the refrigerator. Or they can be frozen for longer storage.

MAKES 12

---

*It has to be brown rice to cook in the same amount of time as the lentils.

Chili Burgers

½ cup chili sauce
1 tablespoon chili powder
Olive oil
2 green bell peppers, seeded and
    chopped

1 jalapeño pepper, seeded and
    minced*

Blend the chili sauce and powder into the burger mix. Form into 12 burgers (⅓ cup each). Fry in a skillet coated with olive oil, adding the green and jalapeño peppers to the pan.

Curry Burgers

1 tablespoon curry powder
½ cup finely chopped walnuts
1 tablespoon chopped fresh
    cilantro (optional)

Olive oil
1 garlic clove, crushed

Blend the curry powder, walnuts, and cilantro into the basic burger mix. Form into 12 burgers (⅓ cup each). Fry in a skillet coated with olive oil, adding the garlic to the pan. (Discard the garlic later.)

*Use rubber gloves to handle hot peppers.

Baked Sugar Pumpkin

SUPERFOODS: pumpkin

Often overlooked as a vegetable, even by frozen vegetable manufacturers, the plump pumpkin is a powerhouse of beta-carotene! A fresh uncut pumpkin will often keep as long as a month in a cool room or enclosed porch.

One 2½- to 3-pound whole sugar   *¼ cup brown sugar*
   pumpkin*   *½ teaspoon ground cinnamon*
½ teaspoon salt
1 tablespoon butter, softened

Preheat the oven to 350 degrees F.

Cut off the top of the pumpkin to make a lid. Clean out the seeds and stringy pulp. Separate the seeds from the pulp and reserve them if you wish to make the roasted pumpkin seeds (recipe follows on the next page).

Brush the soft butter over the inside of the pumpkin. Sprinkle the sides and bottom with the salt, brown sugar, and cinnamon. Cover with the lid.

Bake for 50 minutes to 1 hour, until very tender. Cut into wedges to serve (*or make ahead and prepare the pumpkin casserole that follows on page 414*).

---

*Ask your grocer. Sugar pumpkins are especially grown for cooking rather than for decoration.

Pumpkin Casserole: Peel leftover baked pumpkin, and puree it in a food processor or mash by hand, adding 1 to 2 tablespoons soft butter, more cinnamon, and a few dashes of ground cloves. Spoon it into a casserole. *The recipe can be prepared 1 day ahead. Keep refrigerated.* Top with ¼ cup chopped peanuts and bake in a 350 degree F. oven for 25 to 30 minutes, until piping hot. Or omit the peanuts, and sprinkle a few roasted pumpkin seeds on top just before serving (otherwise, they will overbrown).

Roasted Pumpkin Seeds: Mix the seeds with a tablespoon of vegetable oil and ½ teaspoon of salt, and spread them out on a cookie sheet. Bake in a 250 degree F. oven for 1 hour or until dry; don't let them brown. Use as a snack, a salad topping in place of croutons, or as garnish on leftover pumpkin, as in preceding recipe.

MAKES 6 OR MORE SERVINGS

Poached Pears with Cranberries

SUPERFOODS: pears, cranberries

3 large pears	½ cup sugar
⅓ cup orange juice	1 cinnamon stick
⅔ cup water	1 cup fresh cranberries

Peel, seed, and quarter the pears.

Combine all the ingredients in a deep saucepan. Bring to a simmer, stirring to dissolve sugar, and continue to cook, uncovered, for 20 to 30 minutes, stirring occasionally, until the cranberries break open and the pears are tender.

Let the pears cool and the syrup thicken before serving.

MAKES 6 SERVINGS

T.G.I.F. SUPPER FOR FOUR
WHO ARE REALLY STRESSED OUT

Sautéed Peas and Zucchini with Pasta♦
Panzanella (Bread Salad)♦
Italian Fruit Ices and Amaretti

*M*ake the Panzanella first, so that it can marinate deliciously while you prepare the pasta. Peas, pasta, and bread in this easy supper add up to plenty of carbohydrates to soothe your spirit. Keeping protein to a low profile will speed the effect.

Sautéed Peas and Zucchini with Pasta

SUPERFOODS: onion, red pepper, peas, pasta

A quick, lazy pasta dish that's ready in a few minutes.

3 tablespoons olive oil
½ cup each chopped onion and
    diced red bell pepper
1 medium zucchini, diced
One 10-ounce package frozen
    peas
1 tablespoon minced fresh
    marjoram, or ½ teaspoon
    dried oregano

Salt and pepper
¾ pound small elbow macaroni
⅓ cup freshly grated Romano
    cheese

Heat the olive oil in a large skillet, and sauté the onion and red pepper until they're sizzling, about 2 minutes. Add the zucchini, and continue sautéing over medium heat, stirring often, until the zucchini begins to turn golden brown. This takes 7 to 10 minutes and shouldn't be rushed since the sweetness of the zucchini depends on its being fried.

Add the peas (in a frozen block is okay), herbs, and seasonings. Cover and cook 3 minutes. Remove the cover and blend the peas with the zucchini. Cook 1 to 2 minutes longer, until the peas are just tender but not overcooked.

Meanwhile, cook the elbows according to package directions. Mix the elbows into the vegetables, spoon onto a platter, and top with the cheese.

MAKES 4 SERVINGGS

Panzanella

(Bread Salad)

SUPERFOODS: olive oil, onion, tomatoes

Actually, this Mediterranean favorite is a tomato salad with lots of fresh croutons sopping up the delicious juices. The amount of oil has been reduced from the original, but a good fruity virgin oil will deliver the flavor.

4 cups 1-inch bread cubes cut from Italian bread, including crust	½ cup chopped red onion
¼ cup virgin olive oil	2 tablespoons snipped fresh basil
2 tablespoons red wine vinegar	4 cups chopped vine-ripened tomatoes
¼ cup pitted and slivered Greek olives	Salt and freshly ground black pepper

Heat the oven to 300 degrees F.

On a baking sheet, toast the bread cubes for 15 minutes or more, until lightly golden and dry. Cool.

In a salad bowl, combine the oil, vinegar, olives, onion, and basil. Stir in the tomatoes and salt and pepper to your taste. Allow the mixture to marinate at room temperature for a half-hour or so, stirring occasionally.

About 15 minutes before serving, stir in the bread cubes. Yes, some of the bread will soften, but that's the idea of this salad.

Some Different Versions: Finely diced cucumber or yellow bell pepper is sometimes added to the tomatoes. A finely minced garlic clove can be substituted for the onion. Four mashed fillets of anchovy and 1 tablespoon of drained capers can replace the black olives. Or mix and match as you wish!

MAKES 4 GENEROUS SERVINGS

AFTER-WORK EASY DINNER
FOR FOUR

Pastina in Broth with Shredded Spinach♦
Tuna and Chickpea Salad♦
Whole Wheat Focaccia
Instant Blueberry "Ice Cream"♦

After a difficult day, when you still have things to do or places to go, you'll want easy preparation and you'll need nourishment that's both comforting and energizing. This model menu is quickly made, light on fat and rich in vitamins and minerals, with comforting carbohydrates in pasta and bread, energizing but light protein in tuna and yogurt—and "all of the above" in chickpeas.

Pastina in Broth with Shredded Spinach

SUPERFOODS: pastina, spinach

1 quart (two 13-ounce cans reduced-sodium) chicken broth	2 cups loosely packed, finely shredded spinach
½ cup pastina*	Pepper
	Grated Parmesan cheese

*Acini de pepe, otherwise known as "soup mac," can be substituted. Cook 8 to 10 minutes.

Choose a pot large enough to allow for expansion, since this soup tends to bubble up.

Heat the broth to boiling. Add the pastina, and cook uncovered over medium-high heat 5 to 8 minutes, stirring often, until tender. If the broth threatens to boil over, adding a teaspoon of oil will calm it.

Turn off the heat. Add the spinach, cover, and let stand 5 minutes.

Add pepper to your taste, and pass grated cheese at the table.

MAKES ABOUT 1 QUART

Tuna and Chickpea Salad

SUPERFOODS: tuna, chickpeas, scallions

Italian tuna has a superb flavor, compared to water-packed American tuna. To compensate for the oil that clings even to well-drained tonno, there's no added oil in this salad.

Two 6-ounce cans imported Italian oil-packed tuna
One 20-ounce can chickpeas, drained and rinsed
12 Kalamata olives, pitted and halved
3 to 4 tablespoons red wine vinegar

4 scallions, chopped
Freshly ground black pepper
½ head romaine lettuce, torn into bite-size pieces (4 cups)
Red bell pepper or grated carrot for garnish

Drain the tuna well and flake it, but don't mash it, with a fork. Mix with all the remaining ingredients except the lettuce. Taste to correct seasoning. You may want more vinegar.

Line a bowl with the lettuce, and spoon the salad into the center. Top with rings of red bell pepper or a heap of coarsely grated carrot.

Instant Blueberry "Ice Cream"

SUPERFOODS: blueberries, yogurt

And not a trace of fat!

1 cup frozen blueberries*	*¼ cup brown sugar*
1 cup plain nonfat yogurt	*½ teaspoon ground cinnamon*

Combine all ingredients in the work bowl of a food processor, and blend until smooth and creamy.

Serve at once—in which case the texture will be like soft "dairy freeze"—or set the dessert in the freezer for a little while (while you're having dinner, for instance) for a firmer texture. Stir before spooning into dessert dishes (preferably sherbet glasses).

MAKES 4 SERVINGS

*The berries must be solidly frozen.

SIMPLY CHEERY AND HEARTY DINNER FOR FOUR

Creamy Sweet and White Potato Soup with Brown Onions♦
Pumpernickel Bread
Steamed Asparagus Garnished with Chopped Hard-Cooked Egg
Beet, Cucumber, and Yogurt Salad♦
Honey-Hazelnut Cake♦
or
Apples Wedges and Honey for Dipping

Starchy carbohydrates, with hardly any fat, cheer up those SAD (seasonal affective disorder) winter blues—but that's not all there is to this menu. There's beta-carotene in the sweet potatoes and carrots (hidden in the cake), folate in the beets and asparagus, calcium in the yogurt, to name just a few nutritional bonuses.

Creamy Sweet and White Potato Soup with Brown Onions

SUPERFOODS: sweet and white potatoes, olive oil, onions

A deliciously "creamy" soup without a drop of cream.

3½ cups peeled, sliced potatoes (2   1 large onion, chopped
   sweet and 2 white)   ¼ teaspoon white pepper
3½ cups chicken broth   A few dashes of grated nutmeg
2 tablespoons olive oil

Combine the potatoes and broth in a 2-quart saucepan. Bring to a boil, reduce heat, and simmer for 10 to 15 minutes, covered, until the potatoes are very tender.

Meanwhile, heat the olive oil in a small skillet, and sauté the onion until it is browned and crisp, but not burned, about 6 minutes.

Scoop out the potato with a slotted spoon, and puree it in a food processor. Gradually add the broth through the feed tube. Be cautious with this; hot food foams up high. (Alternatively, if you use a blender, blend the soup and potatoes together, in 2 batches.)

Return the soup to the saucepan, and stir in the onion, white pepper, and nutmeg. Taste to correct seasoning; you may want more seasoning or a little salt. If the soup seems too thick, whisk in some additional broth.

The soup can be made 1 day ahead. Keep refrigerated. Reheat in the top of a double boiler or in a glass casserole in the microwave; whisk occasionally while heating.

MAKES ABOUT 1½ QUARTS

Beet, Cucumber, and Yogurt Salad

SUPERFOODS: beets, onion, yogurt

1 cucumber
1 cup cooked and finely diced or coarsely grated beets
¼ cup finely diced sweet onion
1 cup Thickened Yogurt (see page 534)
2 tablespoons red wine vinegar

1 tablespoon olive oil
1 tablespoon minced fresh dill
¼ teaspoon each white pepper, salt, and sugar
A small head of bibb lettuce
Sprigs of fresh dill for garnish

Cut the cucumber lengthwise, and scrape out the seeds with a grapefruit spoon. Finely dice the cucumber, salt it, and let it drain for 30 minutes. Rinse off the salt, and press out the excess moisture.

Combine the cucumber, beets, and onion in a bowl. Blend the yogurt, vinegar, oil, and seasonings. Mix the yogurt with the vegetables, and let the salad marinate in the refrigerator for an hour or so.

Line chilled salad dishes with torn leaves of bibb lettuce. Divide the cucumber-beet salad among the plates, and garnish with sprigs of dill.

Serve very cold with thinly sliced pumpernickel bread.

MAKES 4 SERVINGS

Honey-Hazelnut Cake

SUPERFOODS: carrots, hazelnuts

Leftover cake, wrapped in foil and refrigerated, will keep several days.

1¾ cups sifted all-purpose flour
1 teaspoon baking powder
½ teaspoon baking soda
¼ teaspoon each ground ginger, grated nutmeg, ground cloves, ground cinnamon, and salt
2 eggs

½ cup sugar
2 tablespoons vegetable oil
½ cup mashed cooked carrots (2 large carrots)
⅓ cup honey
¼ cup strong brewed hazelnut coffee* or regular coffee
½ cup shelled hazelnuts

Preheat the oven to 325 degrees F. Oil an 8- or 9-inch square cake pan and line the bottom with oiled waxed paper cut to fit.

Sift together the flour, baking powder, baking soda, spices, and salt.

With an electric mixer or by hand, whisk the eggs until thick. Beat in the sugar, oil, carrots, honey, and coffee, one at a time, until the mixture is quite light, about 5 minutes. Stir the dry ingredients into the egg mixture, and fold in the hazelnuts. Pour the batter into the prepared pan.

Bake on the middle shelf for 30 to 35 minutes, or until a cake tester inserted in the center comes out dry. Cool the cake in the pan on a wire rack for 5 minutes. Remove from pan, invert the cake, and gently strip off the waxed paper. Finish cooling the cake right side up before cutting.

Note: Chopped dates can be substituted for the hazelnuts.

MAKES 8 TO 12 SERVINGS

*Just if you happen to have it on hand.

MEDITERRANEAN COMFORT
BY THE FIRESIDE—FOR FOUR

Antipasto of Prosciutto, Fresh Fennel, and Radishes
Sicilian Potatoes♦
Dandelion and Romaine Salad
Whole-Grain Italian Bread
Tangerines and Roasted Chestnuts♦

Here's a comforting potato dish that's hearty enough to be a main dish. Wafer-thin prosciutto will not overload this menu with protein—and less protein means a faster delivery of the amino acid tryptophan, to activate serotonin and promote a cheerful calmness.

Sicilian Potatoes

SUPERFOODS: garlic, onion, green peppers, tomatoes, potatoes (also peas and anchovies, if using)

My mother's recipe. I remember with pleasure the wonderful fragrances when she opened the oven door to stir the dish.

2 tablespoons olive oil

1 garlic clove, minced

1 medium onion, chopped

4 anchovy fillets (optional)

2 green bell peppers, seeded and chunked

1 dried hot pepper

One 28-ounce can whole tomatoes

6 potatoes (2 pounds), peeled and cut into thirds

½ teaspoon each dried oregano and salt

¼ teaspoon Spicy Pepper Mix (see page 539) or black pepper

One 10-ounce package frozen peas (optional)

2 tablespoons chopped fresh flat-leaf parsley

Heat the oil in a Dutch oven, and sauté the garlic, onion, anchovies (if using), and green peppers until they are softened but not brown, about 3 minutes. Add all the remaining ingredients except the peas and parsley. Bring to a boil, reduce the heat, and simmer, uncovered, stirring occasionally, for 10 to 12 minutes, until the potatoes are just beginning to soften.

Meanwhile, heat the oven to 400 degrees F.

Put the simmering dish into the oven, uncovered, and bake 30 to 40 minutes, stirring occasionally, until the potatoes are quite tender and the tomatoes have become a sauce. If using the peas, add them during the last 5 minutes of cooking.

Stir in the parsley and remove the dried hot pepper.

MAKES 4 SERVINGS

Roasted Chestnuts

SUPERFOODS: chestnuts

There's something very cosy and cheery about roasting anything on an open fire, although it is a most uneven form of cooking. Chestnuts are especially high in vitamin B$_6$ for enhanced calcium and magnesium absorption.

12 to 16 fresh chestnuts

Soak the chestnuts in warm water for 30 minutes. Drain. Cut an *X*, through the shell but not into the meat, on the rounded side of the nut.

By the fireside: You need a heavy pan with a handle that won't burn, and one that you won't mind blackening. I use my ancient cast-iron frying pan. Set the pan of chestnuts in glowing embers, but naturally not in the midst of the fire. Use an oven mitt to give it an occasional shake, exercising great care in working around the open fireplace.

When the crosses peel open and the nuts smell delicious, about a half-hour, they are probably cooked. But timing on open-fire cooking is far from specific. Cool one nut a bit, peel, and taste it for a test.

Wrap the nuts in a towel for a few minutes before peeling.

On the grill: Follow the same procedure and cook over medium gas or nonflaming coals. The chestnuts may take less time.

In the oven: Bake at 400 degrees F. for about 20 minutes.

MAKES 4 SERVINGS

10

MORE BRAIN FOOD

How the Chemicals in Food Influence Your Mind

The food-mood connection extends far beyond the effect of carbohydrates alone. Every food you eat contains chemicals that can have an influence on how you feel emotionally, how you learn and remember, and how quickly your mind works in making those associations that are the basis of creativity. The relationship between food and mood is the subject of much current research, and fascinating new links are being discovered—and disputed—right now. This is an exciting new field of nutrition that women will want to follow closely.

CHOLINE MAY BE A MEMORY BOOSTER

Besides helping the body to maintain membrane fluidity, choline is also used to synthesize acetylcholine, one of the neurotransmitters involved in emotions, behavior, and memory. Evidence of enhancing short-term memory through the use of choline has appeared in several studies "of mice and men." The validity of these results is disputed, however, by other scientists, who feel the evidence has not been sufficient to support the theory. Still, anyone whose short-term memory is sometimes a bit fuzzy will welcome the news that research into this problem is going forward and that provocative results are being obtained.

Choline is a component of lecithin, a phospholipid, related to lipids (fats). Some researchers have found that lecithin helps to lower cholesterol, but according to other doctors, more studies are needed before any conclusions can be reached.

Along with exploring the choline-memory connection, scientists have been researching the effects of choline on related disorders. Although lecithin and choline can be made by the body itself as well as ingested, patients with Alzheimer's disease appear to have an impaired ability to make or use the neurotransmitter acetylcholine, which is employed by nerve cells involved in memory processing and storage. While lecithin and choline supplements have not proved effective in relieving this problem, research is continuing. The hope is that some supportive compound can be found that will work with choline to produce acetylcholine in these patients.

Subjects with a predispostion to depression have been further depressed by *high* doses of choline, but those with manic symptoms have felt their symptoms become more controlled. Neurological disorders characterized by abnormal muscular movements have responded favorably to lecithin.

TRY AN ORDER OF CHOLINE, "SUNNY SIDE UP"

Because of its particular ability to meld water and fat, lecithin is a common food additive—one that is actually nutritious—in ice cream, mayonnaise, and margarine. Choline in the diet is derived from the lecithin in eggs, organ meats, whole wheat, soybeans and other beans, and fish. So, if you're eating the superfoods recommended in this book, you're probably getting plenty of choline already. Nevertheless, if you have an egg for breakfast once in a while, why not choose to have it on days when you especially need a crisp, sharp memory? It's even better with whole wheat toast.

Superfood Sources of Choline

Beans, especially soybeans   Wheat germ, whole wheat
Fish   containing the germ

Note: While not included in my list of superfoods, both liver and eggs are excellent sources of choline but high in cholesterol. If cholesterol is not a problem, an occasional snack of chopped chicken liver or an omelet will boost choline intake.

SNACK ON CHOLINE . . .

A champion breakfast of whole wheat flakes
A scoop of chopped chicken liver
Salmon pâté on whole wheat crackers
Hard-boiled egg with whole wheat melba toast

TYROSINE FOR A QUICKER RESPONSE TO LIFE'S CHALLENGES

Speaking of the days when you need to be sharp, consider the effect of the amino acid tyrosine.

A sensible, varied, nutrient-rich diet will make you stronger mentally as well as physically, but it's possible to be even more specific. You can manage certain elements in your diet to produce desired effects of alertness or relaxation depending on what you choose to eat and when you eat it. The previous chapter explained how consuming pure carbohydrates with little protein or fat will allow tryptophan to reach the brain, thus producing more of the neurotransmitter serotonin to make you feel calm, relaxed, focused, and able to concentrate amid distractions. Moreover, taken at bedtime, pure carbohydrates function like a sleeping pill in helping you get your *ZZZZZs*!

Tyrosine, another amino acid, has a quite different effect—it's an energizer. Carried across the protective filters called the blood-brain barrier, tyrosine stimulates your brain to produce more of the neurotransmitters dopamine and norepinephrine. Soon after this happens, you'll begin to feel more mentally alert, energetic, confident, ready and willing to meet the day's challenges in a winning way. I guess we can all use a little of that on Monday mornings!

THE RX FOR ALERTNESS

According to the research done by Judith Wurtman, a nutrition scientist at M.I.T., it's simply a matter of eating a "power breakfast." (Or "power lunch" or "power dinner," depending on when you expect those challenges to arise.) In this case, the power is protein. Tyrosine is made available to your brain after a meal filled with protein, eaten alone or with a side dish of carbohydrate (not carbohydrate as a first course, however). It's important when planning this invigorating repast that you skip the fat that would slow down your digestion and everything else. So obviously, a bagel and cream cheese or a waffle with butter and syrup are not the breakfasts that are going to set you up to take a 10:00 A.M. meeting by storm. Or if it's an afternoon meeting, a quarter-pound beefburger and fries for lunch is not going to leave you sparkling at 2:00 P.M. (Neither will a glass of wine. When it's serious business, stick with the caffeine boost of coffee or tea.)

Some doctors have prescribed tyrosine supplements to relieve symptoms of PMS. On the negative side, tyrosine supplements can trigger migraine attacks in women who are susceptible, and excessive amounts can raise blood pressure.

So how much protein do you need to trigger the alertness chemicals? Three or 4 ounces, says Dr. Wurtman. The response is self-limiting; more protein than that won't make you feel any perkier—and too many calories in any one meal are liable to weigh down that desirable vibrant response.

Superfood Sources of Protein (and Therefore, Tyrosine)

Beans Tofu
Cheeses, low-fat Turkey
Fish and shellfish Yogurt

HIGH PROTEIN, LOW FAT: FAST FIRST AID FOR THE BRAIN

A dish of nonfat yogurt and fruit
A shrimp cocktail
Sliced turkey in a pita pocket (no fat in pita bread)
A scoop of hummus (chickpea spread) and nonfat crackers

THE WELL-OILED BRAIN

With the nutrition press continually urging us to eat a low-fat diet, it's important to remember this shouldn't be taken to mean a *no-fat* diet. Our bodies definitely require some lipids (fats) along with other nutrients to maintain good health (although we note that some fats are much better for us than others). It's probably less generally known that our brains, too, need lipids to keep them functioning. In fact, the brain is the organ of the body with the greatest concentration of lipids—half its dry weight.

Of particular importance to maintain a "well-oiled" brain are the essential fatty acids.

BRAIN ESSENTIALS—LINOLEIC AND ALPHA-LINOLENIC ACIDS

Linoleic acid (LA), a polyunsaturated fatty acid, is now universally recognized as an essential nutrient for the brain and nervous system. Some nutrition experts are concerned that infants bottle-fed on formula lacking linoleic acid may be short-changed on their intelligence potential. Alpha-linolenic acid (LNA), an essential fatty acid found in grapeseed and corn oils, among others, has also, more recently, joined the essential list. A diet low in this nutrient has been shown to affect the learning behavior of animals.

LA and LNA are found in vegetable oils, not necessarily the same ones. But walnut, wheat germ, and soybean oils are good sources of *both* LA and LNA, as are margarine and cheese. Whole grains, nuts, and seeds, from which many of these oils are pressed, are other sources of essential fatty acids.

THE RX FOR BRAIN POWER

Jean-Marie Bourre, M.D., director of research at the Institut National de la Recherche Medicale in Paris, and an expert on neurology and nutrition, writes that "it's primarily a balanced and appropriate supply of fatty acids that defends the brain against toxic, immunological, and viral attacks, and that prevents premature aging." Recommending that we consume a variety of oils, he suggests "a combination of some sort" rather than switching from one to another or using just one oil to the exclusion of others.

Olive oil, a monounsaturated oil which has been featured in this book for its many other nutritional benefits, has lesser amounts of LA than some other oils and only a trace of LNA. One can, however, eat the superfoods—wheat germ, nuts, and seeds—that are rich in both LA and LNA plus so many other important nutrients. Adding a little walnut oil to a vinaigrette salad dressing, using safflower oil in homemade baked goods, or enjoying a reasonable amount of cheese or margarine should round out the "brain prescription."

Dr. Bourre recommends 2 grams of alpha-linolenic acid and 10 grams of linoleic acid every day for a "well-oiled" brain. There are 14 grams in a tablespoon of oil. Of oils at the top of these two lists, walnut contains 8 percent alpha-linolenic acid and grapeseed contains 70 percent linoleic acid.

FATTY FISH FUELS THE BRAIN, TOO

More brain nutrients are contained in the omega-3 fatty acids found in fish and shellfish. Pregnant and nursing mothers are especially urged to include seafood in their diets on a regular basis to nourish the brain development of the unborn and just born.

MANAGING THOSE ESSENTIAL FATTY ACIDS

There is no RDA for fats, but nutritionists recommend at least 1 tablespoon of polyunsaturated fat to supply the essential fatty acids. They warn that fats should not exceed 30 percent of your daily calories, and that the major proportion must be monounsaturated and polyunsaturated oils. Also considered beneficial to the heart and brain and therefore a proper part of your "fat ration" is the fat in oily fish.

Thirty percent of one's calories is *not*, however, thirty percent of one's *food*—the calories in fat are highly concentrated. Thirty percent of a 2,000-calorie day would be 600 fat calories—about the equivalent of six tablespoons of margarine or five of vegetable oil. Since our daily meals probably include some combination of meat, dairy products, nuts, seeds, and/or grains, all of which contain their own fat calories, we should probably restrict ourselves to one to two tablespoons of "brain food" oils a day.

Superfood Sources of Linoleic and Alpha-Linolenic Acid

Vegetable oils:
grapeseed, sunflower,   wheat germ, soybean,
walnut, safflower, corn,   peanut, rapeseed, olive

A QUICK DISH OF ESSENTIAL FATTY ACIDS
FOR BRAIN POWER

Just make a salad and dress it with the following mixture of vegetable oils:

All-Purpose Salad Oil Blend

Makes 1¼ cups
Mix yourself a cruet of essential fatty acids for brain power. Use this blend for recipes in which the oil will not be subject to heat. (For sautéing and frying, use plain olive oil, and continue enjoying its multiple health benefits.)
¼ cup grapeseed oil
¼ cup walnut oil
¼ cup soybean oil
½ cup olive oil

SUPPLEMENTS VERSUS WHOLE FOODS

In evaluating differing views on choline, tyrosine, and some other nutrients, such as the B vitamins, one discovers an ultra-conservative attitude throughout nutritional research—coupled with strong opposition in medical circles to self-diagnosis and self-medication in the form of readily available, unregulated supplements. Agreement is general in the entire medical community that dosing—often *over*dosing—oneself with supplements of isolated food chemicals can be dangerous.

The source of foot-dragging in the field of nutrition may be based on this primary problem with supplements: While a surplus of some nutrients is harmlessly excreted, an excess of some others is retained in toxic porportions. It's often the case in nature's pharmacy that a little is good medicine, while a lot is poison.

You can feel perfectly comfortable, however, consuming some of the good whole foods that contain these substances, since it's nearly impossible to overdose on chemicals and nutrients obtained in that natural way (providing you don't do anything as foolish as drinking *gallons* of carrot juice).

Not only are they safer than supplements, fresh whole foods offer a synergism of nutrients and phytochemicals (nonnutrient food chemicals, some of which help to prevent diseases) in particularly effective combinations. And perhaps there are some as yet undiscovered benefits, too. No supplement can replace the amazing food power of a simple orange!

Tips, menus, and recipes for smart meals follow.

SUPERMEALS FOR BRAIN POWER

Recipes indicated by a ♦ follow the menus.

A SMART SATURDAY NIGHT SUPPER FOR SIX

Spicy Baked Soybeans♦
Fried Scrod with Mint Sauce♦
Cabbage Salad with Walnuts and Walnut Oil♦
Apple Brown Betty♦
or
Apples and Molasses Cookies

*F*rom soybeans to scrod to wheat germ (hidden in the Brown Betty), this menu is a choline feast. Walnut oil and walnuts add linoleic and alpha-linolenic acids for a well-oiled brain.

Not in the mood to make soybeans from scratch? Buy canned soybeans at a whole-foods market, spice 'em up with a little of the same seasonings, and bake until bubbly.

Spicy Baked Soybeans

SUPERFOODS: soybeans, tomato sauce, molasses

It takes time but almost no effort to make a basic pot of beans. A good-looking bean pot is a handsome addition to any kitchen and invites you to try your hand at this Saturday afternoon sport.

1½ cups dried soybeans	2 slices fresh ginger (optional)
1 medium onion,	2½ cups boiling water
½ cup each soy sauce, molasses,	½ teaspoon salt
and tomato or chili sauce	Pepper

Put the soybeans into a 4-quart pot, pour in about 3 quarts of cold water, and let the beans soak overnight in a cool room. The next day, drain and rinse the beans, discarding the soaking liquid.

Preheat the oven to 300 degrees F.

Put the onion in the bottom of a bean pot or heavy casserole with a lid, such as a Dutch oven. Add the beans, soy sauce, molasses, tomato or chili sauce, and ginger, if using. Pour the boiling water over all.

Bake the beans, covered, for 4 hours or until tender. Remove the lid, stir in the salt and pepper to your taste, and bake 30 minutes longer. Add a little more hot water if the beans seem dry.

The beans can be made 3 to 4 days ahead and kept refrigerated or frozen for longer storage. Pint containers are a good size. Reheat in a skillet on the range top or in a microwave-safe dish in the microwave, adding a little water if necessary, until bubbling throughout.

MAKES 1 QUART

Fried Scrod with Mint Sauce

SUPERFOODS: scrod

6 serving-size pieces scrod, about ¾ inch thick (2 pounds total)	About 1 cup seasoned dry bread crumbs
2 eggs beaten with 2 tablespoons water, or ½ cup prepared egg substitute	Olive oil
	Mint Sauce (recipe follows)

Rinse and pat dry the scrod. Put the egg in a shallow dish, the crumbs on a sheet of waxed paper. Dip the fish into the egg, then the crumbs, to coat the fillets lightly on all sides. Chill to set the crumbs.

When ready to cook, coat a 12-inch skillet with olive oil. Heat the pan and fry the scrod until the pieces are golden on both sides, 6 to 8 minutes, adding more oil if necessary.

Serve the fish with Mint Sauce.

MAKES 6 SERVINGS

Mint Sauce

1 cup fresh mint leaves, loosely
  packed*
½ cup apple jelly, melted over
  low heat

¼ cup white wine vinegar
¼ teaspoon salt

Finely mince the mint leaves. If they're really dry, you can do this in a food processor. Put the minced leaves into a gravy boat. Combine the remaining ingredients, and stir to dissolve the salt. Add the liquid to the mint leaves, and let stand at room temperature for an hour or so. Stir occasionally.

Cabbage Salad with Walnuts and Walnut Oil

Superfoods: cabbage, walnut oil, walnuts, raisins

When other greens wilt and fail, you can always count on cabbage for a good nutritious winter salad. A food processor makes shredding a snap!

1½ pounds green cabbage, very
  finely shredded
3 tablespoons walnut oil
2 tablespoons white wine vinegar
1 teaspoon sugar

½ teaspoon salt
¼ teaspoon white pepper
⅓ cup walnut pieces
3 tablespoons raisins

*Available in bunches (like parsley) in some supermarkets.

In a large bowl, combine the cabbage, oil, vinegar, and seasonings. Toss well. Stir in the walnuts and raisins. Chill the salad for at least 1 hour.

The salad can be made 1 day ahead. Keep refrigerated.

Before serving, toss again and taste to correct seasoning, adding more oil or vinegar to your taste.

MAKES 6 SERVINGS

Apple Brown Betty

SUPERFOODS: whole wheat bread, apples, wheat germ

6 slices whole wheat bread
*6 cooking apples, peeled and
  sliced*
¾ cup brown sugar
½ teaspoon ground cinnamon

¼ teaspoon salt
½ cup water
2 tablespoons toasted wheat germ
2 tablespoons butter, melted

Preheat the oven to 250 degrees F.

Dice the bread small, put the pieces on a baking sheet, and bake until they are dry and firm but not brown, about 20 minutes. Crush the bread even smaller into large crumbs.

Turn oven to 350 degrees. Sprinkle one-third of the crumbs in a buttered 2- to 3-inch-deep casserole with a 2-quart capacity. Layer half the apples on top. Mix the brown sugar, cinnamon, and salt, and sprinkle one-third of that over the apples. Add another third of the crumbs, the rest of the apples, and one-third of the sugar mixture. Cover with the remaining one-third crumbs and one-third sugar. Pour the water over all, sprinkle on the wheat germ, and drizzle with butter.

Cover the casserole with foil or a lid and bake for 40 minutes. Uncover and bake 15 minutes longer or until the apples are tender. Serve warm or cold. Nonfat frozen vanilla yogurt makes a super accompaniment.

MAKES **6** SERVINGS

MEMORY BOOSTER
FOR FOUR

Lucy's Chicken Liver Spread♦
with Whole Wheat Melba Toast
Baked Haddock in a Potato Crust♦
Pinto Bean, Tomato, and Endive Salad♦
Sliced Kiwis with Nonfat Mango Yogurt

Boost your memory for that after-dinner game of Trivial Pursuit or Scrabble with these choline-rich foods: chicken liver, eggs, whole wheat, fish, and beans. Although liver is high in fat, appetizer portions can be small. The rest of the meal contains only a moderate amount of oil.

Lucy's Chicken Liver Spread

This perennially popular starter is a great source of iron as well as choline.

1 tablespoon vegetable oil	*1 hard-boiled egg, finely chopped*
½ pound chicken livers	*2 tablespoons finely chopped red*
½ tablespoon minced fresh	*onion*
parsley	*2 tablespoons mayonnaise*
Freshly ground black pepper	*Pinch of salt*

Heat the oil in a nonstick skillet, and sauté the chicken livers with the parsley and black pepper until they are cooked through, about 5 minutes. Remove the livers with a slotted spoon.

Put the livers through a meat grinder (not a food processor, which will turn them to mush!). Blend the ground livers with all the remaining ingredients. Chill.

The spread can be made up to 2 days ahead. Keep refrigerated.

Serve with whole wheat melba toast.

MAKES ½ POUND

Baked Haddock in a Potato Crust

SUPERFOODS: potatoes, olive oil, shallots, haddock

Leftovers of this dish could easily become a next-day chowder.

2 to 3 large potatoes (1½ pounds)   2 tablespoons Dijon mustard
About 2½ tablespoons olive oil   Paprika
Salt and pepper
¼ cup chopped shallots
1 haddock fillet, about 1½
   pounds

Peel, wash, and cut the potatoes into thin half-rounds. Dry them in a towel.

Heat 2 tablespoons oil in a large skillet (nonstick or seasoned cast-iron require less oil) and fry the potatoes slowly until they are tender and golden, 25 to 30 minutes, loosening from the bottom of the skillet and stirring often. Salt and pepper them to your taste.

Preheat the oven to 400 degrees F.

Oil a baking dish and add the shallots. Put the pan into the heating oven until the shallots are sizzling. Remove the pan.

Rinse and pat dry the fillet. Lightly score the skin in a criss-cross pattern. Brush the fillet with some of the shallots, and place it skin side down in the pan.

Brush the fish with the mustard. Lay the potatoes in an overlapping pattern (something like fish scales) over the fillet. Sprinkle with paprika.

Bake on the top shelf for 20 minutes, or until the fish flakes apart easily at the center.

MAKES **4** SERVINGS

Pinto Bean, Tomato, and Endive Salad

SUPERFOODS: pinto beans, tomato, onion

Vinaigrettes—like dry martinis—have many possible proportions, depending on how the cook feels about vinegar. The bland sweetness of beans goes well, however, with a really vinegary vinaigrette like this half-and-half version.

*One 20-ounce can pinto beans,
    rinsed and drained**
1 large ripe tomato, diced
½ cup chopped red onion
*Several leaves fresh basil,
    chopped*

Salt and pepper
3 tablespoons red wine vinegar
*3 tablespoons All-Purpose Salad
    Oil Blend (see page 436) or
    any vegetable oil*
1 small head endive

Put the beans, tomato, onion, and basil in a bowl. Add salt and pepper to your taste. Add the vinegar and oil; toss gently. Refrigerate several hours to develop the flavor.

The recipe can be made to this point 1 day in advance.

Taste to correct seasoning. You may want more vinegar and/or oil.

Separate the endive into leaves. Rinse and shake them dry. Place them, pointed ends out, on a circular platter, and scoop the bean mixture into the center.

MAKES 4 TO 6 SERVINGS

*Or shell beans.

PROTEIN POWER (MINUS MOST OF THE FAT) FOR FOUR

Chicken and Swiss Chard with Fresh Fettuccine♦
Sliced Tomatoes with Chopped Scallions
Whole Wheat French Bread
Chocolate Raisin Pudding♦

Make the dessert first so that it can chill and set while you have dinner. "Light" protein sources in this menu are the skinless chicken breasts plus nonfat yogurt in the pudding. Because this easily prepared menu is low in fat, it allows the amino acid tyrosine to stimulate your mental energy.

Chicken and Swiss Chard with Fresh Fettuccine

SUPERFOODS: Swiss chard, garlic, pasta

About 1 pound Swiss chard
1 tablespoon olive oil
2 garlic cloves, minced
1½ pounds boneless, skinless
   chicken breasts, cubed
Cornstarch
1 tablespoon butter

½ teaspoon mixed dried herbs:
   choose from rosemary, thyme
   leaves, tarragon, basil,
   oregano, or any other favorite
Salt and pepper
⅔ cup dry vermouth, white wine,
   or chicken broth
One 8- to 9-ounce package fresh
   fettuccine*
Grated Parmesan cheese

Wash the chard well. Cut away the ribs to separate them from the leaves. Chop the leaves. If the ribs are large (over ½ inch wide), slice them thin; otherwise, dice them.

Heat the oil with the garlic in a 12-inch skillet. Stir-fry the ribs until they are almost cooked through, about 3 minutes; add the leaves and continue cooking until both are tender, about 2 minutes. With a slotted spoon, remove and reserve the chard.

Dust the chicken cubes lightly on both sides with cornstarch. Add the butter to the skillet, and stir-fry the chicken cubes until they are golden brown and just cooked through, about 5 minutes. If necessary, add a teaspoon more oil. Sprinkle the chicken with herbs, salt, and pepper to your taste. Remove and reserve the chicken.

Deglaze the hot pan with the wine or broth, scraping to loosen any brown bits. Boil the pan juices rapidly, stirring, until it's reduced to about ⅓ cup. Return the greens and chicken to the pan just to heat them through.

*Look for fresh pasta in a refrigerator case at the supermarket.

Meanwhile, cook the fresh fettuccine according to the package directions; it takes only a few minutes. Drain and toss the pasta with the chicken and greens.

Pass the grated cheese at the table.

MAKES 4 SERVINGS

Chocolate Raisin Pudding

SUPERFOODS: yogurt, raisins

Reasonably guiltless! Besides the protein in milk and yogurt, cocoa is rich in zinc and raisins in iron.

1 cup milk (whole milk works best)
½ cup sugar
3 tablespoons each cornstarch and cocoa
⅛ teaspoon salt

1 cup plain nonfat yogurt
1½ teaspoons vanilla extract
¼ cup raisins

Combine the milk, sugar, cornstarch, cocoa, and salt in a deep saucepan. Whisk until well blended, then whisk in the yogurt.

Bring to a boil over medium heat while whisking constantly. (A hand-held electric mixer with a whisk attachment makes this task easier.) Reduce the heat to warm, and simmer 2 minutes, whisking.

Remove the pudding from the heat; stir in the vanilla and raisins. Divide the pudding among 4 dessert dishes. Chill the puddings until set.

MAKES 4 SERVINGS

A LIGHT MEAL FOR A LITTLE HEAVY THINKING FOR FOUR

Quick White Bean and Chive Soup with Browned Shallots♦
Whole Wheat French Bread
Tomatoes Stuffed with Shrimp♦
Wine-Glazed Baked Pears♦

All make-ahead dishes in this menu! Beans and whole wheat served together equal complete protein, and there's more protein in the shrimp with yogurt dressing. This low-fat, high-protein supper is the kind of meal that will energize those "little gray cells"!

Quick White Bean and Chive Soup with Browned Shallots

SUPERFOODS: shallots, white beans

1 tablespoon olive oil
⅓ cup coarsely chopped shallots
1½ cans (20-ounce size) white beans (cannellini)
¼ to ¾ teaspoon white pepper, or to taste

½ teaspoon salt
2 cups chicken broth
3 tablespoons finely chopped fresh chives

Heat the olive oil in a large saucepan, and sauté the shallots, stirring often, until they are golden brown but not dark brown, about 3 minutes. Watch closely!

Rinse and drain the beans. In a food processor, puree the beans with the pepper and salt. Gradually add the chicken broth. (If you use a blender, the liquid can be added from the beginning—but mix in 2 batches to avoid overflowing.) Taste to adjust the pepper.

Pour the pureed mixture into the saucepan with the shallots, and bring it to a simmer. Simmer 3 to 5 minutes, stirring often, to develop the flavor.

The recipe can be made ahead to this point. Keep refrigerated. When ready to serve, reheat in the top of a double boiler over simmering water or in a microwave-safe bowl in the microwave.

Remove from the heat and stir in the chives.

MAKES 1 QUART

Tomatoes Stuffed with Shrimp

SUPERFOODS: tomatoes, shrimp, yogurt

When you need to use really ripe tomatoes or pears, you have to buy them about three days ahead and ripen them at room temperature. You don't need any fancy kind of ripening contraption. Just put them in a bowl with an apple or two; apples give off a gas that ripens fruit.

4 large firm ripe tomatoes	1 tablespoon minced fresh chives
Salt	¼ teaspoon dried dill
½ pound cooked cleaned shrimp	⅛ teaspoon each white pepper
½ cup plain nonfat yogurt	and sugar
1 tablespoon lemon juice	Watercress sprigs for garnish

Slice the tops off the tomatoes; clean out the seeds and juice. Sprinkle the insides with salt, and turn them upside down to drain while making the shrimp salad.

Save 4 shrimp for garnishing. Chop the rest roughly. Blend all the remaining ingredients, except the watercress, in a small bowl. Combine this dressing with the chopped shrimp.

Shake the juice out of the tomatoes, and stuff them with the shrimp mixture. Garnish each tomato with a whole shrimp and watercress sprigs.

The tomatoes can be stuffed several hours ahead. Keep refrigerated.

MAKES 4 SERVINGS

Wine-Glazed Baked Pears

SUPERFOODS: pears

The alcohol in the glaze will evaporate, leaving the lovely fruity flavor of red wine. Pears are a great source of soluble fiber.

4 very large and ripe d'Anjou   ½ cup Merlot or other dry red
  pears   wine
¼ cup sugar

Halve the pears, but don't peel them. Remove the core, leaving an oval hollow in each half.

Preheat the oven to 350 degrees F.

Sprinkle the sugar in a 10- to 12-inch glass pie plate. Pour the wine on top. Place the pears on the wine, cut sides down. Bake for 25 minutes or until quite tender. Carefully turn the pears right side up, and place each half on a plate.

Measure the pan juices. If there is more than ⅓ cup, pour the juice into a small saucepan and boil rapidly until reduced to ⅓ cup. Watch carefully!

Divide the sauce among the pears, pouring some into the hollows left from the cores and the rest over all. Serve the pears at room temperature or chilled.

The pears can be made 1 day ahead. Keep refrigerated.

MAKES 4 SERVINGS

11

FIBER, A VITAL NONNUTRIENT

For Defense Against Heart Disease, Cancer, Diabetes, and Obesity, and for a Healthy Digestive System

Earlier in this century, fiber was known as "roughage" and people were urged to eat plenty of it in order to remain "regular." True enough—but a rather rudimentary view of fiber. Recently, however, fiber has become more than the subject of some quiet advice from Grandma—and has taken its rightful place in the healthy diet. In fact, it's so touted in food advertising, you can't have missed knowing that your diet ought to include sufficient fiber. Not bad for a nonnutrient!

Fiber is called a nonnutrient because, being mostly indigestible, it supplies no nourishment to the body. Nevertheless, fiber has a vital supporting role as a regulator of the digestive system, a protector of the cardiovascular system, and much more.

The real reason Americans are not getting enough fiber is that most of our food has been highly refined, either to appeal to childish tastes for soft white stuff or to improve shelf life. But manufacturers who used to process foods to rid them of fiber are now jumping on the bandwagon and putting back some of the fiber, often charging more for the "new, natural" products.

While we're assaulted on all sides with the high-fiber message, some questions naturally arise. How much fiber? What kinds? And why? The answers are not as simple as the brightly lettered claims printed on cereal boxes.

THE RX FOR FIBER

First, *how much fiber?* If you're typical, about twice as much as you're eating now. Recent USDA surveys tell us that the average woman between the ages of 19 and 50 consumes only about 12 grams of fiber a day. (For vegetarians, however, this figure is probably higher.) Although at present there is no RDA for fiber, the National Cancer Institute is recommending 20 to 30 grams, with an upper limit at 35 grams. The same amount is recommended by the American Dietetic Association. Some individual nutritionists would push that figure higher, 40 to 60 grams.

While sensibly increasing your fiber intake will definitely help to keep you slim and trim as well as healthy, it's important to remember that you *can* have too much of a good thing. An excess of fiber—over the NCI's upper limit, for instance—may push out of your system some minerals essential to women, such as iron, calcium, and zinc. Also, if not introduced gradually into your customary diet, the sudden onslaught of high fiber also can cause abdominal distress. That's because fiber, while edible, is the least digestible portion of the foods we eat. It's composed of substances that give plants—fruits, vegetables, and grains—their structure. So fiber isn't found in animal products—meat or milk.

Although fiber is not digested in the small intestine, some of it is digested in the large intestine, particularly soluble fiber. In answering the question, *what kinds of fiber?*, two categories must be considered: soluble and insoluble.

Gums, mucilages, and pectins are soluble fibers, found in fruits, vegetables, dried beans and peas, and oats. (Pectins are also known for their ability to turn fruit juice into jelly.) Cellulose, hemicellulose, and lignin are insoluble fibers, found in the brans of wheat, rye, rice, corn and the skins, white membranes, and woody parts of plant foods in general.

SOLUBLE FIBER DEFENDS AGAINST HEART DISEASE AND DIABETES

Soluble fiber dissolves in water to form gels; it's associated with lowering cholesterol and improving sugar control in diabetes.

A study of 31,000 health professionals revealed that those who ate the most fruit (the equivalent of five apples daily), a significant source of soluble fiber, had the least risk of developing high blood pressure. The fruit fiber seemed to be even more beneficial than vegetable and cereal fiber. Another study showed a lowering of cholesterol in hamsters who were fed apples along with their regular diet. Converted in the large intestine to short-chain fatty acids, soluble fiber works by inhibiting cholesterol synthesis. For women, a high-fiber diet has been found to reduce the risk of heart disease by as much as 30 percent.

Soluble fiber also significantly improves glucose tolerance by slowing the digestion and absorption of carbohydrates, and therefore the rise of sugar in blood levels, following meals. A number of studies have shown that a high-fiber diet benefits both Type I and Type II diabetes.

PREVENT INTESTINAL PROBLEMS WITH INSOLUBLE FIBER

Insoluble fiber, which doesn't dissolve but does absorb large amounts of water, increasing stool bulk, prevents constipation and is believed to help prevent diverticulosis (pockets in the intestinal wall that become inflamed) and hemorrhoids (swollen veins) as well. If diverticulosis develops—and the chances increase with advancing years—it's often treated with 15 to 30 grams of supplementary fiber. Irritable bowel syndrome is another intestinal disorder treated with fiber.

INCREASING FIBER IS A REAL DIET AID

The fact that most diet aids sold over the counter contain various kinds of fiber is an indication of its weight-controlling value. (How much more enjoyable, though, to dine on actual high-fiber foods!) Crude fiber gives a feeling of fullness in lieu of calories, helping to prevent overeating. Researchers theorize that fiber also interferes with the digestion and absorption of other foods, either by speeding them through the intestine or by blocking the action of certain digestive enzymes. At any rate, what can be observed is that more fat is eliminated from the body after a high-fiber meal than after a meal low in fiber. The basis of some popular eat-real-food-and-lose-weight diets is simply more fiber and less fat—a healthful diet change you can choose to make for yourself as a forever lifestyle, not merely a temporary diet.

FIBER'S ROLE IN CANCER PREVENTION

There have been mixed results from various studies evaluating whether increasing fiber and/or decreasing fat in the diet lowers the risk for breast cancer. While some studies have found evidence to support these theories, the wide-ranging Nurses' Health Study found no evidence of a negative influence from dietary fat or a positive one from dietary fiber on breast cancer risk.

It's a different story with colon cancer, however; there's a lot of evidence that a low-fat, high-fiber diet does decrease the risk. Insoluble fiber is thought to help keep the lower intestine free of cancers of the colon and rectum by reducing the amount of time that foods (and the traces of cancer-causing chemicals they may contain) stay in the intestine before being eliminated.

SUPERFOODS ARE HIGH-FIBER FOODS

So in answer to the question, *why increase fiber?*, there are all these good reasons for making low-fat, high-fiber your dietary goal. Since your body needs both kinds of fiber, you'll want to be aware of which foods fulfill these requirements. Many of them, happily, are the same superfoods that contain other essential nutrients as well. Serving plentiful vegetables, fruits, and nuts, plus whole-grain breads and cereals will ensure that your meals contain a good supply of dietary fiber. Even better if beans replace fatty burgers, whole grains replace French fries, and raw apples replace apple pie.

AVOIDING FIBER DISTRESS—FROM BRAN TO BEANS

Some women have trouble tolerating bran, one of the best-advertised sources of insoluble fiber. If you're one of these, keep in mind that bran is not the *only* source of fiber—there are plenty more from which to choose. If one particular high-fiber food causes distress, concentrate on the others rather than giving up the effort.

Other women complain of the gas caused by foods like broccoli and cauliflower. For those sulphurous vegetables, try a very gradual addition of them to your regular fare. Allowing your body a leisurely chance to get in harmony with any new regime is a smart move. Most women will find a gradual increase of fiber from a number of sources is the most comfortable course of action.

Beans are another problem food, notoriously "gassy." Home-made beans, an old-fashioned staple, were soaked in 4 times their volume of cold water overnight (8 hours minimum) to leach out some of the hard-to-digest sugars they contained. To speed up this process, beans can be boiled for 3 minutes, then allowed to soak off heat for 2 hours. In either case, *the soaking water must be drained off* and the beans cooked in fresh cold water.

Newer methods of preparing homemade beans frequently omit this soaking step, increasing cooking time instead. Recently, it's been claimed that soaking doesn't eliminate the gas problem at all. Any such analysis is bound to be subjective. If you like to make homemade beans, try it both ways and decide which works for you. When you soak beans overnight, set them in a cool place, which is the way kitchens used to be at night in earlier times.

If you don't have time to hang around the kitchen while a pot of beans is cooking, canned beans may be rinsed in cold water to rid them of some of their pesky sugars. (Do this anyway to remove excess salt.) Also, there are products on the market such as Beano (often sold in produce departments) that claim to eliminate the gas problem and are worth trying. Beans merit a bit of thought and effort, since a single cup of them contains about 16 grams of fiber, of both the soluble and insoluble kinds— or about half the daily recommendation.

Two other tips on avoiding "fiber distress": Be sure to drink plenty of liquids and to spread fiber consumption throughout the day rather than simply loading up on bran cereal at breakfast or beans at dinner.

AN EASY-DOES-IT FIBER PROGRAM

A sensible start might be any whole-grain bread or cereal plus fruit at breakfast, some really crunchy salad vegetables at lunch, snacks of raw fruit anytime, and a helping of cooked-but-fibrous vegetables like peas plus brown rice or whole-grain bread at dinner.

At the same time, note how far such a beginner's fiber program would go toward fulfilling USDA's latest daily recommendations for at least six servings of grain products, three to five of vegetables, and two to four of fruits. (If the USDA's guide sounds like a whole lot of food, keep in mind that half an English muffin or two large crackers or ½ cup berries is described as one serving.)

The menus and recipes that follow are designed to plump

up your daily fiber intake but not you, since they are reasonably fairly low in fat, which is the real culprit in weight control.

Superfood Sources of Dietary Fiber

Note: Most high-fiber foods contain both kinds of fiber, but the foods exclusively noted for soluble or insoluble fiber are so indicated below.

Beans and peas
Berries (insoluble)
Corn, popcorn, whole
  cornmeal
Cruciferous vegetables
  (soluble): broccoli, Brussels
  sprouts, cabbage,
  cauliflower
Fruits (soluble): apples,
  apricots, bananas, citrus,
  kiwi, peaches, pears, and
  pineapple
Fruits, dried: prunes, dates,
  apricots

Nuts and seeds
Oats (soluble), especially
  oat bran
Okra (soluble)
Onions (soluble)
Parsley
Potatoes (soluble), white
  with skins, sweet
Rice, brown and wild
  (insoluble)
Rye
Squash (soluble), winter
Wheat (insoluble),
  especially wheat bran

SUPERMEALS FULL OF FABULOUS FIBER

Recipes indicated by a ♦ follow the menus.

A "MELTING POT" DINNER
FOR FOUR

Cumin Chicken with Black Beans♦
Citrus and Cucumber Salad♦
Mulled Prunes with Yogurt Custard Sauce♦

Chicken with black beans comes from Cuba, the salad is strictly Mediterranean, and the dessert steps out of the American 1940s. Mixed traditions, yet they all share a healthy fiber content found in beans, citrus fruits, and prunes.

Cumin Chicken with Black Beans

SUPERFOODS: olive oil, onion, green pepper,
black beans, garlic

In order to reduce the oil needed for frying, be sure the oil is really heated before adding the chicken, and then cook the pieces very slowly. Slow-frying also makes them delightfully crusty even though skinless.

2 whole boneless, skinless
    chicken breasts
¼ cup all-purpose flour
3 teaspoons ground cumin
½ teaspoon dried thyme
Salt and pepper

2 tablespoons olive oil
1 small onion, chopped
1 green bell pepper, seeded and
    chunked
2 cups Cuban Black Beans*
    (recipe follows)

Cut each chicken breast into 2 pieces lengthwise, and pound with a mallet to flatten them slightly.

On a sheet of waxed paper, blend the flour, cumin, and thyme with salt and pepper to your taste. Dredge the chicken pieces in the seasoned flour.

Heat the olive oil in a large skillet. Be sure it's hot before adding the chicken. Cook over very low heat until golden on one side, about 8 minutes. Turn the chicken, adding the onion and green pepper to the pan. Slowly brown the chicken on the second side, 6 minutes. (If the chicken pieces are large, you may have to cook them in 2 batches.)

Heat the beans and serve them with the chicken.

MAKES 4 SERVINGS

CUBAN BLACK BEANS

One 1-pound package dried
    black beans
6 cups water
1 tablespoon chopped garlic
½ teaspoon each dried thyme
    and dried oregano

½ teaspoon salt
Black pepper
2 tablespoons each olive oil and
    wine vinegar
1 cup chopped pickled peppers**

*A 1-pound can black beans, rinsed, can be substituted. In this case, season the beans with half the olive oil, wine vinegar, and pickled peppers called for in the black bean recipe that follows.
**You'll find these in various ethnic sections of supermarkets, usually labeled "sweet pickled peppers," but don't let that fool you; no sugar had been added— "sweet" simply means "not hot." If you decide to use hot peppers instead, you may want to reduce the amount.

Pick over and rinse the beans. Put them into a large pot with 4 times their volume of water and soak them overnight in a cool place. The next day, drain the beans, discard the water, rinse them, and put them back into the pot with the 6 cups fresh cold water, garlic, and herbs.

Bring the beans to a simmer, and cook over very low heat with cover ajar for 3 hours or until tender. Stir in the salt, black pepper to taste, oil, vinegar, and pickled peppers.

The beans can be made up to 3 days in ahead. Keep refrigerated. Or freeze them in pint containers for longer storage.

MAKES **2** QUARTS

Citrus and Cucumber Salad

SUPERFOODS: grapefruit, orange, olive oil

1 cucumber
1 red grapefruit
1 seedless orange
2 scallions with green tops, chopped

Salt and freshly ground black pepper
3 tablespoons extra-virgin olive oil

Peel the cucumber, unless it's unwaxed and organically grown. Slice it thin and arrange the slices on a platter.

Peel the grapefruit and orange, removing all the white membrane as well as the skin. Slice them; cut the grapefruit slices into quarter-rounds, the orange into half-rounds. Lay the citrus slices over the cucumber. Scatter the scallions over all. Dress the salad with salt, pepper, and olive oil.

MAKES **4** SERVINGS

Mulled Prunes with Yogurt Custard Sauce

SUPERFOODS: prunes, yogurt

Prunes have improved over the years, becoming pitted, soft, and quick-cooking without sacrificing their great nutrition. Fiber, yes—and prunes are also a powerhouse of iron, vitamin B$_6$, and potassium.

1½ cups pitted prunes
1 cup water*
½ cup dry red wine* or red grape juice
2 tablespoons sugar

1 cinnamon stick
½ teaspoon whole cloves, tied into cheesecloth
Yogurt Custard Sauce (see page 535)

Combine all the ingredients, except the sauce, in a saucepan. Bring to a simmer and cook, with cover ajar, for 15 minutes or until the prunes are very tender. Remove the prunes with a slotted spoon to dessert dishes. Strain the juice and discard the cloves; pour some of the juice over each serving. Pass the Yogurt Custard Sauce at the table.

MAKES 4 OR MORE SERVINGS

*You can use all water, or a larger proportion of wine, as you wish. Alcohol evaporates during the cooking process, and the flavor of red wine really peps up prunes.

SIMPLY SUMPTUOUS DINNER
FOR FOUR

Pan-Fried Swordfish with Grapes♦
Lucy's Mashed Potato Casserole♦
Brussels Sprouts Salad♦
Apricot Streusel Cake♦

Those cruciferous vegetables like Brussels sprouts that are so good for you in other ways are also chock-full of fiber. And there's more fiber in grapes, potatoes, apricots, and that oatmeal in the cake's disguise.

Pan-Fried Swordfish with Grapes

SUPERFOODS: swordfish, grapes

Ideally, this sauce is made with Champagne or asti spumante (the Italian equivalent). Should you find yourself with a leftover glass of Champagne gone flat, think of this recipe! Otherwise, any dry white wine will work.

Red grapes are a good source of the anticancer phytochemical quercetin.

4 serving-size pieces swordfish, about ¾ inch thick (about 1½ pounds total)
Seasoned bread crumbs
1 tablespoon each butter and olive oil

1 cup dry white wine or Champagne
½ tablespoon cornstarch, stirred into 1 tablespoon cold water until dissolved
2 cups seedless red grapes

Dust the swordfish with crumbs. Heat the butter and oil in a large skillet, and cook the swordfish until golden and cooked through, about 3 minutes per side. Remove the swordfish and keep it warm.

Add the wine to the hot pan, and let it boil fast until reduced to ½ cup, about 3 minutes. Reduce the heat, add the cornstarch mixture, and stir until the glaze thickens. Add the grapes and simmer for 2 minutes. Pour the sauce over the fish.

MAKES 4 SERVINGS

Lucy's Mashed Potato Casserole

SUPERFOODS: potatoes, garlic

Thanks to Emily Calandrelli, who described this dish, and to my daughter Lucy-Marie, who developed the recipe.

2 to 3 tablespoons chopped fresh chives
1 garlic clove, pressed in a garlic press
4 cups mashed potatoes*

4 ounces shredded part-skim mozzarella
2 tablespoons grated Romano cheese
Paprika and additional chopped chives

*Takes about 2 pounds. Whip them with enough skim milk to make them creamy in texture, and season them with salt and pepper to your taste.

Blend the chives and garlic into the potatoes, taking care to distribute the garlic evenly throughout. Layer half the potatoes in a buttered casserole. Add a layer of mozzarella. Top with the remaining potatoes. Sprinkle with Romano cheese plus paprika and additional chives.

The recipe can be made to this point 1 day ahead. Keep refrigerated.
Preheat the oven to 350 degrees F.

Bake uncovered for 30 to 40 minutes, until heated through and slightly brown on top.

MAKES 4 TO 6 SERVINGS

Brussels Sprouts Salad

SUPERFOODS: brussels sprouts, yogurt

1 pound Brussels sprouts, fresh, or 16-ounce bag frozen	*½ cup or more "Light" Russian Dressing (see page 532)*

Pull off any loose outer leaves of the sprouts and trim the stems; cut an *X* in the bottom of each to allow for even cooking. Boil the sprouts in a large pan of salted water until they are tender, 5 to 8 minutes, depending on size. Drain, cover them with cold water for a few minutes, then drain again very well.

If you use frozen sprouts, cook according to package directions.

Cut the sprouts in half and mix them with the dressing. Chill until ready to serve.

The salad can be made several hours ahead. Keep refrigerated. Leftovers will still be good the next day.

MAKES 4 TO 6 SERVINGS

Apricot Streusel Cake

SUPERFOODS: oats, dried apricots

Leftover cake will keep for 3 days; cover the pan with foil and refrigerate.

For the topping

3 tablespoons brown sugar

2 tablespoons quick-cooking oats (not instant)

1 tablespoon flour

¼ teaspoon ground cinnamon

1 tablespoon butter or margarine, softened

For the cake

1½ cups sifted all-purpose flour

½ cup granulated sugar

1 tablespoon baking powder

¾ teaspoon ground cinnamon

½ teaspoon salt

1 cup quick-cooking oats (not instant)

1 cup milk (can be skim)

¼ cup vegetable oil

1 egg or ¼ cup prepared egg substitute

½ cup chopped dried apricots (or snipped with a kitchen scissors)

Preheat the oven to 375 degrees F. Butter a 9-inch square baking pan, perferably ceramic.

Stir all the topping ingredients together, rubbing or cutting in the butter until the mixture is evenly coarse. Set aside the topping.

Sift together the flour, sugar, baking powder, cinnamon, and salt into a large bowl. Stir in the oats.

Beat together the milk, oil, and egg.

Pour the liquid cake ingredients into the dry, and stir to blend. Fold in the apricots. Spoon the batter into the prepared pan, and smooth the top with a spatula.

Place the pan in the top third of the oven. Bake 25 minutes, or until a cake tester inserted in the center comes out dry.

Cool on a wire rack; serve from the pan.

MAKES **8** SERVINGS

SUMMER DELIGHTS
FOR SIX

Double-Corn Polenta with Fresh Shell Beans♦
Onion Cups Stuffed with Homemade Turkey Sausage♦
Whole Wheat French Bread
Sliced Tomatoes with Fresh Basil and Olive Oil
Fresh Peaches with Ricotta and Honey

There's spicy sausage flavor without the fat when you make your own mixture using very lean ground turkey. Onions, corn, cornmeal, shell beans, whole wheat, and peaches add up to big fiber.

———————

Double-Corn Polenta with Fresh Shell Beans

SUPERFOODS: cornmeal, corn, beans

Fresh shell beans are such a pleasant change from dried beans—and they cook much more quickly! Look for them in July and August; their cranberry-and-white pods should look bright and fresh, not moldy. Since their season is so short, why not cook an extra batch for the freezer?

3 cups hot cooked Polenta (see
   page 519)
1 cup white shoepeg frozen corn*
   or any frozen corn,
   unthawed
2 pounds shell beans in pods
1 medium onion

Several whole cloves
½ teaspoon each dried summer
   savory and salt
1 tablespoon butter
White pepper
Minced fresh cilantro as garnish

After the polenta is cooked, stir in the frozen corn. Spoon the polenta into a 9- or 10-inch glass pie pan, and smooth the top. Chill.

Shell the beans; you should have 2¼ to 2½ cups. Put them into a medium saucepan, and cover them with water. Add the onion, stuck with whole cloves, and the remaining ingredients except the pepper. Bring to a simmer and cook for 20 to 30 minutes, until tender.

The polenta and beans can be made 1 day in ahead, and stored separately, covered, in the refrigerator.

Reheat the beans, if made ahead. Drain, discard the onion, and stir in the pepper.

*If available, 1 cup cooked fresh corn cut from an ear can be substituted.

Cut the polenta into 6 wedges. Fry them in a lightly oiled skillet until just hot throughout (overcooking will disintegrate the wedges), or reheat in a glass pie pan in the microwave. Top each wedge with about ⅓ cup beans and garnish with cilantro.

MAKES 6 SERVINGS

Onion Cups Stuffed with Homemade Turkey Sausage

SUPERFOODS: onions, turkey

3 large sweet onions, such as
  Vidalia or Spanish*
1 cup herb stuffing mix,
  moistened
White wine or water
1¼ pounds lean ground turkey

1 teaspoon salt
½ teaspoon each freshly ground
  black pepper, fennel seeds,
  and paprika
⅛ to ¼ teaspoon cayenne pepper

Make the onion cups. Cut off tops and the root ends of the onions (½ inch to make a flat surface) and peel them. Parboil them for 1 minute in a pot of boiling water (taking care not to splash when you place them in it). On one side of each onion, make a vertical cut from the outside ring to the center, and carefully remove the whole outer rings, which will look like cups. (Save the inner portions for another use.) If necessary, when you get to the second rings, dip the onions for a few seconds in the boiling water. Choose the best-looking 6 rings for stuffing.

*I usually figure on 1 extra onion in case I break some onion cups. Ideally, you should get 2 cups out of each onion.

Mix the sausage. Moisten the stuffing mix with just enough white wine or water to dampen it. Mix the stuffing mix, turkey, and all the remaining ingredients.

The recipe can be prepared to this point several hours ahead. Keep the ingredients refrigerated.

Preheat the oven to 350 degrees F.

Assemble the onions. Divide the stuffing among the 6 cups. Overlap the verticle cuts a bit to enclose the stuffing, and place the cups in an oiled baking dish that will hold them upright. Bake them for about 40 minutes or until the turkey is cooked through.

Country Sausage: Substitute 1 teaspoon ground sage for the anise seeds and paprika. The cayenne is optional.

MAKES 6 SERVINGS

READ-THE-*TIMES*-WHILE-IT-ROASTS SUNDAY DINNER FOR FOUR

Roasted Veal Breast Stuffed with Vegetables and Bran♦
Baked Sweet Potatoes with Gorgonzola♦
Chicory and Romaine Salad
Sliced Kiwi and Raspberries with Granola Cookies

*P*reparing the veal takes a little time, so save this menu for when you feel like fooling around in the kitchen. But once you get the meat and potatoes in the oven, you'll have plenty of time to relax. Bran in the veal stuffing, sweet potatoes, kiwi, raspberries, and granola all contribute deliciously to your soluble and insoluble fiber intake for the day.

Roasted Veal Breast Stuffed with Vegetables and Bran

SUPERFOODS: green pepper, shallots, garlic, wheat bran, tomatoes

This labor of love is an Italian favorite that might be served between the pasta and the roast at a grand holiday dinner, but for our smaller appetites serves as the main dish. Anchovy fillets sometimes find their way into the stuffing, but not this time, when sweet potatoes are the accompaniment.

3- to 4-pound veal breast, bones in or boned

1½ teaspoons olive oil

1 cup chopped fennel

1 green bell pepper, seeded and diced

2 shallots, chopped

1 garlic clove, minced

1½ cups herb stuffing mix

1½ cup wheat bran, toasted*

2 plum tomatoes, diced

Freshly ground pepper

½ teaspoon dried rosemary

1 cup chicken broth, plus more as needed

Trim all extra fat from the veal. Use a boning knife to cut a pocket between the layers of meat (next to the ribs, if any) as large as possible without making a hole in the pocket. When the pocket is made, trim away any internal fat also.

In a skillet, heat the oil and sweat the vegetables—except tomatoes—for 10 minutes; they should turn golden but not brown. If the pan gets dry, add a tablespoon of broth or white wine.

Preheat the oven to 350 degrees F.

*Packaged in jars or boxes, sold with toasted wheat germ and other cereals.

Mix the vegetables, stuffing mix, bran, tomatoes, pepper to your taste, and about half the rosemary. Stir in ½ cup or more broth; the stuffing should be moistened throughout but not mushy. Stuff the veal pocket and either tie it closed with kitchen twine or skewer it with small metal skewers, sometimes called ''nails.''

Put the stuffed veal into a roasting pan with a fitted lid, such as a Dutch oven. Pour the remaining broth into the pan, rub oil over the veal, and sprinkle it with the remaining rosemary. In lieu of a lid, you can cover the pan tightly with foil.

Roast the veal, covered, for 2 hours. When it is fork-tender, uncover the veal and bake another 30 minutes or until nicely browned, adding more broth to the pan as needed to cover the bottom with ½ inch. When you uncover the veal, if there is any extra stuffing, you can bake it alongside in a small casserole, moistened with a tablespoon of the veal pan juices and covered.

Remove the twine or skewers, and let the roast rest for 10 minutes. To carve, use a well-sharpened carving knife to cut across the layers (between any ribs) so that each slice includes both meat and stuffing.

MAKES 4 SERVINGS WITH LEFTOVERS

Baked Sweet Potatoes with Gorgonzola

SUPERFOODS: sweet potatoes

4 sweet potatoes

About 1 cup crumbled
Gorgonzola cheese

Scrub the potatoes and prick them with a fork in several places. Bake for about 1 hour in a 350 to 400 degree F. oven (350 degrees F. to accommodate the roasting veal, 400 degrees F. if alone), or 20 minutes on high (for 4 potatoes) in a microwave, until quite tender.

Slit the potatoes lengthwise, divide the cheese among them, and mash it into the halves slightly. Serve at once.

MAKES 4 SERVINGS

A MOSTLY MAKE-AHEAD
MEATLESS MENU FOR SIX

Roman Beans♦
Romaine Lettuce and Roasted Red Pepper (see page 523) Salad
Squash and Vidalia Onion Bread♦
Fresh Pears and Walnuts

When you're trying to increase fiber, think beans! But don't think boring, because there are a great many kinds and preparations from which you can choose. Whole-foods markets are more likely to have a variety of canned beans to make quick menus more interesting. Meanwhile, in this supper, not only beans but also squash, onion, pears, and walnuts are fine sources of fiber.

Roman Beans

SUPERFOODS: roman beans, olive oil, onion, red pepper, garlic, tomato paste

This is the quick method of soaking beans to soften them and to remove some of the sugars that cause gas.

One 1-pound package dried
  Roman beans or pinto
  beans*
¼ cup olive oil
1 large onion, chopped
1 red bell pepper, seeded and
  diced
3 to 4 garlic cloves minced

4 or more cups water
¼ cup tomato paste
2 tablespoons chopped fresh flat-
  leaf parsley
1½ teaspoons dried oregano
1 teaspoon salt
½ teaspoon Spicy Pepper Mix (see
  page 539) or black pepper

Spill the dry beans onto a tray to check for foreign particles. Rinse the beans well in a fine-meshed strainer.

Put the beans into large pot. Add 4 quarts of water, bring to a boil, and cook for 3 minutes, Turn off the heat, and let the beans stand for 2 hours. Drain the beans and discard the soaking water.

In the same pot, heat the oil and sauté the onion, red pepper, and garlic until the vegetables are softened. Add the drained beans, 4 cups of fresh water, and all the remaining ingredients.

Simmer the beans over low heat, stirring occasionally, for 2 hours, or until quite tender. If the mixture gets too thick and is in danger of sticking, add another cup of water.

The beans can be prepared ahead and refrigerated for 2 or 3 days or frozen in plastic containers for 6 months.

MAKES ABOUT 1½ QUARTS

*Two 20-ounce cans of Roman or pinto beans, rinsed and drained, can be substituted. Reduce the water to 1 cup and the salt to ¼ teaspoon; reduce all the remaining ingredients by half, and simmer for 30 minutes to develop the flavor.

Squash and Vidalia Onion Bread

SUPERFOODS: whole wheat flour, squash, yogurt, onion

1 tablespoon butter

2 cups unbleached all-purpose
  flour

1 cup sifted whole wheat flour

2 tablespoons sugar

4 teaspoons baking powder

1 teaspoon salt

¼ teaspoon white pepper

3 eggs or ¾ cup prepared egg
  substitute

½ cup vegetable oil

One 10-ounce package frozen
  squash, thawed completely

⅓ cup plain nonfat yogurt

1 teaspoon dried cilantro

1 cup chopped Vidalia or any
  other sweet onion

Preheat the oven to 375 degrees F.

Melt the butter in a 10-inch cast-iron skillet or 2-inch-deep cake pan. Brush the melted butter over the sides and bottom of the pan.

Sift together the flours, sugar, baking powder, salt, and white pepper into a large bowl. In another bowl, whisk together the eggs, oil, squash, yogurt, and cilantro.

The recipe can be prepared to this point several hours ahead. Keep the squash mixture refrigerated, and preheat the oven when ready to bake.

Stir the squash mixture into the dry ingredients all at once, and blend but don't overbeat. Fold in the onion.

Spoon the batter into the prepared pan. Bake in the top third of the oven for about 30 minutes, until a cake tester inserted in the middle comes out dry.

When the bread has cooled, remove leftovers from the pan, and wrap in foil to store.

MAKES 12 SLICES

A BRUNCH WITH FIBER PUNCH
FOR SIX

Scrambled Eggs in Whole Wheat Pitas
Oatmeal Pancakes with Sautéed Bananas♦
Very Berry Compote♦

There's more to breakfast fiber than just cereal! Whole wheat and oatmeal in pitas and pancakes, plus bananas and berries, can offer a different sort of fiber bonanza for a Sunday morning.

Oatmeal Pancakes with Sautéed Bananas

Superfoods: skim milk, oats, wheat germ, bananas

A deliciously different twist to plain old cereal and bananas. The batter needs to rest for an hour, perhaps while you read the Sunday papers. Or make it the night before.

1 cup milk (can be skim)
1 tablespoon white vinegar
1 cup quick-cooking oats
¼ unbleached all-purpose flour
3 tablespoons sugar
2 tablespoons wheat germ
½ teaspoon each baking powder
   and baking soda
¼ teaspoon each ground
   cinnamon and salt

1 egg, beaten, or ¼ cup prepared
   egg substitute
About 2 tablespoons butter,
   melted
2 bananas
Dry unflavored bread crumbs
Cinnamon Sugar (see page 540)
Maple syrup

Combine the milk and vinegar and let the mixture stand to "sour" the milk, about 10 minutes.

In a bowl, stir together all the dry ingredients (except the bread crumbs).

Blend the milk, egg, and 1 tablespoon of the melted butter into the dry ingredients. Let stand 1 hour to thicken the batter. *The recipe can be made to this point the night before. Keep refrigerated.*

Cut the bananas in half lengthwise, and again across, yielding 4 pieces from each banana. Roll them in the bread crumbs.

Heat a griddle to 375 degrees F. or use a large skillet. Brush the griddle with some of the remaining melted butter. Drop the batter by large spoonfuls onto the hot griddle and cook the pancakes in batches. Turn them when bubbles cover the surface of one side—carefully, because these cake are not as stiff as regular pancakes. When browned on both sides, keep the pancakes warm.

Brush the griddle with more melted butter, and sauté the bananas until golden on both sides. Sprinkle them with cinnamon sugar, and serve them with the pancakes.

Pass maple syrup at the table.

MAKES 12 PANCAKES

Very Berry Compote

SUPERFOODS: raspberries, strawberries, blueberries

*One 10-ounce package frozen
  raspberries in syrup, partly
  thawed
1 pint fresh strawberries**

1 pint fresh blueberries
⅓ cup orange juice
Sugar
8 to 12 fresh mint leaves***

Wash and pick over the berries. Slice the strawberries.

Combine the partly thawed raspberries, fresh berries, and orange juice in a glass bowl. Taste to correct sweetening, adding sugar to your taste (but there may be enough sugar in the raspberries to sweeten all).

Crush the mint leaves slightly between your fingers, and stir them into the compote.

Let stand a few minutes to finish thawing the raspberries.

MAKES 6 SERVINGS

*Frozen, partly thawed, unsweetened berries can be substituted if the fresh

**Don't substitute dried leaves.

12

HERBS, SPICES, AND TEAS

Plant Medicines of Ancient Times Are Still Potent Healers

Interwoven with myth and legend, the medicinal properties of herbs are sometimes dismissed as folklore. Don't believe it! Those pungent conveyors of condensed flavor can be equally strong in their pharmacological effects. Many of today's medicines are extracted from herbs and spices or are the synthetic replications of the plants' active principles. The source of the original birth control pill, for instance, was the Mexican wild yam.

Asian and Indian systems of medicine have been deeply involved in herb lore for centuries and these cultures have not abandoned their traditional remedies in modern times, so it's not surprising that current research into the efficacy of herbs and spices often comes from the East. Many of these preliminary studies will need follow-up research, but some are already well established. It has been amply demonstrated, for example, that ginger is an excellent no-side-effects remedy for nausea arising from motion sickness or pregnancy. What a good excuse to nibble ginger snaps!

Herbs and spices are available in other forms besides those you may grow on a sunny windowsill or purchase at the supermarket. Herbal supplements that advertise themselves as remedies for every ailment known to womankind may be found in health-food stores. It would be helpful if these highly advertised compounds were required to list their active ingredients, along with how much of each is actually contained in the bottle, right there on the packaging. That law will be coming; meanwhile, the pros and cons of supplements are beyond the scope of a cookbook, so this chapter will concentrate on the cook's collection of herbs and spices you probably have right there in your kitchen—from energizing cayenne to sedating celery leaves—plus a few soothing herbal teas you may wish to stock in the pantry.

Knowing the pharmacological effects of herbs and spices makes using them even more meaningful and pleasurable. But as with any nutritious food item, it's the better part of wisdom not to overdose with a single flavoring agent. Be guided by the amounts that taste good in dishes, or if you wish to benefit from the action of herbal teas, enjoy those steaming, aromatic brews in moderation.

Several herbs, as I have noted on the following pages, are reported by herbalists to help induce menstruation when consumed in medicinal amounts: celery seed, peppermint, parsley, cinnamon. Herbal references (see Bibliography) warn pregnant women to avoid medicinal amounts of these herbs. This should not be taken to mean that *culinary use* of a sprinkle of minced parsley or chopped celery is unsafe. Again, it's a question of moderate, sensible use. *Medicinal amounts* involve using the concentrated juice (parsley) or the essential oil (peppermint and cinnamon) of an herb, or one to two teaspoons of the seed (celery) to make tea.

Among the recipes that follow are several classic spice mixtures. They're easy and fun to make, they add interest to one's spice shelf, and being all assembled they save time. You'll only need to take down that one jar of *fines herbes*, for example, instead of four or five different herbs to season an omelet or a vinaigrette. Labels are important as well as a decorative touch for your homemade herb blends.

Along with the recipes in this chapter, numerous recipes throughout this book are flavored with these herbs and spices.

CALMING CELERY

Celery seed is noted for calming the nerves and the digestive system. In Chinese studies, celery also was found to lower blood pressure. Herbalists recommend the seed for its diuretic properties, and it's listed among remedies for premenstrual water retention—even though celery has a high natural sodium content.

In folklore, drinking celery juice was thought to bring on menstruation. Herbalists report that the seed stimulates uterine contractions in animals. Munching the odd stalk is not thought to have much effect; it's the seed that contains the strong chemicals.

Celery Salt

A flavorful salt to use in soups, stews, salad dressings, and any kind of fresh pickles.

¾ cup kosher salt   ¼ cup celery seeds

Combine the salt and seeds in a blender or food processor, and pulverize the mixture. This takes about 3 minutes. Sieve the salt through a tea strainer, using only what will pass through. Discard the rest of the solids.

Store the salt in a tightly covered jar. Stir before measuring for recipes.

MAKES 1 SCANT CUP

Fresh Pickled Cucumbers

2 large cucumbers	2 to 3 tablespoons sugar
1/3 cup white wine vinegar	3/4 teaspoon celery salt
1 tablespoon minced fresh dill, or	1/4 teaspoon white pepper
1 teaspoon dried	

Peel the cucumbers unless they are organically grown and unwaxed, in which case you won't need to peel them. Slice them, and place the slices in a deep bowl.

Combine the remaining ingredients in a jar, close it tightly, and shake to blend. Pour the dressing over the cucumbers.

Chill the cucumbers for several hours or overnight before serving. Stir them once or twice while they are marinating, during which time they will give off juice and increase the volume of dressing and also dilute it. Taste to correct the seasoning; you may want more salt, sugar, or vinegar.

MAKES 4 SERVINGS

AROMATIC CINNAMON AND CLOVES

Cinnamon, the inner bark of the cinnamon tree, and cloves, buds of the clove tree, have been shown to inhibit oral bacteria—and they taste good, too! Oil of clove is familiar as a toothache remedy. Recent studies suggest that both spices may be anticoagulants (preventing blood clots)—especially cloves—and that cinnamon boosts insulin activity.

Cinnamon Honey Butter

Try spreading this treat on whole wheat raisin toast!

½ cup (1 stick) butter or
    margarine, softened
½ cup dark clover honey, or any
    other honey

1 teaspoon ground cinnamon

Cream the butter, blending in the honey and cinnamon thoroughly.
    *Keeps refrigerated for up to 2 weeks, but bring to room temperature
for serving.*

MAKES 1 CUP

Chinese Five Spice Powder

A classic Asian flavoring mixture.

1 tablespoon anise seeds
½ tablespoon fennel seeds
1 tablespoon ground cinnamon

1 teaspoon ground cloves
1 teaspoon black pepper

Use a mortar and pestle or clean coffee grinder to pulverize the
anise and fennel seeds. Sieve the mixture into a small bowl,
and discard the chaff. Blend the anise-fennel powder with the
remaining ingredients. Store the powder in a jar.
    Use ½ teaspoon or more of the powder to flavor Asian marinades and sauces.

MAKES ¼ CUP

Pumpkin Pie Spice Blend

It's not just for pumpkin pie! Use this mixture to flavor cookies, sweet muffins, sautéed apple rings—or with a little brown sugar in a squash casserole.

2 tablespoons ground cinnamon   1 teaspoon grated nutmeg
1 tablespoon ground ginger   ½ teaspoon ground allspice
1 teaspoon ground cloves

Blend the spices well, and store the mixture in a jar. Keep in mind when you use this mixture that it's not sugared and, depending on how you're using it, may need a companion sweetener.

You can substitute 1 tablespoon (3 teaspoons) of this blend for the combination of spices called for in pumpkin, squash, or sweet potato pie recipes.

MAKES ¼ CUP

COCOA AS A PICK-ME-UP

Some researchers claim that this "devil's food" releases brain chemicals that cause a slightly euphoric feeling, akin to falling in love. Whether true or not, cocoa *is* a good source of zinc and magnesium as well as being rich in caffeine, the universal pick-me-up. Other chemicals in cocoa soothe the stomach and relax the digestive tract. A cup of cocoa is reported to relieve chest congestion.

On the flip side, some of cocoa's chemicals may trigger headaches in migraine sufferers or be implicated in irritable bowel syndrome and its caffeine content can cause insomnia if taken at bedtime.

Cocoa has fewer calories and less fat than chocolate. All cocoa is not created equal, however; that which is termed "Dutch-processed" has a far superior flavor.

Cocoa for Two

Much tastier than those instant mixes! Chocolate makes milk more digestible to the lactose intolerant.

2 cups milk (can be skim)	*2 tablespoons sugar*
2 tablespoons Dutch-processed unsweetened cocoa	*2 marshmallows (optional but nice!)*

Heat the milk but don't boil it. Mix the cocoa and sugar in a cup. Slowly add ½ cup of the hot milk, stirring to blend smoothly. Whisk this mixture into the milk remaining in the pan. Bring the cocoa to the point of scalding, and immediately remove it from the heat.

If desired, whisk until frothy. Pour into 2 large cups, and top each with a marshmallow.

Note: Some people prefer cocoa stronger and/or sweeter. Once you've tried this recipe, in future you can alter the proportions of cocoa and sugar to suit your taste.

SUPERBULBS GARLIC AND ONION ARE VEGETABLE HEALERS

Revered for their medicinal properties since ancient times, garlic and onion have been legitimatized in extensive current research.

Sulphur-containing compounds that give garlic its powerful taste also give the superbulb its healing power against heart disease. Garlic has been demonstrated to lower cholesterol and blood pressure. Both garlic and onion inhibit the blood clotting that can lead to strokes. Onion contains compounds that raise the blood level of HDL, the helpful cholesterol.

That both bulbs are anticancer vegetables has been confirmed by many studies and extensively reported in the scientific literature. In general, they rev up the immune system to fight off many diseases and disorders. Garlic is antibacterial, antiviral, and antifungal, thus working against herpes, flu, colds, and yeast infections.

In recent studies, Japanese researchers have reported garlic to be at least 60 percent as effective as Valium in decreasing stress.

All this and great flavor, too! What would we do without garlic and onions to animate our soups, stews, entrees, vegetables, and salads? How reassuring to reflect, as you chop, mince, and mash these marvelous flavorers, that you're infusing your dishes with a potent insurance against "the thousand natural shocks that flesh is heir to."

Roasted Garlic

Spread peeled and mashed roasted garlic on any grilled meat, or on whole-grain Italian bread toast as an accompaniment to soups. You can also make a savory spread by mixing the garlic puree with thickened plain nonfat yogurt (see page 534) and herbs of your choice.

4 to 5 whole bulbs of garlic   Olive oil
½ cup chicken broth

Preheat the oven to 350 degrees F. Slice off about ½ inch from the tops of the garlic bulbs, and put them into a small gratin dish. Add the broth, and drizzle oil over all. Bake for 45 to 50 minutes, until soft.

A Quick, Hot, Garlicky Dish of Pasta

Skip the Valium! Joust away those jitters with a fragrant dish of garlic-potent pasta. You can have it ready in twenty minutes, counting the preparation time.

7 tablespoons olive oil (½ cup less   ½ to 1 teaspoon hot red pepper
  1 tablespoon)   flakes*
2 teaspoons finely minced garlic   ½ cup freshly grated Romano
  (4 cloves)   cheese**, plus more to pass
1 cup chopped canned tomatoes   at the table
  with puree   1 pound linguine
½ cup chopped fresh flat-leaf
  parsley

In a 12-inch skillet, heat the oil and sauté the garlic over very low heat until it just begins to soften and turn golden; do not brown it. Turn off the heat and stir in the remaining ingredients except for the cheese and linguine.

*1 teaspoon makes this dish mighty hot.
**If you substitute store-grated cheese with a fine powdery consistency, reduce the measurement to ⅓ cup.

The sauce can be prepared 1 to 2 hours ahead and held at room temperature.

Cook the linguine in a large pot of boiling salted water until it reaches the tenderness you prefer.

Drain well, and scoop the linguine into the skillet, tossing until all strands are coated with the sauce. Add the cheese, and toss again. Serve immediately on 4 heated plates. Pass more cheese at the table.

A salad of dark leafy greens and some fresh Italian bread are the required accompaniments to this meal. Because the sauce is oily, I usually dress the salad with vinegar only (seasoned rice vinegar is a good mild choice).

MAKES 4 SERVINGS

Aunt Marie's Onion Sandwiches

You must use very sweet onions, such as Vidalia, for this savory treat! My aunt served these as an afternoon restorative, with hot black tea.

8 slices "toasting" white bread   Paper-thin slices of Vidalia onion
Softened butter or margarine

Toast the bread until it's perfectly golden, and spread the slices with softened butter. Arrange a layer of onion on 4 of the slices, top with the remaining bread slices. Cut the sandwiches into triangles.

MAKES 4 SERVINGS

PEPPERY GINGER CURES NAUSEA, HELPS ARTHRITIS

For the nausea that accompanies early pregnancy, or for queasiness resulting from anything—motion sickness to overindulgence—ginger is handy, effective, and has no nasty side effects (in reasonable amounts, of course—as with any food). An aid to digestion since very ancient times in China, and later in Greece and Rome, its antispasmodic action makes it helpful for menstrual cramps as well.

Pungent principles in ginger produce heat in the body limbs. Ginger has been found to lessen the pain and swelling of arthritis with none of the adverse side effects of other potential anti-inflammatory drugs that were tested.

To keep fresh ginger on hand for that occasional recipe, buy a large root and slice, peel, and freeze the slices on a tray. When they have frozen solid, store the slices in a small plastic container in the freezer. A few minutes at room temperature will thaw as many as you need.

Gingered Cran-blueberry Sauce

SUPERFOODS: cranberries, blueberries, ginger

The peppery taste of ginger gives this sauce zing! Cranberries are a time-honored preventive of and remedy for urinary tract infections— a folk remedy endorsed by recent research.

2 cups whole fresh cranberries	*½ cup sugar*
1 cup blueberries, fresh or frozen	*6 slices fresh ginger, peeled**
½ cup water	

**No substitutes.

Wash the cranberries. Combine all the ingredients in a medium saucepan, and bring them to a simmer, stirring until the sugar is dissolved. Simmer over low heat for 10 to 12 minutes.

Cool to room temperature. Refrigerate to chill.

The sauce can be made up to 3 days ahead.

Remove the ginger slices. Finely mince 1 or 2 slices and stir them into the finished sauce, which will make it a great deal hotter. Save the remaining slices for another use, such as simply nibbling them if you like the flavor—especially if you are feeling in distress from too much roast turkey.

MAKES ABOUT 2 CUPS

Peppery Ginger Tea

My very favorite tea, not only as a remedy after a heavy meal but also because it's so deliciously warming.

½ teaspoon to 1 teaspoon black   Several paper-thin slices fresh
   tea   ginger
1 cup boiling water

Heat a single-serving tea pot with hot water, then drain. Add the tea and boiling water. Steep 3 minutes, keeping the pot warm, then strain into a cup, adding the fresh ginger slices.

As the hot tea softens them, press the ginger slices with the back of a spoon so that they release their juices. A teaspoon of honey and/or a slice of lemon can be added.

If fresh ginger is not too hot for your taste, nibble on one of the softened slices.

Note: On the other hand, if what you want is a deliciously cooling drink, make iced tea by your usual method (not the instant stuff, please!), stirring 1 teaspoon grated fresh ginger and 2 tablespoons sugar into 1 quart of tea while it's hot. When you add the ice later, you'll have a refreshing, eye-opening cross between tea and ginger ale.

MAKES 1 SERVING

THE CHEERING MINTS AID DIGESTION

Peppermint is the most widely known of the herbal digestive remedies. Several over-the-counter digestive aids owe their minty flavor to peppermint. It's helpful in relieving gas, diarrhea, cramps, and the general stomach miseries. Less well known are research findings indicating that the mints may inhibit micro-organisms responsible for such nasty afflictions as colds, flu, sinusitis, mumps, pneumonia, and yeast infections. Peppermint tea is widely available wherever herbal teas are sold.

Peppermint's essential oil contains menthol, an ingredient in many topical anesthetics.

In folklore and in traditional herbal medicine, all the mints are believed to have a cheering effect on one's spirits, to strengthen and calm the nerves.

Catnip, another member of the mint family, is equally effective as a digestive aid, if you can convince a feline companion to share its favorite herb with you. Despite the way it energizes cats, catnip's potent chemicals have a sedative effect on humans. Catnip tea is reputed to be a soporific that induces sleep.

Herbalists report that catnip helps to relieve menstrual cramps and that peppermint brings on menstruation.

Try a drop or two of oil of the mint pennyroyal—popularly known as fleabane—on the brush (not on the skin) when you groom your dog. It leaves a delightfully spicy aroma and discourages fleas. Essential oils of herbs and spices can be found in whole-foods markets and herb specialty shops. Many essential oils of common spices (cinnamon oil, for instance) are too strong for internal use—but for this topical use, pennyroyal is a time-honored pet-saver.

Pineapple-Mint Raita

SUPERFOODS: yogurt, pineapple, onion

This is based on a chilly Indian condiment meant to accompany fiery foods, but it's also very nice with grilled pork chops or baked fish.

1 cup plain nonfat yogurt	1 tablespoon finely chopped fresh
1 cup finely chopped fresh	mint
pineapple	Salt
2 tablespoons finely chopped red	
onion	

Combine all ingredients, and chill for an hour or more before serving.

MAKES 2 CUPS

PARSLEY POWER—RICH IN ANTIOXIDANTS

A member of the carrot family, it's not surprising that parsley is rich in vitamin A as well as vitamin C. Parsley is reported to be a diuretic, an aid to digestion, an expectorant, and a breath freshener. Strong infusions of parsley may induce menstruation.

Many a sprig of parsley is left to languish on the plate. Instead of garnishing with the herb, chop it fine, stir it in, munch it up— for its marvelous antioxidant properties.

Tomato and Parsley Salad

SUPERFOODS: tomatoes, parsley, onion, olive oil

Try this spicy salad in a pita bread pocket.

2 cups chopped ripe tomatoes
½ cup finely chopped fresh flat-
    leaf parsley
½ cup finely chopped red onion

Freshly ground black pepper and
    salt
3 tablespoons virgin olive oil

Combine all ingredients in a bowl, and allow the salad to marinate at room temperature for 20 to 30 minutes before serving.

MAKES 2 SERVINGS

Vermicelli with Oysters and Parsley

SUPERFOODS: olive oil, garlic, tomato, oysters, parsley,
pasta

*The taste of parsley is more than a hint in this quick dish, which
you can have ready in less than twenty minutes.*

3 tablespoons olive oil	8 ounces shucked oysters, liquor
1 or 2 garlic cloves, finely minced	drained and strained
1 dried hot red pepper	Freshly ground black pepper
6 slivers lemon rind (no pith)	¼ cup finely chopped fresh flat-
1 medium yellow tomato, diced	leaf parsley
small	½ pound vermicelli

Put a large pot of water on to boil for the vermicelli.

In a small skillet, combine the olive oil, garlic, red pepper, and
lemon rind. Cook over very low heat for 10 minutes; the garlic
should not brown. If the garlic does begin to color, immediately
remove the pan from the heat and go on to the next step.

Add the tomato and sauté for 5 minutes. Add the oysters and
⅓ cup of their liquor. Cook over low heat until the edges of the
oysters curl, indicating that they are cooked, which takes only
a few minutes.

Remove the sauce from the heat; remove the red pepper. Stir
in black pepper to taste and the parsley.

Cook the vermicelli in a large pot of salted water according to
package directions, adjusting the recommended time to your
preference; taste to test for doneness. Toss with the sauce.

MAKES 2 SERVINGS AS AN ENTREE

ZESTY HOT PEPPERS, GOOD FOR HEART AND RESPIRATION

What about hot spices being bad for your stomach? One study of ulcers showed that chili powder had no detrimental effect on duodenal ulcers and proposed that the daily pepper ingestion may have a beneficial adaptive response. If hot spices don't agree with your personal digestive system, however, it would be wise to avoid them, since this is an area in which more studies need to be done. But if you do tolerate and enjoy the spicier touches that pepper and chili powder give, go for it! The stuff is really good for you.

Capsaicin, the active heat in peppers, is "hot" medical news, reported to help prevent blood clots by breaking them down through enzymatic action. For those suffering with chest congestion due to colds, a few dashes of hot pepper sauce in that bowl of chicken soup will help loosen secretions and unclog respiratory passages.

As an ingredient in topical creams, capsaicin has proved to be a helpful anesthetic for the relief of nerve disorders affecting the skin.

Kiwi Salsa

SUPERFOODS: kiwi, onion, jalapeño peppers

Here's some cool green hot stuff to accompany any plain meat or fish.

3 large ripe kiwifruits, peeled and coarsely chopped
¼ cup finely chopped red onion

2 minced fresh jalapeño peppers*
1 tablespoon minced fresh cilantro, or 1 teaspoon dried

*Use rubber gloves when handling hot peppers. Including the seeds will make the condiment even hotter.

Mix all ingredients, cover, and marinate several hours in the refrigerator to develop the flavor.

MAKES ABOUT 1¼ CUPS

Chili Oil

SUPERFOODS: hot peppers, olive oil

Use this oil to add spiciness to Asian stir-fries.

Dried hot red chilies   *1 cup olive oil*

Combine several dried hot red peppers with the olive oil in a jar. Crush the peppers slightly to release the seeds. Allow the oil to ripen at room temperature for at least 3 days. Store at room temperature indefinitely.

MAKES 1 CUP

FRAGRANT THYME RELAXES MUSCLES

This culinary herb has exhibited antibacterial qualities in laboratory experiments. In some studies, small amounts of thyme as an herb (not the essential oil, which is too strong) has relaxed uterine muscles and so may help to relieve menstrual cramps. Thyme also relaxes muscles of the gastrointestinal tract, which explains its traditional reputation as a digestive aid. It is one of the herbs used in Benedictine liqueur.

Fines Herbes

This classic mixture of herbs has its origins in French cuisine. Some recipes also include chives and/or parsley, but since these two herbs are best added fresh, I haven't included them in this useful "spice rack" mixture.

1 tablespoon dried thyme	*1 tablespoon dried tarragon*
1 tablespoon dried chervil	*1 tablespoon dried marjoram*

Buy the dried leaves, not the ground herbs. Blend the herbs well, and store them in a jar.

Use Fines Herbes to flavor omelets, sautéed mushrooms, cream cheese (with lots of white pepper), split pea soup, sautéed chicken breasts, or anything else that strikes your fancy. Toast French bread, brush with virgin olive oil, and sprinkle with Fines Herbes as an accompaniment to soup.

MAKES ¼ CUP

Thyme for Tea

Include a little boost of caffeine with muscle-soothing thyme.

½ teaspoon black tea	*1 cup boiling water*
½ teaspoon dried thyme	

Heat a single-serving tea pot with hot water, then drain. Add the tea, thyme, and boiling water. Steep 5 minutes, keeping the pot warm, then strain into a cup. If the tea is too dark for your taste, dilute with very hot water as desired. A teaspoon of honey and/or a slice of lemon can be added.

MAKES 1 SERVING

SPICE SHELF CHEMOPREVENTION

In Indian experiments (seeking the scientific basis for their traditional system of medicine, Ayurveda) turmeric and cumin were found to inhibit platelet aggregation—in other words, help to prevent the clotting that leads to strokes.

Other studies in India found a number of common herbs and spices to suppress carcinogenesis in mice and therefore were thought to be effective protective agents against cancer. The anticancer herbs and spices on the list that are commonly found in American kitchens are cumin, poppy seeds, turmeric, basil, garlic, black pepper, and sesame seeds. Or if they're not already in your kitchen, perhaps you should put them there.

There's a trace of morphine in poppy seeds—not enough to cause a narcotic effect, but enough to throw off a drug urine test, as it did for one woman who'd merely indulged in a poppy seed muffin before the test.

Experiments with saffron in the lab found that it inhibited DNA and RNA synthesis in malignant cells. In mice, this most precious of spices was found to be an antitumor antioxidant.

Curry Powder

Several of the preceding spices are found in traditional curry powders. Homemade curry powders are, of course, subject to infinite variation, of which the following is a fairly hot version.

1 teaspoon ground cumin	*½ teaspoon cayenne pepper**
1 teaspoon ground coriander	*½ teaspoon ground ginger*
1 teaspoon black pepper*	*½ teaspoon ground fenugreek***
1 teaspoon turmeric	*⅛ teaspoon ground cloves*
1 teaspoon ground cardamom	

Blend all the ingredients well, and store the mixture in a tightly closed jar.

MAKES A SCANT ¼ CUP

A Quick Curry Sauce for Plain Chicken

SUPERFOODS: yogurt

1 cup chicken broth	*2 teaspoons curry powder*
2 tablespoons cornstarch	*1 cup plain nonfat yogurt*

*Use less for a milder curry.
**Available in specialty stores.

Heat the broth in a saucepan (not to the point of boiling). With a whisk, thoroughly mix the cornstarch and curry powder with the yogurt. Stir the mixture into the broth, and keep whisking until the sauce boils and thickens. Simmer 2 minutes, whisking constantly. (Brisk whisking is important to prevent the sauce from separating.) If your range is electric, turn off the burner for the simmering, using just the heat that remains.

MAKES 2 CUPS

SOME PREPARED TEAS OF NOTE

Teas containing the following herbs may be found wherever herbal teas are sold. Some are strictly herbal; others are combined with caffeine-rich black or green tea.

RASPBERRY LEAF TEA

Dried leaves of the red raspberry make a tea that's commonly used to treat nausea or to relieve menstrual cramps. They contain astringent tannins that may be helpful in treating diarrhea.

CHAMOMILE TEA

Probably the most popular and potent of herbal remedies, but those who are allergic to ragweed should avoid this tea, which could trigger an allergic reaction. Others may benefit from its calming effect—a real nerve tranquilizer in times of anxiety and/ or insomnia.

GINSENG TEA

With the time-honored reputation as a cure-all, ginseng has been recommended for everything from disease prevention to stimulating sexual appetite. Soviet researchers have reported that the root boosts immunity, inhibits cancer, and improves physical stamina.

In other studies, extract of ginseng seemed to improve the memory of laboratory animals given the task of searching through a maze for food.

Herbalists prescribe ginseng tea to help relieve unpleasant symptoms of menopause. Because of its steroid-like chemical structure, ginseng may work something like estrogen. Ginseng is also recommended as a mental and physical stimulant—for occasional and not continuous use.

JAPANESE GREEN TEA

Studies in Japan on the eating habits and mortality rates of two different areas have suggested that a diet that combines green tea with a high intake of fruits, vegetables, and miso soup may lower the risk of stomach cancer. Separate studies in China credited green tea (even as small a "dose" as one cup per week!) with helping to prevent cancer of the esophagus. Skeptical U.S. nutritionists point out that the scientific studies of green tea are only at a beginning stage. Still, if you like green tea, which is available in specialty stores and natural-food stores, why not enjoy a steaming cup regularly while East and West are still arguing its merits?

In general, green tea is reported by Asians to be antibiotic and antiviral, a remedy for diarrhea, and an anticoagulant to help prevent dangerous blood clots. (So is black tea, but to a lesser degree.) In Asian medicine, green tea is considered to be effective in all-around disease prevention.

Green tea, ginger tea, raspberry leaf, mint, gingseng, and even wonderful black teas like Earl Grey—why not stock a whole "pharmacy" of teas for every need and mood?

An afternoon "tisane" (as Hercule Poirot would call it) is a pleasantly relaxing custom, even if you're in the middle of a crisis—or maybe, *especially* if "the slings and arrows of outrageous fortune" are flying. Close your door, put your feet up, and take a few minutes to nourish yourself—you deserve it!

13

Mix 'n' Match
Menus

For a Beautiful Balance of Nutritional Pluses

Many of the preceding chapters have concentrated on one particular nutritional need that women have—with the menus and recipes to help boost intake of that special substance, such as iron or antioxidants or calcium. Optimum nutrition over the long run, however, naturally calls for a balance, so it's important to choose a variety of superfoods from day to day and thus benefit from the best of everything.

All the recipes in this cookbook have "mix 'n match" possibilities; they can be combined and recombined into multidimensional menus for a balanced approach to overall good health. To get you started, here are a dozen menus with recipes culled from these various chapters. The important thing is to treat yourself to the entire spectrum of superfoods—to prevent disease, to resist the signs of aging, and to keep on looking and feeling great.

A RELAXED SUPPER FOR
FOUR TO SIX

Herb-Marinated Grilled Tuna (page 279)
Stir-Fried Asparagus with Tofu and Cashews (page 255)
Crusty Whole Wheat Rolls
Practically Instant Strawberry Tiramisù (page 313)

Grilling and stir-frying must be the two most relaxed ways to cook! Besides those important omega-3 fatty acids, tuna is also high in iron for energy and in niacin, a heart protector and nerve builder. Tofu offers more iron plus calcium, asparagus is rich in folate and potassium, and cashews add vitamin E. The B vitamins in the whole wheat rolls and vitamin C with potassium in the strawberries round out a take-it-easy supper.

For six people, increase the dessert recipe by half to make two more portions.

DINNER FOR FOUR WITH
A MEDITERRANEAN FLAIR

Pasta Autunno (page 190)
Tuna and Chickpea Salad (page 419)
Whole-Grain Italian Bread
Almond "Cream" Puddings with Sliced Fresh Peaches (page 385)

*B*roccoli, carrots, and peaches are rich in beta-carotene, pasta is a soul-satisfying complex carbohydrate food, and garlic helps to boost immunity. Tuna is rich in iron; chickpeas add more, plus fiber. Whole-grain bread is another source of fiber in this menu, as well as rich in B vitamins. There's plenty of calcium in the dessert and with the addition of cheese to the pasta. Almonds are a great source of riboflavin, the exerciser's vitamin.

A SIMPLY SUPER DINNER FOR FOUR

Broiled Swordfish with Lime and Mint (page 106)
Green Bean Salad à la Grecque (page 294)
Baked Sweet Potatoes with Gorgonzola (page 473)
Chocolate Raisin Pudding (page 448)

*T*his densely nutritious menu goes together easily, although the potatoes will take about an hour to bake. Swordfish is rich in omega-3 fatty acids and niacin to protect the heart. Sweet potatoes are fairly bursting with beta-carotene, plus potassium, riboflavin, and vitamin C. Walnuts in the salad, along with fish, are good brain food. Both of the vegetables add to your daily fiber intake. And the dessert provides calcium, manganese, and iron, not to mention the joy of chocolate.

For this menu, omit the feta cheese in the green bean salad in favor of the melting gorgonzola on the sweet spuds.

COMFORT FOOD
FOR SIX

Escarole in Chicken Broth (page 309)
Macaroni 'n' Cheese with Salsa (page 380)
Carrot Salad with Ginger Vinaigrette (page 196)
Italian Baked Apples (page 382)

There is plenty of calcium, complex carbohydrates, and zinc in the entree, plus potassium in dark leafy greens and carotenoids in both greens and carrots. Along with fiber, apples provide boron for strong bones.

For this menu, increase the broth in the soup recipe by 2 cups for six people; omit the julienne carrot so as not to upstage the salad.

EASY-DOES-IT DINNER
FOR FOUR

Chicken Cutlets
with Red Pepper and Braised Carrots (page 154)
Sautéed Spinach and Tofu (page 260)
Whole Wheat French Bread
Wine-Glazed Baked Pears (page 452)

A rainbow of carotenoids for cancer defense in red bell pepper, carrots, and spinach. There's lots of iron in spinach, but it's not easily absorbed. When combined with the iron in chicken and tofu and the vitamin C in peppers, however, spinach iron becomes more available. Choose whole-grain breads for B vitamins and fiber. Pears are a great source of boron.

AFTER-A-DAY-OUT
SUPPER FOR FOUR

Shrimp and Broccoli Salad (page 73)
Mixed Mushroom Sauté (page 360)
Whole Wheat Pita Bread
Easy Golden-Baked Peaches (page 131)

Suppose you've just arrived home from a day of sun and fun. Everyone's hungry and tired, and that includes you. Here's a quick and easy dinner to revive you with iron-rich shrimp in a nearly fat-free yogurt dressing, the cruciferous and calcium defense of broccoli, vitamin C in the salad's tomato garnish, the immune-system benefits of mushrooms, whole wheat for the nerves, and antioxidant-rich peaches for dessert. Repeat as needed!

DINNER FOR FOUR—ON THE RUN

Spanish-Style Scallops with White Beans (page 53)
Broccoli with Oil and Lemon (page 275)
Crusty Italian Bread
Very Berry Compote (page 480)

Each of these dishes takes only a few minutes to prepare and cook. If you're really pressed for time, barely cooked frozen broccoli can be substituted for parboiled fresh broccoli. And what a bonanza of nutrition! There's plenty of iron for energy in the scallops, a bevy of B vitamins like folate and thiamin in beans, which are also a fortifying complex carbohydrate food. And there's calcium and beta-carotene in cruciferous broccoli, vitamin C galore in berries. Great fiber in beans, broccoli, and berries.

HEART-TO-HEART DINNER
FOR FOUR

Seared Salmon Fillets with Dilled Yogurt (page 84)
"Shuffled" Chard and Potatoes (page 195)
Warm Banana "Splits" with Blueberries (page 108)

To paraphrase a famous commercial, nothing says lovin' like a heart-healthy dinner. Although they come from different chapters, just about all the heart savers are stressed in this one selection of recipes: salmon, high on the list for important omega-3 fatty acids; soluble fiber in potatoes and blueberries; stroke-fighting garlic; calcium in yogurt; potassium in chard and bananas. Potatoes, fruits, yogurt, and garlic are also foods that help lower the risk of cancer.

In this menu for four, you may wish to reduce the chard recipe somewhat—or enjoy the leftovers.

FAIRLY FAST FOOD
FOR FOUR

Penne with Tomato-Yogurt Sauce (page 292)
Tuna and Mixed Greens Salad (page 200)
Anise Oranges (page 59)

If you haven't made the thickened yogurt called for in the pasta recipe, it's okay to use yogurt just as it comes from the container (the sauce will be a bit thinner). In plumping up that nutritional advantage, it's not time spent in cooking but in planning that counts. The iron in tuna and yogurt will be more readily absorbed because of the vitamin C in tomatoes and oranges. Tuna is high on the fish list for heart health, complex carbohydrates in pasta provide sustained energy, and dark, leafy greens along with yogurt add calcium. A fillip of garlic and onion helps with all-round immunity.

MAKE-IT-NOW, COOK-IT-LATER DINNER FOR FOUR

Baked Haddock with Tomatoes and Peppers (page 88)
Lucy's Mashed Potato Casserole (page 465)
Spinach Salad with Pecans (page 42)
Macedonia di Frutta (page 303)

Everything can be prepared hours ahead and tucked into the refrigerator. When ready to cook, bake the fish and potatoes in a half-hour or so, and toss the salad. Vitamin C in tomatoes and in the fruit dessert enhances iron absorption from haddock and spinach. Great carbohydrates in potatoes accompany calcium in the casserole's melting heart of cheese. Pecans are high in zinc, a component of the antioxidant package. In general, a diet rich in fruits and vegetables reduces the risk of cancer.

For this menu, cook both fish and potatoes at 375 degrees F. (instead of 400 and 350 degrees F., respectively); the fish may take a few minutes longer. Omit the optional blue cheese in the salad.

EASYGOING ELEGANCE
FOR FOUR

Sauté de Veau Chasseur (Hunter's Veal Stew) (page 296)
Brown Basmati Rice (page 524)
Asparagus Vinaigrette (page 211)
Gingered Figs (page 161)

*S*o many good things can be simmered into stew! In this French
dish, tomatoes and mushrooms add a potassium bonus. Asparagus
is rich in folate as well as vitamins C and E. The comforting
carbohydrates of brown rice contain many B vitamins. Figs are
especially high in thiamin, a vitalizer vitamin.

In this menu for four, reduce the asparagus to 1 pound and
use a bit less dressing.

AN APPETIZER BUFFET
FOR A BUNCH

Grilled Bruschetta with Walnut Pesto (page 277)
Marinated Vegetable Appetizer (page 129)
Smoked Salmon Spread (page 65)
Cannellini Puree (page 66)
Sweet 'n' Sour Pepper Relish (page 135)
Oven-Fried Eggplant Sticks (page 283)
Spinach-Stuffed Mushrooms (page 191)
Tabbouli (page 307)
A Selection of Cocktail Ryes and Whole-Grain Crackers

A really good-for-you spread of easy, savory make-ahead party appetizers, without the usual overdose of nitrates and salt. Fat is kept at a minimum (compared to the usual cold cuts and cheeses), and it's beneficial olive oil. You'd never guess you're nibbling on calcium, cruciferous vegetables, carotenoids, B vitamins, iron, and all the other nutrients women need most. Every recipe can be doubled—and more! If you err on the side of abundance, leftovers are a lovely bonus.

___ 14 ___
SUPERFOOD BASIC RECIPES

Basic recipes like these are the foundation of many healthy dishes, in and out of this cookbook. In some cases, such as with tomato sauce and low-fat salad dressings, store-bought alternatives are indeed possible when you're short of time and energy. But none of these recipes is really difficult (as compared, say, to puff pastry) and homemade always tastes best. Not only that, but homemade also tastes different from the last time you made it. Since you're not a machine of perfect measurement, one time your hand may be a little heavy with the pepper, another time with the garlic. Store-bought stuff, however, is always boringly the same (especially the tomato sauce).

Half-and-Half Tomato Sauce

Superfoods: tomatoes, olive oil, garlic

A combination of fresh tomatoes, for that summery taste, and canned tomatoes for a smoother, thicker sauce. If you happen to have some pesto, homemade (see page 526) or from a jar, it can always be substituted for the fresh basil called for in this and many other recipes—in fact, this sauce may taste even better with a dollop or two of pesto.

2 pounds ripe tomatoes	*¼ teaspoon or more freshly*
¼ cup olive oil	*ground black pepper*
2 garlic cloves, minced	*One 1-pound can ground*
1 dried hot red pepper	*imported Italian tomatoes*
2 tablespoons minced fresh basil	*2 tablespoons minced fresh flat-*
¾ teaspoon salt	*leaf parsley*

Pour boiling water over the fresh tomatoes, and let them stand until the skins loosen. Drain, peel, seed, and chop the tomatoes.

Heat the olive oil in a 12-inch skillet, and sauté the garlic until it sizzles, about 2 minutes, but don't let it brown. Add all the remaining ingredients except the canned tomatoes and parsley. Cook uncovered, over medium heat, for 15 minutes, stirring occasionally. Add the canned tomatoes, and simmer over low heat for 20 to 30 minutes, until a sauce consistency is reached. Taste the sauce. If very acidic, ½ teaspoon or so of sugar can be stirred in.

Remove the sauce from the heat, discard the hot red pepper, and stir in the parsley.

The sauce can be made up to 3 days ahead. Keep refrigerated, or freeze for longer storage.

MAKES 1 QUART

A Quick Sicilian Tomato Sauce

Superfoods: garlic, green pepper, tomatoes

Sicilian fast food! Keep the sauce thin for thin spaghetti.

2 tablespoons olive oil

One 2-ounce can flat anchovies, drained

1 garlic clove, finely minced

1 green bell pepper, seeded and chopped

One 14-ounce to 1-pound can imported Italian plum tomatoes in puree

½ teaspoon dried oregano

2 tablespoons Basil Pesto (see page 526), or ½ teaspoon dried basil

1 dried hot red pepper or pinches of hot red pepper flakes

⅛ teaspoon or more black pepper

Heat the oil in a medium skillet, and sauté the anchovies over very low heat until they are dissolved. Stir in the garlic and green pepper, and continue to cook over low heat for 3 to 5 minutes.

Add all the remaining ingredients, and simmer uncovered for about 20 minutes.

The sauce can be made up to 2 days ahead. Keep refrigerated, or freeze for longer storage.

MAKES ABOUT 2 CUPS

Brown Mushroom-Tomato Sauce

SUPERFOODS: mushrooms, garlic, olive oil, tomatoes

This rich dark sauce can substitute for a meat sauce.

8 to 12 ounces brown
  mushrooms, such as
  portobello, cleaned and sliced
1 to 2 garlic cloves, minced
¼ cup olive oil
One 2-pound can imported
  Italian tomatoes in puree

½ cup strong beef broth*
1 tablespoon minced fresh basil,
  or 1 teaspoon dried
¾ teaspoon salt
½ teaspoon black pepper
2 tablespoons minced fresh flat-
  leaf parsley

In a large skillet, sauté the mushrooms and garlic in the oil until sizzling but not brown. Add all the remaining ingredients except the parsley, bring to a simmer, and cook, stirring occasionally and breaking up the tomatoes, for 30 to 45 minutes. Remove from the heat and stir in the parsley.

The sauce can be made up to 3 days ahead. Keep refrigerated, or freeze for longer storage.

MAKES ABOUT 1 QUART

---

*1 cup canned beef broth reduced by boiling to ½ cup.

Polenta the Easy Way

SUPERFOODS: cornmeal

A native food of the Americas, when cornmeal was introduced into the Mediterranean cuisine, it became comforting, versatile polenta, the perfect foil for any number of flavorful sauces, such as smoky Grilled Fresh Tomato Sauce (see page 408).

Polenta also may be served with a topping of mushrooms, garlic, and oil. In Italy, this would be grilled fresh porcini mushrooms, but here we have to be satisfied with portobello or another earthy brown type. Quickest of all, hot polenta can simply be dressed with crumbled Gorgonzola cheese melting deliciously on top.

Besides being served hot from the pot, polenta is often chilled, sliced, and reheated later—a kind of continental cousin to New England's fried cornmeal mush.

Although many polenta recipes instruct you to stir for 30 minutes with a wooden spoon, this recipe's effortless alternative method produces equally smooth results. Use a good-quality, sturdy metal whisk instead of a stirring spoon.

2 cups chicken broth
¾ cup coarse-grained yellow cornmeal*
1 cup cold water

3 tablespoons grated Parmesan cheese
¼ teaspoon freshly ground black pepper or more

In the top of a 2-quart double boiler, bring the broth to a boil over direct heat. In a small pitcher, blend the cornmeal into the cold water until smooth. Stir again just before pouring the cornmeal mixture into the boiling broth while whisking constantly with your other hand. Continue whisking until cornmeal thickens; lower heat and cook, stirring, for 3 minutes.

*Preferably not degerminated.

Meanwhile, bring 2 inches of water to boil in the bottom of the double boiler. Cook the polenta over the boiling water, with cover ajar, for 45 minutes, whisking about 3 times. Check occasionally that the water doesn't boil out. Remove from heat; whisk in the cheese and pepper.

MAKES 4 SERVINGS

Italian Chicken Broth

This wonderful broth is the basis of so many favorite Italian soups. For a typical holiday soup, add escarole and tiny meatballs. For minestrone, add vegetables, beans, and pasta.

One 3-pound chicken	¼ cup coarsely chopped fresh flat-
2 celery stalks with their leaves,	leaf parsley
chopped	Sprigs of fresh rosemary and
1 large onion, chopped	thyme, or pinches of dried
¼ cup minced shallots	1 teaspoon salt
1 carrot, scraped and sliced	Several peppercorns
4 plum tomatoes (fresh or	2½ quarts water
canned), chopped	

Wash the chicken well in salted water. Discard internal fat. Save the giblets, if you wish, for another use.

Put all the ingredients into a large pot, and bring the soup to a boil. Scoop off any froth that rises to the top, and reduce the heat to a simmer. Cook with cover ajar for 1½ to 2 hours.

Strain the soup through a small-meshed strainer. Discard the vegetables, herbs, peppercorns, and skin from the chicken. Refrigerate the chicken immediately, moistened with a little of the broth. Cool the rest of the broth and refrigerate it. Skim off the congealed fat before using the broth.

The cooked chicken is a bonus, the base of a host of great dishes, from a simple chicken sandwich to chicken supreme.

MAKES ABOUT 2 QUARTS BROTH

Stewed Lentils

SUPERFOODS: lentils, onion, garlic, celery, carrot, tomatoes

So nice to have on hand for everything from soups to salads!

One 1-pound bag of lentils
3 tablespoons olive oil
1 large onion, chopped
2 garlic cloves, minced
2 celery stalks with leaves, diced
1 carrot, finely diced

6 to 7 cups water
1 cup crushed tomatoes or tomato
    sauce
1 teaspoon each dried oregano
    and salt
Pepper

Pick over (looking for field debris such as small stones) and rinse lentils in a close-meshed strainer.

Heat the olive oil in a large pot, and sauté the vegetables until they are softened and fragrant, about 5 minutes. Add the lentils, 6 cups water, tomatoes, oregano, and salt.

Simmer the lentils for 1 hour, with cover ajar, stirring occasionally, until very tender. If the mixture seems to get too dry, add more water. When cooked, stir in pepper to taste.

The lentils can be made up to 3 days ahead and stored in the refrigerator, or frozen for up to 6 months; pint containers are a useful size.

MAKES ABOUT 2 QUARTS

Oven-Sautéed Eggplant

SUPERFOODS: eggplant, garlic

This no-work, no-watch method is so much easier than frying (and it uses so much less oil), you may never go back to the range top.

Besides the recipes in this book, versatile sautéed eggplant can be stirred into a risotto, spooned into a frittata, sprinkled on a pizza, tossed into a pasta, or served plain as an appetizer.

One 1- or 1¼-pound eggplant	1 garlic clove, minced
1 teaspoon salt	Pepper
2 tablespoons olive oil	

Peel and dice the eggplant, unless you happen to have an organically grown, young and firm vegetable, in which case leave it unpeeled. Sprinkle with salt, toss to distribute it, and leave the eggplant to drain in a colander for 30 minutes to 1 hour.

Preheat the oven to 400 degrees F.

Rinse off the salt. Put the eggplant in a dishtowel, and press to squeeze out the moisture.

Toss the eggplant with the oil, and spoon it into a baking pan that will fit the pieces in 1 layer.

Bake for 20 minutes. Add the garlic and toss well. Bake an additional 10 minutes, or until tender. Add pepper to taste.

(If you're not using the eggplant in a recipe, season it with dried herbs, such as marjoram and/or basil, and a few dashes of dried red pepper flakes.)

The eggplant can be made 1 day ahead. Keep refrigerated.

MAKES ABOUT 2 CUPS

Roasted Red Peppers

SUPERFOODS: red peppers, olive oil

Italian soul food!

6 large red bell peppers	*1 garlic clove, crushed*
Salt	*½ cup olive oil or more as needed*

Put the peppers on a broiler tray. Broil them about 6 inches from the heat, turning often with tongs, until they are partly browned on all sides.

Put the peppers in a plastic bag until they are cool enough to handle. Halve the peppers and remove the seeds. Peel off the skins, which will have loosened from the steam in the plastic bag.

Cut the peppers into strips, and salt the strips to your taste. Put them in a jar with the garlic and enough oil to cover them. Stir occasionally while they marinate for an hour, to distribute the garlic flavor.

The peppers will keep for about 5 days refrigerated. The oil makes a tasty addition to salad dressings.

MAKES ABOUT 1 PINT

Sweetened Red Onion Rings

Try these onions in a winter salad with sliced oranges!

1 large red onion   ½ *cup red wine vinegar*
1 tablespoon sugar

Peel the onion, slice it, and separate the slices into rings, discarding the small white center of each ring. In a soup plate, stir the sugar into the vinegar until dissolved. Marinate the onion rings in this mixture for ½ to 1 hour at room temperature, turning often. Drain off and discard the vinegar before using.

The onions can be made up to 2 days in advance. Cover well and keep refrigerated. The longer they marinate, the sweeter they will be.

Brown Basmati Rice or Brown Rice

Basmati is a particularly nutty-flavored rice grown in India and Pakistan. The unrefined brown variety can be bought in whole-foods markets that feature organic foods. It should be looked over (for foreign particles) and rinsed before using.

If you can't find brown basmati, regular brown rice can be substituted, 40 minutes cooking time, or use refined basmati, 15 to 20 minutes.

2 quarts of water   1 teaspoon salt
½ tablespoon vegetable oil   1½ cups brown basmati rice

Bring the water to a boil, add oil, salt, and rice, and stir once. Lower the heat to medium-high and cook until the rice is just tender 40 to 45 minutes. Taste is the best test. Drain well.

Alternative steamer method: (Even better, if you have the equipment, producing firmer, more separate grains.) After 30 minutes of boiling, drain the rice and steam it, covered, over an inch of boiling water for 10 to 15 minutes. You can use a conventional steamer or improvise one from a large, close-meshed strainer that will fit in a pot you can cover. The bottom of the strainer should not touch the boiling water. Transfer the rice to a bowl and fluff it with a fork. If using the rice for salad, spread it out on a platter to cool quickly without clumping.

Brown and Wild Rice: Substitute ½ cup wild rice for ½ cup of the brown basmati or other brown rice. Do not try this with white rice or refined basmati, which cooks too fast for the wild rice.

MAKES ABOUT 4 CUPS

Arborio Rice

Italian short-grain rice is a delicious choice when plain white rice is wanted. Besides all the dishes it "goes with," try arborio rice plain, with just a dusting of Parmesan, when your stomach feels a bit jumpy. Instantly soothing!

2 quarts water	*½ teaspoon salt (optional)*
1 teaspoon olive oil	*1 cup arborio rice*

In a 3-quart saucepan, bring the water to a boil. Add the oil and salt, if using. Add the rice. Reduce the heat to medium, stir once, and keep at a lively simmer for about 12 minutes, or until cooked al dente. Drain well.

Return the rice to the warm pan, fluff it with a fork to separate the grains, and let it stand 2 to 3 minutes. Serve hot.

MAKES ABOUT 2 CUPS

Basil Pesto

Useful as a condiment as well as a pasta topping, try stirring a spoonful into a plate of soup.

2 cups fresh basil leaves, main
  stems removed
1 to 2 garlic cloves
½ cup lightly toasted pine nuts
½ teaspoon salt

¼ teaspoon freshly ground black
  pepper
⅓ to ½ cup extra-virgin olive oil
¼ cup grated Parmesan cheese

Rinse and thoroughly dry the basil leaves. In a food processor with the motor running, toss the garlic down the feed tube to mince it. Stop the motor. Add the basil, pine nuts, salt, and pepper to the work bowl. Process until finely minced.

With the motor running, slowly pour the oil down the feed tube in a thin stream until the mixture reaches a pastelike consistency, neither too thick to drop off a spoon nor runny. You'll have to stop, stir, and check a few times.

Transfer the pesto to a bowl, then stir in the cheese.

The pesto will keep 1 week, refrigerated. Cover with plastic wrap so that it touches the entire surface of the pesto. Or freeze for later use. I do this in an ice cube tray coated with cooking spray. When the cubes are solid, I remove them, with the assistance of a sharp paring knife, to a plastic bag or container stored in the freezer. This makes conveniently available a tablespoon or two of pesto whenever it is wanted.

MAKES ABOUT ¾ CUP

Parsley Pesto

A nice touch on cold chicken.

1 to 2 garlic cloves	¼ teaspoon freshly ground black
4 cups parsley leaves, main stems	pepper
removed	About ½ cup extra-virgin olive
½ teaspoon salt	oil

Follow the directions for Basil Pesto in the previous recipe.

MAKES ABOUT 1¼ CUPS

Lemon-Garlic Mayonnaise

Especially good in fish salads, such as lobster, shrimp, or tuna.

1 garlic clove	*½ cup olive oil*
⅓ cup lemon juice	*⅓ cup canola oil*
⅓ cup prepared egg substitute	*¼ teaspoon white pepper*
1 teaspoon Dijon mustard	*Salt**

Processor method: With the motor running, toss the garlic down the feed tube and process until it is minced. Stop the motor; add the lemon juice, egg substitute, and mustard. Process until well blended. Combine the oils in a small pitcher, and with the motor running, slowly pour the mixture through the feed tube. When all the oil has been added, blend in the pepper. Taste to correct seasoning; add salt if desired.

Blender method: Press the garlic through a garlic press into the work bowl. Proceed as above.

By hand: Press the garlic. Proceed as above, whisking the juice, egg, and mustard by hand. Add the oil very slowly while whisking constantly.

Keeps 5 to 7 days, refrigerated.

MAKES ABOUT 1 CUP

*The mustard adds some salt.

Greek-Style Salad Dressing

To get those hard little lemons to yield more juice, soak them in hot tap water for 15 minutes or press and roll them on the kitchen counter before squeezing. Or both.

⅓ cup fresh lemon juice
1 cup olive oil
1 teaspoon dried oregano
½ teaspoon salt

¼ teaspoon freshly ground black pepper
2 garlic cloves, crushed

Combine all the ingredients in a pint jar. Cover the jar tightly, and shake to blend. Let the mixture stand at room temperature for about an hour to develop its flavor. After that, remove the garlic, and refrigerate the dressing until needed. *The dressing keeps 1 week to 10 days.*

MAKES 1½ CUPS

Herb Vinaigrette

To dress a four-serving salad lightly, try ⅓ cup dressing. Each serving will average about 1 tablespoon oil.

¼ cup rice wine vinegar
2 tablespoons red wine vinegar
1 tablespoon Dijon mustard
¾ cup olive oil
½ teaspoon dried cilantro or
   tarragon
½ teaspoon dried basil or
   marjoram

½ teaspoon dried dill
¼ teaspoon dried thyme leaves
¼ teaspoon freshly ground black
   pepper
½ teaspoon celery salt or regular
   salt*

In a blender or food processor, whisk together the vinegars and mustard. With the motor running, slowly pour the oil through the feed tube until the dressing is thick and emuslified. Stir in the remaining ingredients.

The vinaigrette will keep a month or more stored in a jar in the refrigerator. Bring to room temperature before using.

Caper Vinaigrette: Omit the herbs. Use regular salt rather than celery salt. Substitute lemon juice for red wine vinegar. After blending, remove the dressing to a jar and stir in 2 tablespoons drained capers.

MAKES ABOUT 1 CUP

---

*But don't use garlic or onion salt; their acrid flavors overpower the herb essence. If you want garlic flavor, squeeze some garlic into the dressing just before using. If you want onion, add fresh onion to the salad.

Honey-Mustard Dressing

When preparing a salad ahead of time, pour the dressing into the bottom of the bowl. Stir in any ingredients that might turn brown when exposed to air, such as chopped avocado, fennel, apple, or that might improve by being marinated, such as chopped onions or cabbage. Put the crisp greens on top, but don't toss again until serving time.

¼ cup rice vinegar	*1 tablespoon honey*
2 tablespoons Dijon mustard	*¼ teaspoon freshly ground black*
¾ cup olive oil	*pepper*

In a blender or food processor, whisk together the vinegar and mustard. With the motor running, slowly pour oil through the feed tube until the dressing is thick and emulsified. Stir in the remaining ingredients.

The dressing will keep a month or more stored in a jar in the refrigerator. Whisk before using, if necessary.

Poppy Seed Dressing: Stir 2 teaspoons poppy seeds into Honey-Mustard Dressing.

MAKES ABOUT 1 CUP

"Light" Russian Dressing

Naturally good on a shrimp salad, or try it on a sandwich.

1 cup plain nonfat yogurt	⅓ cup sliced stuffed green olives
⅔ cup chili sauce	3 tablespoons chopped pickles*
⅓ cup mayonnaise	¼ teaspoon hot pepper sauce

Mix all ingredients and store in a jar in the refrigerator. *The dressing will keep as long as the date on the yogurt package indicates.*

MAKES ABOUT 2½ CUPS

Yogurt-Mint Dressing

A good companion for cold roast lamb.

1 cup plain nonfat yogurt	1 tablespoon lemon juice
1 garlic clove, pressed in a garlic press or finely minced	8 fresh mint leaves, minced
	½ teaspoon dried dill
1 tablespoon minced fresh parsley	¼ teaspoon each salt, white pepper, and sugar

Mix all the ingredients, and chill until needed. *The dressing will keep 5 days, refrigerated.*

MAKES 1 CUP

*As long as you choose crisp pickles, they can be sweet, sour, or dill—according to your taste.

Caesar Yogurt Dressing

A flavorful, lighter version!

⅔ cup plain nonfat yogurt
⅓ cup mayonnaise*
¼ cup grated Parmesan cheese
2 to 4 anchovy fillets, well
  mashed**
2 small or 1 large garlic clove,
  pressed in a garlic press or
  finely minced

1 teaspoon each *Dijon mustard*
  and Worcestershire sauce
White pepper to taste

Whisk together all ingredients. Store in a jar. *Can be made up to 3 days ahead. Keep refrigerated.*

MAKES ABOUT 1¼ CUPS

*For a really low-fat dressing, use 1 cup yogurt and no mayonnaise.
**Or 2 teaspoons anchovy paste.

Blue Cheese–Yogurt Dressing

1 cup plain nonfat yogurt   1 teaspoon Dijon mustard
2 tablespoons rice vinegar   ½ cup crumbled blue cheese
1 tablespoon mayonnaise

Whisk together the yogurt, vinegar, mayonnaise, and mustard. Stir in the blue cheese, mashing it slightly. Store in a jar in the refrigerator. *Keeps 4 to 5 days.*

MAKES 1½ CUPS

Thickened Yogurt or Yogurt Cheese

Regular nonfat yogurt can be too thin and watery for many recipes. When you need a thicker yogurt or a yogurt cheese, follow the easy steps given below.

Some kitchen shops sell a yogurt-cheese funnel made of porous plastic; I don't think it works as well as a paper coffee filter or cheesecloth. Cheesecloth is sold in supermarkets (sometimes), hardware stores, and kitchen shops; you'll find it a worthwhile investment for really fine straining, such as is needed for consommé, fruit jelly, or this recipe.

Fit a paper coffee filter into a 1-quart wire-mesh strainer. Or use a double thickness of rinsed cheesecloth cut large enough overlap the top.

Place the strainer over a bowl or pan that will hold it at least 3 inches above the bottom. Spoon yogurt into the strainer, and cover it with a small plate or the cheesecloth overlap. One quart yogurt can be strained in a cheesecloth-lined large strainer. A paper coffee filter will take about 2 cups yogurt; repeat the process after making the first batch.

For thickened yogurt: Strain in the refrigerator for an hour. Spoon the yogurt into a container. Discard the water at the bottom of the bowl.

For yogurt cheese: Strain in the refrigerator overnight and proceed as above. If desired, mix with seasonings such as chopped herbs, white pepper, and/or finely minced garlic.

MAKES 2 TO 2½ CUPS

Yogurt Custard Sauce

This recipe can easily be doubled or tripled, as needed.

½ cup plain nonfat yogurt	¼ cup sugar
2 teaspoons cornstarch	1 egg, beaten
½ cup whole milk	1 teaspoon vanilla extract

In a cup, sprinkle the yogurt with the cornstarch, and stir with a small whisk until very well combined.

In a small saucepan, whisk together the milk, sugar, and egg over low heat until the sugar is dissolved. (Do not boil yet.) Whisk in the yogurt mixture, and keep whisking over medium heat until the mixture bubbles and thickens. Cook about 1 minute longer.

Remove the sauce from the heat and stir in the vanilla.

Can be made 1 day ahead. Keep covered with plastic wrap over the surface of the sauce; refrigerate until needed. Whisk well before using.

MAKES ABOUT 1 CUP

Almond Paste

Great for stuffing dried fruits or including in pastries and tarts!

2 cups slivered blanched almonds   ½ teaspoon natural almond
⅓ cup honey, or more   flavoring

In a food processor, grind the almonds until they begin to get pasty. Occasionally stop the motor to scrape up the ground nuts that fall below the steel blade. Gradually add honey through the feed tube, until the mixture forms a soft, kneadable paste that will hold its shape, like clay. Be cautious with the honey; you don't want the mixture too soft. Add the almond flavoring.

Wrap the almond paste in plastic wrap, then foil, and refrigerate.

The almond paste will keep for weeks, refrigerated. Bring the paste to room temperature when you're ready to work with it.

MAKES ABOUT 1 CUP

Vegetable Oil Pastry

This is not the meltingly flaky butter-and-solid shortening pie crust favored by pastry purists, but a healthful substitute. Besides not glutting your arteries, it has the advantage of rolling out quite neatly between two sheets of paper. But don't substitute whole wheat pastry flour for all-purpose white flour; the combination of whole wheat and oil produces a pastry that falls apart when you roll it out.

2¼ cups unbleached all-purpose   *½ to 1 teaspoon salt*
   flour   *½ cup vegetable oil*
2 teaspoons sugar (optional)   *⅓ cup cold milk (can be skim)*

Mix the flour, sugar, and salt together with a fork. Measure the oil and milk into a cup. Pour the liquids all at once into the dry ingredients, mixing with a fork until just blended.

Since the consistency of flour does vary, you may want to add a teaspoon or so more milk if the pastry seems too dry, or pat in more flour if it seems too wet.

Form the pastry into 2 balls; flatten each slightly. Roll out half the pastry between 2 sheets of floured waxed paper or plastic wrap into a 12-inch circle. Handle gently to avoid toughening the pastry. As you roll, turn the pastry over, paper and all, from time to time, straighten out any wrinkles in the bottom sheet, and dust with flour if necessary.

Peel off the top sheet and fit the dough, bottom sheet up, into an 8- or 9-inch pie or tart pan. Remove the second sheet of paper. Trim the pastry ½ inch beyond the edge of the pie plate. Flute the edge.

Or, for a double-crust pie, after filling the pastry, roll out the top crust. Trim the top crust ½ inch beyond edge of pie plate. Fold extra pastry under the bottom crust. Flute the edge, pressing the 2 crusts together, or seal the edge with a floured fork.

To bake an unfilled single-crust pie or tart shell, preheat the oven to 400 degrees F. Prick the pastry shell all over with a fork and bake it on the bottom shelf of the oven until it's golden, about 12 minutes. Keep an eye on its progress. If part of the shell rises in a hump, prick it with a fork to allow the steam to escape. Cool the shell before filling.

Note: This pastry dough does not freeze well.

MAKES ENOUGH FOR 1 DOUBLE-CRUST PIE OR 2 SINGLE-CRUST TARTS

Butter or Margarine Pastry

2½ cups unbleached all-purpose   12 tablespoons (1½ sticks)
  flour   unsalted* butter or
1 teaspoon sugar (optional)   margarine
½ teaspoon salt   6 to 7 tablespoons ice water

Mix the flour, sugar, and salt. Slice the cold butter or margarine into ½ tablespoon pieces, and add them to the flour.

In a food processor with on/off turns of the motor, or using a pastry cutter, cut in the butter or margarine until the mixture looks like coarse crumbs, some of them as large as oatmeal flakes or very tiny peas. If using a processor, transfer the mixture to a bowl.

Pour the water into a small pitcher, and add 2 ice cubes. Sprinkle the water by tablespoons over the flour, mixing lightly with 2 forks after each addition. After 4 to 5 tablespoons have been added, use your fingertips instead of forks to mix in the rest. This will enable you to feel when the right amount of moisture has been added so that the pastry will hold together and form a ball.

Divide the pastry into halves and pat the halves into 8-inch circles. Roll out half the pastry on a floured surface into the desired size. As you roll, use a spatula to loosen the pastry and turn it from time to time, dusting with flour. Do everything gently to avoid toughening the pastry.

Fit the dough into an 8- or 9-inch pie pan. Proceed as in the previous recipe.

MAKES ENOUGH FOR 1 DOUBLE-CRUST PIE OR 2 SINGLE-CRUST TARTS

Spicy Pepper Mix

This pungent blend can be used, measure for measure, in place of plain black pepper.

2 teaspoons black pepper   1 teaspoon white pepper
1 teaspoon cayenne pepper

Combine all ingredients. Stir gently (to prevent sneezing!) and store the mix in a salt shaker.

Ginger Sugar

This is a soothing tea sweetener when one's stomach is a bit nervous and upset.

Mix 2 tablespoons ground ginger and ⅓ cup sugar. Store in a jar or salt shaker.

MAKES A SCANT ½ CUP

Cinnamon Sugar

Before baking, sprinkle this on cakes you don't plan to frost—or use it to make cinnamon toast from plain whole wheat, or to add a spicy flavor to hot oatmeal.

Mix 2 tablespoons cinnamon with ⅓ cup sugar. Store in a large salt shaker.

MAKES A SCANT ½ CUP

Cocoa Sugar

Try a dusting of cocoa sugar on berries or vanilla yogurt or plain, unfrosted cakes.

Blend together 2 teaspoons unsweetened cocoa and 2 tablespoons confectioners' sugar. Store in a shaker with large holes.

MAKES 2½ TABLESPOONS

BIBLIOGRAPHY

American Heart Association. *American Heart Association Cookbook, 5th Edition*. New York: Random House, 1991.

Boston Women's Health Book Collective. *The New Our Bodies, Ourselves*. New York: Simon & Schuster, 1992.

Bourre, Jean-Marie. *Brainfood*. Boston, Massachusetts: Little, Brown, 1993.

Bremness, Lesley. *Herbs*. London: Dorling Kindersley, 1994.

Brody, Jane. *Jane Brody's Nutrition Book*. New York: Bantam Books, 1988.

Carper, Jean. *Jean Carper's Total Nutrition Guide*. New York: Bantam Books, 1989.

———. *Food—Your Miracle Medicine*. New York: HarperCollins, 1993.

Castleman, Michael. *The Healing Herbs*. Emmaus, PA: Rodale Press, 1991.

Dean, Ward, and John Morgenthaler. *Smart Drugs & Nutrients*. Santa Cruz, CA: B & J Publications, 1990.

Foley, Denise, and Eileen Nechas. *Women's Encyclopedia of Health and Emotional Healing*. Emmaus, PA: Rodale Press, 1993.

Gebhardt, Susan E., and Ruth H. Matthews, United States Department of Agriculture. *Nutritive Value of Foods*. Washington DC: U.S. Government Printing Office, 1981.

Hendler, Sheldon, M. D. *The Doctor's Vitamin and Mineral Encyclopedia*. New York: Simon & Schuster, 1991.

Herbert, Victor, and Genell J. Subak-Sharpe. *The Mount Sinai School of Medicine Complete Book of Nutrition*. New York: St. Martin's, 1990.

Hongladarom, Gail Chapman, Ruth McCorkle, and Nancy Fugate Woods. *The Complete Book of Women's Health*. Englewood Cliffs, NJ: Prentice-Hall, 1982.

Keys, Ancel, and Margaret Keys. *How to Eat Well and Stay Well, the Mediterranean Way*. Garden City, New York: Doubleday, 1975.

Levander, O. A., and Lorraine Cheng, eds. *Micronutrient Interactions: Vitamins, Minerals, and Hazardous Elements*. Volume 355. New York: New York Academy of Sciences, 1980.

Margen, Sheldon, et al. *The Wellness Encyclopedia of Food and Nutrition*. Berkeley, CA: University of California at Berkeley, 1992.

McIntyre, Anne. *Herbs for Common Ailments*. New York: Simon & Schuster, 1992.

Mindell, Earl. *Earl Mindell's Herb Bible*. New York: Simon & Schuster, 1992.

Mowrey, Daniel B. *The Scientific Validation of Herbal Medicine*. New Canaan, CT: Keats Publishing, 1986.

Nutrition Search, Inc. *Nutrition Almanac*. New York: McGraw-Hill, 1979.

U.S. Department of Agriculture. *Good Sources of Nutrients*. Washington DC: U.S. Government Printing Office, 1990.

U.S. Department of Health and Human Services. *The Surgeon General's Report on Nutrition and Health*. Washington DC: U.S. Government Printing Office, 1988.

Wolfe, Sidney M. *Women's Health Alert*. Reading, MA: Addison-Wesley, 1991.

Wurtman, Judith J. *Managing Your Mind & Mood Through Food*. New York: Harper & Row, 1986.

REFERENCES

Introduction

Ahmed, F. E. "Effect of Nutrition on the Health of the Elderly." *Jour. Amer. Diet. Assoc.* 1992;92(9):1102–1108.

Barker, D. J. P. et al. "Why Londoners Have Low Death Rates from Ischaemic Heart Disease and Stroke." *British Med. Jour.* 1992;305(6868):1551–1554.

Block, G. et al. "Fruit, Vegetables, and Cancer Prevention: A Review of the Epidemiological Evidence." *Nutrition and Cancer.* 1992; 18(1):1–29.

Brabin, L. et al. "The Cost of Successful Adolescent Growth and Development in Girls in Relation to Iron and Vitamin A Status." *Amer. Jour. of Clinical Nutr.* 1992;55(5):955–958.

Buckley, D. I. et al. "Dietary Micronutrients and Cervical Dysplasia in Southwestern American Indian Women." *Nutr. Cancer.* 1992;17(2):179–185.

Bunin, G. R. et al. "Relation Between Maternal Diet and Subsequent Primitive Neuroectodermal Brain Tumors in Young Children." *New Engl. Jour. Med.* 1993;329(8):536–541.

Chandra, R. K. "Nutrition and Immunoregulation." *Jour. Nutr.* 1992;122(3 Suppl):754–757.

Farinaro E. et al. "Diet and Cardiovascular Risk Among Women in Italy." *Ann. Ist. Super. Sanita.* (in Italian) 1992;28(3):349–353.

Gey, K. F. et al. "Increased Risk of Cardiovascular Disease at Suboptimal Plasma Concentrations of Essential Antioxidants: An Epidemiological Update with Special Attention to Carotene and Vitamin C." *Amer. Jour. Clin. Nutr.* 1993;57(5 Suppl):787s–797s.

Haines, P. S. et al. "Eating Patterns and Energy and Nutrient Intakes of U.S. Women." *Jour. Amer. Diet. Assoc.* 1992;92(6):698–704, 707.

"Daily Vitamins Boost Immunity." *Harvard Medical Letter,* May 1993;4–5.

Helser, M. A. et al. "Influence of Fruit and Vegetable Juices on the Endogenous Formation of N-nitrosoproline and N-nitrosothiazolidine-4-carboxylic Acid in Humans on Controlled Diets." *Carcinogenesis* 1991;13(12):2277–2280.

Johnson, K. et al. "Preventative Nutrition: An 'Optimal' Diet for Older Adults." *Geriatrics* 1992;47(10):56–60.

Kelley, D. S. et al. "Salmon Diet and Human Immune Status." *Euro. Jour. Clin. Nutr.* 1992;46(6):397–404.

Levi, F. et al. "Dietary Factors and the Risk of Endometrial Cancer." *Cancer* 1993;71(11):3575–3581.

Lloyd, T. et al. "Nutritional Characteristics of Recreational Women Runners." *Nutritional Research* 1992;12(3):359–366.

MacDonald, H. B. "Meat and Its Place in the Diet." *Canadian Jour. of Public Health.* 1991;82(5):331–334.

"Recommendations for the Use of Folic Acid to Reduce the Number of Cases of Spina Bifida and Other Neural Tube Defects." *MMWR Morb. Mortal. Wkly.* 1992;41(RR-14):1–7.

Popkin, B. M. et al. "Dietary Changes in Older Americans, 1977–1987." *Amer. Jour. Clin. Nutr.* 1992;55(4):823–830.

Prasad, M. P. "Esophageal Cancer and Diet—A Case-control Study." *Nutr. Cancer* 1992;18(1):85–93.

Ryan, A. S. "Nutrient Intakes and Dietary Patterns of Older Americans, a National Study." *Jour. Gerontol.* 1992;47(5):M145–150.

Schapira, D. V. "Nutrition and Cancer Prevention." *Prim-Care.* 1992; 19(3):481–491.

Williamson, D. F. et al. "Weight Loss Attempts in Adults: Goals, Duration, and Rate of Weight Loss." *Amer. Jour. of Public Health* 1992;182(9):1251–1257.

Wolff, M. A. et al. "Blood Levels of Organochlorine Residues and Risk of Breast Cancer." *Jour. Natl. Cancer Inst.* 1993;85(8):648–652.

1 IRON-RICH FOODS FOR SUPER ENERGY

Borigato, E. V. M. et al. "Iron Incorporation in Brazilian Infant Diets Cooked in Iron Utensils." *Nutr. Research* 1992;12(9):1065–1073.

Bunin, G. R. et al. "Relation Between Maternal Diet and Subsequent Primitive Neuroectodermal Brain Tumors in Young Children." *New Engl. Jour. Med.* 1993;329(8):536–541.

Byers, T. et al. "Effect of Vitamin C Supplementation on Iron Deficiency Anemia in Chinese Children." *Biomed. Environ. Sci.* 1992;5(2):125–129.

Cook, J. D. et al. "Calcium Supplementation: Effect on Iron Absorption." *Amer. Jour. Clin. Nutr.* 1991;53(1):106–111.

Gizis, F. C. "Nutrition in Women Across the Life Span." *Nurs. Clin. North Amer.* 1992;27(4):971–982.

Lamanca J. J. et al. "Effects of Low Ferritin Concentration on Endurance Performance." *Int. Jour. Sport Nutr.* 1992;2(4):376–385.

Lyle, R. M. et al. "Iron Status in Exercising Women: The Effect of Oral Iron Therapy vs Increased Consumption of Muscle Foods." *Amer. Jour. Clin. Nutr.* 1992;56(6):1049–1055.

Salonen, J. T. et al. "High Stored Iron Levels Are Associated with Excess Risk of Myocardial Infarction." *Circulation* 1992;86(3):803–811.

Scholl, T. O. et al. "Anemia vs. Iron Deficiency: Increased Risk of Preterm Delivery in a Prospective Study." *Amer. Jour. of Clinical Nutr.* 1992;55(5):985–988.

Sherman, A. R. "Zinc, Copper, and Iron Nutriture and Immunity." *Jour. Nutr.* 1992;122(3 Suppl):604–609.

2 Fabulous Fish

Berlin, E. et al. "Effects of Omega-3 Fatty Acid and Vitamin E Supplementation on Erythrocyte Membrane Fluidity, Tocopherols, Insulin Binding, and Lipid Composition in Adult Men." *Jour. of Nutr. Biochemistry.* 1992;3(8):392–400.

Farinaro, E. et al. "Diet and Cardiovascular Risk Among Women in Italy." *Ann. Ist. Super. Sanita.* (in Italian) 1992;28(3):349–353.

Feskens, E. J. et al. "Inverse Association Between Fish Intake and Risk of Glucose Intolerance in Normoglycemic Elderly Men and Women." *Diabetes Care* 1991; 14(11):935–941.

"Heart Disease and Women." *Johns Hopkins Women's Health* 1993;1(1):3.

Nettleton, J. A. "Are N-3 Fatty Acids Essential Nutrients for Fetal and Infant Development?" *Jour. Amer. Diet Assoc.* 1993;93(1):58–64.

Neugut, A. I. "Dietary Risk Factors for the Incidence and Recurrence of Colorectal Adenomatous Polyps." *Ann. Intern. Med.* 1993;118(2):91–95.

Roach, P. D. et al. "Fish Oil and Oat Bran in Combination Effectively Lower Plasma Cholesterol in the Rat." *Atherosclerosis* 1992;96(2–3):219–226.

Stephenson, J. "Rheumatoid Arthritis: Fishing for a Dietary Connection?" *Harvard Medical Letter*, Jul 1993:4–5.

Thompson, G. N. et al. "Protein Turnover in Pregnancy." *Euro. Jour. of Clin. Nutr.* 1992;46(6):411–417.

3 THE CRUCIFEROUS KINGDOM

Baldwin, W. S. et al. "The Anti-carcinogenic Plant Compound Indole-3-carbinol Differentially Modulates P450-mediated Steroid Hydroxylase Activities in Mice." *Chem. Biol. Interact.* 1992; 83(2):155–169.

Chung, B. L. et al. "New Potential Chemopreventative Agents for Lung Carcinogenesis of Tobacco-Specific Nitrosamine." *Cancer Res.* 1992;52(9 Suppl):2719s–2722s.

Steinmetz, K. A. et al. "Vegetables, Fruit, and Lung Cancer in the Iowa Women's Health Study." *Cancer Res.* 1993;53(3):536–543.

Swanson, C. A. et al. "Dietary Determinants of Lung-cancer Risk: Results from a Case-control Study in Yunnan Province, China." *Int. Jour. Cancer* 1992;50(6):876–880.

"Broccoli Revisited." *Tufts University Diet and Nutrition Letter,* May 1992.

4 ANTIOXIDANTS TO THE RESCUE

Barbone, F. et al. "Diet and Endometrial Cancer." *Amer. Jour. Epidemiol.* 1993;137(4):393–403.

Bolton, S. C. et al. "The Scottish Heart Health Study." *Eur. Jour. Clin. Nutr.* 1992;46(2):85–93.

Bunin, G. R. et al. "Relation Between Maternal Diet and Subsequent Primitive Neuroectodermal Brain Tumors in Young Children." *New Engl. Jour. Med.* 1993;329(8):536–541.

Deucher, G. P. "Antioxidant Therapy in the Aging Process." *EXS.* 1992;62:428–437.

Eichholzer, M. et al. "Inverse Correlation Between Essential Antioxidants in Plasma and Subsequent Risk to Develop Cancer, Ischemic Heart Disease and Stroke Respectively." *EXS.* 1992;62:398–410.

Feher, J. et al. "The Role of Free Radical Scavengers in Gastrointestinal Diseases." *Orv. Hetil.* (in Hungarian) 1993;134(13):693–696.

"Diet May Play an Important Role in Lowering Endometrial Cancer Risk." *Health After 50.* 1993;5(5):1.

Hennekens, C. H. et al. "Antioxidants and Heart Disease: Epidemiology and Clinical Evidence." *Clin. Cardiol.* 1993;14(4 Suppl 1):110–113; 113–115.

Herrero, R. et al. "A Case-control Study of Nutrient Status and Invasive Cervical Cancer." *Amer. Jour. Epidemiol.* 1991;134(11):1335–1346.

Levi, F. et al. "Dietary Factors and the Risk of Endometrial Cancer." *Cancer* 1993;71(11):3575–3581.

Reznick, A. Z. et al. "The Threshold of Age in Exercise and Antioxidants Action." *EXS.* 1992;62:423–427.

Rohan, T. E. et al. "Dietary Fiber, Vitamins A, C, and E, and Risk of Breast Cancer." *Cancer Causes Control* 1993;4(1):29–37.

Sies, H. et al. "Antioxidant Functions of Vitamins." *Annual N.Y. Acad. Sci.* 1992;669:7–20.

VITAMIN C

Buettner, G. R. "The Pecking Order of Free Radicals and Antioxidants: Lipid Peroxidation, Alpha-tocopherol, and Ascorbate." *Arch. Biochem. Biophys.* 1993;300(2):535–543.

Darr, D. et al. "Topical Vitamin C Protects Porcine Skin from Ultraviolet Radiation-induced Damage." *Br. Jour. Dermatol.* 1992:127(3):247–253.

el Nahas, S. M. et al. "Radioprotective Effect of Vitamins C and E." *Mutat. Res.* 1993;301(2):143–147.

Enstrom, J. E. et al. "Vitamin C Intake and Mortality Among a Sample of the United States Population." *Epidemiology* 1992;3(3):194–202.

Lupulescu, A. "Ultrastructure and Cell Surface Studies of Cancer Cells Following Vitamin C Administration." *Exp. Toxicol. Pathol.* 1992;44(1):3–9.

Lysy, J. et al. "Ascorbic Acid Status in Diabetes Mellitus." *Nutrition Research* 1992;12(6):713–720.

Menzel, D. B. "Antioxidant Vitamins and Prevention of Lung Disease." *Ann. N.Y. Acad. Sci.* 1992;669:141–155.

Simon, J. A. "Vitamin C and Cardiovascular Disease: A Review." *Jour. Amer. College of Nutr.* 1992;11(2):107–125.

Steinmetz, K. A. et al. "Vegetables, Fruit, and Lung Cancer in the Iowa Women's Health Study." *Cancer Res.* 1993;53(3):536–543.

Willett, W. C. et al. "Dietary Fat and Fiber in Relation to Risk of Breast Cancer. An 8-year Follow-Up." *JAMA* 1992; 268(915):2037–2044.

VITAMIN E AND SELENIUM

Barone, J. et al. "Vitamin Supplement Use and Risk for Oral and Esophageal Cancer." *Nutr. Cancer.* 1992;18(1):31–41.

Bendich, A. "Vitamin E Status of US Children." *Jour. Amer. Coll. of Nutr.* 1992;11(4):441–444.

Lai, K. et al. "Effects of Selenium, Vitamin A and E on Human Breast Cancer Cell Proliferation." *Acta Nutrimenta Sinica* (in Chinese) 1992;14(1):48–53.

London, S. J. et al. "Carotenoids, Retinol, and Vitamin E and Risk of Proliferative Benign Breast Disease and Breast Cancer." *Cancer Causes Control* 1992;3(6):503–512.

Longas, M. O. et al. "Dietary Vitamin E Reverses the Effects of Ultraviolet Light Irradiation on Rat Skin Glycosaminoglycans." *Biochim. Biophys. Acta* 1993;1153(3):239–244.

Meydani, M. "Protective Role of Dietary Vitamin E on Oxidative Stress in Aging." *Age* (Omaha) 1992;15(3):89–93.

Meydani, M. "Modulation of the Platelet Thromboxane A2 and Aortic Prostacyclin Synthesis." *Biol. Trace Elem. Res.* 1992;33:79–86.

Mickle, D. A. et al. "Future Directions of Vitamin E and Its Analogues in Minimizing Myocardial Ischemia-reperfusion Injury." *Can. Jour. Cardiol.* 1993;9(1):89–93.

"E & C Not Best for Breast." *Nutrition Action Health Letter* 1993;20(8):4.

Oldfield, J. E. "Some Implications of Selenium for Human Health." *Nutrition Today,* Jul/Aug 1991:6–11.

Ringstad, J. et al. "The Tromso Heart Study: Relationships between the Concentration of Selenium in Serum and Risk Factors for Coronary Heart Disease." *Jour. Trace Elem. Electrolytes Health Dis.* 1987;1(1):27–31.

Spiller, G. A. et al. "Effect of a Diet High in Monounsaturated Fat from Almonds on Plasma Cholesterol and Lipoproteins." *Jour. Amer. Coll. Nutr.* 1992;11(2):126–130.

Stampfer, M. J. et al. "Vitamin E Consumption and the Risk of Coronary Disease in Women." *N. Engl. Jour. Med.* 1993;328(20):1444–1449.

Tanaka, M. et al. "Aging of the Brain and Vitamin E." *Jour. Nutr. Sci. Vitaminol. Tokyo.* 1992; Spec. No.:240–242.

Zheng, W. et al. "Serum Micronutrients and the Subsequent Risk of Oral and Pharyngeal Cancer." *Cancer Res.* 1993;53(4):795–798.

VITAMIN A AND THE BETA-CAROTENE BONUS

Barone, J. et al. "Vitamin Supplement Use and Risk for Oral and Esophageal Cancer." *Nutr. Cancer* 1992;18(1):31–41.

Candelora, E. C. et al. "Dietary Intake and Risk of Lung Cancer in Women Who Never Smoked." *Nutr. Cancer* 1992;17(3):263–270.

Chug-Ahuja, J. K. et al. "The Development and Application of a Carotenoid Database for Fruits, Vegetables, and Selected Multicomponent Foods." *Jour. Amer. Diet Assoc.* 1993; 93(3):318–323.

Colditz, G. A. et al. "Increased Green and Yellow Vegetable Intake and Lowered Cancer Deaths in an Elderly Population." *Amer. Jour. Clin. Nutr.* 1985; 41:32–36.

Coultas, D. B. et al. "Occupational Lung Cancer." *Clin. Chest Med.* 1992;13(2):341–354.

"Vitamin A: Qualified Link to Breast Cancer." *Environmental Nutr.* 1993;16(9):1.

Friedenreich, C. M. et al. "A Cohort Study of Alcohol Consumption and Risk of Breast Cancer." *Amer. Jour. Epidemiol.* 1993;137(5):512–520.

Hankinson, S. E. et al. "Nutrient Intake and Cataract Extraction in Women: a Prospective Study." *BMJ* 1992;305(6849):335–339.

Huang, C. et al. "A Case-control Study of Dietary Factors in Patients with Lung Cancer." *Biomed. Environ. Sci.* 1992;5(3):257–265.

"Breast Cancer: A Women's Health Update." *Johns Hopkins Women's Health* 1993;1(2):1-4.

Katsouyanni, K. et al. "Diet and Urine Estrogens Among Postmenopausal Women." *Oncology* 1991;48(6):490-494.

Lai, K. et al. "Effects of Selenium, Vitamin A and E on Human Breast Cancer Cell Proliferation." *Acta Nutrimenta Sinica* (in Chinese) 1992;14(1):48-53.

Menkes, M. S. et al. "Serun Beta-carotene, Vitamins A and E, Selenium, and the Risk of Lung Cancer." *New Engl. Jour. Med.* 1986;315(20):1250-1254.

Murakoshi, M. et al. "Potent Preventive Action of Alpha-carotene against Carcinogenesis: Spontaneous Liver Carcinogenesis and Promoting Stage of Lung and Skin Carcinogenesis in Mice are Suppressed More Effectively by Alpha-carotene than by Beta-carotene." *Cancer Res.* 1992;52(23):6583-6587.

Sandford, M. K. et al. "Neural Tube Defect Etiology: New Evidence Concerning Maternal Hyperthermia, Health, and Diet." *Dev. Med. Child Neurol.* 1992; 34(8):661-675.

"Avoiding Breast Cancer Through Food Choices." *Tufts Univ. Diet & Nutr. Letter* 1993;11(7):1.

Zheng, W. et al. "Serum Micronutrients and the Subsequent Risk of Oral and Pharyngeal Cancer." *Cancer Res.* 1993;53(4):795-798.

ZINC

Deucher, G. P. "Antioxidant Therapy in the Aging Process." *EXS.* 1992; 62:428-437.

Good, R. A. et al. "Nutrition and Cellular Immunity." *Int. Jour. Immunopharmacol.* 1992;14(3):361-366.

Hunt, C. D. et al. "Effects of Dietary Zinc Depletion on Seminal Volume and Zinc Loss, Serum Testosterone Concentrations, and Sperm Morphology in Young Men." *Amer. Jour. Clin. Nutr.* 1992;56(1):148-157.

Narang, R. L. et al. "Levels of Copper and Zinc in Depression." *Indian Jour. of Physiology & Pharm.* 1991;35(4):272-274.

Sherman, A. R. "Zinc, Copper, and Iron Nutriture and Immunity." *Jour. Nutr.* 1992:122(3 Suppl):604-609.

Utley, R. "Nutritional Factors Associated with Wound Healing in the Elderly." *Ustomy Wound Manage.* 1992;38(3):22, 24, 26-27.

5 AMAZING YOGURT AND TOFU

Halpern, G. M. et al. "Influence of Long-term Yogurt Consumption in Young Adults." *Int. Jour. of Immunotherapy* 1991;7(4):205-210.

Peters, R. K. et al. "Diet and Colon Cancer in Los Angeles County, California." *Cancer Causes Control* 1992;3(5):457-473.

Takeuchi, S. et al. "Benzaldehyde as a Carcinostatic Principle in Figs." *Agric. Biol. Chem.* 1978;47(7):1449-1451.

6 THE MEDITERRANEAN SECRET

Block, E. "The Chemistry of Garlic and Onions." *Scientific American* 1985;252(3):114–119.

Bosaeus, I. et al. "Olive Oil Instead of Butter Increases Net Cholesterol Excretion from the Small Bowel." *Euro. Jour. of Clin. Nutr.* 1992;46(2):111–115.

el Nahas, S. M. et al. "Radioprotective Effect of Vitamins C and E." *Mutat. Res.* 1993;301(2):143–147.

Farinaro E. et al. "Diet and Cardiovascular Risk Among Women in Italy." *Ann. Ist. Super. Sanita.* (in Italian) 1992;28(3):349–353.

Gatti, E. et al. "Differential Effect of Unsaturated Oils and Butter on Blood Glucose and Insulin Response to Carbohydrate in Normal Volunteers." *Euro. Jour. of Clin. Nutr.* 1992;46(3):161–166.

Gavaler, J. S. et al. "The Association Between Moderate Alcoholic Beverage Consumption and Serum Estradiol and Testosterone Levels in Normal Post-menopausal Women." *Alcohol Clin. Exp. Res.* 1992;16(1):87–92.

Kritchevsky, David. "The Effect of Dietary Garlic on the Development of Cardiovascular Disease." *Nutr. Res.* 1991;14(41):3–4.

Reichman, M. E. et al. "Effects of Alcohol Consumption on Plasma and Urinary Hormone Concentrations in Premenopausal Women." *Jour. Nat. Cancer Inst.* 1993;85(9):722–727.

Renaud, S. et al. "Wine, Alcohol, Platelets, and the French Paradox for Coronary Heart Disease." *Lancet*, N. Amer. ed. 1992;339(8808):1523–1526.

"The New Thinking about Fats." *Univ. of Calif. at Berkeley Wellness Letter* 1993; 9(12):4–5.

Vialettes, B. "Mediterranean Nutrition: a Model for the World?" *Arch. Mal. Coeur. Vaiss.* (in French) 1992:85 Spec No. 2:135–138.

7 WHOLE GRAINS AND B VITAMINS FOR THE WHOLE NERVOUS SYSTEM

Bell, I. R. et al. "Vitamin B1, B2, and B6 Augmentation of Tricyclic Antide-pressant Treatment in Geriatric Depression with Cognitive Dysfunction." *Jour. Amer. Coll. Nutr.* 1992;11(2):159–163.

Czeizel, A. E. et al. "Prevention of the First Occurrence of Neural-tube Defects by Periconceptional Vitamin Supplementation." *New Engl. Jour. Med.* 1992;327(26):1832–1835.

Levi, F. et al. "Dietary Factors and the Risk of Endometrial Cancer." *Cancer* 1993;71(11):3575–3581.

Levitt, A. J. "Folate, Vitamin B12 and Cognitive Impairment in Patients with Alzheimer's Disease." *Acta Psychiatrica Scandinavica* 1992;86(4):301–305.

"Another Vote for Vegetables." *Harvard Women's Health Watch*, Sep 1993: 7.

Mills, J. L. et al. "Maternal Vitamin Levels During Pregnancies Producing Infants with Neural Tube Defects." *Jour. Pediatr.* 1992;120(6):863–871.

Niebyl, J. R. "Drug Therapy in Pregnancy." *Curr. Opin. Obstet. Gynecol.* 1992; 4(1):43–47.

Ohta, T. et al. "Daily Activity and Persistent Sleep-Wake Schedule Disorders." *Prog. Neuropsychopharmacol. Biol. Psychiatry* 1992;16(4):529–537.

Reynolds, E. H. "Multiple Sclerosis and Vitamin B$_{12}$ Metabolism." *Jour. Neuroimmunol.* 1992;40(2–3):225–230.

Rosenberg, I. H. "Good Choices at Mealtimes Can Slow the March of Years." *Providence Journal-Bulletin's Good Life,* May 1993.

Rosenberg, I. H. et al. "Nutritional Factors in Physical and Cognitive Functions of Elderly People." *Amer. Jour. Clin. Nutr.* 1992;55(6 Suppl): 1237S–1243S.

Sabate, J. et al. "Effects of Walnuts on Serum Lipid Levels and Blood Pressure in Normal Men." *New Engl. Jour. Med.* 1993;328(9):603–607.

Turnlund, J. R. et al. "Vitamin B-6 Depletion Followed by Repletion with Animal or Plant Source Diets and Calcium and Magnesium Metabolism in Young Women." *Amer. Jour. of Clinical Nutr.* 1992;56(5):905–910.

Weekes, E. W. et al. "Nutrient Levels in Amniotic Fluid from Women with Normal and Neural Tube Defect Pregnancies." *Biol-Neonate* 1992;61(4): 226–231.

Winters, L. R. T. et al. "Riboflavin Requirements and Exercise Adaptation in Older Women." *Amer. Jour. Clin. Nutr.* 1992;56(3):526–532.

8 CALCIUM AND VITAMIN D

Alvir, J. M. et al. "Premenstrual and Menstrual Symptom Clusters and Response to Calcium Treatment." *Psychopharmacol. Bull.* 1991;27(2):145–146.

Chapuy, M. C. et al. "Vitamin D3 and Calcium to Prevent Hip Fractures in the Elderly Woman." *New Engl. Jour. Med.* 1992;327(23):1637–1642.

Farinaro, E. et al. "Diet and Cardiovascular Risk Among Women in Italy." *Ann. Ist. Super. Sanita.* (in Italian) 1992;28(3):349–353.

Gizis F. C. "Nutrition in Women Across the Life Span." *Nurs. Clin. North Amer.* 1992;27(4):971–982.

Harris, S. et al. "Rates of Change in Bone Mineral Density in the Spine, Heel, Femoral Neck and Radius in Healthy Postmenopausal Women." *Bone Miner.* 1992;17(1):87–95.

"Osteoporosis." *Harvard Women's Health Watch,* Nov 1993:3–5.

Heany, R. P. "Calcium in the Prevention and Treatment of Osteoporosis." *Jour. Intern. Med.* 1992;231(2):169–180.

Hernanadez, A. et al. "Caffeine and Other Predictors of Bone Density Among Pre- and Perimenopausal Women." *Epidemiology* 1993;4(2):128–134.

"Diet May Play an Important Role in Endometrial Cancer Risk." *Johns Hopkins Medical Letter, Health After 50* 1993;5(5):1.

"Osteoporosis." *Johns Hopkins Women's Health* 1993;1(2):5.

Lukert, B. et al. "Menopausal Bone Loss Is Partially Regulated by Dietary Intake of Vitamin D." *Calcif. Tissue. Int.* 1992;51(3):173–179.

Mazess, R. B. "Bone Density in Premenopausal Women." *Amer. Jour. Clin. Nutr.* 1991;53(1):132–142.

Nordin, B. E. et al. "Osteoporosis and Vitamin D." *Jour. Cell. Biochem.* 1992:49(1):19–25.

"Mom Was Right." *Nutrition Action Health Letter* 1993;20(8):4.

Peters, R. K. et al. "Diet and Colon Cancer." *Cancer Causes Control* 1992;3 (5):457–473.

Recker, R. R. "Prevention of Osteoporosis: Calcium Nutrition." *Osteoporos. Int.* 1993;3(Suppl. 1):163–165.

Recker, R. R. et al. "Bone Gain in Young Adult Women." *JAMA* 1992;268(17):2403–2408.

Tolstoi, L. G. et al. "Osteoporosis—The Treatment Controversy." *Nutr. Today,* Jul/Aug 1992:6–9.

"Yet Another Reason to Drink Your Milk." *Tufts Univ. Diet & Nutr. Letter.* 1992;9(11):1.

Turnlund, J. R. et al. "Vitamin B–6 Depletion Followed by Repletion with Animal or Plant Source Diets and Calcium and Magnesium Metabolism in Young Women." *Amer. Jour. of Clinical Nutr.* 1992;56(5):905–910.

"A Lifelong Program to Build Strong Bones." *Univ. of Calif. at Berkeley Wellness Letter* 1993;9(10):4–5.

Weaver, C. M. "Calcium Bioavailability and Its Relation to Osteoporosis." *Proc. Soc. Exp. Biol. Med.* 1992;200(2):157–160.

9 COMPLEX CARBOHYDRATES, NATURE'S ATTITUDE ADJUSTERS

Bancroft, J. et al. "Perimenstrual Complaints in Women Complaining of PMS, Menorrgagia, and Dysmenorrhea." *Psychosom. Med.* 1993;55(2):133–145.

Banosbo, J. et al. "The Effect of Carbohydrate Diet on Intermittent Exercise Performance." *Int. Jour. . of Sports Med.* 1992;13(2):152–157.

"Ten Tips for Weight Control." *Harvard Women's Health Watch,* Sep 1993:4.

Levi, F. et al. "Dietary Factors and the Risk of Endometrial Cancer." *Cancer* 1993;71(11):3575–3581.

Ludbrook, C. et al. "Energy Expenditure and Nutrient Intake in Long-distance Runners." *Nutr. Research* 1992;12(6):689–699.

Moller, S. E. "Serotonin, Carbohydrates, and Atypical Depression." *Pharmacol. Toxicol.* 1992;71(Suppl. 1):61–71.

Rohan, T. E. et al. "Dietary Fiber, Vitamins A, C, and E, and Risk of Breast Cancer." *Cancer Causes Control* 1993;4(1):29–37.

Sandler, R. S. "Diet and Risk of Colorectal Adenomas." *Jour. Natl. Cancer Inst.* 1993;85(11):884-891.

"Real Men Eat Broccoli." *Tufts Univ. Diet & Nutr. Letter* 1993;2(9):8.

Williams, C. et al. "The Effect of a High Carbohydrate Diet on Running Performance During a 30-km Treadmill Time Trial." *Eur. Jour. Appl. Physiol.* 1992;65(1):18-24.

10 MORE BRAIN FOOD

Bourre, J. M. et al. "Function of Dietary Polyunsaturated Fatty Acids in the Nervous System." *Prostaglandins Leukot. Essent. Fatty Acids.* 1993;48(1):5-15.

Nettleton, J. A. "Are N-3 Fatty Acids Essential Nutrients for Fetal and Infant Development?" *Jour. Amer. Diet Assoc.* 1993;93(1):58-64.

Wurtman, J. J. *Managing Your Mind & Mood Through Food.* New York: Harper & Row, 1986.

11 FIBER, A VITAL NONNUTRIENT

Bolton, S. C. et al. "The Scottish Heart Health Study." *Eur. Jour. Clin. Nutr.* 1992;46(2):85-93.

Harlan, L. C. et al. "Estrogen Receptor Status and Dietary Intakes of Breast Cancer Patients." *Epidemiology* 1993;(4)1:25-31.

"Five Apples a Day?" *Harvard Medical Letter*, Feb 1993:4-5.

Howe, G. R. et al. "Dietary Intake of Fiber and Decreased Risk of Cancers of the Colon and Rectum." *Jour. Natl. Cancer Inst.* 1992;84(24):1887-1896.

Kashtan, H. et al. "Wheat-bran and Oat-bran Supplements' Effects on Blood Lipids and Lipoproteins." *Amer. Jour. of Clinical Nutr.* 1992;55(5):975-980.

Kushi, L. H. et al. "Dietary Fat and Postmenopausal Breast Cancer." *Jour. Natl. Cancer Inst.* 1992;84(4):1092-1099.

Richardson, S. et al. "The Role of Fat, Animal Protein, and Some Vitamin Consumption in Breast Cancer." *Int. Jour. Cancer* 1991;48(1):1-9.

Rohan, T. E. et al. "Dietary Fiber, Vitamins A, C, and E, and Risk of Breast Cancer." *Cancer Causes Control* 1993;4(1):29-37.

Sable-Amplis, R. et al. "Hepatic Acylcoenzyme A: Cholesterol Acyltransferase Activity Is Low in Hamsters Fed Apples in Addition to a Standard Diet." *Ann. Nutr. Metab.* 1993;37(1):1-7.

Sandler, R. S. "Diet and Risk of Colorectal Adenomas." *Jour. Natl. Cancer Inst.* 1993;85(11):884-891.

Sandstrom, B. et al. "An Eight-Month Controlled Study of Low-Fat, High-Fibre Diet: Effects on Blood Lipids and Blood Pressure in Healthy Young Subjects." *Eur. Jour. Clin. Nutr.* 1992;46(2):95-109.

12 HERBS, SPICES, AND TEAS

Aruna K. et al. "Plant Products as Protective Agents Against Cancer." *Indian Jour. Exp. Biol.* 1990;28(11):1008–1011.

Crespo, M. E. et al. "Antibacterial Activity of the Essential Oil of Thymus Serpylloides." *Microbios.* 1990;61(248–49):181–184.

Eldershaw, T. P. et al. "Pungent Principles of Ginger (Zingiber Officinale) Are Thermogenic in the Perfused Rat Hindlimb." *Int. Jour. Obes.* 1992;16 (10):755–763.

"Research Hints Garlic May Be Wonder Bulb Against Disease." *Environmental Nutrition* 1994;17(1):1,6.

Marotta R. B. et al. "Diet and Nutrition in Ulcer Disease." *Med. Clin. North. Amer.* 1991;75(4):967–979.

Nasu, K. et al. "Differences of Food Intake and Nutritional Status Between the Areas with Low and High Standardized Mortality Ratio for Stomach Cancer in Shizuoka Prefecture." *Japanese Jour. of Nutr.* 1992;50(3):133–144.

Petkov, V. D. et al. "Memory Effects of Standardized Extracts of Panax Ginseng, Ginkgo Biloba, and Their Combination Gincosan." *Planta. Med.* 1993;59(2):106–114.

Saeki, Y. et al. "Antimicrobial Action of Natural Substances on Oral Bacteria." *Bull. Tokyo Dent. Coll.* 1989;30(3):129–135.

Srivastava, K. C. "Extracts from Two Frequently Consumed Spices—Cumin and Turmeric—Inhibit Platelet Aggregation and Alter Eicosanoid Biosynthesis in Human Blood Platelets." *Prostaglandins Leukot. Essent. Fatty Acids.* 1989;37(1):57–64.

Srivastava, K. C. et al. "Ginger (Zingiber Officinale) in Rheumatisum and Musculoskeletal Disorders." *Med. Hypotheses* 1992;39(4):342–348.

Unnikrishnan M. C. et al. "Tumour Reducing and Anticarcinogenic Activity of Selected Spices." *Cancer Lett.* 1990;51(1):85–89.

INDEX

Entries in *italics* indicate health issues.

ABOUT THE AUTHOR

DOLORES RICCIO is the author of nine previously published books, including five cookbooks. She lives in Warwick, RI, with her husband and is the mother of two grown children.